THE MERTON ANNUAL

Studies in Culture, Spirituality, and Social Concerns

Volume 17   2004

Edited by

Victor A. Kramer

Guest Editor
for selected 2003 International Thomas Merton Society Papers

Lynn Szabo

THE MERTON ANNUAL
Studies in Culture, Spirituality, and Social Concerns

THE MERTON ANNUAL publishes articles about Thomas Merton and about related matters of major concern to his life and work. Its purpose is to enhance Merton's reputation as a writer and monk, to continue to develop his message for our times, and to provide a regular outlet for substantial Merton-related scholarship. *THE MERTON ANNUAL* includes as regular features reviews, review-essays, a bibliographic survey, interviews, and first appearances of unpublished, or obscurely published Merton materials, photographs, and art. Essays about related literary and spiritual matters will also be considered. Manuscripts and books for review may be sent to the editor.

EDITOR

Victor A. Kramer
University Catholic Center for Emory
1753 North Decatur Road
Atlanta GA 30307
Email: victorak@bellsouth.net

PRODUCTION MANAGER

Glenn Crider
University Catholic Center for Emory
1753 North Decatur Road
Atlanta GA 30307
Email: wcrider@emory.edu

Grateful acknowledgement is expressed to The Merton Legacy Trust for permission to publish the extract from the unpublished manuscript of *Peace in the Post-Christian Era*, and, as well, for permission to reuse the original Merton calligraphy image, which was embossed on the cover of Vol. 1 of *The Merton Annual* (AMS Press, 1988).

PUBLISHED BY:

Fons Vitae
49 Mockingbird Valley Drive
Louisville KY 40207
502.897.3641
Email: Fonsvitaeky@aol.com
http://www.fonsvitae.com

ALSO AVAILABLE THROUGH:

The Thomas Merton Foundation
211 Payne Street
Louisville, KY 40206
502.899.1991
Email: info@mertonfoundation.org

For members of the International Thomas Merton Society, available for $15.00, plus shipping and handling.

Individual copies are available through bookstores and direclty from the publisher for $19.95.

Cover artwork is a drawing by Thomas Merton. Used with permission of the Merton Legacy Trust and the Thomas Merton Center at Bellarmine University.

Library of Congress Control Number: 2004115748

ISBN 1887752773

The Merton Annual

Volume 17	2004

REVIEWS

Introduction:
A Simplicity of Wonder: Merton's Honor
for the Particular Extending Outward

Victor A. Kramer

A Geography of Success and Failure

My successes are never my own.
The path to them was prepared
by others.
The fruit of my labor is not my own.
For I am preparing the way
Toward the achievements of others.

Nor are my failures my own.
They may spring from the failure
of another;
Yet failures are often compensated
by another's achievement.
Therefore, the meaning of life is

Seen only
In the complete integration
of my successes and failures
With the achievements and losses
of my entire generation,
My own society, and time.[1]

Like life itself, moving in a rhythm which allows flexibility as all things supporting life grow, evolve, change, life in a family or monastery or in any institution moves in cycles. It is not surprising that a publication like this *Annual* should also reflect cyclical change. The project of an annual collection of Merton scholarship has been part of my life now for almost two decades. In 1985-1986 the concept for such a book emerged and the original editors thought it would attract longer manuscripts. This volume will be published in 2004, and at that time Volume 18 (2005) should be well on the way toward completion.

What I have come to appreciate as I have watched this cycle develop each year is the complexity of each year's book and the many talents needed to bring it to completion. One is reminded of constant interconnections. Myriads of people contribute to each volume and thereby become like separate stars illuminating aspects of Merton's life's work which keeps revealing itself to us in still more ways. The work of the International Thomas Merton Society has become part of this developing pattern.

It occurs to me that as the many essays were refereed and refined for earlier thematic collections in volumes of *The Merton Annual* (Vol. 12, Monasticism; Vol. 14, the Feminine; Vol. 16, Spirituality) in each of these instances Thomas Merton's rootedness in particular places and a sometimes paradoxical desire to be elsewhere was often demonstrated in many fascinating ways, and thus, is fundamental to his life's journey and to the challenge of the spiritual life which calls us to see the whole. Therefore, the choice of theme for the 2003 Vancouver ITMS General Meeting which emphasized Merton's fascination with geography and his love of particular landscapes inevitably was a topic which could draw a wide range of commentators. Merton's own early global peregrinations are well known. His later imaginative journeys, triggered by constant reading and poetic imagination, became ever more crucial to his own widening spiritual development as he matured and thereby grew in compassion for all persons and places as animated by God's presence.

The grouping of articles which has developed from presentations at the 2003 Vancouver ITMS General Meeting demonstrate how Merton embraced all. He could draw well on his absorption and blessing of a particular landscape and love of place to then build toward a personal, theological, or spiritual point of view which always became cosmic, yet also reminds us of Christ's participation in our world. Edited by Professor Lynn Szabo, these articles could stand as a small book. They refract the insights which Merton drew from pondering the relationship of his love for experiences of the particular in relation to his own unfolding affirmation of humankind's connection with, and responsibility for, the entire globe brooded over by God.

II

These ten scholarly essays were refereed and chosen as the most representative pieces which developed from a meeting which generated many different methods to examine Merton's paradoxical love of place. They often simultaneously manifest a desire for and glimpses of the transcendence of place. Necessary detachment, Merton teaches us, allows then a development and a widening in spirit, yet a spirit always still rooted in the particular.

Thomas Merton's developing global concerns and his definite disappointment with cultures which are destructive of the particulars of any place, or person, is clearly a recurrent passion revealed in these essays because of these passionate concerns. It is appropriate that as Merton's spiritual life unfolded and developed he became more appreciative of each dimension of the local, more appreciative of every unique individual and moment. It also seems especially appropriate at this moment (as *The Merton Annual* moves into a new and, we think, broader phase of inclusion of more persons involved in its writing and editing) that our unpublished Merton manuscript should be an excerpt from his *Peace in the Post-Christian Era*. Truly, Merton's love for God made it imperative that he think as widely as possible, indeed, globally. Patricia Burton's editorial note and detailed article both clarify why this text still speaks to us today. I am very pleased that after we decided to publish this chapter, arrangements were made for the entire Merton manuscript to be published by Orbis.

We are also extremely appreciative of the thorough and complete index which Patricia Burton has also made for Volumes 1-16. This will make it easier for scholars to pursue topics earlier investigated by other scholars in preceding volumes, but now perhaps forgotten. Over and over, Merton reminds us, our hidden roots sprout seeds of contemplation yet not to comfort us, rather to extend outwardly to the wider world of God's presence.

Still additional parallel connections beyond Merton's Abbey of Gethsemani, or even the United States, are reflected both in the interview included in this volume with Donald Allchin and in the bibliographic essay prepared by David Belcastro. The interview, which I arranged in 1998, is with Rev. A.M. (Donald) Allchin, Anglican priest, friend of Merton, and ecumenical scholar. It shows how Merton was constantly building connections. This interview was conducted in Atlanta, Georgia just after Fr. Allchin participated in a conference at Emory University about "Merton and Ecumenism."

Allchin's interest in the Orthodox Church, American culture and Catholicism have continued to form his consciousness which is open to the wider world of religion. He stands as a model of someone who learned from Merton and as a model of someone who, in being open, can teach others to remain open to God's manifestations. It was not an accident but rather a providential moment that Allchin and Merton should have been together on the very day of Martin Luther King, Jr.'s death. All three of these men witness to global visions. Such a wideness of vision is what also unites many Merton scholars.

Many of the persons who are mentioned in this introduction possess that global vision. The major gathering of articles derived from the ITMS General Meeting in Vancouver reflect an overall theme which emphasizes global awareness too. Members of the ITMS Publication Committee (Monica Weis, Bonnie Thurston, Patrick O'Connell, and the current ITMS President, Erlinda Paguio) have all contributed supportive ideas which have helped this new series of *The Merton Annual* to develop. I thank them. I thank other members of the Board who expressed wishes for further ITMS collaboration with *The Merton Annual*. I also thank Bob Toth of The Merton Foundation and Gray Henry at Fons Vitae Publishing for their courage to push this volume through.

Even more significantly, I am especially thankful of the careful and sustained work done by Lynn Szabo, Patricia Burton, Glenn Crider and David Belcastro—without whom the farewell postscript in Volume 16 would have, indeed, been the end. I am quite happy to see that my hopes for a new cycle of *The Merton Annual* have materialized. David Belcastro's analytical bibliograpical study of recent writings by, and about Merton, is yet another reminder of our continuing need to keep rereading "misreadings" so that we can perceive more ways to see beyond ourselves and into the local with more appreciation of what is beyond us, never to be fully understood, but celebrated.

III

Someone, I am reminded, once told Walker Percy he must be "Benedictine" and in his reply, included in *Conversations with Walker Percy*, he agreed there was some truth to such an assessment. He agreed that a recurrent pattern in the Benedictine rhythm includes an alternating building up, then cultural change and always diminution followed by renewal. This, too, apparently happens with all life. Once Fr. Louis commented that until someone has experienced a particular place throughout the rhythm of its seasons, one cannot fully know that place. He is right, and interestingly what I now realize is that Merton's mystical quest ultimately included his endorsement and prayer for all persons in all places.

An additional acknowledgement needs to be made. I was fortunate to be a research scholar at the St. John's University Institute for Ecumenical and Cultural Research during the academic year 2003-2004. So was another one of our contributors in the year preceding. This introduction, therefore, and one of the Vancouver essays were both written at an Institute which has as its goal, encouraging ecumenical seekers. Therefore, Merton's love of the local extending outward triggered another thought as I prepared the introduction. This thought is about the mysterious intersections of place and time which should make every moment and every place a providential moment, revealing a unity. I recall three such intersections which I am sure have now led to this book's flavoring of articles, essays and book reviews which will, in turn, stimulate others: 1) Memphis, March, 2002 when I gave a talk there on Merton and Civil Rights, sponsored by the Memphis ITMS Chapter; 2) Louisville, June 2002 at the ITMS Board Meeting; 3) Vancouver, June, 2003 at the ITMS General Meeting. All of these were times when various members of the ITMS thanked me and encouraged me to continue to seek ways to keep *The Merton Annual* published.

Interestingly, one of the very persons whom I had met in Memphis was also in Vancouver, Paul Dekar. Earlier, as I was preparing to spend the year at St. John's Institute of Ecumenical and Cultural Research I learned that Dekar was already on sabbatical there and studying Merton. Later that year, when I arrived at the Institute, I learned that Dekar and I had both been assigned the same apartment. Chance perhaps, but provident. I was then quite pleased when in late fall, 2003, I received Dekar's submission which ties together so well with the broad vision of Merton and his wonder about all places and his respect for all persons. The knowledge that our particular years at this Institute were nurturing for both of us suggests the Benedictine rhythms of "prayer and work," as rooted in the particular, keep blooming into an awareness and respect for all persons and cultures.

IV

As Volume 17 of *The Merton Annual* goes to press, I emphasize that I cannot be other than grateful for the many persons who shared the editorial work which has allowed this book to be fashioned as it is. A year ago it seemed probable that the preceding volume was perhaps the last. Now I see that we have moved into new opportunities for Merton investigation. When we first started refereeing manuscripts for Volume 1 (1988) there lingered an element in the Merton work being done then of, if not the hagiographical, at least an almost unquestioning attitude about Merton's work. In the period which has followed, many significant questions have been introduced by critics and commentators, especially in Volumes 12, 14 and 16, where we gathered essays about Merton as a monastic; in relationship to the feminine; and about his influences upon contemporary culture. In all of these categories we found Merton's work serving not just as unquestioned influence, but rather as a catalyst for action and thinking. This has largely been the work of ITMS members. Now with the involvement of ITMS presenters who have fashioned their papers into articles and with the work of four new editorial contributors (Szabo, Belcastro, Burton and Crider) we have actually changed the way *The Merton Annual* functions.

Here we have pieces gathered, edited, indeed, written by a range of persons—most of them active in the International Thomas Merton Society—something not capable of even having been dreamt in 1986 when *The Merton Annual* started, and indeed not exactly what I (and others) hoped for as *The Annual* unfolded with many good developments in Volumes 6 through 16, while its editors were still hoping for articles which would be reflections of a wider range of cultural and critical commentary. This has still not yet happened. The fact is, as has been pointed out in earlier editor's remarks, Merton readers and commentators remain within a fairly narrow spectrum. This often ITMS-encouraged mode of ecumenical investigation is clearly reflected throughout all of *The Merton Annual's* preceding volumes.

Merton is loved; he is a prophet; but we also now see that his writings, in fact, serve well as a reflection of the thinking and changing public face of the Church—no longer just adulatory acceptance—but rather a loving embrace of the fact that the Church, with its collective and ongoing spiritual journey stands as both Incarnation and as a continuing contemplative prayer with each moment always a potential movement "towards crisis and mystery."

A year ago it was impossible to imagine the contents for this volume. Now, in retrospect, this "inexorable" moment is clear, and because of the generous contributions of many, more of Merton's mystery shines. Volume 17 stands as proof that many people were waiting in the wings to help. When we ponder Merton's expanding love of the cosmos and all its particular beauty we know, as Robert Faricy expresses it,

> The risen Jesus' presence permeates everything: it shines at the heart of all things all around us. Teilhard [de Chardin] writes, 'Christ is physically active in order to control all things . . . . He ceaselessly animates, without disturbing, all the earth processes. The universal influence of the risen Jesus' love extends not only to every human heart but to the heart of the world and to every single part, every atom and molecule, every rock and breeze. His love holds all things together and moves them forward'.[2]

This volume exists as testament to Merton's affirmation of the continuing unity we affirm as persons and of the presence of God's grace working within our generation.

Notes

1. Variation on Merton's "Success and Failure" from *No Man is an Island* in *Blaze of Recognition: Throughout the Year with Thomas Merton: Daily Meditations*. Selected and edited by Thomas P. McDonnell (New York: Doubleday, 1983) p. 103.

2. Robert Faricy, *The Lord's Dealing: The Primacy of the Feminine in Christian Spirituality* (New York: Paulist Press, 1988) p. 25.

Editorial note concerning Thomas Merton's *Peace in the Post-Christian Era*, Chapter 15

Patricia A. Burton

From the evidence of the manuscript of *Peace in the Post-Christian Era*, the chapter titled "Christian Perspectives in World Crisis" was the last piece of the puzzle inserted just as the work was being typed on mimeograph stencils. In the manuscript, this chapter was constructed by inserting part of the essay "Christian Action in World Crisis" after the chapter "Red or Dead—the Anatomy of a Cliché." The last page of that chapter had been hand-numbered by Merton as page 82 of the manuscript. The insert was given page numbers 82a through 82q. Merton divided the section into two chapters, the first of which is presented here as "Christian Perspectives in World Crisis," representing pages 82a through 82i of the manuscript, 109 to 119 of the mimeograph.

In editing the chapter, Merton amended words and phrases in the text, struck out some passages, and added inserts, hand-written in blue ink, on the blank back of the pages of the carbon copy. Textual analysis of the chapter shows that almost 70% of the text does not overlap with the original essay, "Christian Action in World Crisis," but is new, with parts of the original essay now embedded throughout the new chapter.

Merton cites scripture and Papal pronouncements to support his argument. The manuscript was written before the publication of Pope John XXIII's encyclical *Pacem in Terris*. Merton and other Catholic writers about peace had to comb through Christmas Messages and other speeches to try to ascertain the papal position on war in the nuclear age.

This chapter is central to Merton's message: that all Christians must take responsibility for bringing about peace, since love, peace and nonviolence were the original Christian message. It speaks of his original concern that Christians were allowing moral apathy to overcome them. Peace must be integral to Christian life, a concept not just spoken but lived, as the monastic life is lived: social action begins with prayer and arises from it.

The full text of Merton's book, *Peace in the Post-Christian Era,* will be published by Orbis Books in the fall of 2004, with a Foreword by Jim Forest and an Introduction by Patricia A. Burton.

15: Christian Perspectives in World Crisis

Thomas Merton

It should be clear from the moral and mental confusion of our time that the present world crisis is something far worse than a merely political or economic conflict. It goes far deeper than ideologies. It is a crisis of man's spirit. It is a completely[1] moral upheaval of the human race that has lost its religious and cultural roots. We do not really know half the causes of this upheaval. We cannot pretend to have a full understanding of what is going on in ourselves and in our society. That is why our desperate hunger for clear and definite solutions sometimes leads us into temptation. We oversimplify. We seek the cause of evil and find it here or there in a particular nation, class, race, ideology, system. And we discharge upon this scapegoat all the virulent force of our hatred, compounded with fear and anguish, striving to rid ourselves of our dread and of our guilt by destroying the object we have arbitrarily singled out as the embodiment of all evil. Far from curing us, this is only another paroxysm which aggravates our sickness.

The moral evil in the world is due to man's alienation from the deepest truth, from the springs of spiritual life within himself, to his alienation from God. Those who realize this try desperately to persuade and enlighten their brothers. But we are in a radically different position from the first Christians, who revolutionized an essentially religious world of paganism with the message of a new religion that had never been heard of.

We on the contrary live in an irreligious post-Christian world in which the Christian message has been repeated over and over until it has come to seem empty of all intelligible content to those whose ears close to the word of God even before it is uttered. In their minds Christian is no longer identified with newness and change, but only with the static preservation of outworn structures.

But why is this? Is it merely that the spiritual novelty of Christianity has worn off in twenty centuries? That people have heard the Gospel before and are tired of it? Or is it perhaps because for centuries the message has been belied and contradicted by the conduct of Christians themselves? Christianity is essentially the revelation of the Divine Mercy in the Mystery of Christ and His Church. Infinite mercy, infinite love are revealed to the world, made *evident* to the world in the sanctity of the Mystical Body of Christ, united in charity, nourished by the sacramental mystery of the Eucharist in which all participate in the divine *agape*, the sacrifice of the Word made Flesh. To say Christianity is the revelation of love means not simply that Christians are (or should be) nice charitable people. It means that love is the key to life itself and to the whole meaning of the cosmos and of history. If Christians, then, are without love they deprive all other men of access to the central truth that gives meaning to all existence.

"By this shall all men know that you are my disciples, if you have love for one another" (John 13:35). "That they all may be one in us, as thou Father in me and I in thee; so that the world may believe that Thou hast sent me" (John 17:21). "My peace I give unto you... I do not give peace as the world gives it" (John 14:27). "The wisdom that comes from above is marked chiefly indeed by its purity but also indeed by its peacefulness... It carries mercy with it and a harvest of all that is good; it is uncensorious and without affectation. Peace is the seed ground of holiness and those who make peace will win its harvest. What leads you to war, what leads to quarreling among you? ... The appetites which infest your mortal bodies. Your desires go unfulfilled and so you fall to murdering" (James 3:17-4:2).

It must be admitted therefore that if the Gospel of Peace is no longer convincing on the lips of Christians, it may well be because they have ceased to give a living example of peace, unity and love. True, we have to understand that the Church was never intended to be absolutely perfect on earth, and she is a Church of sinners, laden with imperfection. Christian peace and Christian charity are based indeed on this need to "bear one another's burdens," to accept the infirmities that plague one's own life and the lives of others. Our unity is a struggle with disunity and our peace exists in the midst of conflict.

But the fact remains that a warring and warlike Christendom has never been able to preach the Gospel of charity and peace with full conviction or full success. As Cardinal Newman so rightly said, the greatest victories of the Church were all won before Constantine, in the days when there were no Christian armies and when the true Christian soldier was the martyr, whose witness to

Christ was nonviolent. It was the martyrs who conquered Rome for Christ with a conquest that has been stable for twenty centuries. How long were the crusaders able to hold Jerusalem?

This should teach us that though the words of the Gospel still objectively retain all the force and freshness of their original life, it is not enough now for us to preach and explain them. It is not enough to announce the familiar message that no longer seems to be news. Not enough to teach, to prove, to convince. Now above all is the time to embody Christian truth in action even more than in words. No matter how lucid, how persuasive, how logical, how profound our theological and spiritual statements may be, they are usually wasted on anyone who does not already think as we do. That is why the serene and classic sanity of moralists exposing the traditional teaching of Christian theologians on the "just war" is almost a total loss in the general clamor and confusion of half truths, propaganda slogans, and pernicious clichés, many of which are preached and disseminated by Christians themselves, not excluding the clergy.

What is needed now is the Christian who manifests the truth of the Gospel in social action, with or without explanation. The more clearly his life manifests the teaching of Christ, the more salutary it will be. Clear and decisive Christian action explains itself, and teaches in a way that words never can.

Christians must not only assert the existence of a moral order and of natural law in the midst of a world where law and order are questioned or even completely forgotten. Christians above all must act in all things, in their work, their social relations, their political life as if justice and objective right were to them vital and essential realities, not just consoling ideas.

Pope John XXIII said in *Mater et Magistra*:

Let men make all the technical and economic progress they can, there will be no peace nor justice in the world until they return to a sense of their dignity as creatures and sons of God, who is the first and final cause of all created being. Separated from God man is but a monster, in himself and toward others, for the right ordering of human society presupposes the right ordering of man's conscience with God, who is Himself the source of all justice, truth and love (215).

And Pius XII said in his Christmas Message of 1955 that Christians have a most serious obligation to help build a society based on genuinely Christian principles:

> If ever Christians were to neglect this duty of theirs by leaving inactive insofar as in them lies the guiding force of faith in public life they would be committing treason against the God-Man.[2]

What is wanted now is therefore not simply the Christian who takes an inner complacency in the words and example of Christ, but who seeks to follow Christ perfectly, not only in his own personal life, not only in prayer and penance, but also in his political commitments and in all his social responsibilities.

We have certainly no need of a pseudo-contemplative spirituality that claims to ignore the world and its problems entirely, and devotes itself supposedly to the things of God, without concern for human society. All true Christian spirituality, even that of the Christian contemplative, is and must always be deeply concerned with man, since "God became man in order that man might become God" (St. Irenaeus). The Christian spirit is one of compassion, of responsibility and of commitment. It cannot be indifferent to suffering, to injustice, error, untruth. Precisely for that reason then a genuine Christian spirituality must be profoundly concerned with all the risks and problems implied by the mere existence of nuclear stockpiles and biological weapons.

In the presence of an international politic based on nuclear deterrence and on the imminent possibility of global suicide, no Christian may remain indifferent, no Christian can allow himself a mere inert and passive acquiescence in ready-made formulas fed to him by the mass media.

Still less can a Christian conscience be content with an ethic that seeks to justify and permit as much as possible of force and terror, in international politics and in war. The Christian is formally obliged to take positive and active means to restrain force and bring into being a positive international authority which can effectively prevent war and promote peace. The whole world faces a momentous choice. Either our frenzy of desperation will lead to destruction, or our loyalty to truth, to God and to our fellow man will enable us to perform the patient, heroic task of building a world that will eventually thrive in unity, order and peace.

In the present crisis, Christian action can be decisive. That is why it is supremely important for us to keep our heads and refuse to be carried away by the wild projects of fanatics who seek an oversimplified and immediate solution by means of ruthless violence. Power alone is not the answer.

In a world that has largely discarded moral imperatives and which indeed no longer seriously considers the violent death of one hundred million human beings as a moral issue, but only as a pragmatic exercise of power, the Christian must regard himself as the custodian of moral and human values, and *must give top priority to their clarification and defense.*

This implies first of all, the duty of unremitting study, meditation, prayer and every form of spiritual and intellectual discipline that can fit him for so serious a task. Obviously this responsibility is first of all binding on the clergy and religious, and above all on those entrusted with their education and spiritual formation.

In this all-important matter we have to rediscover the sources of Christian tradition, and we must come to realize that we have to a great extent abandoned the early Christian ideal of peace and nonviolent action. Surely it is curious that in the twentieth century the one great political figure who has made a conscious and systematic use of the Gospel principles for nonviolent political action was not a Christian but a Hindu. Even more curious is the fact that so many Christians thought Gandhi was some kind of eccentric and that his nonviolence was an impractical and sensational fad.

Christians have got to speak by their actions. Their political action must not be confined to the privacy of the polling booth. It must be clear and manifest to everybody. It must speak loudly and plainly the Christian truth, and it must be prepared to defend that truth with sacrifices, accepting misunderstanding, injustice, calumny, and even imprisonment or death. It is crucially important for Christians today to adopt a genuinely Christian position and support it with everything they have got. This means an unremitting fight for justice in every sphere—in labor, in race relations, in the "third world" and above all in international affairs.

This means reducing the distance between our interior intentions and our exterior acts. Our social actions must conform to our deepest religious principles. Beliefs and politics can no longer be kept isolated from one another. It is no longer possible for us to be content with abstract and hidden acts of "purity of intention" which do nothing to make our outward actions different from those of atheists or agnostics.

Nor can we be content to make our highest ideal the preservation of a minimum of ethical rectitude prescribed by natural law. Too often the nobility and grandeur of natural law have been debased by the manipulations of theorists until natural law has become indistinguishable from the law of the jungle, which is no law at all. Hence those who complacently prescribe the duty of national defense on the basis of "natural law" often forget entirely the norms of justice and humanity without which no war can be permitted. Without these norms, natural law becomes mere jungle law, that is to say crime.

Many Christians will with complete docility accept opinions and decisions that bear the stamp of jungle law rather than that of the Gospel. They will submit without protest to such directives, and they will feel little or no uneasiness of conscience, even though someone who has lost his faith in God may be shocked by such insensitivity and scandalized by this apparent perversion of the moral sense.

It is unfortunate that a spirit of minimalist legalism has in the past distorted the Christian perspectives both of the laity and the clergy. Hence we have sometimes allowed our consciences to be content with pharisaism and spiritual trifling, "straining [at] gnats and swallowing camels." Undoubtedly one of the most important objectives of John XXIII in calling the Second Vatican Ecumenical Council is to favor and encourage the great movement of renewal that is making itself felt in the Church today. The Holy Father obviously feels there is a real hope of the Church turning the tide of secularism and violence by

> taking the perennial, vital divine power of the Gospel and injecting it into the veins of the human society of today which glories in its recent scientific and technological advances at the same time as it is suffering damage to its social order. (*Humanae Salutis*, Dec. 25, 1961)

But at the same time this will not be possible, says Pope John, unless the grave dangers of the time "point up the need for vigilance *and make every individual aware of his own responsibilities.*" In particular the Pope refers specifically to questions of social justice, international relations and the whole climate of secularism and materialism in modern thought.

Nuclear war is certainly a case in point. It is quite certain that many Catholics who are spontaneously revolted by the natural injustice involved in the threat to answer "intolerable political provocation" with the annihilation of enemy cities, may swallow their repugnance and accept the prospect with docility, believing that "the leaders know best" and that in this case, as well as in any other case, it is always more Christian to suspend judgment and leave the decision to someone else. But how can this be true if the decision is left in the hands of men without firm moral standards, or compassion, or humanity? Worse still if it really depends on men of whom we know nothing, and who determine the policies and decisions of leaders we hopefully trust?

Lloyd George said that if the Churches had resolutely refused their blessing and cooperation, the First World War would never have been fought. It is quite true that the Popes and other religious spokesmen have come out tirelessly with clear, uncompromising directives to avoid violence: but these directives have either been minimized or set aside as inopportune by Catholics in countries that were actually at war. One can certainly appreciate the difficult position of the Churchmen, for instance in Nazi Germany during World War II. The fact remains that their cooperation with Hitler's unjust war effort is something of a scandal.*

The Popes have repeatedly pleaded with Christians to show themselves in all things disciples of Christ the Prince of Peace, and to embody in their lives their faith in His teaching. "All His teaching is an invitation to peace" says Pope John XXIII in the 1961 Christmas message. Deploring the ever increasing selfishness, hardness of heart, cynicism and callousness of mankind, as war becomes once again more and more imminent, Pope John says that Christian goodness and charity must permeate all the activity, whether personal or social, of every Christian. The Pontiff quotes St Leo the Great in a passage which contrasts natural ethics with the nonviolent ethic of the Gospel: "To commit injustice and to make reparation—this is the prudence of the world. On the contrary, *not to render evil for evil, is the virtuous expression of Christian forgiveness.*" These words, embodying the wisdom of the Church

---

* See Gordon Zahn, *German Catholics and Hitler's Wars* (New York: Sheed and Ward, 1962)[Merton's footnote].

and the heart of her moral teaching, are heard without attention and complacently dismissed as if they could not seriously apply to the present international crisis.

Here we come face to face with a serious ambiguity, which is very near the heart of the problem.

It is quite true that the blunt, unqualified statement that one "must not render evil for evil" seems disconcerting and hopelessly impractical when it is brought face to face with any concrete political problem, here and now. What possible relevance can such a principle have, we ask, when Khrushchev is threatening to rain down H-bombs on western Europe and America?

To say that we must not "render evil for evil" seems to mean that we must placidly fold our hands and allow ourselves to be enslaved or destroyed. But this is not the meaning of this basic Christian principle, otherwise how could such a principle ever be applied in politics? To take the principle as if it meant that alone is to understand it in an absurd sense.

It is obvious, too, that appeals to nonviolent action or even to unilateral disarmament tend to create the same false and absurd impression. It is certainly neither practical nor even sane to expect that thousands of military bureaucrats who people the Pentagon will suddenly have a change of heart and listen to the message of nonviolence one fine day, close down all their offices, cancel all the orders for new missiles, tear up all the defense contracts, and retire to *ashrams*.

Of course the "realist" who has finally discarded the thought of "not rendering evil for evil" as purely meaningless has perhaps something to be said for him. He has simplified his life. He has abolished the need to make his practical action conform to deep spiritual norms of morality. He has abolished a definitely uncomfortable and frustrating state of inner contradiction. When the enemy threatens him with a thousand megatons he can reply with a threat of ten thousand, and no nonsense about good and evil.

The sincere Christian cannot have it that easy. He is bound by his religious commitment to live with this inner conflict between seemingly irreconcilable extremes. Yet he is also bound to attempt, as far as he can with the grace of God, to reconcile them.

In reality the plea not to render evil for evil must retain some meaning even for a General in the age of nuclear war. What can that meaning be? Obviously it is not that one who has all his life lived in and for and by war and threat of war, should suddenly renounce all thought of retaliation when he is threatened. But nevertheless the principle is there, and one has to begin somewhere to observe it.

The point at which even a military strategist should consider himself bound not to render evil for evil is at least this: that an evil which takes the form of a political or military *threat* and which is most probably a bluff, is not to be met, ethically, *with the evil of actual force*. Not only that, but he should strive, if possible, to refrain from meeting it with an equally sinister or even more sinister political threat, and, while maintaining his defensive capacity, he should do all that he can to reduce tensions and to work for an eventual elimination of this evil altogether, by other than violent means.

This is certainly not unreasonable, and though it may not measure up to the perfection of the Gospel, it is at least a good start and one who can do this in our time has no reason to be ashamed.

But in actual fact politicians and military strategists in general tend to reject the uncomfortable principle of "not rendering evil for evil" altogether. They can do so quite easily by *simply refusing to take it in any other than an absurd sense.*

It is a tragic fact that one of the effects of the "Cold War mentality" is precisely this. Not only militarists but also theologians, priests and bishops have come to the point where, in the context of the Cold War crisis, they are *practically unable to take this basic principle seriously*. As Christians they will give it a formal nod of assent, but in a concrete political situation their complete obsession by Cold War phobias makes it *morally impossible for them to take the principle in any sense which is not absurd*. In a word, they cannot see it in any light that makes it worth considering, and hence they reject it from their practical judgments. It may end by having no influence whatever in the decisions of their conscience regarding nuclear war.

That is why, in practice, we tend to assume that the teaching of Christian forgiveness and meekness applies only to the individual, not to nations or collectivities. The state can go to war and exert every form of violent force, while the individual expresses his Christian meekness by shouldering his gun without resistance and obeying the command to go out and kill. The state need never forgive. The state can hate with impunity. The state can render evil for evil, and indeed even evil for good! This is not Pope John's idea at all. He utters a solemn warning to rulers of nations:

With the authority we have received from Jesus Christ we say: *Shun all thought of force; think of the tragedy of initiating a chain reaction of acts, decisions and resentments which could erupt into rash and irreparable deeds.* You have received great powers not to destroy but to build, not to divide but to unite, not to cause tears to be shed but to provide employment and security. (Christmas Message, 1961)

On the contrary, Pope John insists that peace must be based on an

appreciation of true brotherhood, for a resolution of sincere cooperation that stays clear of all intrigue and of those destructive factors that we will once again call by their proper names without any disguise: pride, greed, callousness, selfishness.

In this same Christmas Message the Pope says that the mentality of suspicion and hatred is unfortunately encouraged and strengthened by those who possess the art of forming public opinion and have a partial monopoly over it! In very serious terms he warned these men "to fear the stern judgment of God and of history and to proceed cautiously with respect and a sense of moderation."

He added, "We say this regretfully but frankly—the press has helped to create a climate of hostility, of animosity, of sharp division."

Notes

1. Although the term "a completely moral upheaval" may seem ungrammatical, there is a reason why Merton expressed himself in this way. The paragraph is one which appeared in a slightly altered form in the essay "Christian Action in World Crisis," reprinted in Thomas Merton, *Passion for Peace: The Social Essays,* edited by William H. Shannon (New York: Crossroad, 1995), 83. In the original essay, Merton had written "a great religious and moral upheaval." The change to "a completely moral upheaval" indicates that he was trying to focus on the problem as a question of morality, not introducing at this point the question of religion. The paragraph, and indeed the book itself, tries to address the moral question to the widest possible audience of readers who, in being "post-Christian," feel the necessity to address moral questions

even if they subscribe to no particular religious group. The word "entirely" might have made the sense clearer. The expression may seem inelegant, but the meaning is there.

2. Pope Pius XII used the term "God-Man" to refer to Christ. The complete text of the sentence is "If ever Christians neglect this duty of theirs by leaving inactive the guiding forces of the faith in public life, to the extent that they are responsible, they would be committing treason against the God-Man Who appeared in visible form among us in the cradle of Bethlehem." See Vincent A. Yzermans, ed., *The Major Addresses of Pope Pius XII, Vol II: Christmas Messages* (St. Paul: Northern Central Publishing Co., 1961), 205. This is a slightly different translation than Merton was using.

Forbidden Book: Thomas Merton's
Peace in the Post-Christian Era

Patricia A. Burton

In the summer of 1998, checking bibliography in the University of Toronto library system, I discovered that the University of St Michael's College Library had copies of several Merton mimeographs in their Rare Books collection. I was particularly interested in *Peace in the Post-Christian Era* (*PPCE*), Merton's book on the issue of nuclear war which had appeared only in mimeograph. Having carefully traced the parts of it through the Breit and Daggy bibliography,[1] I thought I knew what the copy would look like, and was surprised to find that the mimeograph in St Michael's library was different from the Breit and Daggy description.

Had Merton written two different versions of it? Using the published letters and journals, I worked out a timeline which showed when he might have done so (he made no direct mention of a rewrite anywhere). Through textual comparison with the mimeograph, I was able to ascertain how much of it had been published in articles and later in books such as *Seeds of Destruction*,[2] *The Nonviolent Alternative*[3] and *Passion for Peace*.[4] I could not explain, however, why the Breit and Daggy version (as I had assembled it) had only 93 pages, whereas the mimeograph had 138 pages, and why some of the sections of the mimeograph were not recorded at all in Breit and Daggy.

The Chief Librarian at the John M. Kelly Library, St Michael's, suggested that an exchange of copies might be arranged with the Thomas Merton Center at Bellarmine University in Louisville, so that I could delve more deeply into this apparent mystery. Through the good offices of both libraries, and with the approval of the Merton Legacy Trust, the trade of copies was done.[5]

What I expected to see when the copy arrived from the TMC was a 93-page mimeographed "short version" of *Peace in the Post-Christian Era* which matched the Breit and Daggy description. What was actually in the parcel was not a different version of the book, but a copy of the complex haystack of material which Merton had handed to the long-suffering typist who had made the mimeograph. I had been wrong about the possible existence of a shorter version. There were in fact about 170 pages (although the last page was hand-numbered 93), held together by various numbering and lettering systems, bristling with inserts and even whole extra chapters developed on the fly, all bearing signs of haste and also a monastic thrift about both text and paper. For some reason the bibliography had been based on this manuscript rather than the mimeograph made from it, and the manuscript is so complicated that it requires a copy of the mimeograph and the original articles to help decipher it. Thus this notoriously "forbidden" book had not been fully documented. My investigation had also shown that the book's history was an intriguing one, told only partially in the biographies and analyses I had read. The chance to evaluate a neglected Merton manuscript was an amazing opportunity, and examining it provided far more interesting insights than I had could have anticipated from any comparison of versions.

In treatments of Merton's life and writing, *Peace in the Post-Christian Era* is a rather shadowy piece about which certain ideas linger: the description "unpublished" is the principal one. There are oft-quoted self-deprecating remarks Merton made, as though he had given up on it, and a rather triumphant passage in his journal which has been interpreted to mean that he did get to publish the whole thing after all, in *Seeds of Destruction*. This is not the case: the story is much more complex. A recent article in *The Merton Journal* reports a discussion at a "Pilgrimage to Prades" tour: "in '63 the Pope himself published the encyclical *Pacem in Terris* and Merton became free to write openly again."[6] As we shall see, exactly the opposite happened.

In order to focus more sharply on *Peace in the Post-Christian Era* in this account, I have not described all the other writing Merton was doing at the same period of his life, since many good accounts exist.[7] Masked by the other myriad details of his writing, the story of Merton's defense of the book looks scattered, random; without the other details it looks almost obsessive in its determined return to the subject time after time.

Textual comparisons and word counts indicate that approximately 45% of the text does not match with any of the published articles. Merton did not simply bridge together a few articles already written, but worked in a great deal of new text, and after its appearance in mimeograph he fought for it for the better part of two years and managed to salvage part of it with great difficulty.

In this study I hope to show that an accurate description and history of *Peace in the Post-Christian Era* deserve a place in the Merton canon.

Why Write about War?

Why was a monk (and famous spiritual author) commenting on social questions? There is a sound monastic and clerical tradition in respect of that kind of writing, in which well-known monastics and mystics wrote letters to the great and powerful, often with complaints about the ethics of their actions. Merton already had his exemplar: in 1953 he had written a Foreword to a translation of letters of Bernard of Clairvaux addressed to a wide variety of people, including the politically powerful. Merton remarked that although Bernard's letters were often angry, there was another side to his character: "gentle and longsuffering ... tender as a mother," and concluded "perhaps our own century needs nothing so much as the combined anger and gentleness of another Bernard."[8]

Whether in imitation of Bernard or not, Merton began to write and collect letters which he ultimately published in mimeographed form. He had set himself the task of "getting into contact with the others most concerned" in the autumn of 1961.[9] William Shannon marks the year of Merton's greatest activity against nuclear war as "The Year of the Cold War Letters" (October 1961 to October 1962)(*PFP*, 6). It is certainly true that Merton put his most intense efforts into peace writing during this time, but it seems also to be generally accepted that after the activity of that year, Merton (understandably as a result of repeated refusals from Superiors) abandoned his writing against nuclear war and let the issue drop. This assumption needs to be tested not only against Merton's writing but also against his actions during and after that year. Merton's tenacity was well-known when he felt conviction over an issue. Challenged directly, he tended to fall back and seemed to acquiesce; when changed circumstances offered a new opportunity, he took the initiative again.

Contemplation and Activism

On August 22, 1961, Merton had used a book by Christopher Dawson, *Understanding Europe*, to help articulate a mission for himself:

I have a clear obligation to participate, as long as I can, and to the extent of my abilities, in every effort to help a spiritual and cultural renewal of our time. This is the task that has been given me, and hitherto I have not been clear about it, in all its aspects and dimensions. ... This for the restoration of man's sanity and balance, that he may return to the ways of freedom and of peace, if not in my time, at least some day soon. (*TTW*, 155)

In Merton's situation in 1962 "action" had come to mean his own kind of activism on current issues like nuclear war (and the need for the abolition of all war) "Primarily of course by prayer. I remain a contemplative"(*TTW*, 175). His journals in 1961 are full of entries about writing in a time of crisis, from August 29, 1961: "I have been considering the possibility of writing a kind of statement—'Where I stand'...There is *no other activity* available to me"(*TTW*, 157), to November 25, 1961: "Yesterday afternoon at the hermitage, surely a decisive clarity came. That I must definitely commit myself to opposition to, and non-cooperation with, nuclear war" (*TTW*, 182). On October 29, 1961 he recorded, "Yesterday I finished an article on Peace: Christian duties and perspectives. Discussed it a little with the novices, which was a good idea. It will certainly not please many people"(*TTW*, 174). The article, later twice rewritten, was the first in a series which would come to be associated with *Peace in the Post-Christian Era*.

Whatever the hesitations and arguments against writing, there were equivalent forces pushing Merton to act: in many of his letters from the early 1960s, particularly those published in *The Hidden Ground of Love*, one theme repeatedly cropped up: his worry about what appeared to be the moral passivity of American Catholics, who were content to accept the lead of the Church even on questionable moral issues like the threat of nuclear annihilation inherent in the Cold War. To Etta Gullick he wrote:

...it is absolutely necessary to take a serious and articulate stand on the question of nuclear war. And I mean against nuclear war. The passivity, the apparent indifference, the incoherence of so many Christians on this issue, and worse still the active belligerency of some religious spokesmen, especially in this country, is rapidly becoming one of the most frightful scandals in the history of Christendom.[10]

Power versus Influence

Merton never had any official power in the hierarchy of the Church, but as a well-known author, he had traded power for influence: he wrote to two Popes, to the sister-in-law of the U.S. President, to a U.S. Secretary of State, to the mayor of Hiroshima, to a Zen master and several Muslims—in short, to anyone with whom he wanted to share communication. During his inner debate about writing for peace, he had recorded a dialogue in his journal:

> A monk said to Joshua—"What is the way?"
> He replied: "Outside the fence."
> The monk said, "I mean the great way: what is the great way?"
> Joshua replied, "The great way is that which leads to the Capital." Remember this in this war business, please. Stay on the way where you now are and don't get off it to run all over the countryside shouting "peace! peace!" But stay on the great way which leads to the Capital. (*TTW*, 176)

How was one to stay on the great way and also outside the fence? In 1954, writing *The Last of the Fathers*, Merton quoted advice from a letter of Bernard of Clairvaux to William of Saint Thierry, advice which Merton later passed on to Daniel Berrigan (also in trouble because of his activism for peace):

> But putting aside what both of us wish, as it is right we should, is safer for me and more advantageous for you if I advise you as I think God wishes. Therefore I say hold on to what you have, remain where you are.... Do not try to escape the responsibility of office while you are still able to discharge it...[11]

Merton's advice to Berrigan was:

> ...if you get yourself censured or kicked out or something, even though a benevolent bishop may eventually with many sighs grab you just before you hit the left field fence, you will spell out too unmistakably for comfort that the Church is plenty conservative and still profoundly asleep in some areas where she ought to be most awake. (*HGL*, 77)

In other words, stay where you are, do what you can, and remember that you are seen as a representative of the Church. The irony is, of course, that you cannot leave without jeopardizing your influence.

Eventually, when writing about criticism of his peace book from E. I. Watkin in September 1962, Merton once again painfully confronted the same choices, and said in his journal:

> [Watkin] asserts he would listen to *no* authority against conscience on this issue. But my position loses its meaning unless I can continue to speak from the center of the Church. Yet that is exactly the point: where is that true center? From the bosom of complacent approbation by Monsignors? (*TTW*, 244-245)

Even influence had its price, and Merton would come to know that more and more as time went on. As in the case of William and of Berrigan, to be most effective he had to stay put.

Whence the Title?

February of 1962 found Merton debating the place and influence of Christianity on the wider culture. Bruno Paul Schlesinger had sent him an essay by George Tavard; Merton remarked in a letter of February 10, 1962:

> I agree, too of course, as anyone with eyes and ears must inevitably agree, that "Christendom" has ceased to exist and that we are *bel et bien* [well and truly] in the post-Christian era."(*HGL*, 544)

The term "post-Christian" could be seen as the philosophic nexus of Merton's turn to the world. As an idealistic young man, in a 1941 letter to Catherine de Hueck Doherty he had speculated about whether there could be a "completely Catholic government," and even went on to say that he imagined Vatican City as a place where "politics would be, all down the line, subordinated to salvation"(*HGL*, 5). By the time he wrote his "Peace book" he knew more about what was to be expected from politics and the relative place of the Church in the world. The use of the term "post-Christian" automatically put the viewpoint of Merton's book in a larger world where the Church was no longer the focal point. The Christian philosophers Merton was reading might have been able to get away with such a title, but its use by a religious was risky (it would be absolutely guaranteed to annoy the Abbot General).

Merton only directly attributed the source of the term "post-Christian" once, in a small pamphlet he wrote for the Sisters of Loretto: "Christian dissent is all the more essential as we enter what C. S. Lewis has called the *post-Christian* era" (italics Merton's).[12] C. S. Lewis had described the term in his 1954 inaugural lecture at Cambridge, in which he spoke of the era as follows:

> roughly speaking we may say that whereas all history was for our ancestors divided into two periods, the pre-Christian and the Christian, and two only, for us it falls into three - the pre-Christian, the Christian, and what may reasonably be called the post-Christian. [...] [T]he second change is even more radical than the first. Christians and Pagans had much more in common with each other than either has with a post-Christian. The gap between those who worship different gods is not so wide as that between those who worship and those who do not.[13]

Lewis did not believe that the onset of this "new age" meant a mere "relapse into Paganism": on the contrary, the possibility of a simple historical reversal did not exist:

> that Europe can come out of Christianity "by the same door as in she went"...is not what happens. A post-Christian man is not a Pagan; you might as well think that a married woman recovers her virginity by divorce. The post-Christian is cut off from the Christian past and therefore doubly from the Pagan past.[14]

Merton was later to admit that the phrase "post-Christian era" might sound provocative.[15] The idea is reworked and more clearly articulated in *Conjectures of a Guilty Bystander* (and by 1966 when it was published, Merton had done some careful alterations to his language):

> The Church is now in a world that is culturally "post-Christian." (Theologically, one cannot really speak of a "post-Christian era." The "Christian era" is the time of the end, the last era ...) Tavard's

idea is that, by turning to the world and working with those who are not explicitly Christian, we can perhaps in our convergence with them bring about a resurrection of basically Christian values in secular culture.[16]

The Published Articles

In a letter to Daniel Berrigan, December 7, 1961, Merton demonstrated that his internal struggles about this writing had continued to evolve into action:

> I am getting out an ingenuous, wide-eyed article on peace in the Christmas *Commonweal* [the article was later deferred to February 1962] ... I have been asked to write for *The Nation*, and may perhaps do something on "Christian Ethics and Nuclear War." Laying down a barrage all around, and then when the smoke clears we'll see what it did. Probably not much. (*HGL*, 72)

In his journal, the interior debate went on:

> About peace. Maybe the best is to say quickly and wisely and fully all that I have to say, all at once, and then let the blow fall. [...] No point in saving up the ammunition for later, there may be no later. (*TTW*, 187)

By the beginning of 1962, the Merton's "barrage" was in place. In short order several essays made it through censorship and were published; one in particular (ominously) would be refused:

• "Nuclear War and Christian Responsibility" in *Commonweal* in February, followed by controversy and a rewrite in *The Catholic Worker* in May-June 1962, called "We Have to Make Ourselves Heard." This version was later to be used as the basis for "Peace: A Religious Responsibility" in *Breakthrough to Peace*, and as a framework for *Peace in the Post-Christian Era*;
• "Christian Ethics and Nuclear War" in *The Catholic Worker* in March, before it had passed the censors (resulting in another rewrite, published as "Religion and the Bomb" in *Jubilee*, in May 1962);
• "Red or Dead: Anatomy of a Cliché" in *Fellowship* in March 1962, and included in a Fellowship pamphlet;
• "Christian Action in World Crisis" in *Blackfriars* in June 1962;

- "Target Equals City," a mimeograph Merton started mailing to friends in about February 1962, although it was not otherwise published in his lifetime. It appears that this article in particular got him into censorship trouble.[17]

By the spring of 1962 Merton had at hand carbon copies (and in one case a mimeograph) of various versions of all of these articles: textual comparison with the manuscript makes it clear that he used these as a basis for the book *Peace in the Post-Christian Era*. The book had been requested: in a letter of March 4, 1962 to Jay Laughlin, Merton wrote "Macmillan offered me a ten thousand dollar advance for a book on peace, after the recent *Commonweal* article."[18]

Breakthrough to Peace

As if it were not enough to be embroiled in writes and re-writes, Merton had also suggested another project in a letter to James Laughlin, his friend and publisher at New Directions, at the end of October 1961: "An idea has occurred to me for a [New Directions] paperback for next spring, on Peace. It could be a kind of anthology..."(*TMJL*, 183). Laughlin was enthusiastic about the idea, and Merton began to gather articles by other authors, casting his net wide in order to get as many well-known contributors as possible. The anthology would eventually be called *Breakthrough to Peace* and would contain a long article by Merton (the fourth rewrite of that first article of October 1961) which he also used as a framework upon which to build *Peace in the Post-Christian Era*. Because the gestation of *Breakthrough to Peace* was more or less simultaneous with that of *Peace in the Post-Christian Era*, some editors of Merton material have confused the two.[19]

Editing *Breakthrough to Peace* was an important formative experience for Merton. The roster of authors and range of themes in the book could hardly have been faulted, which makes it seem even stranger that the Cistercian Abbot General would later tell Merton not to write about nuclear war because he knew nothing about the issues.[20]

Dating the Mimeograph

Merton did not generally make it easy for scholars and bibliographers by systematically referring in his journals to what he was writing. The journal reference to the article he read to the novices finally dates the essay initially called "Peace: Christian Duties and Perspectives" to October 29, 1961(*TTW*, 174). In Merton's lifetime this version of the article was available only as a mimeograph. Gordon Zahn included it in *The Nonviolent Alternative* and wrote a footnote about its similarities with "Peace: A Religious Responsibility."[21] William Shannon, in his introduction to the essay "Nuclear War and Christian Responsibility" refers to the piece published by Zahn as "fairly close to the original [i.e. "Nuclear War and Christian Responsibility"], but toned down a bit."[22]

The earlier dating in Merton's journal of that first essay shows that the order of events was in reality reversed, making a little more evident that Merton was not necessarily carrying on a course of "toning down and diluting" his ideas in order to get the censors' approval. It is important to recognize the date order of the essays in the context of his friends' later arguments about whether he had "gone far enough." The article "Peace: Christian Duties and Perspectives" came first and was elaborated in a string of rewrites ("tuned up" rather than "toned down," one might say).

As to the exact time when Merton wrote *PPCE*: there is negative evidence in the relatively small amount of other writing he did in April of 1962: he had been averaging 14 journal entries per month at the time, but for April there are only four. Similarly, in March of 1962 he wrote 24 letters, in May another 21, but in April only ten.[23] Two of his letters further identify the time he was working on the manuscript. To Abdul Aziz on April 4 he wrote: "I want to write a book against nuclear war and am engaged in this now"(*HGL*, 52). On April 12 he wrote to the atomic physicist Leo Szilard that he wished "to devote a notable part of the royalties of a book I am currently writing, on peace, to your cause."[24] By April 29, he was able to write to Jim Forest "I have been trying to finish my book on peace, and have succeeded in time for the ax to fall"(*HGL*, 266). The only direct mention of the book in Merton's journal at the time is an April 26, 1962 entry: "I read to the novices in a conference a bit of the Peace ms - on Machiavelli - and Teller"(*TTW*, 215).

How Merton Worked: the Evidence of the Manuscript

The manuscript of *Peace in the Post-Christian Era* is a palimpsest incorporating layers of writing and editing built up over months. To construct the book, Merton used a carbon copy of one version of "Peace: A Religious Responsibility," physically disassembling it into parts, and then inserting parts of other essays into it as chapters, keeping the whole together by writing a large new page number with a circle around it in the upper right corner of each page, the last being 93.[25] It is evident that the Breit and Daggy bibliography used the pagination of this manuscript rather than of the mimeograph made from it.

Merton edited the material extensively and carefully. A good deal of new text was written in on the blank facing pages of the carbon-copied parts. Careful textual comparison indicates that Merton sometimes even used carbons of different versions of the same essay. Each represented a stage in the development of a particular article, and in the end nothing perfectly matched anything else (the carbons vary in some details from the published versions). That Merton had more than one typist is indicated in the varying typewriter pitches and different page-numbering styles used by individual typists. It is possible to detect, for example, that he used pages from two different versions of "Peace: A Religious Responsibility" and that each of these differed somewhat from the published versions of the essay.

Matthew Kelty recounts that as a novice he had experience as Merton's typist:

> He'd assign me to type stencils for him. That was his work style. He used to write out, type out his articles, and then revise them, I think in red, and then revise them again in black, and then we would type it out on a stencil and mimeograph it, and then he would send it out to a lot of his friends.[26]

In addition to recycling material he already had, Merton also added whole extra sections after he had done his initial 93-page layout: a five-page insert to page 61 (numbered 61a, 61b etc.), in order to further discuss theological views of war; a new chapter at page 77 (77a through 77g), to discuss the scientists' views of nuclear strategy, describing particularly the contrast between the ideas of physicists Leo Szilard and Edward Teller.[27] After his circled page 82, he interpolated two whole chapters with pages numbered 82a through 82q (using as a foundation the Blackfriars essay "Christian Action in World Crisis"[28]), which may have been included late in the process because of censorship delays with the original essay.

There is evidence in the manuscript that Merton carried the piece around with him and worked whenever he got the chance. In the case of the manuscript page 12, he typed an initial paragraph, removed the page and put it into a different typewriter to continue, then edited the whole by hand.

The manuscript looks as though it had been done in bursts of great speed and energy. It also shows an organizing intelligence which kept the many seemingly ramshackle parts from collapsing into chaos.[29]

New Material

It is important to note also that there is a central section of the book which was not based on previously published articles. That this section was new is demonstrated by the quality of the copy in the manuscript, which is either in handwriting or in Merton's error-prone rough draft typing style. It became evident later that this was a part of the book which Merton did want to publish (and it was probably the same part which later caused criticisms from his friends). There is evidence in Merton's notes on the first page of the manuscript of a pre-existing draft or outline called "Peace-A Christian Responsibility," the parts of which evolved under the following headings:

- "Can We Choose Peace?"
- "The Christian as Peacemaker"
- "War in Origen and St Augustine"
- "The Legacy of Machiavelli"

In the manuscript, these involve an 8-page section "Can We Choose Peace?" and a section of 19 pages, numbered in the draft 8a, 8b, etc., up to 8s, following on page 8 of the section called "The Christian as Peacemaker." These are unmistakably in rough draft form, but show evidence of having been edited after the initial writing.

These newly-written parts of the book set the peace question in the framework of Church's traditional view of the just war, and in the context of Christian morality. What Merton did subsequently showed that he had not forgotten which parts of the manuscript came from copies of existing articles, and which he had written specifically to place the crisis in terms of Christian history.

The Abbot General's Order

On April 27, 1962, Dom James Fox handed Merton a letter dated January 20, 1962 from the Abbot General of the Cistercians, Dom Gabriel Sortais, requesting that Merton no longer write on the issues of war and peace. Along with this was a refusal by a censor[30] and a request that Merton not send him any more articles of the kind. Merton wondered what was to become of the "book that is practically finished for Macmillan." Dom James seemed "inclined to let the book go through and be censored at least, then published if passed." Merton flirted with the idea of giving up on the whole thing, and wondered what was God's will in the matter.[31]

The element of time in enforcing the ban is noted by William Shannon in *Silent Lamp*: Dom James delayed notification from January to April of 1962, allowing Merton to publish several key articles(*SL*, 222-23). The Abbot must also have given Merton permission to mimeograph the text, using monastery labor. It took the rest of April and May and part of June, to finish typing the mimeograph stencils, and even then the Abbot could have stopped it at any time. Dom James may simply have been providing what seemed a reasonable safety valve, perhaps seeing no harm in a limited distribution of copies.

As soon as he had received the order about peace writing, Merton immediately wrote to Dom Gabriel on behalf of the book, explaining that it was a rewrite of articles already censored (but with additions and changes), asking that he at least be allowed to submit it to the censors.[32] Dom Gabriel's reply did not arrive for a month, and in that time Merton still entertained hopes, although he did inform J. Laughlin and Jim Forest that his peace writing had met resistance.[33] In a letter to Ernesto Cardenal on May 22, 1962 Merton was still hoping that he could send royalties to Leo Szilard to help with his peace movement.[34]

The reply from Dom Gabriel arrived on May 26, 1962, and left no doubt that Merton was to give up the idea of the book and "de vous abstenir désormais d'écrire sur ce sujet de la guerre atomique...[35] ["That you abstain from writing *from now on* about the subject of nuclear war" (Italics mine).] Merton wrote to the General on the same day, saying "I accept your decision joyfully"(*SCH*, 144), (although he still could not refrain from trying to defend it again in the letter) and confirmed this in his journal entry of the day (*TTW*, 221). As he had done before in other circumstances, Merton said it was a relief, but the matter was far from over.

Obedience, Censorship and Publication

The situation was drifting in an extraordinary direction: Merton was about to become a well-known writer against war who was not allowed to write against war. It was a decade when people were demonstrating, marching in the street with banners, burning draft cards, spending time in jail. Marching out the front door of the monastery and joining the peace movement on the street was not an option Merton was considering, but he found his own way: in the end, his "banner carried in the street" consisted in being silenced and letting people know about it, meanwhile making sure as many people as possible saw the "forbidden book." Contact through correspondence with an ever-widening circle of friends had given Merton an informal channel which he would greatly need as time went on.

Merton was by 1961 fully experienced at dealing with Dom Gabriel's strictures. When the Abbot General told Merton not to write about Teilhard de Chardin's *The Divine Milieu*, Merton wrote in his journal

> I have *no obligation* to form my thought or my conscience along the rigid lines of Dom Gabriel. I will certainly accept and obey his decision, but I reserve the right to disagree with him. (*TTW*, 65)

When confronted by Superiors, Merton tended to give way; however, when he had assimilated a subject so thoroughly as this one, he could not automatically stop thinking about it, and it inevitably emerged both in his writing and in his actions. In this struggle there was also an interior process of growth going on. Mott's biography notes that Merton's knowledge of his own vulnerability and need for approval made the decision to try to publish the peace material even more difficult (Mott, 368). An additional factor in the problem was Merton's concern for the Church itself. Whereas another writer might have responded to the publication ban with wounded *amour-propre* and indignant demands for free speech, Merton's main worry was what the ban meant in terms of the way the Church was regarded.

As to whether the ban had upset him or not: by June 4, Merton seemed to have adopted a sort of devil-may-care attitude and said in a letter to W. H. Ferry, "I am not sore, not even very much interested any more...Have been going back to Origen and Tertullian"(*HGL*, 212). When Merton went out of his way to say he did not feel something, it often meant that he did, but was too overwhelmed at the moment to be able to sort it out. His letters to Robert Lax were usually more honest, although couched in a private language:

I have been silence. I have been nacht und nebel for my war book....I have been put in the calabozo. I have been shut up in a tin can. I have been shrewdly suppressed at the right moment. I have been stood in the corner. I have been made to wear the cap. I have been tried and tested in the holy virtue of humility. I have been found wanting and tested some more. I have been told to shut up about the wars, wars is not for Christians except to support.
Hence my dear Charlot the laments in the current Jubilee is my finale. It comes a little agent with too big an overcoat and false glasses with a copy of contraband war book in about six weeks. Nobody to print, nobody to show. Just read the dmn war book.

Lax replied in kind:

am thanking you for the book of thoughts on you-know-what. very good,strong, powerful, well-thought-out bk. [...]
ora (plenty) for nos intransigeants.
it is the time of the mop.[36]

Merton went on to obey the direct order from the Abbot General in the most literal and careful manner possible, warning editors and friends not to publish any of his writing on nuclear war after the ban, especially noting the phrase "from now on." He clung, however, to the pieces which had been passed by censors as if they were still to be allowed because the ban was a matter of timing.

Criticism from Friends

Merton mentioned in letters to Catherine de Hueck Doherty and John Heidbrink that the mimeograph stencils had just been finished when the order to stop writing had arrived, saying "I will run off a few copies anyway and friends can see it."[37] In a letter to James Laughlin, he said "the Abbot General vetoed it…The Peace Book[38] will be mimeographed shortly"(*TMJL*, 207-208). The mimeographed copies were ready in mid-June of 1962, and Merton sent copies immediately to his "peace friends," including Jim Forest, Daniel Berrigan, Etta Gullick, Dorothy Day, John Harris, Sister Emmanuel de Souza e Silva and Charles S. Thompson, the publisher of *Pax Bulletin* in England.[39]

As to his own opinion of his mimeographed book, Merton was as usual self-deprecating. A statement to Jim Forest in a letter of July 6, 1962 has been generally adopted as Merton's definitive judgment of his book and his intentions for it. Responding to Forest's comments about his apparent equivocation in order to please the censors of his order, he said:

> I was bending in all directions to qualify every statement and balance everything off, so I stayed right in the middle and perfectly objective, and so on, and then at the same time tried to speak the truth as my conscience wanted it to be said. In the long run the result is about zero.[…] My feeling is that it is not worth the trouble to do anything more with this book. Let it die. There is plenty of good stuff coming out now… [40]

The way Merton embraced the criticisms of *Peace in the Post-Christian Era* indicates that they may have been ironically comforting to him: recognizing that the book was not perfect made its suppression less painful for the author. At the time, he was only allowed one chance to get it right. If the book had gone through a normal editing and censorship process, some of its problems might have been ironed out. But as Merton said in a September 1962 letter to E. I. Watkin, "It did not even get to the censors, so I did not have a chance to find out if what I said accorded with the teaching of the Church" (*HGL*, 579). For the Church's purposes, the book simply did not exist, while for Merton's purposes it was only a mimeograph, and thus "unpublished." As those who manned the guns at Fort Knox might have said, it flew under the radar.

It also turned out that regardless of what Merton had said about the book, he did not stop mailing it, promoting it in letters, and trying to get another chance at rewriting it.

More Copies

By July 7, 1962, when Merton wrote his self-deprecating letter to Jim Forest, there were only "about a dozen" mimeo stencils left(*HGL*, 269). In early August Merton mentioned to John Heidbrink that he was going to "run off a few more copies and will send you half a dozen"(*HGL*, 409). There had been a few occurrences on other fronts to encourage him.

At the end of August 1962, copies of the anthology *Breakthrough to Peace* arrived from the printer, and Merton at last got a chance to rejoice a little: "I am glad of it and proud of it. What I wanted to do last August, I have done. I have taken my position, and it is known"(*TTW*, 240). Through the summer of 1962 Merton had also been working with Thomas P. MacDonnell on *A Thomas Merton Reader* for Harcourt, Brace. He noted in a letter to W. H. Ferry that he had

all the most outspoken stuff concentrated in one place so that if they didn't know before, the Squares will know now that I am on the other side of some fence. (*HGL*, 213)

Merton put most of "Religion and the Bomb" in the *Reader*, renaming the first part of it "May 1962" as if to memorialize his own silencing.[41]

In September, 1962 Merton learned from Jim Forest that the National Committee for a Sane Nuclear Policy (SANE) were doing their bit by re-mimeographing the text. Merton nervously hoped they would be careful about publication (*HGL*, 270). He lamented again in his journal about being powerless if he could not write, and even thought about the writing as a sort of last will, in the context of his own death: "Now is the time to give what I have to others, and not reflect on it" (*TTW*, 249, 253).

Along the way, Merton had also gained another supporter and friend in Leslie Dewart, a philosophy professor at St Michael's College, University of Toronto, to whom he sent a copy of the second printing. Dewart noted the arrival date of the mimeograph on the cover of his copy "August 27, 1962," thus giving us further evidence for the date of the second run of the mimeograph.

Witness to Freedom includes a section of text (*WTF*, 288-293) which Merton sent to Dewart in the hope that it could somehow be worked into the book Dewart was developing, *Christianity and Revolution-The Lesson of Cuba.*[42] Dewart used the text and other parts of their correspondence to craft a dialogue between the two of them, which he thought might be used as an appendix to his book. Merton approved of Dewart's work: "This appendix is great, and really packs a wallop." He went on to describe in careful detail how much Dewart could quote directly from him (*WTF*, 293-294). The appendix was not included in Dewart's book, but eventually appeared as an article in *Continuum* under Dewart's name, with a title that echoed that of Merton's mimeograph, and characterized the essence of the debate between them: "A Post-Christian Age?"[43] Dewart was so careful in the way he used Merton's text and his name, that the article has escaped the bibliographers.

The Pressure of Events

Merton had need of the extra mimeograph copies he had made up in August. Two events of October 1962 brought the issues to life again. One was the Cuban Missile crisis; going back and forth to Louisville, Merton heard bits of the story and worried over it, not only because the world had come close to nuclear war but also because he feared some might feel an indecent sense of triumph at a "cold war victory"(*TTW*, 260ff.). The other event was the beginning of Vatican II on October 11, 1962. Merton's friends Jean and Hildegard Goss-Mayr were preparing a submission on peace for the Council. He concentrated on plying them with information, including copies of *Peace in the Post-Christian Era*, calling it the "most complete text I have written" on the subject and asking if he should be sending copies of things "to any bishops."[44] Not wasting another opportunity in his campaign to convince the General, he added: "Incidentally I suggest you go see our Abbot General, Dom Gabriel Sortais, and give him a strong push in favor of my writing about peace," and went on to give advice on the right way to handle Dom Sortais (*HGL*, 327-328, 330).

At Christmas 1962, more copies went off, to Abdul Aziz and Edward Deming Andrews among others.[45] Mailings to a wider circle of friends indicated that Merton now felt that the peace writing had a central position in his work, no matter what his superiors thought, and that he should share it with all his friends. He even recommended to Jacques Maritain that mimeography might be a good way to publish Raïssa Maritain's *Journal*: "Through a little book of my own on peace, whose publication was forbidden, I can vouch for the fact that private circulation goes much further"(*CFT*, 35). In February of 1963 he sent a copy to Maritain, and in the accompanying letter made it evident that he was still smarting from the Abbot General's rebuke that his defense of peace

> *"fausserait le message de la vie contemplative"*...a hateful distraction, withdrawing one's mind from Baby Jesus in the Crib. Strange to say, no one seems concerned at the fact that the crib is directly under the bomb. (*CFT*, 36)

The tone is reminiscent of his Christmas message sent to Lax in their usual code, where humour hid despair:

> as for me my dear Charlot I sit in my hutch mimeographing forbidden books with the help of fifty-nine uncouth Albanian novices all highly irregular and dissipated ready for the most desperate acts. For the rest our situation is too awful to be described.[46]

Pacem in Terris

Merton's journal entry of April 23, 1963 recorded that Pope John XXIII's encyclical *Pacem in Terris* had been read in the refectory at Gethsemani: "The document is in every way sane, lucid and admirable"(*TTW*, 315). In his peace articles and in *Peace in the Post-Christian Era*, Merton had quoted all the papal statements he could find which might be interpreted as condemnations of nuclear war; there were Christmas messages and other speeches, but up to that point no definitive papal statement on war. When *Pacem in Terris* was published, Merton wrote to Abbot General Sortais, to request that he be allowed "to recast this book [*PPCE*] while commenting on *Pacem in Terris*"(*SCH*, 166). He once again aired his reasons for doing so. This time the answer was not long in coming. In both his Journal (*TTW*, 317-318) and a letter to Dewart, Merton records Sortais' answer,

> categorically refusing me permission to publish Peace in the PCE and ordering me to drop all thought of doing so, with or without comments on the encyclical. His reasons: I am a contemplative monk and my business is silence and solitude. Besides that, ... the encyclical ...does not deprive a nation of the right to acquire nuclear weapons and arm with them for its self-defense...And

finally I am just incompetent anyhow and my opinions are of no value since I don't know what I am talking about in the first place.[…] [T]he book goes on the shelf. (*WTF*, 286)

This was the third time the General had specifically stepped on Merton's peace writing. Merton consoled himself by writing a letter to Ethel Kennedy, sister-in-law of the President of the United States, on May 14, 1963:

I wrote a book on peace which the Superiors decided I ought to bury about ten feet deep behind the monastery someplace, but I still don't think it is that bad. I mimeographed it and am sending you a copy, just for the files or, who knows, maybe the President might have five minutes to spare looking at it. If you think he would, I will even send him a copy. (*HGL*, 447)

As time went on Merton still had not forgotten about his "unpublished" book, and mentioned it in a letter in January 1964 to Bishop John J. Wright, who had been enthusiastic enough about it to circulate it among some of the *periti* at Vatican II. Merton, encouraged, had offered more copies and commented "Even though the book is not published, I am happy to think that the work was not wasted"(*HGL*, 609). It had been two years since Merton had started in on this work, and his efforts on its behalf had resulted only in reinforcement of the ban.

Seeds of Destruction: A New Crisis

Merton did have hopes that at least some of his peace articles and letters might be published in a new book of essays for Farrar, Straus, Giroux, to be called *Seeds of Destruction*. In March of 1964, however, he experienced yet another rebound effect of the dispute with Dom Sortais in 1962. To Naomi Burton Stone, he wrote on March 3:

..the unthinkable has happened. […] A letter from the new Abbot General [Dom Ignace Gillet] came in concerning the articles on peace in *Seeds of Destruction*. … [He] dug out all the correspondence, had a meeting with the definitors, and said that these articles are not to be "republished" in book form and implicitly in any other form […] Hence […] we have to take out the articles on war. I am sick about this… (*WTF*, 142-143)

So sick, in fact, that Merton went on to question his own vocation and wondered if it was all "the most monumental mistake"(*WTF*, 143). The sorrow expressed in his journal entry of the day was clearly not just because of his own feelings but because the ban provided a "grim insight into the stupor of the Church, in spite of all that has been attempted, all efforts to wake her up!" and once more stating "I cannot leave here in order to protest since the meaning of any protest depends on my staying here."[47]

This was the low point in Merton's struggle over his peace writing. Within three days he had become more philosophical, and was able to write to Dom Ignace saying that he was "dropping this type of work" and assuring him of his "genuine loyalty and obedience"(*SCH*, 209). Merton was still sore and sad enough about it all to mention the problem in letters to Jim Forest, Leslie Dewart and W. H. Ferry.[48]

What were the articles Merton wanted to use in *Seeds of Destruction*? A letter in the research files of William H. Shannon answers that very question. The letter is from Robert Daggy, and it describes

the first 'uncorrected proofs' of *Seeds of Destruction*. In the typescript Merton had inserted the mimeograph and cut pages from three articles written in 1962—he makes it plain in the first proofs that these articles appeared almost without change just as they had appeared in journals. They were:

1. "Nuclear War and Christian Responsibility," *Commonweal* 75 (9 February 1962)
2. "Religion and the Bomb," *Jubilee* 10 (May 1962)
3. "Christian Action in World Crisis," *Blackfriars* 43 (June 1962)
[…] one set of proofs has these three totally removed-the other set still has them with (Naomi thought in Bob Giroux's handwriting) the notation "Kill pp.36-59"[49]

So Merton had gone back to the original text of three published articles, hoping that what had passed the censors once would do so again. He had not attempted to use the rewritten versions which appeared as chapters in *Peace in the Post-Christian Era*, or any of the newer, uncensored material there, but his care over the censorship issue had been for nothing. Two years into the dispute there still seemed to be no hope that Merton would ever be able to publish these articles in book form.

What saved the situation was the intervention of Robert Giroux. Merton said in his journal,

> [A] call came from Bob Giroux in New York. It appears that the problem of publishing *Seeds of Destruction* is being finally resolved. (Giroux wrote to the General and got a settlement. One essay on war may be printed if I will "transform" it.)(*DWL*, 107)

What the "transformation" required is noted in Mott's biography: Merton "could write about peace, not war—he was not to show pessimism"(Mott, 400).

"the real heart"

Over an astonishing ten days between June 2 and June 12, 1964, as he described to Leslie Dewart, Merton rewrote

> about a third of [*Seeds of Destruction*]. The earlier stuff on the bomb which had been permitted is now no longer licit and I have to do it all over, writing about peace without treating the question of the bomb. I suppose the next thing I can do is write about marriage without referring to sexual love. (*WTF*, 297)

When he needed a new, full-length article, Merton knew just where to find the basis for it in the *PPCE* mimeograph. By October 1964 Merton had told Jim Forest that he had "no more copies [of *Peace in the Post-Christian Era*], but the essence of it is going to be in my new book..." (*HGL*, 282). This indicates that by June he probably had only his personal copy left, and it is likely that he used that. If he followed the same pattern with "The Christian in World Crisis" as he had with *Peace in the Post-Christian Era* (bearing in mind his usual thrift about text) he would simply have pulled out pages 6 to 16 and 29 to 49 of the mimeograph (text which he knew had never appeared elsewhere), made his annotations, written the new material around them, and handed the revised whole to the typist.[50] The items he used were the section "Can We Choose Peace?" and those which treated of philosophical and theological tradition, "War in Origen and St Augustine," "The Legacy of Machiavelli" and "The Christian as Peacemaker."

My textual comparisons showed that he did not extensively edit the recycled material, but fitted it up with new sections to change the focus. There is a very small overlap with "Peace: A Religious Reponsibility" at the beginning, but the rest came from the parts of the manuscript which had not been published elsewhere. The shape of these particular parts of *Peace in the Post-Christian Era* must have remained in Merton's mind over the two years of ups and downs about the book. He called the new article "The Christian in World Crisis: Reflections on the Moral Climate of the 1960's."[51] It contained an entirely new concluding section called "The Reply of *Pacem in Terris*."

He described the new article to Gordon Zahn in a letter as "a long rewritten piece on *Pacem in Terris*, basically the same as [*Peace in the Post-Christian Era*] but without controversy on the bomb, just peace peace"(*HGL* 653). The comment and others like it may have led to the idea that (as the Mott biography states) Merton published the whole of *PPCE* in *Seeds of Destruction* (Mott, 400).

Finally, a month after he had submitted the new article for censorship, there was a jubilant entry in the journal. *Seeds of Destruction* was to go ahead with the new article, so "the real heart of the forbidden book, *Peace in the Post-Christian Era*, is to be published after all"(*DWL*, 127). The evidence of the mimeograph text shows us that the term "the real heart" was literal. Merton had torn out of the mimeograph the crucial pages which he needed.

New details of the censorship story have come to light in an interview with Dom M. Laurence Bourget published in *The Merton Annual* 12. Interviewer Jonathan Montaldo's questions pursued the story of the relationship between Dom Gabriel Sortais, his secretary Father Clement de Bourmont, and Merton. Dom Bourget gives a highly nuanced description of each of these men from his personal recollection, and his assessment is invaluable to anyone pursuing the censorship issue. The interviewer's question had been whether Father Clement had been "an 'enemy' of Merton's literary career," as Merton and others had suspected (Mott, 374). Father Clement's better command of the English language meant he was in a position to comment to Dom Sortais about works in that language, and he was secretary to both Dom Sortais and Dom Gillet. What had been his involvement in the final chapter of the censorship story?

As it turned out, Dom Bourget had inadvertently intervened, without knowing what was involved, at a crucial moment. Called into Dom Ignace Gillet's office in July 1964, he was handed a manuscript, with the request:

'Would you read this text of Merton and tell me if you find anything objectionable in it? We have no time to send it to the Censor because the printer is waiting for it to complete a book.'

I did read the text very carefully and returned it promptly to the General with the comment, 'Far from finding anything objectionable in it, I find what it says is pure Gospel!'

Dom Bourget finishes the anecdote with the comment

What still mystifies me, however, is that at that time (July 1964)Fr Clement was still the General's secretary and I now wonder if I was only called in because he happened to be absent from Rome. The ways of Divine Providence indeed![52]

The new article also developed a life of its own: part of it was later included in a pamphlet called *Therefore Choose Life*, published by the Center for the Study of Democratic Institutions for the New York conference on the papal encyclical. An edited version of the pamphlet was reprinted in the *Saturday Review* in a special section on February 13, 1965: "*Pacem in Terris*, Commentaries by Robert McAfee Brown, Norman Cousins, Everett E. Gendler, Thomas Merton, and Hermann J. Muller." Merton's essay was called "The Challenge of Responsibility."[53]

A Burnt-Out Case

Merton's "demonstration" had certainly cost him, to the point that he considered whether his vocation might be at an end. He had thought and written a great deal about the authenticity of the interior life. The struggle to work for something he sincerely felt was morally right and just, but which had put him into direct conflict with his Order, had hollowed him out. The pain of living the internal conflict comes out in a remarkable passage in an August 1964 letter to Daniel Berrigan, where Merton describes himself:

As a priest I am a burnt-out case, repeat, burnt-out case. So burnt out that the question of standing and so forth becomes irrelevant. I just continue to stand there where I was hit by the bullet. [...] [W]ord will go around about how they got this priest who was shot and they got him stuffed sitting up at a desk propped up with books and writing books, this book machine that was killed. [...] When I fall over, it will be a big laugh because I wasn't there at all. [...]

I am sick up to the teeth and beyond the teeth, up to the eyes and beyond the eyes, with all forms of projects and expectations and statements and programs and explanations of anything, especially explanations about where we are all going... (*HGL*, 84)

The Fate of the Mimeograph

When the Merton Center received the manuscript of *PPCE*, it was not treated as most holograph manuscripts are, but was bound in a cover and given a tentative date "[1962?]." Manuscripts are nowadays not treated in such a way, but the practice in the 60s seems to have been to bind them.[54] This may have been the reason that the bibliography entries in Breit and Daggy were done on the basis of this bound final draft, which has a much more imposing appearance than the rather flimsy mimeographed copies, especially since the work had never been published.

The mimeograph had done what Merton wanted: it carried a message out under the radar, and assured the fact that the text itself would survive somewhere. However, the fatal flaw in the strategy of defining the work as "unpublished" (and thus removing official attention from it) was that it worked all too well. "Unpublished" came to mean unpublishable. The controversy defined the book, as the suppression helped define the author. In the end, only relatively few readers were able to judge the full text for themselves. Later editors republishing Merton's peace material passed over *Peace in the Post-Christian Era*: after all Merton had both criticized it and also said he had published the "real heart" of it. It was simpler to reprint the articles it was based on. In the end, time passed it by, and the work virtually disappeared from the Merton canon.

As for the text itself: the careful "objectivity" for which the author's friends criticized him is more than offset by Merton's passionate involvement in the issues. He had been caught for a time between two forces: his "peace friends" who hoped he would be more activist and extreme, and his Church connections who thought that writing about nuclear war was not fitting for a monk. As always he had tried to find the line by which he could communicate with everyone. In doing so he demonstrated an astonishing breadth of argument: who but Merton would have been comfortable discussing Origen, Augustine and Machiavelli in one chapter and Leo Szilard and Edward Teller in the next? Some sections of the book are eerily prophetic of the international situation four decades later, and we need to hear again that the just war does not include pre-emptive strikes.

Who can now gauge the effect that this work had, even in mimeograph? In its time it had made its way to quite a few readers, some of them undoubtedly influential in the course of historical events. The appeal of a "forbidden book by Thomas Merton" must certainly have been a factor in making readers curious about it. Copies circulated among the *periti* at Vatican II. There is an intriguing observation about one of them, in a footnote in James Forest's *Living with Wisdom*: "Bob Grip tells me that he came upon a copy of *Peace in the Post-Christian Era* on a window sill in the library of the Vatican's North American College in Rome."[55] Merton must have sent a copy when he wrote to Leo Szilard: it is still on file as part of Szilard's papers at the University of California at San Diego.[56]

Aftermath

Having developed contacts at Vatican II through friends and mailed mimeographs, Merton had busied himself behind the scenes in regard to the document called "Schema XIII" which dealt with the Church and modern war. He wrote an "Open Letter to the American Hierarchy" which was published in 1965 in *Unity*, *Worldview*, and *Vox Regis*.[57] Once more, he stated the themes that had carried through the forbidden book, especially as regards the moral indefensibility of nuclear war on any grounds, and the Christian necessity of "choosing peace"(*WTF*, 88-94).

Merton's position on war had enough currency that Archbishop George Bernard Flahiff sent him a copy of the relevant text from the draft Schema in Latin. Merton demonstrated his usual versatility by commenting on the Latin text and offering suggestions(*HGL*, 246-248). Once vilified for allegedly defending pacifism "against the Church," Merton could now offer advice at least in the tempering of text. In the final irony, the man forbidden to write about nuclear war was now consulted as an expert.

With this we have come full circle. Worry about the apathy of American Catholics and the need to make the issues clear had led to Merton's determination to write what he could, regardless of obstacles. His ability to publish had been severely limited, but he had done what he could. During the same time period he had written many other things, focusing on varied subjects, to the extent that this particular thread almost vanished into the fabric. Indeed it had not disappeared but rather had become part of him, and in the end, regardless of the ban, one of the primary things he is known for is his writing about peace.

The manuscript of *Peace in the Post-Christian Era* begins with the author's note to himself and his blessing on the book. This essay ends there:

+

Xtian Action
1) Towards <u>change</u>—prophetism
2) That men may be masters of things and not mastered by them
3) Recognition of new situation—understanding meaning and creative value of crisis.

Notes

1. Marquita Breit and Robert Daggy, *Thomas Merton: A Comprehensive Bibliography*. (New York: Garland Publishing, 1986). The bibliography does not list *Peace in the Post-Christian Era* as a separate item (as though it were a book) but lists only articles associated with it. The list of articles is incomplete, and the pagination is that of the manuscript, not of the mimeograph.

2. Thomas Merton, *Seeds of Destruction* (New York: Farrar, Straus, Giroux, 1964).

3. Thomas Merton, *The Nonviolent Alternative*, ed. Gordon Zahn (New York: Farrar, Straus, Giroux, 1980); subsequent references will be cited as "*NVA*" parenthetically in the text.

4. Thomas Merton, *Passion for Peace*, ed. William H. Shannon (New York: Crossroad, 1995); subsequent references will be cited as "*PFP*" parenthetically in the text.

5. My thanks to Louise Girard, Chief Librarian, and Noel McFerran, Head of Public Services for the Kelly Library, and Thomasine O'Callaghan, Merton Legacy Trustee, who helped carry out the exchange at a time when the Director of the Merton Center in Louisville was ill.

6. Larry Culliford, "Pilgrimage to Prades," *Merton Journal* 9.2 (2002): 40.

7. Among the best of these is William Shannon's account in *Silent Lamp* (New York: Crossroad, 1992), 218-223. Subsequent references will be cited as "*SL*" parenthetically in the text. Shannon's account focuses on the development of the *Commonweal* article "Nuclear War and Christian Responsibility" and comes to a close with Dom Gabriel Sortais'

writing ban (223). Other excellent accounts by contemporaries are: Jim Forest, "Thomas Merton's Struggle with Peacemaking," 15-54; and Gordon Zahn, "Thomas Merton, Reluctant Pacifist," in *Thomas Merton: Prophet in the Belly of a Paradox*, ed. Gerald Twomey (New York: Paulist Press, 1978), 55-79.

8. Foreword by Thomas Merton in Bruno Scott James, editor and translator, *St Bernard of Clairvaux Seen Though his Selected Letters* (Chicago: Regnery, 1953), v-viii.

9. Thomas Merton, *Turning Toward the World: The Journals of Thomas Merton* Volume 4, 1960-1963 (San Francisco: HarperCollins, 1996), 176; subsequent references will be cited as *"TTW"* parenthetically in the text.

10. Thomas Merton, *The Hidden Ground of Love: The Letters of Thomas Merton on Religious Experience and Social Concerns*, selected and edited by William H. Shannon (New York: Farrar, Straus, Giroux, 1985), 349; subsequent references will be cited as *"HGL"* parenthetically in the text. See also: to Dorothy Day, 139; to Daniel Berrigan, 71; to Jim Forest, 271.

11. Thomas Merton, *The Last of the Fathers* (New York: Harcourt Brace, 1954), 34-35.

12. Thomas Merton, "Loretto and Gethsemani," in *The Springs of Contemplation* (Notre Dame: Ave Maria Press, 1992), 206. The date for the pamphlet is given as "the spring of 1962" on p. 202.

13. C.S. Lewis, *"De Descriptione Temporum"* in *They Asked for a Paper* (London: Geoffrey Bles, 1962), 14.

14. *Ibid.*, 20.

15. Letter to Jean and Hildegard Goss-Mayr, January 15, 1964, *HGL*, 332.

16. Thomas Merton, *Conjectures of a Guilty Bystander* (Garden City, NY: Doubleday 1966), 197; subsequent references will be cited as *"CGB"* parenthetically in the text. Merton further works out the definition in a footnote when describing the philosophy of Sartre, 301.

17. The progression of articles which were the foundation of *PPCE* is listed and charted in Patricia A. Burton, *Merton Vade Mecum* (Louisville: Thomas Merton Foundation, 2001), 162-164.

18. *Thomas Merton and James Laughlin, Selected Letters* (New York: W.W. Norton, 1997) 196; subsequent references will be cited as *"TMJL"* parenthetically in the text.

19. As for example in a note about a letter to Mark Van Doren, January 18, 1962: "J [Laughlin] was here...We have pretty well planned the peace book." Thomas Merton, *The Road to Joy: The Letters of Thomas Merton to New and Old Friends*, selected and edited by Robert E. Daggy. (New York: Farrar, Straus, Giroux, 1989), 44. The peace book was misidentified by the editor of the letters as *Peace in the Post-Christian Era*; Merton was working with Laughlin on *Breakthrough to Peace*, but did not do so on *PPCE*, as it never got to a stage where a publisher saw it.

20. *Breakthrough to Peace: Twelve Views on the Threat of Thermonuclear Extermination* [with essays by Herbert Butterfield, Norman Cousins, Allan Forbes, Jr., Jerome D. Frank, Erich Fromm and Michael Maccoby, Howard E. Gruber, Joost A. M. Meerloo, Thomas Merton, Lewis Mumford, Walter Stein, Tom Stonier and Gordon C. Zahn] (New York: New Directions, 1962). Merton is not listed as editor but only as a contributor: he was worried that his difficulties with censorship would jeopardize publication (see *TMJL*, 194).

21. Gordon Zahn (editor) in *NVA*, 12.

22. *PFP*, 38. See also the chart indicating the order of essays involving *Peace in the Post-Christian Era* in *Merton Vade Mecum*, 162.

23. *Merton Vade Mecum*, 30-31.

24. Thomas Merton, *Witness to Freedom: The Letters of Thomas Merton in Times of Crisis*, selected and edited by William H. Shannon. (New York: Farrar, Straus, Giroux, 1994), 49-50; subsequent references will be cited as "*WTF*" parenthetically in the text. Szilard had been one of the physicists who developed the bomb, but afterwards campaigned against nuclear proliferation.

25. See "The Book That Never Was: Thomas Merton's Peace in the Post-Christian Era," on file in the Merton Center at Bellarmine University. The author of the present essay did this detailed analysis in 1998, and included a colour-coded map of the manuscript, describing the various components in detail.

26. Matthew Kelty OCSO, "Looking Back to Merton: Memories and Impressions; An Interview," conducted by Victor A. Kramer, edited by Dewey Weiss Kramer *Merton Annual* 1 (1988): 58.

27. This section, which demonstrates the author's ease with contemporary material as well as traditional teaching, has never been published anywhere.

28. The article was missed in the Breit and Daggy bibliography: pages from the middle of it formed the basis of two chapters of the book: "Christian Perspectives in World Crisis" and "Christian Conscience and National Defence."

29. The black and white photocopy of the manuscript I worked on initially does not show how the editing was done; the original manuscript has corrections and edits in different sections in pencil and ballpoint pen in black, blue, red and green, indicating that the carbon copied parts had generally been edited at least twice, sometimes oftener. Each pen colour represents a "layer" of editing within a part of the manuscript, and some sections show several colours, indicating several reworkings.

30. The censor specifically rejected "Target Equals City," as Merton later reported in a letter to Daniel Berrigan in *HGL*, 74.

31. All quotes in this paragraph from *TTW*, 216.

32. Thomas Merton, *The School of Charity: The Letters of Thomas Merton on Religious Renewal and Spiritual Direction*, selected and edited by Patrick Hart OCSO (New York: Farrar, Straus, Giroux, 1990), 141-143; subsequent references will be cited as *"SCH"* parenthetically in the text.

33. To Laughlin (April 28, 1962), *TMJL*, 200 ff; to Forest (April 29, 1962), *HGL*, 266-268 (a particularly poignant assessment of his situation).

34. Letter to Szilard (April 12, 1962), *WTF* , 49-50. Letter to Cardenal, Thomas Merton, *The Courage for Truth: Letters to Writers*, selected and edited by Christine M. Bochen (New York: Farrar, Straus, Giroux, 1993), 133; subsequent references will be cited as *"CFT"* parenthetically in the text.

35. Michael Mott, *The Seven Mountains of Thomas Merton* (Boston: Houghton Mifflin, 1984), 379; subsequent references will be cited as "Mott" parenthetically in the text.

36. Thomas Merton and Robert Lax, *When Prophecy Still Had a Voice: The Letters of Thomas Merton and Robert Lax*, edited by Arthur Biddle (Lexington KY: University Press of Kentucky, 2001), 237-238.

37. To Catherine de Hueck (June 4, 1962), *HGL*, 19; to John Heidbrink (May 30, 1962), *HGL*, 408.

38. "The Peace book...": Merton here refers to *Peace in the Post-Christian Era*, misidentified by the editor of Laughlin's letters as *Breakthrough to Peace*, which was published by New Directions, not mimeographed.

39. All references in *HGL*: to Forest (June 14, 1962), 269; to Berrigan (June 15, 1962), 74; to Gullick (June 16, 1962), 353; to Dorothy Day (June 16, 1962), 145; to Harris (June 8, 1962), 398; to Sister Emmanuel (June 18, 1962), 188; to Thompson (July 19, 1962), 573.

40. To Forest, *HGL*, 269; Merton reiterated these comments in a letter to Henry Miller (July 9, 1962), *CFT*, 275.

41. Thomas Merton, *A Thomas Merton Reader* (New York: Harcourt, Brace and World, 1962), 288-297.

42. Published by Herder in 1963: see *WTF*, 282 and 288-293.

43. Leslie Dewart, "A Post-Christian Age?" *Continuum* 1:4 (1964): 556-567.

44. *HGL*, 329-330. His largest shipment to the Goss-Mayrs included *Breakthrough to Peace*, one copy of *Peace in the Post-Christian Era* (by air, with others to follow by sea), and separate copies of "Target Equals City" and "Red or Dead."

45. To Aziz (December 26, 1962), *HGL*, 53; to Andrews (December 28, 1962), *HGL*, 38.

46. Thomas Merton and Robert Lax, *A Catch of Anti-Letters* (Kansas City: Sheed and Ward, 1978), 7.

47. Thomas Merton, *Dancing in the Water of Life* (San Francisco: HarperCollins, 1997), 84; subsequent references will be cited as *"DWL"* parenthetically in the text.

48. To Forest (March 16, 1964), *HGL*, 279; to Dewart (April 24, 1964), *WTF*, 295; to Ferry (May 27, 1964), *HGL*, 217.

49. Letter to William H. Shannon from Robert E. Daggy, June 13, 1986.

50. Merton treated a mimeograph of the "Cold War Letters" in the same way: a copy in the library at St Bonaventure University describes loose pages with editorial markings. "All pages have edge holes to accomodate comb binding." web.sbu.edu/friedsam/mertonweb/mimeos&photocopy2.htm

51. Thomas Merton, *Seeds of Destruction* (New York: Farrar, Straus, Giroux, 1964), 93-183.

52. Bourget, Dom M. Laurence, "Thomas Merton: A Monk Who 'Succeeded ': An Interview by Correspondence," conducted and edited by Jonathan Montaldo *Merton Annual* 12 (1999): 45, 48.

53. Thomas Merton, "The Challenge of Responsibility," *Saturday Review*, 13 February, 1965, 19-30.

54. Paul Pearson, Director of the Merton Center in Louisville, reports that several of the original manuscripts of Merton's books were bound.

55. James Forest, *Living with Wisdom.* (Maryknoll, NY: Orbis Books, 1991), 223 (footnote 241).

56. http://orpheus.ucsd/speccoll/findaids/science/szilard, at the Mandeville Special Collections Library, listed in the Register of Leo Szilard Papers among the items sent to Rare Books or General Collections.

57. It reappeared when the question of nuclear weapons recurred in the 1980s, when it was reprinted in the *National Catholic Reporter* as "Merton Plea on Nukes: 'Avoid Fine Moral Distinctions'," (29 April 1983).

Thomas Merton's Sacred Landscapes: Perspectives from the Vancouver Conference

Lynn R. Szabo

The Eighth General Meeting of the International Thomas Merton Society held in Vancouver in June of 2003 attracted a robust response to its theme, "The Hawk's Dream: Thomas Merton's Sacred Landscapes." The title is an allusion to a favorite poem of Merton's by Robinson Jeffers, the rugged Californian poet with whom Merton was taken in the late sixties, especially when he visited the Monastery of the Redwoods on the West Coast in 1968. Merton's sacred landscapes captured the imagination of presenters from all hemispheres of the globe, reflecting Merton's own wide-ranging geographic, intellectual and spiritual spheres of inquiry and insight. In this volume of *The Merton Annual*, ten of the presenters have honed their papers into articles which broaden the discussions undertaken at that meeting. It has been very rewarding and enlightening to work closely and collegially as a guest editor with these writers whose disciplines and expertise lend new and careful thought about Merton as a figure of influence in the past and present centuries.

Deborah Kehoe explores three of Merton's early poems with intelligent sensitivity and graceful eloquence. Each of the poems begins with vivid sensory details describing specific features of the monastery at Gethsemani. This study reveals that the poems move beyond the physical realm, however, to recreate the poet's metaphysical encounters with a plane of existence in which perfection, unity, and peace are realized.

Angus Stuart also focuses on the relationship between inner space and the sense of place in the geography of solitude, exploring an amplitude of texts from Merton's substantial writings on this subject, especially in the late sixties. Thomas Merton's experience is juxtaposed on that of the Beat poets, who occupied themselves as Fire Lookouts in the North Cascade Mountains of America during the mid-1950s.

Gray Matthews combines his interest in American philosopher, Henry Bugbee, with his reading of Merton to suggest a possible dialogue of ideas between these two American contemplative thinkers and writers. Their mutual indebtedness to the wisdom of Meister Eckhart, Henry David Thoreau, Daisetz Suzuki, Max Picard and Gabriel Marcel testifies to the fact that Merton and Bugbee were working on many of the same ideas in relation to contemporary culture. Matthews' scholarly intensity and discipline provide us with a fine and rewarding study and an excellent research source.

Ron Dart continues this method of inquiry by making a comparison of worldview principles between Merton and the significant Canadian contemplative philosopher and iconoclast, George Grant. The two were contemporaries and although of very different personal histories, they proffer many of the same illuminations about societal and personal responsibility in relation to the church and the world.

Edward K. Kaplan, renowned Jewish scholar from Brandeis University, offers a compelling and profound reading of Merton's receptivity to the feminine, Judaism and religious pluralism. Kaplan's intellectually stimulating and sophisticated prose examines this enormous topic with deftness and perceptivity. He posits that later in life Merton reintegrated the "feminine" within himself, as is demonstrated by his seminars with the Sisters of Loretto and his love of "Margie"; these were foreshadowed by Merton's fantasized relationship with "Proverb" and his opening to Judaism. Kaplan finds parallels between the Shekhinah and the Virgin Mary in Merton's writing and experience.

In his analysis of Merton's famous diarized essay, "Fire Watch," **David Leigh SJ** dialogues with Ross Labrie's conference presentation, "The Unanswered Question in Thomas Merton's 'Fire Watch.'" Although Labrie's paper does not appear in this volume, it has been published in *Christianity and Literature* (2003) and might well be read in concert with Professor Leigh's article which here explores dimensions of Merton's use of fire and water imagery in his journals, autobiography and poetry, as expressions of purification, the desire for contemplation, and the painful consolation of the divine presence in human experience.

From the perspective of Asian studies, **Patrick Bludworth** explores Merton's "outlaw lineage" in relation to the desert fathers and Asian masters. His article discovers possible stages by which

Merton became convinced that the key to unlocking the treasures of Christian as well as Asian spiritual traditions was the institution of the guru; that Merton recognized great value in the teacher-disciple relationships that existed among the Christian Desert Fathers and which continue to exist within various Asian traditions.

The subsequent article by **Joe Raab** offers "some notes" on Merton's epiphany at Polonnaruwa—one of the more studied and significant of Merton's enlightenments because of its location in his Asian journey and its proximity to the time of his death. As Raab sees it, within Merton there is a complementary interpenetration of contexts, Buddhist and Christian, but that his interest in the former always included the faith commitments he had made within the latter. Merton's contemplative Catholicism provided him with a place from which to move into the Buddhist world; a first language with which to correlate meanings within a new linguistic frame of reference.

This collection of revised conference papers nets a human interest story, as well, with **Kenelm Burridge's** summary of his anthropologist's view of Merton and the Cargo Cults. What is of singular interest here is that Burridge's book, *Mambu: A Melanesian Millenium* (1960) actually prompted Merton to write his well-known essay on the cargo cults of the South Pacific which from the nineteenth to well into the middle of the last century have been interpreted psychologically, sociologically, and as "derivatives of Christian outpouring."

The last word is left to **Paul Dekar** who returns us to the present moment with his exploration of Merton and technology, "What the Machine Produces and What the Machine Destroys." As Dekar interprets Merton, technology must be approached with wisdom and applied with caution. It emerges as a sustained force, contributing to the distortion, distraction and denial of our condition, and fostering alienation and even placing human survival at risk.

Early Reflections in a "Nothing Place":
Three Gethsemani Poems

Deborah P. Kehoe

Lyndall Gordon concludes her 1998 biography of T. S. Eliot, *T. S. Eliot: An Imperfect Life*, by emphasizing the famous writer's ultimate understanding that his life had been an imperfect search for God. Although the search necessarily took him deep into the solitude of his own soul, Eliot knew he was not alone. According to Gordon, Eliot "spoke to choice souls of the future, 'the posterity of the desert' who would reenact his lone watch."[1]

Certainly one such "choice soul" to whom Eliot "spoke" even well before he died was Thomas Merton. In *The Sign of Jonas*, in an entry dated March 14, 1948, Merton extols the virtues of Eliot's then-recently-published *Four Quartets* and vows to learn from the older poet's mastery: "As a poet, I have got to be sharp and precise like Eliot—or else quit."[2] In one of the recorded conferences with the novices at Gethsemani during the 1960s, Merton again speaks enthusiastically of *Four Quartets*, especially "Little Gidding." Merton feels a connection with Eliot's work which is more than simple admiration for the poet's craft; this feeling is evident in his talk focused on Eliot and prayer.

Merton's sympathetic response can be said to derive in part from a shared belief between the two poets that prayer sanctifies any location in which it occurs consistently. The setting for the poem "Little Gidding," the village of Little Gidding, site of a Seventeenth- century Anglican community, is one such location. Harry Blamires comments on its symbolic significance:

> Little Gidding stands as a symbol of reconciliation . . . a peculiarly powerful symbol of reconciliation between the Way of Negation and the Way of Affirmation, between the practice of austerity and the acceptance of life's revelatory richness. . . .[3]

In the poem, Eliot simply calls Little Gidding a place "where prayer has been valid."[4] Earlier, he establishes that Little Gidding is not the only such prayerful place on earth:

> There are other places
> Which are also the world's end[5]

The monastery of Our Lady of Gethsemani is one of those "other places."

"Gethsemani is like Little Gidding," Merton proposes to the novices in his talk.[6] He develops the comparison by pointing out the unremarkable, even unattractive, external attributes of the two locations. Certainly no example of stunning architectural design or landscaping, Little Gidding features a plain little chapel half-hidden by a pig sty, while Merton jokingly agrees with one of the novices who states that the monastery's main building "looks like a barrel factory."[7] Merton, however, qualifies the good-natured insult by insisting, "God knows how or why, but prayer here has been valid," a declaration he punctuates by exclaiming, "Saints have been here!"[8]

The tie that binds Little Gidding to Gethsemani in Merton's mind is their shared history of contemplative prayer. The physicality of the places is significant, not because of any stunning beauty, but because they are not distracting to the eye in any remarkable way. The physical surroundings are significant primarily because they initiate a journey which can lead one to the unitive stage of prayer. The material aspects stimulate the first response of a creature, that of the senses. The ultimate response, however, is surrender, not to sensory stimuli, but to the spirit, to the enlivening and sanctifying of the created elements of the place, a place made holy by repeated acts of self-renunciation. One comes to such locations to do as others, who are now dead, did in the past: to kneel in prayer of submission to the will of God and, by doing so, connect one's soul with eternity.

As Eliot explains in the poem, this kind of prayer is not a simple "order of words."[9] It is a kind of prayer that Merton describes in *New Seeds of Contemplation* in which one not only speaks to God or even listens to God, but allows oneself to become the language of God. Merton explains from personal experience: "There exists some point at which I can meet God in a real and experimental contact with His infinite actuality, [a point at which] God utters me like a word."[10]

For both writers, the living word of God takes the form of poetry. Poetry and contemplation, as Merton eventually concludes, are compatible experiences; one stimulates rather than militates against the other.[11] Merton holds that poetry has unique properties. It introduces one to another dimension, what he calls "the angelic realm," a meeting place between God and flesh where spirit is in complete harmony with the created world. In this sphere, material and spiritual elements are reconciled and mutually blessed. Poetry recognizes this unity and assumes that communication between, among, and within these elements is possible.[12] Only in poetry, Merton claims, can one be so bold as to assert, "Here is a place where prayer has been valid." Such a statement would be irresponsible, he explains, if made in a scientific context because it cannot be measured or proved. But in the angelic realm, the speaker speaks the infinite truth of God self-evident to anyone who meets God through contemplation.[13]

Helen Gardner writes of *Four Quartets*, "These poems do not begin from an intellectual position or truth. They begin with a place ...."[14] The same description applies to several of Merton's poems written during his first six years as a Trappist, representing that period in which he produced what George Woodcock classifies as "the poetry of the choir."[15] These poems center upon the specifics of the one place in which the restless monk would honor his vow of stability for 26 years. The geography of Gethsemani provides the setting for the story of Thomas Merton's maturing soul. It is where Merton makes both a beginning and an ending and where he learns to see the two as one. The place can be described, using Merton's blunt phrases, as a "total non-entity," "a null and void nothing place," like Little Gidding.[16] But when seen through the eyes of the contemplative poet open to the revelatory grace of God, the "nothing place" becomes replete and consequential and talks of things beyond itself,[17] saying that here is another place where time and timelessness intersect.

The comparison provides a basis for studying representative early poems by Merton. As Gethsemani (the place) is like Little Gidding (the place), Merton's Gethsemani poems—those poems written early in his career as a poet-turned-monk—are like "Little Gidding," the poetic masterpiece. They reveal Merton's affinity with Eliot's concept (so captivatingly illustrated in *Four Quartets*) that a place can be hallowed by tradition, arrested in time, and neutralized to the senses and, therefore, conducive to ecstatic and transcendent experience. In Eliot's end, one might say, is Merton's beginning.

Three of these poems "After the Night Office—Gethsemani Abbey," "The Trappist Cemetery—Gethsemani," and "Spring: Monastery Farm" draw their considerable vitality from paradox; in them, the poet recognizes the fullness of emptiness, the light within darkness, life amid the province of the dead, freedom that comes only from surrender, and spring which never leads to winter; in a semblance of contradiction which is the heart of the apophatic or Negative Way of seeking to know an unknowable God. The three poems originate with descriptions of physical details of place, vivid and precise images, such as Merton admired in the work of Eliot, but they move beyond the level of sensory encounter to recreate the poet's experience with the source of that significance, a recreation and a reconciliation which can be conveyed only through paradox.

"After the Night Office—Gethsemani Abbey" is an ecstatic statement by a seeker-of-light who is in love with the darkness. The poem anticipates future expressions of Merton's long-lived attraction to the night as a time of spiritual liberation and clarification for the monks of Gethsemani. For example, in *The Sign of Jonas*, in an entry dated April 8, 1950, Merton writes: "At the end of the Night Office, when the whole choir sank into the darkness of death and chanted without the faintest light, I thought of the darkness as a luxury, simplifying and unifying everything."[18] In yet a later entry, he resumes the topic and offers the same perspective, this time in more concise terms: "The night, O My Lord, is a time of freedom. You have seen the morning and the night, and the night was better."[19]

This poem also illustrates Merton's own critical standard that "[a]ll really valid poetry (poetry that is fully alive and asserts its reality by its power to generate imaginative life) is a kind of recovery of paradise."[20] In "After the Night Office," the poet's imagination thrives in the darkness which blankets the monastery at this particular time and vividly renders the recovery of its innocence, a process which Merton would later refer to as being "[b]aptized in the rivers of night."[21]

Appropriately, the poem opens with the rhetoric of *apophasis*,[22] in which the speaker affirms by negation:

> It is not yet the gray and frosty time
> When barns ride out of the night like ships:
> We do not see the Brothers, bearing lanterns,
> Sink in the quiet mist . . .[23]

By describing clearly what he cannot see, he calls special attention to the physical details of a place with which he has become intimately familiar. Like Eliot, who gives directions in "Little Gidding" in a series of statements beginning with the clause "If you came this way" and ending with a description of what one would find there, Merton directs the would-be pilgrim with the assurance of one who has memorized the geography of which he speaks. The speaker comfortably delineates, as well as anticipates, the features and routines of the monastery he has come to know in the few years he has lived there. The speaker not only points out what has just taken place but what he knows will appear when the day eventually dawns. This familiarity—intensified by the simple fact that the monk's life is, by design, lived within strict boundaries—makes the current state of visual obscurity no hindrance to the speaker's awareness.

The suggestion that the place is familiar enough that the poet can describe it, even in the dark, captures an important aspect of Merton's view of the sanctity of place. In his discussion of "Little Gidding," Merton emphasizes the following passage:

> If you came this way,
> Taking any route, starting from anywhere,
> At any time or at any season,
> It would always be the same.[24]

Merton considers the most important words in this passage to be "always" and "the same." The antecedent of "it" is the place, and its sameness is a mysterious quality, distinguishing the holiness it has developed through its history as a place of prayer. This sameness "neutralizes the accidentals" of the place, subordinating the externals to the internal.[25]

The characteristic of "always the same" is also suggested of Gethsemani in the opening stanza of "After the Night Office— Gethsemani Abbey." The darkness is the metaphor for God's ineffable grace, the sanctifying power that renews Gethsemani. It restores Gethsemani's Edenic purity while it also conveys and reinforces its sameness, leaving the speaker confident that the "barns [will] ride out of the night like ships," just as they always do, and the Brothers will return from the mists into which they only just hours before sank "bearing lanterns"—to greet a new but unchanging day. The day will be new in that it will have only recently dawned, but what it will hold for the monks is sure to be similar to that which was offered by the day before.

The poem immediately moves from the predictable to the disorienting, however, when it presents a portrait of disorder in which the speaker and his brothers, fresh from their office, are now out of sync with time:

> But now our psalmody is done.
> Our hasting souls outstrip the day:
> Now, before dawn, they have their noon.[26]

Their prayers have hastened their souls' movement beyond that of the clock and have propelled the poet into a zone of awareness in which paradoxically his temporary blindness has clarified his spiritual vision. He sees not through his physical eyes, but with "the secret eye of faith." This faith resides in a soul freed by the blessed darkness to "drink [the] deeps of invisible light," a synesthetic image which calls to mind a reversal of the famous Miltonic oxymoron in which the essence of Hell is captured in one terrifying phrase: "darkness visible."[27] The synesthesia continues into the third stanza, as does the speaker's confidence, an assurance of well-being which transcends the knowledge of his ordinary sensory experiences: the life-giving rays of the "invisible light," perceptible now only through touch and hearing, are nevertheless still shining.

The penultimate stanza, framed by the poet's echo of John Donne's futile scolding of the rising sun—although here the sun arrives not too early, but too late, having been supplanted by a superior light—reveals the poet's reluctance to yield to the mere light of day. The speaker reinforces his unwillingness to greet the sun by directing it to "hide behind Mount Olivet" and announcing that the "flying [that is, disappearing] moon" is being "held prisoner" by the juniper tree, [28] striking images that suggest Merton's early attraction to the work of Donne and other Metaphysical Poets of the Seventeenth century, such as George Herbert and Andrew Marvell.[29] In these fanciful words, a gentle irony exists, however, in that Mount Olivet and the juniper tree are familiar features of the landscape of the poem's setting. The irony arises from the speaker's specific identification of them. Even in his transcendent state, transported by his poetic and contemplative vision far from the mundane details of home, the speaker still effortlessly calls by name those geographical elements which are clearly visible only in the light of day but with which he shares a spiritual connection, unbroken by his fidelity to the obscuring darkness.

Certain identifying properties of Gethsemani, such as the steeple and the water tower, recur throughout Merton's writing. In *The Seven Storey Mountain,* for instance, he notes that in his first viewing of the monastery, the steeple "shone like silver in the moonlight."[30] In one of his early journal entries, he writes of the water tower appearing "fierce and efficient."[31] In the final stanza of "After the Night Office—Gethsemani Abbey," the two objects appear again. The steeple is again portrayed in terms of a precious metal—here, along with the water tower, it is gold in the sunlight as it appears in a description which suggests a lingering resentment on the part of the speaker toward the rising sun:

> But now the lances of the morning
> Fire all their gold against the steeple and the water-tower.[32]

Morning is depicted through mixed metaphors of violence; it is portrayed as a force that wields weapons (sharp objects and firearms) against the landscape to which it comes. The steeple and water tower stand tall as if they are both targets and first lines of defense against the invading sun. While the word "lance" also denotes an act to promote healing, it is an effective measure only when it causes painful bloodshed. Clearly, the speaker is conflicted; he has not yet completely reconciled himself to the fact that the period of luxurious, simplifying, and unifying darkness has ended.

The bellicose implications of the description suddenly give way, however, as the poem reaches a peaceful climax. As the sun arrives, so does consciousness for the inhabitants of Gethsemani who, along with the speaker, find themselves miraculously blessed. Finally, the steeple and water tower (as well as the juniper tree), because they are images of height, can be seen as emblems of the steadfast heavenly aspirations of their earthly setting—ordinary and familiar features, yet extraordinary because they too have been "soaked in grace, like Gideon's fleece."[33]

The significance of the monastic cemetery in the holy landscape of Gethsemani is also significant in Merton's sacred vision of the place. In a passage from *The Sign of Jonas* dated December 20, 1948, he writes of celebrating the 100th anniversary of the monastery by standing in the cemetery looking up at the sky where he thinks "of the sea of graces . . . flowing down on Gethsemani" and envisions the crosses on the graves speaking to him, as if "the jubilant dead were just about to sit up and sing." [34]

"The Trappist Cemetery—Gethsemani Abbey" is Merton's loving if somewhat effusive address to "the jubilant dead" and is compatible with his declaration that Gethsemani is a place where saints have been. As in "After the Night Office—Gethsemani," this poem pulses with paradox. The speaker praises the dead by assuring them of their anonymity. The physical graves, rather than memorializing the individuals who lie there, serve instead to "hide [their] characters."[35] The graves are not marked by grand monuments, but by "simple crosses."[36] The simplicity subdues rather than proclaims the glory of the dead brothers; such absence of ornamentation contributes to the holiness of the place. The magnificence is not external, but within. It is not individual, but collective. It exists in the sustained lives of prayer which the brothers led on earth, a habit of prayer which has not ended, but has merely moved on to another plane where it continues its work which "is not yet done."[37]

To adorn their graves would not only constitute an offense against humility, but would be a far too conclusive statement that the monks are dead. The poem illustrates the speaker's refusal to distinguish clearly between life and death by using the contradictory descriptive phrases "green cradles"[38] and "green tombs"[39] to refer to the brothers' graves.[40] The poet's use of these seemingly conflicting images suitably frames this poem, the central focus of which is the paradoxical concept that in death the monks are actually more alive than they were before they died. The poet once again transcends the limitations of his physical setting to enter a plane of existence where ending and beginning meet at the intersection of gone forever and forever present, or as Eliot, in "Little Gidding," terms it, "[n]ever and always."[41]

By remaining faithful to surface routines, in short, by maintaining Gethsemani's sameness, the terrain and natural occupants of Gethsemani protect the sanctity of the souls whose remains lie buried beneath its landscape. Everything goes about its usual business of daily life: birds "bicker in the lonely belfry"[42] while swallows and chimney swifts frolic about the monastery's eaves and steeple, yet all the while the graves of the departed brothers "smile like little children"[43] who know they are safe, far from the potential harm suggested in the description of the world just beyond the monastery grounds where the road carries cars in which "cities pass and vanish," where the air is filled with a "roar," and where the noise assaults the natural world by "[h]urling the air" into the trees, creating an effect of "panic."[44]

But as the monks of the holy place carry on their ordinary practices, protecting the privacy of the departed brothers, they also ensure that they will share in the blessings of eternal glory which the dead monks now enjoy. In fact, the poet considers these elements of place to be saints, too: the hills themselves are canonized by a sun which "exult[s] like a dying martyr."[45] Further, the poet identifies not only with the dead monks but also with the "frogs along the creek" who "[c]hant in the moony waters" offering their nightly devotions "to the Queen of Peace."[46] By virtue of this connection of a temporal place to the eternal souls of the holy living and the holy dead, the beasts and plants of Gethsemani take their place in the poet's eschatological vision with which the poem climaxes:

> Then will creation rise again like gold
> Clean, from the furnace of your litanies:
> The beasts and trees shall share your resurrection,
> And a new world be born from these green tombs.[47]

As Ross Labrie writes, Merton's exquisite descriptions of nature in Gethsemani are often more "than an emptying of the mind in preparation for contemplation of the divine. His aesthetic pleasure in looking out at the world is everywhere evident and affirmed."[48] Such aesthetic pleasure is certainly evident in the poem "Spring: Monastery Farm." As Labrie further comments on this poem, Merton here portrays "the instinctive energy of nature as an emblem of freedom."[49] The poem hails the arrival of spring on the monastery farm by presenting lively visual, aural, and tactile images of the natural world released from the prison of winter. The poem abounds with expressions of movement and activity: the bulls "roam in their pens"; the trees "boom with honey bees"; the streams ("blue-eyed" clean and fresh) "run to meet the sun."[50] This poem sets up a relationship among the flora and fauna of the farm's landscape and its human residents in that all are joined in spring-time revelry. As the opening lines announce, even the mighty bulls in their pens sing of spring in their own unmelodious way, "like trains."[51] This introductory image of joyful movement within confinement subtly points to the poem's paradoxical underpinnings as well as to its ultimate message: only by total surrender of self-will does one become truly free. Spring on the monastery farm offers sensuous pleasure to all its living inhabitants, and the speaker affirms the beauty of the season on the farm for its own sake. His delight is evident in his abundant use of sensory imagery to depict the season. He also makes clear, however, that the monks' happiness at the arrival of spring is intensified by their understanding that while the time of year brings freedom from seasonal captivity, it also signifies the liberation of the soul from the prison of sin.

While the poem begins by suggesting a union between nature and man, it climaxes with a statement of contrast between the natural world and the supernatural transcendent life of the earth-laboring monks. As much as the bulls and the honey bees revel in the arrival of spring, their enjoyment of the season cannot match that of the monks who "glaze the dark earth with a shining ploughshare" with more "ardent" minds and more "insatiable" hearts than those of their animal companions.[52] The reason for this greater degree of happiness is that the natural world depends totally on the promise of the sequence of the seasons for its regeneration, but the monks have "traded April for [their] ransom" and now possess a joy that surpasses the temporal jubilation of the "uncomprehending" natural world.[53] Spring is *not* the "necessity" of the monks who have their Emancipator all year long.[54] Just as the opening of "Little Gidding" speaks of the "heart's heat,"[55] a spiritual warmth that does not go cold in the dead of winter, the monks of Gethsemani enjoy an inner spring which defies the prescribed movement of the seasons. Their spring is not subject to the laws of the physical universe: it is the spring of the eternal domain of the angels.

And yet it is the created landscape of the place in which they live and labor that keeps the monks ever mindful of this truth. In a synesthetic phrase, the poet makes this point quite clear:

> For, in the sap and music of the region's spring
> We hear the picture of Your voice, Creator,
> And in our heartspeace answer You
> And offer You the world.[56]

The term "heartspeace" is reminiscent of the coined language of Gerard Manley Hopkins who also recreates in his poetry an ecstatic acknowledgement of the Creator's presence in the "joy and juice" of early spring.[57] The contentment is so profound that it leads those who possess it to an easy sacrifice; they offer in return nothing less than everything they have. This they do, the poem suggests, as a matter of custom, every spring on the farm, when the saving victory of the Lord is especially evident in the resurrection of the natural surroundings. The poet, however, makes clear in the final lines that the Redeemer is present even when no outward signs declare Him there; His is a presence that is not just seasonal, but perpetual:

...by Your Cross and grace, is made our glory and our Sacrament: As every golden instant mints the Christ Who keeps us free.[58]

This continuous process of recognition and response to a salvific action that knows no end reveals yet another portrait of the immutability of sacred places as seen through the vision of Thomas Merton.

In his recent book, *The Life You Save May Be Your Own: An American Pilgrimage*, a study of the lives and works of Flannery O'Connor, Dorothy Day, Walker Percy, and Thomas Merton, Paul Elie points out that rather early in his monastic writing career, Merton's "romance with the monastery [came] to an end."[59] Elie writes:

From this point forward [the early 1950's] he will strive to be simply a monk in a monastery. Although he will remain faithful to his calling as a Trappist, he will no longer write about Gethsemani as an ideal place, a world unto itself. Rather, he will see it as a place of imaginative possibility.

... He will seek a place outside the monastery or apart from it, in the world, in his surroundings, in the depths of his being or in flights of fantasy; from here on his places and spaces will be longed for, self-made, envisioned, imaginary.[60]

This movement away from the landscape of Gethsemani is certainly traceable in Merton's poetry, as George Woodcock has amply demonstrated. Woodcock explains that once Merton reconciled his two vocations of monk and poet and recognized the relationship between art and spirit, he was free to turn his poet's eye from Gethsemani to different landscapes.[61] The poet no longer needed to depict the actual details of his earthly home with words. Perhaps he had so completely internalized the elements of the place itself that they disappeared altogether from sensory perception and became one with his interior landscape. Perhaps the neutrality—that quality of which he speaks to his novices in the discus-

sion of "Little Gidding"—the hallmark of holy places such as Little
Gidding and Gethsemani, the force that diminishes the accidentals
and clarifies the sacred essence, stilled his impulse to express in
poetry his oneness with Gethsemani and inspired him to celebrate
the union of his soul with sacred spaces accessible only to his inner eye. Perhaps, as William H. Shannon writes, "Gethsemani
root[ed] [Merton], not where Gethsemani is, namely in this earth,
but elsewhere, that is to say, in eternity."[62]

Both T. S. Eliot and Thomas Merton found their nothing places
at the end of the world, and both captured in poetry the para-
doxes they discovered there. In *Four Quartets*, Eliot renders instances of perfect clarity achieved over the course of his imperfect
life, encounters with the eternal that are inextricably bound to the
temporal. In Little Gidding, the time-worn, out-of-the-way refuge
for saints and seekers, the poet recognized a passageway leading
from isolation to unity. In the concluding stanza of Eliot's epony-
mous poem, the essence of the setting it celebrates is summed up
in two lines beginning: "A condition of complete simplicity" and
followed immediately by a parenthetical caveat, offered for rhe-
torical emphasis in the negative: "(Costing not less than everything)."[63] The place bestows its grace (the poet reminds himself)
only on those poor enough to receive it. In Gethsemani, "the poet
of the choir" emerged, flourished, and eventually moved on. Amid
his simple surroundings and through the routines and rituals of
the days and seasons, he found in himself the necessary poverty,
the emptiness which opened him to the infinite wealth of God's
love; "helped him," in Shannon's words, on that inner journey
along the holy way "that knows no geography." [64]

Notes

1. Lyndall Gordon, *T. S. Eliot: An Imperfect Life* (New York: W.W.
Norton, 1998), p. 536.

2. Thomas Merton, *The Sign of Jonas* (New York: Harcourt Brace,
1953), p. 94.

3. Harry Blamires, *Word Unheard: A Guide Through Eliot's Four Quartets* (London: Methuen, 1969), p. 123.

4. T. S. Eliot, "Little Gidding" in *T.S. Eliot: The Complete Poems and
Plays, 1909-1950* (New York: Harcourt, Brace, & World, 1971), pp. 139-
145 (139). Unless otherwise noted, all quotations will be from this collection.

5. Eliot, *Complete Poems and Plays, 1901-1950*, p. 139.

6. *T. S. Eliot and Prayer* (Credence Cassette).

7. *T. S. Eliot and Prayer* (Credence Cassette).

8. *T.S. Eliot and Prayer* (Credence Cassette).

9. Eliot, *Complete Poems and Plays, 1909-1950*, p. 139.

10. Thomas Merton, *New Seeds of Contemplation* (New York: New Directions, 1961), p. 37.

11. Thomas Merton, "Poetry and Contemplation: A Reappraisal," in *The Literary Essays of Thomas Merton*, Patrick Hart, ed. (New York: New Directions, 1985), pp. 338-354 (341).

12. *Poetry: The Angelic Realm* (Credence Cassette).

13. *Poetry: The Angelic Realm* (Credence Cassette).

14. Helen Gardner, *The Art of T. S. Eliot* (New York: Dutton, 1959), p. 57.

15. George Woodcock, *Thomas Merton: Monk and Poet* (New York: Farrar, Straus, Giroux, 1978), p. 51.

16. *T. S. Eliot and Prayer* (Credence Cassette).

17. See Mark Van Doren, "Introduction" in *Selected Poems of Thomas Merton* (New York: New Directions, 1967), p. xiii.

18. Merton, *The Sign of Jonas*, p. 297.

19. Merton, *The Sign of Jonas*, p. 349.

20. Thomas Merton, "Louis Zukofsky—The Paradise Ear," in *The Literary Essays of Thomas Merton*, Patrick Hart, ed. (New York: New Directions, 1985), pp. 128-133 (128).

21. Merton, *The Sign of Jonas*, p. 349.

22. For a thorough explication of the poem in terms of its underlying apophatic theology, see Patrick F. O'Connell, "Thomas Merton's Wake-Up Calls: Aubades and Monastic Dawn Poems from *A Man in the Divided Sea*," *The Merton Annual* 12 (1999), pp. 129-163.

23. Thomas Merton, "After the Night Office—Gethsemani Abbey," in *The Collected Poems of Thomas Merton* (New York: New Directions, 1977), pp. 108-109 (108). Unless otherwise noted, all quotations will be taken from this collection.

24. Eliot, *Complete Poems and Plays, 1909-1950*, p. 139.

25. *T. S. Eliot and Prayer* (Credence Cassette).

26. Merton, *Collected Poems*, pp. 108-109.

27. John Milton, *Paradise Lost*, in *The Complete Poetical Works of John Milton* (ed. Douglas Bush; Boston: Houghton Mifflin, 1965) p. 213.

28. Merton, *Collected Poems*, p. 109.

29. This connection between Merton and the Metaphysical Poets, as well as his technical departure from them, has been documented by scholars of his poetry; see Sister Thérèse Lentfoehr, *Words and Silence: On the Poetry of Thomas Merton* (New York: New Directions, 1979), pp. 52, 89.

30. Thomas Merton, *The Seven Storey Mountain* (Harcourt Brace & Co., 1948), p. 320.

31. Thomas Merton, *Entering the Silence: Becoming a Monk and Writer* (Journals. 2; 1941-1952; ed. Jonathon Montaldo; San Francisco: HarperSanFrancisco, 1996), p. 101.

32. Merton, *Collected Poems*, p. 109.

33. Merton, *Collected Poems*, p. 109.

34. Merton, *The Sign of Jonas*, p. 144.

35. Thomas Merton, "The Trappist Cemetery—Gethsemani," in *The Collected Poems of Thomas Merton* (New York: New Directions, 1977), p. 116. Unless otherwise noted, all quotations will be taken from this collection.

36. Merton, *Collected Poems*, p. 116.

37. Merton, *Collected Poems*, p. 117.

38. Merton, *Collected Poems*, p. 116.

39. Merton, *Collected Poems*, p. 118.

40. This juxtaposition of "green" with an image of death is remarkably similar to Dylan Thomas's phrasing in "Fern Hill" in which he speaks of Time holding him "green and dying." See Dylan Thomas "Fern Hill" in *The Collected Poems of Dylan Thomas: 1934-1952* (New York: New Directions, 1971), pp. 178-180 (180). Given Merton's appreciation of Thomas's poetry, especially at this time—see Sister Thérése Lentfoehr, *Words and Silence: On the Poetry of Thomas Merton* (New York: New Directions, 1979), p. 33—the similarity is worth noting.

41. Eliot, *Complete Poems and Plays*, p. 139. For a more thorough discussion of the poem in terms of this theme of the continuity between death and life, see Patrick F. O'Connell, "Thomas Merton's Wake-Up Calls: Aubades and Monastic Dawn Poems from *A Man in the Divided Sea*," *The Merton Annual* 12 (1999), pp. 129-163.

42. Merton, *Collected Poems*, p. 116.

43. Merton, *Collected Poems*, p. 116.

44. Merton, *Collected Poems*, p. 116.

45. Merton, *Collected Poems*, p. 116.

46. Merton, *Collected Poems*, p. 117.

47. Merton, *Collected Poems*, p. 118.

48. Ross Labrie, *Thomas Merton and the Inclusive Imagination* (Columbia: University of Missouri Press, 2001), p. 84.

49. Labrie, *Thomas Merton and the Inclusive Imagination*, p. 85.

50. Thomas Merton, "Spring: Monastery Farm," in *The Collected Poems of Thomas Merton* (New York: New Directions, 1977), pp. 169-170 (170). Unless otherwise noted, all quotations will be taken from this collection.

51. Merton, *Collected Poems*, p. 169.

52. Merton, *Collected Poems*, p.170.

53. Merton, *Collected Poems*, p.170.

54. Merton, *Collected Poems*, p.170.

55. Eliot, *Complete Poems and Plays 1909-1950*, p. 138.

56. Merton, *Collected Poems*, p.170.

57. See Gerard Manley Hopkins, "Spring" in *Victorian Prose and Poetry* (eds. Lionel Trilling and Harold Bloom; Oxford: Oxford University Press, 1973), p. 682.

58. Merton, *Collected Poems*, p.170.

59. Paul Elie, *The Life You Save May Be Your Own: An American Pilgrimage* (New York: Farrar, Straus and Giroux, 2003), p. 210.

60. Elie, *The Life You Save May Be Your Own: An American Pilgrimage*, p. 210.

61. Woodcock, *Thomas Merton: Monk and Poet: A Critical Study*, p. 69.

62. William H. Shannon. *Silent Lamp: The Thomas Merton Story* (New York: Crossroad Press, 1993), p. 9.

63. Eliot, *Complete Poems and Plays*, 1909-1950, p. 145.

64. Shannon, *Silent Lamp*, p. 10.

THE GEOGRAPHY OF SOLITUDE:
Inner Space and the Sense of Place

Angus F. Stuart

We are exiles in the far end of solitude, living as listeners
With hearts attending to the skies we cannot understand.[1]

The interplay between physical place and the "interior landscape"
of the soul concerns the relationship between spirituality and geographic reality: how our physical surroundings express and influence our spirituality—who we are on the inside. It is therefore about
the search for identity, for the "true self." It is about the search for
sainthood, the path of holiness, the inner journey—an inner journey that finds expression in an outer journey. Potentially, this takes
in questions of pilgrimage and why certain places are deemed *holy*.
It also begs the fundamental question regarding the reason for the
perennial search for *desert places*, for mountaintops and solitary
wilderness places, places of solitude. It is about how contemplation opens our eyes to see the world around us as it is and to recognize it as *sacred space*.

Thomas Merton's journeys to northern California and Alaska
in 1968 provide a focus for the exploration of this interplay between physical and spiritual, inner and outer, landscape and
soulscape. These west coast trips were the first extensive travels
away from the monastery in over 25 years, prior to his last great
journey to Asia in search of *mahakaruna*, the great compassion and
the settlement of the "great affair."[2] In his journal for that last
year he writes about finding a suitable location for a hermitage,
but what was it exactly Merton was looking for? More solitude,
certainly, less interruption from correspondents and visitors, perhaps. But beyond this, why one place rather than another? What
was Merton looking for that he could not have gained simply by
moving a couple of miles further out from the monastery in the
Kentucky backwoods? This paper is not an exercise in locational
analysis but rather an exploration, a teasing out, of the role of place
and how it connected with Merton's own inner journey. In turn,

this relates to the wider, or perhaps more specific, questions which face each of us as we seek to bring into harmony the place in which we dwell within our hearts and our place in the world.

This intersection, or even co-incidence, between *inner* and *outer* is epitomized in Merton's reaction to receiving back one of the photos he had taken during his visit to northern California in May 1968:

> John Griffin sent one of my pictures of Needle Rock, which he developed and enlarged. I also have the contact. The Agfa film brought out the great *Yang-Yin* of sea rock mist, diffused light and half hidden mountain . . . an interior landscape, yet there. In other words, what is written within me is there. "Thou art that."[3]

This comment succinctly articulates the intuition that what is "out there" reflects what is "in here," or perhaps more naturally, what is "in here" reflects what is "out there" in the sense of "tell me where you're from and I'll tell you who you are." There is a sense here of being formed by the environment in which we live, not in a deterministic way but in a dynamic way of interaction. But it works the other way too: what is "out there" reflects what is "in here" in the sense that the environment and the landscapes around us are experienced by us and interpreted according to our own constructs.

One person's "wasteland" is another person's "wilderness," and the same landscape may be both at different times for the same person. The idea is that the landscape is a "metaphor of the soul" or perhaps more strongly a "sacrament of the soul," an outward manifestation of an inward reality: "Thou art that." This is to say that our outward vision enables us to see something of our own true identity. It is about seeing in a new way, a contemplative vision that sees the inner reality of things with clarity. It is also about understanding our interconnectedness with the world in which we live.

There is also a Buddhist inference in Merton's identification of himself with, or in, the photograph of Needle Rock. In D. T. Suzuki's *Manual of Zen Buddhism* we read:

> The world with its expansion of earth, its towering mountains, its surging waves, its meandering rivers, and with its infinitely variegated colours and forms is serenely reflected in the mind-

mirror of the *Yogin*. The mirror accepts them all and yet there are no traces or stains left in it—just one Essence bright and illuminating.[4]

As Merton said, "In other words, what is written within me is there."

Thomas Merton was an intensely "geographical person" who was very conscious of the interrelationship between his physical location and his spiritual identity—the interplay between his inner space and his sense of place. It is perhaps significant that Merton's favorite book of his childhood was a "geography book."[5] The title of his autobiography, *The Seven Storey Mountain*, is itself a geographical metaphor for his spiritual journey, drawn from Dante's *Purgatorio*. Moreover the book itself is very "geographical"—it is full of *places*. In *The Seven Storey Mountain* the reader is very conscious of the location in which particular events and phases of his life *take place*: St. Antonin, Montauban, Oakham, Rome, Cambridge, New York, Olean, Cuba, Gethsemani. One illustration of the vivid sense of place in Merton's story is given in his account of his return to France at the age of ten:

> When I went to France, in 1925, returning to the land of my birth, I was also returning to the fountains of the intellectual and spiritual life of the world to which I belonged....
> Even the countryside, even the landscape of France, whether in the low hills and lush meadows and apple orchards of Normandy or in the sharp and arid and vivid outline of the mountains of Provence, or in the vast, rolling red vineyards of Languedoc, seems to have been made full of a special perfection....
> That day, on that express, going into the south, into the Midi, I discovered France. I discovered that land which is really, as far as I can tell, the one to which I do belong, if I belong to any at all, by no documentary title but by geographical birth. We flew over the brown Loire, by a long, long bridge at Orléans, and from then on I was home, although I had never seen it before, and shall never see it again.[6]

After Merton entered the monastery of Gethsemani in 1941, this interplay between inner and outer for Merton gave rise to an increasing need for solitude and to years of agitation for permission to become a hermit. Yet, when he does finally become a hermit, it is only a couple of years before he finds that he needs more solitude. To be sure, this is partly because he is a "famous monk" and everyone seems to want to have a piece of him; in addition, there is a tension here with his own need for other people (the monk of Times Square)[7]; but the overriding impression given in his journal for the early part of 1968 is of his need for more solitude—more space, more silence, less noise, fewer people—he needs to be alone exteriorly as he is interiorly.

When he comes to the Californian coast in May 1968 he is actively looking for a remote site for a hermitage and he falls in love with the place:

> Friday [May 10] I drove out with Gracie Jones...and this time climbed high upon the slope. It was a bright day and the sea was calm, and I looked out over the glittering blue water, realizing more and more that this was where I really belonged. I shall never forget it. I need the sound of those waves, that desolation, that emptiness.[8]

These are words charged with great emotion, conveying his yearning for a *place* where he really belonged, yet "desolation" and "emptiness" are far from unambiguously positive words—quite the reverse.

As a counterpoint to Merton's experience, I draw here on Jack Kerouac's experience as a fire lookout on Desolation Peak in the North Cascades in the Pacific Northwest of the United States, in 1956. There are many parallels and connections between Merton and Kerouac, perhaps best epitomized in Robert Inchausti's description of Merton as "Jack Kerouac's monastic elder brother."[9] In his various accounts of his solitary summer on top of Desolation, Kerouac gives a gruelling perspective on the negative, as well as the positive, aspects of solitude: "Desolation Adventure finds me finding at the bottom of myself abysmal nothingness worse than no illusion even—my minds in rags—"[10] but there is still, in all the desolation and nothingness, the sense of self-discovery: "*finds me finding* at the bottom of myself." But in this self-discovery, even comforting illusions are destroyed leaving "abysmal nothingness"—*emptiness*. One detects resonance here with the experience of the apophatic mystics such as John of the Cross, and the dark night of the soul. There is a sense of things being reduced to the raw essentials—echoes of transcendentalist Henry Thoreau:

I went to the woods because I wished to live deliberately, to front only the essential facts of life, and see if I could not learn what it had to teach, and not when I came to die, discover that I had not lived…. I wanted to live deep and suck out all the marrow of life…to drive life into a corner, and reduce it to its lowest terms, and, if it proved to be mean, why then to get the whole genuine meanness of it, and publish its meanness to the world….[11]

Kerouac's encounter with himself was perhaps all the more horrifying because it was unexpected:

For I'd thought, in June, hitch hiking up there to the Skagit Valley in northwest Washington for my fire lookout job "When I get to the top of Desolation Peak and everybody leaves on mules and I'm alone I will come face to face with God or Tathagata and find out once and for all what is the meaning of all this existence and suffering and going to and fro in vain" but instead I'd come face to face with myself….[12]

Yet for all the horror and loneliness and boredom, Kerouac did indeed receive a vision, not one perhaps that he expected but nonetheless "the vision of the freedom of eternity which I saw and which all wilderness hermitage saints have seen."[13] This is the experience of "the timeless, the mysterious, and the primordial,"[14] the awareness of a certain permanence underlying all the movements of world history and human lives—"the mountains lookt [sic] the same in 1935…as they do in 1956 so that the oldness of the earth strikes me recalling primordially that it was the same, they (the mountains) looked the same in 584 B.C."[15] There is a sense of timelessness here or, more accurately, a consciousness of a new sense of time within timelessness.

This sense of permanence and timelessness for Kerouac was most incarnated by the imposing presence of Mount Hozomeen towering to the north of Desolation Peak:

The void is not disturbed by any kind of ups or downs, my God look at Hozomeen, is he worried or tearful? Does he bend before storms or snarl when the sun shines or sigh in the late day drowse?…Even Hozomeen'll crack and fall apart, nothing lasts, it is only a faring-in-that-which-everything-is, a passing through….[16]

Kerouac has been plunged into an awareness of his own illusoriness, not even that for illusions have been stripped away, rather his nothingness, emptiness in the void. He sees the mountains hanging in space held there only by gravity, and in this there is a *satori*, a kind of revelatory flash illuminating his place in time and space in the "freedom of eternity." As a metaphor of the soul, this is profoundly disturbing as well as liberating. But the insight is one of a dynamic interaction with the ground of all ground. Belden C. Lane in his book *Landscapes of the Sacred* draws a helpful distinction between space as *topos*—as in "topography," denoting an inert container, exerting no influence—and space as *chora*—as in "choreography," carrying its own energy and summoning participants to a dance.[17]   It is a similar distinction to that between *chronos* time and *kairos* time and calls to mind Merton's passage at the end of *New Seeds of Contemplation* about being "invited to forget ourselves on purpose, cast our awful solemnity to the winds and join in the general dance."[18] Sometimes, though, the dance can be dangerous, to which Kerouac's perilous experience on Desolation bears testimony. For Kerouac, Mount Hozomeen towering another 2000 feet over him on Desolation was a discomforting, threatening presence, by turns a bear and a tiger.

Merton also illustrates the powerful emotions elicited by imposing mountains when he describes his encounter with two volcanoes whilst flying over Alaska in a twin-engine plane in September 1968:

Two volcanoes: *Iliamna*—graceful, mysterious, feminine, akin to the great Mexican volcanoes. A volcano to which one speaks with reverence, lovely in the distance, standing above the sea of clouds. Lovely near at hand with smaller attendant peaks. *Redoubt* (which surely has another name, a secret and true name) handsome and noble in the distance, but ugly, sinister as you get near it. A brute of a dirty busted mountain that has exploded too often. A bear of a mountain. A dog mountain with steam curling up out of the snow crater. As the plane drew near there was turbulence and we felt the plane might at any moment be suddenly pulled out of its course and hurled against the mountain. As if it would not pull itself away. But finally it did. *Redoubt*. A volcano to which one says nothing. Pictures from the plane.[19]

That last note, "Pictures from the plane," is intriguing—a note to himself perhaps that he has taken some pictures but also a comment on what he has just done in the previous lines: provided us with pictures from the plane. These are *contemplative* pictures which allow us to see the window between the inner and outer worlds, in much the same way Merton described his camera as a "Zen camera," a means of provoking an unmediated experience of reality—a photographic *haiku*—a contemplative window that allows us to see both ways and yet actually does neither but opens up a new view: our own view. The experience is analogous to that of an artist and a painting: the artist expresses herself through paint and some of that may be communicated to us as we view the painting but our experience of the picture is not that of the artist; it is our own. It is the essential non-communicability of experience—an insight common to both Zen and contemplation.

Merton takes more haiku-like pictures from the plane, this time conceived as "The new consciousness. Reading the calligraphy of snow and rock from the air," thirty-nine thousand feet over Idaho:

Whorled dark profile of a river in snow. A cliff in the fog. And now a dark road straight through a long fresh snow field. Snaggy reaches of snow pattern. Claws of mountain and valley. Light shadow or breaking cloud on snow. Swing and reach of long, gaunt, black, white forks.[20]

Through contemplation of the world around us we both find and lose ourselves—we appear and disappear. Our senses heighten our awareness of being alive, of existing—we appear—and yet this very consciousness somehow exposes the fiction of ourselves— such that we disappear. It is the difference between the "false" self of the *cogito ergo sum* observing itself thinking and the mysterious, indefinable "true" self of pure being—though I am conscious here that I am trying to articulate the unspeakable. Kerouac expresses it like this:

I saw that if it wasn't for the six senses, of seeing, hearing, smelling, touching, tasting and thinking, the self of that, which is non-existent, there would be no phenomena to perceive at all, in fact no six senses or self.[21]

The "six" senses Kerouac refers to here, rather than the customary five, again reflects Buddhist influence. Kerouac had spent much of the early 1950s studying the traditions and writings of Buddhism, and this is inevitably reflected in his own writings of this period. The six senses are the six *vijnanas* of Buddhist philosophy, which include mind (*manovijnana*) as a sense organ for the apprehension of *dharma*, or objects of thought as for example in the Shingyo Sutra.[22] So Kerouac disappears, whilst at the same time creating some vivid contemplative pictures of his own and so appearing again in the mirror of his own soul:

> The Skagit River at Marblemount was a rushing clear snowmelt of pure green . . . It was the work of the quiet mountains, this torrent of purity at my feet . . . . It was a river wonderland, the emptiness of the golden eternity, odors of moss and bark and twigs and mud, all ululating mysterious visionstuff before my eyes, tranquil and everlasting nevertheless, the hillhairing trees, the dancing sunlight. As I looked up the clouds assumed as I assumed, faces of hermits.[23]

The "emptiness" this time is not desolate but the "golden eternity" as Kerouac assumes here the face of a hermit, inwardly mirroring the clouds "out there." The "face of the hermit" appears once more in Kerouac's "Notes on the Author," part of the introduction to *Lonesome Traveler*:

> Am actually not "beat" but strange solitary crazy Catholic mystic . . . Final plans: hermitage in the woods, quiet writing of old age, mellow hopes of Paradise (which comes to everybody anyway) . . . .[24]

These are words that could almost have been written by the hermit of the Kentucky backwoods himself. But that last year at the hermitage had become increasingly difficult for Merton: "Traffic on the road. Kids at the lake. Guns. Machines, and Boone's dog yelling in the wood at night. And people coming all the time . . . . if I can find somewhere to *disappear* to, I will" (July 29, 1968).[25]

Merton thinks about northern California and speaks of it frequently with much affection and perhaps might have spent part of the year there, or even founded a colony of hermits.[26] In his journal entry for May 24 we find the strongest statement of his desire to return to California and of his sense of alienation at Gethsemani:

> Lonely for the Pacific and the Redwoods. A sense that somehow when I was there I was unutterably happy—and maybe I was. Certainly, every minute I was there, especially by the sea, I felt I was at home—as if I had come a very long way to where I really belonged. Maybe it's absurd, I don't know. But that is the way it feels. I seem to be alienated and exiled here. As if there were really no reason whatever—except a few tenaciously fictitious ones—for being here. As if I were utterly cheating myself by staying where I am only a stranger—and will never be anything else.[27]

These words of alienation and exile poignantly articulate the disjuncture Merton experienced between where he was geographically and where he wanted to be spiritually. In order to get to where he wanted to be *spiritually* he felt the need for a *physical* move. On the Pacific shore, it seems he had found a place where he recognized himself—"Thou art that"—"I need the sound of those waves, that desolation, that emptiness."[28] But even the shore was becoming too populated—too many cars, visitors, hippies, development—one senses his sadness. He thought about Alaska and may well have returned there. He liked it better than Kentucky,[29] though one does not sense the same warmth that he had for California. Ultimately the question of where he might have settled is redundant—he went to Asia and among the Buddha statues of Polonnaruwa found what he was obscurely looking for[30] and ten days later he did, indeed, *disappear*. He had found his place of resurrection. The ultimate place: he was *home*.

It is the concept of "home" that is perhaps key in understanding the relationship between inner and outer, landscape and spirit, geography and solitude. In *The Seven Storey Mountain*, Merton referred to France as the land to which he belonged—the "home" that he had not seen before and would not see again; on the Pacific shoreline he felt he was "at home" having come a long way to where he "really belonged." At the beginning of *The Asian Journal*, he speaks with elation of "going home, to the home where I have never been in this body."[31] "Home" is usually understood in terms of the place where one is from or has grown up or habitually resides over a long period and yet for Merton "home" seems to be a place that he has never been to or is unlikely to return to. In struggling to articulate this after his return from California in May 1968 he stated explicitly, "The country which is nowhere is the real home."[32]

This statement begins the entry for May 30th in *Woods, Shore, Desert* and immediately follows the entry that concludes, "Thou art that" (before adding, "I dream every night of the west"). Merton realises that true home lies beyond physical geography, but he then adds, "only it seems that the Pacific Shore at Needle Rock is more nowhere than this, and Bear Harbor is more nowhere still."[33] Apparently embarrassed, he immediately admits that he was tempted to cross that out but that in these notes he was leaving everything in. He clearly is aware of, and is struggling with, the paradox, if not contradiction, between these notions of home and identity being tied up with his interaction with the physical landscape, the world around him, on the one hand, and on the other hand, the insight that true identity and home lie beyond, or perhaps better, transcend, the physical and geographic. Merton's recognition of "home" at Needle Rock or Bear Harbor articulates his recognition of himself in what he sees. Like Suzuki's Yogin, he sees himself reflected in his "mind-mirror" as he looks upon "the world with its expansion of earth"[34] or, specifically, the "sea rock mist, diffused light and half hidden mountain."[35] But just as Kerouac finds through the experience of solitude on Desolation an empty self of "abysmal nothingness"—literally the nothingness of the abyss—"worse than no illusion even,"[36] so Merton perceives that his own identity lies beyond the reflection of the mind-mirror. His true identity, his real home, is the country that is nowhere. Merton is very much the exile-in-solitude "attending to the skies we cannot understand," skies which nonetheless assume faces of hermits.

Notes

1. From the poem "The Quickening of St. John The Baptist: On The Contemplative Vocation" in *The Collected Poems of Thomas Merton* (New York: New Directions, 1980), p. 201.

2. Thomas Merton, *The Asian Journal* (New York: New Directions, 1973), p. 4; entry for October 15, 1968. Also see: Thomas Merton, *The Other Side of the Mountain* (Journals 7; 1967-1968; ed. Patrick Hart, O.C.S.O.; San Francisco: Harper Collins, 1998), p. 205.

3. Thomas Merton, *Woods, Shore, Desert: A Notebook, May 1968* (Santa Fe: Museum of New Mexico Press, 1968), p. 42. This entry is dated May 22, 1968. Also see: Thomas Merton, *The Other Side of the Mountain, op. cit.* p. 110.

4. D.T. Suzuki, *Manual of Zen Buddhism* (New York: Grove, 1935), p. 72.

5. Thomas Merton, *The Seven Storey Mountain* (London, SPCK, 1990), p. 10.

6. Thomas Merton, *The Seven Storey Mountain, op. cit.* pp. 30-31.

7. This alludes to psychologist Dr. Gregory Zilboorg's charge that Merton's desire for a hermitage was pathological, that he wanted a hermitage in Times Square with a large sign over it saying "Hermit." See: Michael Mott, *The Seven Mountains of Thomas Merton* (London: Sheldon Press, 1986) p. 297.

8. Entry for May 21, 1968 in Thomas Merton, *The Other Side of the Mountain, op. cit.* p. 120.

9. Robert Inchausti, *Thomas Merton's American Prophecy.* New York: SUNY, 1998. p. 5. For a more detailed introduction to the parallels and connections between Merton and Kerouac, see Angus Stuart, 'Visions of Tom: Jack Kerouac's Monastic Elder Brother.' *The Merton Journal* 8:1 (2001), pp. 40-46. See also: http://www.thomasmertonsociety.org/kerouac.htm

10. Jack Kerouac, *Desolation Angels* (New York: Riverhead Books, 1995 (1965)), p. 68.

11. Henry David Thoreau, *Walden* (London & Newcastle-on-Tyne: The Walter Scott Publishing Co. 1886), pp. 88-89.

12. Jack Kerouac, *Desolation Angels, op. cit.* p. 4.

13. *Ibid.* p. 73.

14. Robert Marshall who worked for the United States Forest Service in the 1930s argued for the establishment of "primitive areas" to be kept perpetually free of roads and logging, "To preserve a certain precious value of the timeless, the mysterious, and the primordial." See: John Suiter, *Poets on the Peaks* (Washington DC: Counterpoint, 2002), p. 36.

15. Jack Kerouac, *Desolation Angels, op. cit.* p. 36 (the spelling is Kerouac's own).

16. *Ibid.* p. 5.

17. Belden C. Lane, *Landscapes of the Sacred: Geography and Narrative in American Spirituality* (Baltimore & London: John Hopkins University Press, 2002), p. 39.

18. Thomas Merton, *New Seeds of Contemplation* (London: Burns & Oates, 1999 (1962)). p. 192.

19. Thomas Merton, *The Other Side of the Mountain, op. cit.* pp. 195-196.

20. *Ibid*, p. 94.

21. Jack Kerouac, *Lonesome Traveler* (London: Penguin, 2000 (1960)), p. 116.

22. See D.T. Suzuki, *Manual of Zen Buddhism, op.cit.* pp. 26-30. For more on Kerouac, Merton and Buddhism see: Angus Stuart, 'Grace Beats Karma: Thomas Merton and the Dharma Bums' in *The World in My Bloodstream: Thomas Merton's Universal Embrace,* (ed. Angus Stuart; Abergavenny: Three Peaks Press, 2004), pp. 92-105.

23. Jack Kerouac, *The Dharma Bums.* (London: Flamingo, 1994 (1959)), p. 188.

24. Jack Kerouac, *Lonesome Traveler* (London: Penguin, 2000 (1960)), p. 8.

25. Thomas Merton, *The Other Side of the Mountain, op. cit.* p. 148.

26. *Ibid.* p.139. Merton's entry for July 5, 1968 reads: "[Fr. Flavian] is *very* interested in perhaps starting something out on the Coast. And today, in so many words, he asked me if I were willing to start it: i.e. to go out there and get some sort of small hermit colony going."

27. *Ibid.* p. 122.

28. *Ibid.* p. 120.

29. *Ibid.* p. 193. Merton's entry for September 27, 1968: "Whatever else I may say—it is clear I like Alaska much better than Kentucky and it seems to me that if I am to be a hermit in the U.S., Alaska is probably the place for it."

30. *Ibid.* p. 323. Merton's entry for December 4, 1968: "...I know and have seen what I was obscurely looking for. I don't know what else remains..."

31. Thomas Merton, *The Asian Journal, op. cit.* p. 5; entry for October 15, 1968. Also see: Thomas Merton, *The Other Side of the Mountain, op. cit.* pp. 205-206.

32. Thomas Merton, *Woods, Shore, Desert: A Notebook, May 1968, op. cit.* p. 42. Also see: Thomas Merton, *The Other Side of the Mountain, op. cit.* p. 110.

33. *Ibid.*

34. D.T. Suzuki, *Manual of Zen Buddhism, op. cit.* p. 72.

35. Thomas Merton, *Woods, Shore, Desert: A Notebook, May 1968, op. cit.* p. 42. Also see: Thomas Merton, *The Other Side of the Mountain, op. cit.* p. 110.

36. Jack Kerouac, *Desolation Angels, op. cit.* p. 68.

Reality as Sacred Place: The Parallel Insights of Thomas Merton and Henry Bugbee

Gray Matthews

The monastic Thomas Merton and the philosopher Henry Bugbee were two contemplative adventurers whose quests to live deliberately were alike in many startling ways. Both thinkers strove to transcend the constraints of conceptual thought in order to confront what Thoreau referred to as the "hard bottom and rocks in place, which we can call reality."[1] For Merton and Bugbee, every place was potentially a sacred place if one was fully present there. Home was wherever one stood with one's eyes open.

Although Merton and Bugbee may have never known each other nor been familiar with one another's work, their intellectual paths appear parallel in many intriguing ways, especially when one observes the stream of mutual influences and common interests they shared. Both were born in 1915. Both read and admired Thoreau, loved nature and the joys of solitude and communion with the natural world. Both knew and corresponded with Daisetz Suzuki and were influenced by Kitaro Nishida. Both gleaned valuable insights regarding silence, mystery and wonder from Max Picard and Gabriel Marcel. Both drew wisdom from Meister Eckhart concerning detachment from conceptual thought. Both preferred to write and publish their thoughts in journal form as they sought to know and experience life as poets walking in truth with a deep awareness of living in the present moment.

More significantly, though, Merton and Bugbee both deeply understood the sacred relationship between place and presence in ways that led them to celebrate the transformative realization of communion in coming to view reality, itself, as sacred place. Merton and Bugbee preferred a free-flowing life of openness and reflectiveness, ever reverent and receptive to the communication of Being—a contemplative life—vigilant in resisting the false security of static thought and the lures of conformism. Both thinkers realized, especially, that the natural world was exceptional in its ability to present a ceaseless invitation to experience reality with openness, awareness and reverence.

One might explore key passages in Bugbee's *The Inward Morning* that parallel various statements of Merton's serving to illuminate four axioms of sacred place as posited by Belden Lane.[2] Lane's four axioms will help reveal and bridge a set of common themes and concerns between these two contemplative thinkers. One might posit that Bugbee's approach to contemplation can be appreciated as a philosophical complement to Merton's monastic and spiritual approach, and that, together, their views strengthen one another much in the way which the writer of Proverbs envisions: "As iron sharpens iron, so man sharpens his fellow man" (27.17).

I. An Introduction to the Life and Work of Henry Bugbee

Henry Bugbee (1915-1999) was an American philosopher writing in the tradition of Henry David Thoreau and Ralph Waldo Emerson, yet he was equally influenced by Martin Heidegger and, in particular, Gabriel Marcel. Born in New York City, Bugbee received his A.B. from Princeton in 1936 and his M.A. and Ph.D. from University of California at Berkeley in 1940 and 1947 respectively. He held teaching posts at Nevada, Stanford, Harvard and finally the University of Montana.

The French philosopher and playwright Gabriel Marcel (1889-1973) rivaled Thoreau in terms of his influence on Bugbee's thought. Though Bugbee was not a formal student of Marcel's (Marcel's most famous students were Paul Ricoeur and Emmanuel Mounier), he credited Marcel for helping him find his own philosophical voice. In turn, Bugbee has helped many of his own students, such as philosophers Stanley Cavell and Albert Borgmann, to find their unique personal voices and styles.

Interest in the work of Henry Bugbee was recently revived with the 1999 re-publication of his classic text *The Inward Morning*, which Huston Smith calls "the most 'Taoist' Western book I know— Thoreau's *Walden* not excepted" (back cover endorsement). Marcel penned the original introduction to *Morning*, where he identified Bugbee's philosophy as "a philosophy of the open air."[3] Critic Nathan Scott describes *Morning* as "a most remarkable book" that "still remains largely (and strangely) unknown."[4] American philosophers Albert Borgmann and David Strong both credit Bugbee for helping them ground their own philosophical studies, as recorded in the collection of philosophers talking about their calling in *Falling in Love with Wisdom*.[5] But perhaps *The Inward Morning* belongs to the literature of nature as much as it does to philosophy; this seminal work exemplifies the generic characteristics of the literature of nature, particularly those works that Douglas Burton-Christie identifies as being bound with a philosophical "quest for the sacred."[6]

In addition to *Morning*, a splendid set of critical essays about Bugbee's work was also recently published, edited by Edward F. Mooney (most noted for his works on Kierkegaard), with a foreword supplied by Alasdair MacIntyre.[7] According to Mooney in *The Inward Morning*, Bugbee views reality itself as wilderness through which we travel by real faith, but which also permeates us. "Not only the wilderness of hawks and trout and storms brought to our attention," Mooney explains, "but also human fellowship at sea or in a city."[8] Hence Mooney concludes: "Henry Bugbee's work can be framed as a phenomenological project that renders the full reality of things" in his pursuit to "uncover an experiential ground of felt-compassion that carries the necessity not of law but of the heart—what in reality speaks to the person as a whole."[9]

Bugbee's Approach to Philosophy

Bugbee approaches the work of philosophy from the perspective of a poet: "For me philosophy is in the end an approximation to the poem."[10] He opens *The Inward Morning* by quoting William Carlos Williams: "Form is never more than an extension of content" and a poem is "a structure built upon your own ground...your ground where you stand on your own feet."[11] Such a start would, in my opinion, certainly attract and delight Merton's own attention if he had had the chance to read Bugbee because, for Merton, both the poetic vision and the necessity for standing on your own two feet were primary ways in which he felt the spiritual life was to be lived. Mooney describes Bugbee's style as a form of "lyric philosophy," which serves to "lead us home, or remind us of the home we've left, or reveal a flash of insight that where we stand is now where we belong."[12]

The metaphor of "dawn" pervades Bugbee's journal, giving credence to interpreting his philosophy as a philosophy of inner awakening, hence the journal's title: *The Inward Morning*. Bugbee follows Thoreau in the recognition that "to be awake is to be alive" and therefore "we must learn to reawaken and keep ourselves awake."[13] Such a philosophy of awakening, says Bugbee, cannot be worked out with all the pieces to the puzzle in view, but rather "more like the clarification of what we know in our bones."[14] One cannot rush the inward morning. We can only prepare for inner dawn without force, as he later explains: "When we are imperious, reality withholds its instruction from us. We learn of necessity in all gentleness, or not all."[15] In short, we must ready ourselves to see. Bugbee is certain that we *will* see. We can see reality from within—insight—which one may earn but never steer: "It must find its own articulate form. If it is to become more than sporadic and utterly ephemeral, one must pay attention to it, it must be *worked out*. And to work it out is not to cramp it into a prefixed mould."[16] He advises would-be philosophers, therefore, to work toward insight but not try to capture or entrap it, to let it flow and to trust its liveliness. The inward morning, therefore, is an experience of the dawning of insight and authentic meaning. Bugbee seeks to differentiate his approach to philosophical thinking from the tradition of professional, academic philosophy, which underlines another value of writing in journal format, given its allowances for poetic excursions off the beaten path. In this sense, Bugbee seeks a different operating basis for conducting philosophical thinking and writing philosophical discourse. He intuits a *certainty* that exists outside of any constructs that he might be able to build through rational thought and language, a certainty that "may be quite compatible with being at a loss to say what one is certain of."[17] For Bugbee, rather than a conclusion reached at the end of a complex argument, *certainty* is a basis for action which he compares favorably, to the essence of hope and faith, all as forms of knowledge and kinds of certainty, which we can work from but not possess or control.

I believe it is fair to argue that Bugbee's approach has much in common with Pierre Hadot's perspective of philosophy as spiritual exercise, particularly for the reason that Bugbee finds certainty *in living*, and not in the articulation of philosophical discourse.[18] Merton, as well, realizes the necessity to "develop a certain *kind of consciousness that is above and beyond deception* by verbal formulas."[19] We have to live first before we can put our reasoning to use, which is why Merton advises that the "solution of the problem of life is life itself. Life is not attained by reasoning and analysis, but first of all by living."[20] Thus we see that Merton and Bugbee both share a mystical origin for their philosophical journeys—at the living center of life experience where language springs from and feeds back into a stream of meaning.[21]   Both writers seek to articulate an emphasis upon the *flow* and not the *capture* of reality, an emphasis that undergirds their notions of presence and communion involved in the fluid experiencing of reality as sacred place.

This line of thinking about certainty leads Bugbee to celebrate the philosophical value of wonder, which he contrasts to the "endless business" of explanations. Bugbee writes:

> In wonder it seems as if the presence of things took root in us, and planted in us an intimation of reality not to be understood exclusively by digression, by the ways of explanation. From the time reality has begun to sink into us in wonder, we can begin to realize that our minds are committed to wander.[22]

Bugbee views wonder not merely as an object for reflection but as a source of fundamental truth that beckons us to a greater involvement in the openness of being. He adds that when philosophy is abstracted as mere ideas from the life of a person, our experience of life is dispirited. Bugbee's philosophical task, therefore, is to overcome abstraction in order "to accommodate the life of spirit with all the mind."[23]

Perhaps the best introduction to Bugbee's philosophical approach in regard to place can be found in his own description of performing philosophical work *as a meditation of place*. His account is as follows:

> During my years of graduate study before the war I studied philosophy in the classroom and at a desk, but my philosophy took shape mainly on foot. It was truly peripatetic, engendered not merely while walking, but *through* walking that was essentially a *meditation of the place*. And the balance in which I weighed the ideas I was studying was always that established in the experience of walking in the place. I weighed everything by the measure of the silent presence of things, clarified in the racing clouds, clarified by the cry of hawks, solidified in the presence of rocks, spelled syllable by syllable by waters of manifold voice, and consolidated in the act of taking steps, each step a meditation steeped in reality.[24]

Bugbee persisted in trying to understand what he was thinking and doing while *walking in the presence of things*. It finally dawned on him in the fall of 1941, as he spent time in the Canadian Rockies, that "it was there in attending to this wilderness, with unremitting alertness and attentiveness, yes, even as I slept, that I knew myself to have been instructed for life, though I was at a loss to say what instruction I had received."[25] A short time later, Bugbee served with the U.S. Naval Reserve from 1942-1946, spending three of those years at sea experiencing life on the ocean as continuous with his experience of being instructed by the reality of the mountains, "but with men with whom I lived thoroughly enough to experience the community of men and place; though I did not know it, I lived a meditation of both in communion. The thought which I have been working out in these last three years is definitively based on that experience."[26]

Similarly, Thomas Merton's spiritual journey led him to Cuba, Florida, St. Bonaventure College and Friendship House in Harlem before he experienced an inward dawning in 1941 that propelled him to enter the monastery, and likewise began his own serious reflections on what it means to live in communion with other men in place, a process of thinking that would develop and evolve over the next 27 years as he sought to articulate the instructions he received from the reality of his placed experiences.

Bugbee realizes through communion with the presence of things that communication takes place, despite his incapacity to possess and control the meaning of the experience. Active receptiveness is the key. Bugbee wants to meditate on the phenomena he is experiencing, which he sees is a way to "reestablish ourselves in a deeper vein of experience" (143). Bugbee is intrigued by the idea of linking meditation to prayer. True meditation, for Bugbee, is not merely tilling the ground of one's thoughts, but an opening of oneself through a deepening of candor. In the depths of experience, rather than upon the surface, is where Bugbee claims the inward morning will take place and awaken us.

Thus, in Bugbee we find a philosopher wishing to wonder and experience, the reality he senses as rooted in him as well as outside himself. Bugbee's approach is very much in accordance with David Abram's description of a relational style of thinking "that associates *truth* not with static fact, but with a quality of relationship. Ecologically considered, it is not primarily our verbal statements that are 'true' or 'false,' but rather the kind of relations that we sustain with the rest of nature."[27]

Bugbee's starting point for philosophizing about reality is in the natural world, from which he thinks through experiences as one immersed in the great mystery of living. Bugbee's perspective should strike students of Merton as one very much in keeping with Merton's own sense of wonder and his relentless drive to immerse himself in "hidden wholeness" of reality as sacred place.[28]

II. Bugbee and Merton: Seeds of Insight

The early 1950s marked an especially rich period for Bugbee and Merton. Both Bugbee and Merton were maintaining journals in 1952 and 1953 that would lead to parallel publications in 1958. Bugbee's journal notes would become *The Inward Morning*; for Merton, his meditative notes would become *Thoughts In Solitude*; the books share much in common. In his "Author's Note," Merton acknowledges the inspiration of Max Picard's *World of Silence* woven throughout his reflections in *Thoughts In Solitude*.[29] Interestingly, Picard's classic work on silence includes a wonderful Introduction by Gabriel Marcel, both men who influenced Bugbee's thoughts during this period. In comparison, during the years 1952-3, while Merton struggled with censors and editors over the final version of *The Sign of Jonas*, published in February 1953, Bugbee was struggling with his writing, too, declaring on July 8, 1953, that "for five years I have been writing in an exploratory way, gradually forced to recognize that this was the case and I must accept it, along with its professional consequences."[30] Bugbee explains further, sounding here very much like the struggling writer and emerging master of students, Thomas Merton:

> My task has been to learn to write in a vein compatible with what I can honestly say in the act of trying to discover what I must say. It has been a precarious business. I have found myself thinking quite differently from the majority of men who are setting the style and the standard of philosophy worth doing...It has become apparent that the thought which I am concerned to define is not easy to produce on demand. Often I do not know what I am trying to say[31]

Similarly, Merton was at work at this time penning perhaps his most famous prayer, which begins with the confession: "My Lord God, I have no idea where I am going."[32]

For Merton, the years 1950-1952, immediately preceding his journal notes on solitude, mark a significant period in his life that bear on his later writings about solitude, vocation and the natural world, for it is at this time that Merton begins studying Thoreau in depth as well as taking on the duties of forester for the monastery.[33]

In April 1950, Merton begins to link his vocation with trees: "This afternoon we were out planting trees in the woods. There is no work I can think of that would be more favorable for contemplation than this."[34]   Merton was actively considering parallels between Thoreau and John of the Cross at the end of 1950. Merton became the monastery's timber marker in 1951, and by January 1952, Merton is ready to declare: "I live in the trees."[35]   Merton is so quickly immersed in nature that he experiences the "strange awakening to find the sky inside you and beneath you and above you and all around you so that your spirit is one with the sky, and all is positive night."[36]   Clearly, Merton's vocation has turned to identify "a new level of reality" as prompted by a core sense of awakening through his experiences in the woods around the monastery.[37]   Deeply, Merton begins to realize more fully that

[w]hen your tongue is silent, you can rest in the silence of the forest. When your imagination is silent, the forest speaks to you, tells you of its unreality and of the Reality of God. But when your mind is silent, then the forest suddenly becomes magnificently real and blazes transparently with the Reality of God: for now I know that the Creation which first seems to reveal Him, in concepts, then seems to hide Him, by the same concepts, finally *is revealed in Him*, in the Holy Spirit: and we who are in God find ourselves united, in Him, with all that springs from Him. This is prayer, and this is glory![38]

Merton's fullness of spirit leads him to conclude *The Sign of Jonas* with a beautiful example of this poetic awareness: "There are drops of dew that show like sapphires in the grass as soon as the great sun appears, and leaves stir behind the hushed flight of an escaping dove."[39]   By 1957, Merton begins to associate all monks with trees as he formulates *Basic Principles of Monastic Spirituality*: "In the night of our technological barbarism, monks must be as trees which exist silently in the dark and by their vital presence purify the air."[40]   As Merton's desire for solitude, silence and a relationship to the forest grew, as well as the realization that he could not escape the world by remaining in the woods, his philosophical arguments evolved into a deeper contemplative understanding and fuller sense of dialogical interconnectedness with all of reality in ways that compare favorably with the dawning of similar experiential insights in the life of Henry Bugbee.

III. Bugbee, Merton and the Phenomenology of Sacred Places

Belden Lane argues that there are four basic principles, or axioms, underlying the way in which we experience and understand landscape as sacred. All four axioms relate to how we participate in the sacredness of reality and how such involved encounters influence our experiences of place, including the presence of other beings and objects. From our experiences of sacred places come the narratives upon which we reflect for guidance in centering our busy, displaced lives, what Lane calls the process of mythogenesis.

Bugbee's *Inward Morning* is laced with stories, examples and vignettes steeped in concrete experiences that the author uses not only to explicate his philosophy but to cultivate it from actual experience. These narratives are all acknowledged to be rooted in placed experiences, often in memories that resurface to make meaning upon the waters of reflection, serving to direct Bugbee's thinking about place, presence and communion. Thus Bugbee's stories of going swamping, building a dam as a child, being on the rowing team in college, hiking in the Canadian Rockies, communing with a ship's crew during WWII, helping a drowning man from a river, a road trip to Mexico, fishing for leaping trout—all testify to Bugbee's intention to let life speak and instruct him, to philosophize through living. Almost all of these stories communicate insights about the flow and fluidity of reality. With the patience of a fisherman, Bugbee finds delight waiting for insight. Philosophy, therefore, is simply a means for keeping "one's fingers touching the trembling line" for "it is just in the moment of the leap we both feel and see, when the trout is instantly born, entire, from the flowing river, that reality is knowingly defined."[41]

Merton also wrote about place and the natural world throughout his life, but he wrote as a spiritual writer, and not necessarily as a philosopher or nature writer. The fruit of his constant reflections and insights regarding the natural world can be found throughout his poetry, essays, autobiography and especially in his public and private journals. Thomas Merton was a true monk of the earth in the sense that his spiritual perspective was grounded in the here and now, a view perhaps best represented by his pithy proclamation in the early 1950s: "I do not think that being a monk means living on the moon."[42] Like Bugbee, Merton has stories to tell about stepping into the flowing river of reality. Merton drank deeply from these waters that nourished his awareness of the sacredness of reality, of life.

1. Sacred place is not chosen, it chooses

Lane's first axiom asserts that because God chooses to reveal himself only where he wills, human beings cannot determine or engineer what becomes sacred. Our choice, therefore, is one of choosing to be open to revelation as the way in which we become active participants in the sacralization of place. This insight is clearly operating within Bugbee's philosophical perspective, particularly due to the great emphasis he places on openness and receptiveness as opposed to acts of will and domination. Openness, for Bugbee, is a choice related to wonder in that both are modes for experiencing reality and meaning in depth as reality *chooses* to be made known. Both openness and wonder stand in stark contrast to the reductionism produced by *explaining* reality. "In wonder, however" Bugbee writes, "it seems as if the presence of things took root in us, and planted in us an intimation of reality not to be understood exclusively by digression, by the ways of explanation."[43] Bugbee offers thinkers a choice at this point: We can either continue wandering in search of new and improved explanations, "or we can open ourselves to the meaning of a life in the wilderness and be patient of being overtaken in our wandering by that which can make us at home in this condition."[44] Bugbee argues that the latter choice "involves an openness on the part of the person in his entirety," which he then suggests is a "condition of philosophical truth."[45]

This openness is what Bugbee later refers to as "receptiveness," which is so important to his thinking that he boldly claims that "the readiness to receive is all."[46] Receptiveness is linked to Bugbee's fundamental notion of reality as given: "Here is an essential point: Nothing can be truly given to us except on the condition of active receptiveness on our part."[47] He explains that "givenness is decisive experience of reality," yet he cautions: "to experience reality as given is to be at farthest remove from claiming certain possession of any truth; for the certainty of understanding is contrary to such a claim."[48] Thus reality is a gift that we can only receive: "There is certainty in experience in which reality is given; but this does not seem to be a certainty of knowledge about anything we represent to ourselves and describe."[49] Through the language of openness, receptiveness and givenness, Bugbee argues explicitly that "philosophy is not a making of a home for the mind out of reality. It is more like learning to leave things be: restoration in the wilderness, here and now. By 'leaving things be' I do not mean inaction; I mean respecting things, being still in the presence of things, letting them speak."[50] For Bugbee, therefore, we do not construct reality; we complete reality by responding.

Merton's affection for the philosophy of the Taoist sage, Chuang Tzu, puts him clearly in good company with Bugbee's basic philosophical approach. Merton claims his own "ventures in personal and spiritual interpretation" of Chuang's teachings "have been most rewarding" stating further that he "enjoyed writing this book more than any other."[51] He characterizes Chuang Tzu's philosophy as simple and direct because it goes "immediately to the heart of things" like "all the greatest philosophical thought"; he also finds Chuang Tzu appealing because he "shares the climate and peace of my own kind of solitude, and who is my own kind of person."[52] Merton could have been speaking about Bugbee in arguing that Chuang Tzu's teachings reflect "a certain taste for simplicity, for humility, self-effacement, silence, and in general a refusal to take seriously the aggressivity, the ambition, the push, and the self-importance which one must display in order to get along in society."[53]

One might also find further parallels in Merton's interpretation of Heraclitus's perspective, in which we see another philosophy of awakening. According to Merton, Heraclitus presents "our spiritual and mystical destiny" to be one in which we

"awaken" to the fire that is within us, and our happiness depends on the harmony-in-conflict that results from this awakening. Our vocation is a call to spiritual oneness in and with the logos. But this interior fulfillment is not to be attained by a false peace resulting from artificial compulsion—a static and changeless "state" imposed by force of will upon the dynamic, conflicting forces within us.[54]

Bugbee and Merton both seem to share the same penchant for Heraclitus who by "wielding the sharp weapon of paradox without mercy, seeks to awaken the mind of his disciple to a reality that is right before his eyes but that he is incapable of seeing."[55]

Bugbee's stance, like Merton's, is a contemplative one, although not in the sense of one who, according to Merton, "adopts a systematic program of spiritual self-purification";[56] rather, Bugbee simply seeks to enter into union with the invisible Tao. In contemplation, Bugbee states, "one stands independently and at the same time together with everything other than oneself. Contemplation is governed by omni-relevant meaning. Yet one may respond upon a conclusive meaning of things without being able to say what that meaning is."[57] Bugbee defines the contemplative act as "that in which reality makes firm its grip on us," though he is referring strictly to aesthetic and philosophic forms of contemplation in which one begins to "learn of a sustaining ground in which [one is] rooted."[58] Bugbee recognizes, following Eckhart, that "the heart of true contemplation is disinterestedness"; thus, it is in wonder and openness that we contemplate reality in ways in which our thinking participates and is continuous with the flow of its given sacredness.[59]

In the following quotation, Bugbee almost seems to be describing Merton in the state of contemplation that led him to craft his 1966 essay "Rain and the Rhinoceros."[60] Here, Bugbee is discussing the state of philosophical reflectiveness that brings one to oneself, which can lead one to proclaim along with Merton that as long as the rain talks, we are going to listen:

> One may be struck clean by sunlight over a patch of lawn, by clouds running free before the wind, by the massive presence of rock. What untold hosts of voices there are which call upon one and summon him to reawakening. He remembers, and is himself once again, moving cleanly on his way. Some measure of simplicity again informs the steps he takes; he becomes content to be himself and finds fragrance in the air. He may eat his food in peace. He does not wish to obviate tomorrow's work. He is willing to consider: not to suppose a case, but take the case that is. He becomes patient. Things invite him to adequate himself to their infinity. The passage of time is now not robbery or show; it is the meaning of the present ever completing itself. It is enough to participate in this, to be at home in the unknown.[61]

Merton, in turn, sounding like Bugbee, explains why he listens to the rain instead of the rhinoceros and why *it is enough to participate* in listening to the rain: "because it reminds me again and again that the whole world runs by rhythms I have not yet learned to recognize, rhythms that are not those of the engineer."[62] Certainly, Merton is speaking of the sacred rhythms of reality.

2. Sacred place is ordinary place, ritually made extraordinary

According to Lane, this second axiom refers to the recognition of the sacredness of place through "certain ritual acts that are performed there, setting it apart as unique."[63] For Bugbee, the ritual of reflection, or of contemplation, is the act that must be performed wherever we are in order to see the extraordinariness in the ordinary. We must go through a process of awakening because reality "is a holy place," which Bugbee only recognizes as that "when [one has] been most awake, and [one takes] it as a mark of awakening whenever it dawns upon [one] again as true."[64] For Merton, it is silence that provides the most vital ritual for awakening to the sacredness of ordinary reality.

Like Merton, Bugbee greatly values silence for it reveals to us our need to bear witness to and receive the meanings of reality as it speaks in the dawning of insight. Bugbee studied the work of Max Picard on silence as a corrective to the traditional philosopher's disposition toward speech as the primary mode through which one experiences reality. "From Picard," writes Bugbee, "I retain the idea that sounds, distinct sounds, make sense only as heard articulations of silence. Perhaps sounds are only so heard as we are still. Otherwise they are only abstractly heard, and no matter the order noted between them, they would tend to become a sequence of noises."[65] Silence enables us to hear being, which is an essential criterion for seeing the ordinary stand out as extraordinary. Bugbee records these thoughts on the ritual of being silent and reflective in place:

How welcome everything is, apprehended with such constancy in the immediacy of the flow of meaning, how fluent the articulate world. It is as if it all flowed directly and simply from within oneself and one were receiving the world "from within" as much as "from without." As silence is to the spoken word, so being is to everything distinct. Things are definitely given as being as the issue of silence. They are, are, eternally are. To experience them as being is to know them from within; this knowing them from within is concrete experience.[66]

Bugbee seems to suggest, therefore, that if there is a proper ritual for experiencing the sacredness of reality, then silence helps us become more *responsive to the articulate world around us*; for Bugbee this means that "whatever, then, is truly given, truly perceived, is loved; to love is to understand what is perceived as eternal. Only the truly received is truly given; true reception is active contemplation; it involves completeness, that is purity of response."[67]

Bugbee's philosophical project is centered on *reflecting* during and upon experiences of thinking, a thinking-as-receptiveness that is opposed to merely reasoning about statements concerning such experiences. He defines reflection as "a trying to remember, a digging that is pointless if it be not digging down directly beneath where one stands, so that the waters of his life may re-invade the present moment and define the meaning of both."[68] In other words, Bugbee wants to swim in the river of thinking—live—instead of conducting a slide-show presentation about authentic thoughts afterwards.[69] Quite literally, Bugbee claims that rivers *instruct*: "A river carries with it the sense of reality as I would do justice to it. I could wish for no more than to do justice to the instruction I have received from moving waters."[70] This leads Bugbee to formulate one of the most beautiful and revealing passages in *The Inward Morning*:

> It seems that there is a stream of limitless meaning flowing into the life of a man if he can but patiently entrust himself to it. There is no hurry, only the need to be true to what comes to mind, and to explore the current carefully in which one presently moves. There is a constant fluency of meaning in the instant in which we live. One may learn of it from rivers in the constancy of their utterance, if one listens and is still. They speak endlessly in an univocal exhalation, articulating the silence.[71]

Bugbee seems to be grasping what Merton was writing about in the beginning of *The Waters of Siloe*: "There is intoxication in the waters of contemplation, whose mystery fascinated and delighted the first Cistercians and whose image found its way into the names of so many of those valley monasteries that stood in forests, on the banks of clean streams, among rocks alive with springs...These are the Waters of Siloe, that flow in silence."[72] To truly speak and truly live is what concerns Bugbee more than to think and reason validly. He desires his words to reflect living thought, which for him is authentic thought, and thus he argues that "true words flow from that stillness from which antecedent true words have flowed" and "the authenticity of our deeds is the basic condition of our concrete understanding of reality."[73]

Merton expresses a similar philosophical stance in his essay, "Poetry and Contemplation: A Reappraisal," by arguing that the

> passage from the exterior to the interior has nothing to do with concentration or introspection. It is a transit from objectivization to knowledge by intuition and connaturality. The majority of people never enter into this inward self, which is an abode of silence and peace and where the diversified activities of the intellect and will are collected, so to speak, into one intense and smooth and spiritualized activity which far exceeds in its fruitfulness the plodding efforts of reason working on external reality with its analyses and syllogisms.[74]

For Merton, the woods offer solitude and silence, the necessities of his life. The solitude and healing silence of his hermitage in the woods is the "one central tonic note" that he finds necessary, essential, to hear each day: "I sit in the cool back room, where words cease to resound, where all meanings are absorbed in the *consonantia* of heat, fragrant pine, quiet wind, bird song and one central tonic note that is unheard and unuttered."[75] Merton continues:

> Not the meditation of books, or of pieties, or of systematic trifles. In the silence of the afternoon all is present and all is inscrutable. One central tonic note to which every other sound ascends or descends, to which every other meaning aspires, in order to find its true fulfillment. To ask when the note will sound is to lose the afternoon: it has sounded and all things now hum with resonance of its sounding.[76]

In *Thoughts in Solitude*, published the same year as Bugbee's *Inward Morning*, Merton explains that we share silence with others; we do not possess silence for ourselves. Thus "it is necessary for us to name the things that share our own silence with us, not in order to disturb their privacy or to disturb our own solitude with thoughts of them, but in order that the silence they dwell in and dwells in them, may be concretized and identified for what it is."[77] Silence, in other words, is made real by identifying its reality in ourselves and other beings. In Merton's terms, then, "[t]o name their being is to name their silence. And therefore it should be an act of reverence."[78] Silence enables us to speak reverently about the sacredness of reality.

Far from being a mental stunt cut off from experience, therefore, Merton and Bugbee are teaching us about reawakening to the fullness of life, which begins with silence, in which we are converted to the essential truths that flow through our living experiences of the wholeness of reality and that transform the ordinary into the extraordinary.

3. Sacred place can be tred upon without being entered

With this principle, Lane is asserting that our experiences of sacred landscapes are "intimately related to states of consciousness"; he adds that "being bodily present is never identical with the fullness of being to which humans can be open to time and space."[79] For Bugbee, it seems that the way we gain entrance to the state of consciousness that is most conducive to communing with the presence of sacred places is through our manner of experiencing reality, albeit a process that we cannot dictate nor control. Such experiencing requires that we approach reality as whole beings ready to respond, letting the places in which we move take root within our beings.

The concept of experience in Bugbee's philosophy is a very rich one, and deserves ample attention. Bugbee considers authentic experience to be "permeated with meaning by invasion."[80] He stresses, though, that we do not possess the full meaning of experiences even when we refer to them as "our" experiences. In other words, Bugbee claims "we are not masters of the import of our deeds. We are involved, to the soles of our feet, in the attitudes inflecting the meaning which we realize, or fail to realize, in our on-going experience," but we cannot "predict and control the ebb and flow of meaning."[81] Experience is not apart from us like an object we can observe; rather, "experience is our undergoing, our involvement in the world, our lending or withholding of ourselves, keyed to our responsiveness, our sensibility, our alertness or our deadness."[82] He calls this mode of discovering meaning *experiential* in deliberate distinction from the term empirical. It is in our ability to experience meaning that we become aware that "the presence of things in their definiteness is bound up with understanding reality in its absoluteness," explaining further that "the presence of things does not come home to us except as presence is completed from within ourselves."[83] Thus Bugbee's philosophical goal is to think experientially as one who is immersed in reality, as a full participant but not sole creator. Bugbee uses the term "immersion" to denote "a mode of living in the present with complete absorption; one has the sense of being comprehended and sustained in a universal situation."[84] Immersion is an unforced involvement in reality to its core.

Bugbee employs the metaphor of a "closed circuit" of reality in relation to his notions of presence and immersion in the flow of meaning: "In our experience of things as presences, reality conveys itself and permeates us as a closed electrical circuit in which we are involved with things; the circuit is charged with finality. But in so far as we take things, and think of them, as placed over against us, i.e. objectively, we break the circuit"; thus "to think experientially is to partake in thought of the closed circuit of reality, in which we live and move and have our being."[85]

Merton understood the necessity of not breaking the circuit through which we live in contact with the energy that flows through all of reality. We can see Merton's application of this perspective as manifest in his writings on the relationship between the cloister and the world, and between the interior journey and the social struggle for freedom. Merton fully realized this closed circuit when he declared "I am the world just as you are! Where am I going to look for the world first of all if not in myself?"[86] Merton uses the term "interpenetration" to explain the complexity of our involvement in reality. "We and the world interpenetrate," he writes:

> But this reality, though "external" and "objective," is not something entirely independent of us that dominates us inexorably from without through the medium of certain fixed laws which science alone can discover and use. It is an extension and a projection of ourselves and of our lives, and if we attend to it respectfully, while attending also to our own freedom and our own integrity, we can learn to obey its ways and coordinate our lives with its mysterious movements.[87]

Merton links this ever deepening experience of reality to his vocation in his significant essay "Day of a Stranger." He interprets his peculiar vocation as one in which he senses "an obligation to preserve the stillness, the silence, the poverty, the virginal point of pure nothingness which is at the center of all other loves. I cultivate this plant silently in the middle of the night and water it with psalms and prophecies in silence."[88] In following this call, Merton is forever led to examine his life and reflect on the stakes of a life that is truly worth living.

Bugbee understands such stakes: "for each man there is an absolute stake in life, something absolutely essential in his life; the understanding of what is essential is bound up with understanding man as capable of vocation."[89] Vocation is connected to ethics, for Bugbee, to the extent that a vocation is a calling that "leads directly into the consideration of responsibility. We learn of our position what it is crucial to learn, by responding to a call, in truly vocational action."[90] Merton's response to the woods, in "The Day of a Stranger" therefore, is in part a key element in his vocation as a monk living in the woods *out of necessity.* "Only reality in its necessity," Bugbee affirms, "can give finality to what we say or do."[91] Bugbee's *Inward Morning* is similar to Merton's writings in reflecting this concern to understand reality in terms of necessity, finality and one's vocation. Merton declares, "[i]t is necessary for me to see the first point of light which begins to be dawn. It is necessary to be present alone at the resurrection of Day, in the solemn silence at which the sun appears, for at this moment all the affairs of cities, of governments, of war departments, are seen to be the bickerings of mice."[92]

Merton's admonition that we *attend to* reality respectfully runs parallel to Bugbee's emphasis concerning our need to be *open* through our experiences of reality. Therefore, we see that gaining entrance to the sacredness of placed reality can never be construed to be the result of a method or technique; rather, we wait in attendance and openness in order to respond to, not command, the sacredness of reality.

4. Sacred place is both centripetal and centrifugal, local and universal

Lane's fourth axiom suggests a double impulse inherent in sacred places by which a person is paradoxically drawn to the center of the place while being pushed away. A tension, in other words, is manifest in sacred places that seem to beckon our participation as dwellers while barring us from establishing residency. Perhaps this axiom speaks to the question of who has final control of reality: God or Man? Lane explains it in this way: "We long to be placed in the land of the holy, but on gaining possession of the sanctuary we come quickly to presume upon its guaranteed mystery—only then to be driven from it in search of yet another place, another center of meaning."[93] Bugbee's and Merton's approaches to the center of meaning may help us further comprehend this paradoxical fourth axiom of sacred place.

In his Preface to *The Inward Morning*, Bugbee states that the concept of finality is the unifying theme of the work. "By finality," he explains, "I intend the meaning of reality as realized in true decision. The vein in which it comes to us is the vein of wonder, of faith, of certainty. It is the ground of ultimate human concern with which the will is informed. It comes clearest in every unique deed of purest generosity in which a man gives of himself without stint and with all care."[94] We can find finality, for example, in the tone of a "final word," which is "the tone of reality as definitely given" when someone speaks truly; this is so, says Bugbee, because "finality must harbor all that requires expression as genuine in human life."[95] To be more precise, a final word is that word which a person "can give now, steeped in all that is unknown and cannot be known in our lives. It cannot be made captive in terms themselves, or in any of the cumulative resources at our disposal. It comes to meet us in our acceptance of the frontier of our daily lives."[96] Finality is what is most authentic. Finality is the way reality exists when we see it as uncluttered by our conceptualizations and verbalizations.

Bugbee relates finality to *understanding*. We may understand finality, but we never attain final understanding; hence, finality refers to the state of reality and not to the state of our knowledge of reality—this is what we must understand. Yet, as Bugbee argues, "now you begin to understand and now you don't understand—that is what seems ephemeral about our condition. But as understanding comes upon us and deepens from time to time, strengthening however fleetingly our appreciation of finality, one becomes aware of its relevance to our everyday situation all along," adding that understanding is not something one possesses and that "the spirit to possess it is contrary to the spirit of understanding."[97] Finality is beyond human control, but not of human understanding, because "finality establishes the conditions of its own disclosure; we cannot hold them fast and place them at our disposal."[98] Here, Bugbee is working from Gabriel Marcel's distinction between understanding a problem and understanding a mystery, which is so key to both their philosophies. Bugbee's style of thought strives to appreciate the finality with which "reality makes its stand here and now in existing things"; thus, the finality of reality is *given* reality, reality received but not possessed.[99] This leads Bugbee to the vital recognition of *the sacred*:

> Finality grounds our standing forth; in standing forth we receive the gift of all existent things: coexistence in communion. The sacramental act, and the sacredness of all things—it is to these that reflection on finality must ultimately come. To perceive something truly is to be alive to it in its sacredness; such, at least, is the full implication of the idea of true perception to which I have been led. And the individuality and universality of whatever is so perceived are clarified in the finding of it sacred. The mystery of each thing is the mystery of all things; and this—not generalization or the broadening of our scope of attention to wider and wider complexes of things, is the foundation of the idea of universe: the omnirelevance of the experience of something as sacred.[100]

From the force of his thinking about finality, Bugbee is led to end his published journal with the adoption of a "religious attitude," which he describes as one that "challenges the ultimacy of any interpretation of reality which is 'objective' in the sense of abstracting from the depth of our experience as responsible beings."[101] What Bugbee fundamentally resists is any attitude that demands a conception of God as the basis for religious belief: "I cannot but think that the very notion of object incorporates a mode of thinking with respect to reality which is cut loose from religious attitude."[102] He defines authentic religious attitude as "one of truly universal concern for things, of concern informed with the universality of finite things," which does not mean things in general, but rather a concrete "experience of things in the vein of individuality, for this is precisely the vein in which they are experienced as universal."[103] Therefore, despite his perhaps surprising disclaimers regarding having any association with a religious tradition, Bugbee adopts a spiritual attitude that "always seems to involve humility" that leads him to conclusions regarding faith and reverence, with reverence understood as a mixture of understanding and communion—an "understanding of reality consummated in reverence as understanding-communion."[104]

Bugbee's religious attitude is comparable to what Merton defines as a "sacred attitude" in *The Inner Experience*, an attitude "of reverence, awe, and silence before the mystery that begins to take place within us when we become aware of our inmost self."[105] In contrast, "[t]he secular attitude is one of gross disrespect for reality, upon which the worldly mind seeks only to force its own crude patterns. The secular man is the slave of his own prejudices, preconceptions, and limitations."[106] Merton argues that "that it is therefore a matter of great courage and spiritual energy to turn away from diversion and prepare to meet, face-to-face, that *immediate* experience of life which is intolerable to the exterior man."[107] Merton's emphasis on "immediate" highlights this sense in which reality can be approached as sacred ground.

Merton adopts Gabriel Marcel's stance regarding the philosopher's proper task as the chosen epithet to *Raids on the Unspeakable*: "Today the first and perhaps the only duty of the philosopher is to defend man against himself: to defend man against that extraordinary temptation toward inhumanity to which—almost without being aware of it—so many human beings today have yielded."[108] Merton addresses *Raids*, itself, in the Prologue to the book, expressing his hope that the insights of *Raids* "may perhaps enable a rare person here and there to come alive and be awake at a moment when wakefulness is desirable."[109] Bugbee, likewise, ends his journal in agreement with Marcel that the philosopher's task is to defend humanity from itself: "It is the constant part of a philosopher's job today to guard against the degeneration of basic ideas which have come to traditional embodiment in certain terms, through which they may then suffer inflation and debasement. The language of testimony may always be taken in vain."[110]

Bugbee sounds a great deal like Thomas Merton as he writes toward the end of his seminal work: "These have been days of study, in Tillich, in the book of essays about his work, and I have read the Fourth Gospel and the Book of Job, rounding up on this day of cold and driving rain, with the opening chapters of *Moby Dick*."[111] Bugbee proceeds to compare God's voice in the whirlwind to the dramatic emergence of the great white whale and finds himself, consequently, claiming "the presence of the thing is the cleansing of the man."[112] By the term "cleansing" Bugbee may be suggesting a spiritual emptying, an idea he learned from "the teachings of Meister Eckhart to the effect that we have only to be empty to be filled."[113] Perhaps in a real sense, this is what it means to experience reality as a sacred place in as much as our openness to presences, by being present ourselves, leads to the cleansing—the healing—of the soul. It is a "sacramental act, and the sacredness of all things" Bugbee reminds us, "that reflection on finality must ultimately come. To perceive something truly is to be alive to it in its sacredness."[114] Ultimately then, in regard to Lane's fourth axiom, we cannot establish residency in the sacredness of reality because we are not the sole source of understanding nor do we venture there alone.

Toward the end of his journal, Bugbee suggests that we can gain a deep understanding of reality in being open to all that is ordinary surrounding us. Bugbee wants to assure us that in taking a reverential approach to life we will be better prepared to see and experience the sacredness of landscapes—the sacredness of reality—in which we become present in communion with others. "Anything understood as reality," Bugbee argues, "is understood as old and new and ageless. And this is reverence—the heart of action."[115] For Merton, the sacredness of reality also flows boundlessly, for "[w]hat is really *new* is what was there all the time. I say, not what has *repeated itself* all the time; the really 'new' is that which, at every moment, springs freshly into new existence. This newness never repeats itself. Yet is so old it goes back to the earliest beginning. It is the very beginning itself, which speaks to us."[116]

Merton on Bugbee: Inner Experiences and Inward Mornings

Thus far I have attempted to show significant parallels in the thought of Merton and Bugbee, but in order to fully appreciate their complementarity it is necessary to attend to some important distinctions. In essence, I wish to suggest a few ways in which Bugbee's philosophy could be enriched by Merton's spiritual orientation in contemplating reality. My critique is spurred by a comparison of Bugbee's idea of the inward morning with Merton's notion of the inner experience. Bugbee's inward morning is an awakening to reality through a sense of wonder that deepens into a certainty grounded in our reflective experiences in the moment.

Merton's concept of the inner experience, however, traces this deepening of experience to God, which leads to the discovery of one's inner self and transformation.

It may be helpful to first examine Bugbee's explicit references to theologians and religious language. As noted earlier, Bugbee concludes *The Inward Morning* on a spiritual note, employing a vocabulary more conducive to theologians than philosophers. In those concluding pages Bugbee discusses two theologians in particular, Paul Tillich and Richard Niebuhr. Bugbee faults Tillich for getting too abstract about "ultimate concern" at times, but admires the constant tone of genuineness that operates as a check on his systematic thought. He goes on to praise Tillich for bringing out "the latently religious character of religious issues," adding "it has become clear that the philosophers whose work is in itself of the most constructive value are those who appreciate this fact, and whose work brings out more than latently the religious character of the issues that concern them."[117] It is this predisposition of Bugbee's that I think would have made Merton's writings most appealing to him, particularly Merton's emphases on experience, reflection and a sapiential approach to reading literature, philosophy and theology.

Bugbee gleaned insights from Niebuhr, too, but disagreed with Niebuhr's alleged need to conceive of God as an object in order to avoid extreme subjectivism. As shown earlier, Bugbee resisted any conceptions of God, much in keeping perhaps with Eckhart's influence on him. Bugbee admits that "strange as it may seem, I cannot follow through the idea of creation in terms of a creator."[118] On the other hand, though, Bugbee declares, "nor can I think of man as creator in creative action."[119] Ultimately, it seems, Bugbee attempts to approach reality as gift but cannot completely conceive of a Gift Giver. In this sense, of course, Bugbee is expressing a perspective very much in common with Buddhist thought, and of course Bugbee was deeply impressed by the ideas of Suzuki and Nishida (while at Harvard, Bugbee was given the honored task of escorting D.T. Suzuki to and from his many speaking engagements). Albert Borgmann (1999) has noted Bugbee's seeming unwillingness or inability to acknowledge "only God can save us in our predicament," too, which Borgmann argues is the one simple answer "that resolves the apparent conflict of finality and universality."[120] Yet Borgmann realizes that Bugbee essentially denies only a god that he could name, describe or prove its existence.

In terms of spirituality, Bugbee appears to be more comfortable with an experiential spirituality than he would be with a systematic theology, but as Merton's writings demonstrate, it is unnecessary to divide these approaches into two competing schools of thought. Fairly or unfairly, Bugbee associates "uniformity" with a systematic understanding of reality, and "simplicity" with an experiential understanding of reality (as influenced by Suzuki). Merton, of course, struggled with a similar distinction as he considered his worst books to be born of a systematic understanding of reality instead of, for him, the more accurate experiential approach.

Bugbee's contemplative approach would be strengthened, I think, by Merton's extensive studies of contemplation. Bugbee drew much from Marcel on the subject of contemplation, but Marcel did not treat contemplation as thoroughly or as explicitly as Merton. Bugbee basically writes about two kinds of contemplation, aesthetic and philosophical, but my reading of *The Inward Morning* seems to find an author who is feeling his way toward a deeper understanding of contemplative living. It is unfortunate that Bugbee was never able to read Merton's draft of *The Inner Experience*, in which Merton distinguishes, though not always with perfectly clarity and consistency, more fundamental types of contemplation. Bugbee clearly falls, with some qualification, into the forms of active and natural contemplation. What needs to be qualified here is that Merton viewed both of these forms of contemplation as human activity motivated to commune with God. "Normally," says Merton, "a life of active contemplation prepares a man for occasional and unpredictable visits of infused or passive contemplation."[121] For Merton, it is important to name God. "It is necessary to name Him Whose silence I share and worship," he argues, "for in His silence He also speaks my own name. He alone knows my name, in which I also know His name."[122] For Bugbee, on the other hand, the motivation to contemplation does not involve a search for God; rather it is a mode of being receptive to reality as it presents itself. However, Bugbee does not deny the existence of God the Creator as that would involve closing oneself off to possibilities beyond the inconceivable, thus relying on one's own conceptions of reality as total, which would be bad faith. In his next to last journal entry, Bugbee concludes—with definite reluctance—by employing the term "spiritual" to characterize his philosophical approach, seeming more opposed to soft-headed sentimental religiosity often attached to the term than to any genuine, reflective appreciation of spirituality. He admits that there is much intellectual falsity in refusing to acknowledge perennial, religious truths.

Merton perceives limits to the classical Greek philosophical form of contemplation in which "the essentially religious aspect of contemplation tends to get lost."[123] Bugbee's contemplation is primarily philosophical, to be sure, but it does involve a degree of self-transformation and so is not merely speculative. As noted above, Bugbee eschews mere speculative reasoning as not going far enough, and he does, in fact, see the necessity to adopt a basic religious attitude in contemplating reality, leading him to embrace sacred awe, reverence and mystery as fundamental to an authentic experience of reality. Yet, Bugbee still seems blocked, somewhat, in the end.

Where I believe Merton would be most helpful to Bugbee would be in the translation of the inward morning as an inner experience involving the inner person, Bugbee's own true self. Despite Bugbee's use of personal stories and journal entries, and despite his emphasis on awakening, *The Inward Morning* falls somewhat short of lending full testimony to any personal transformation. One senses that Bugbee's thought life has changed in the course of his writings, but one is left with the question of how Bugbee's whole life has changed. However, perhaps the transformation is a subtle one, not dramatic, and more implicit than explicitly stated. In perhaps the most poignant passage in Bugbee's journal there is his recollection of glimpsing a man drowning but who managed to pull himself out of the water by latching on to a rooted willow. Bugbee rushes to help just as the man is clawing his way up the bank:

> Slowly he raised his head and we looked into each other's eyes. I lifted out both hands and helped him to his feet. Not a word passed between us. As nearly as I can relive the matter, the compassion I felt with this man gave way into awe and respect for what I witnessed in him. He seemed absolutely clean. In that steady gaze of his I met reality point blank, filtered and distilled as the purity of a man. I think of Meister Eckhart's "becoming as we were before we were born."[124]

In reading this, I am reminded of Merton's words from *The Inner Experience*: "the awakening of the inner self is purely the work of love, and there can be no love where there is not 'another' to love."[125] Perhaps Bugbee did, indeed, connect the inward morning to the transformation of the true, inner self.

There is no story of conversionary experiences at the end, but Bugbee's conclusion to *The Inward Morning* does appear to reflect an inward change at least in the form of a greater openness: "I am not content with what I have worked out; but I have worked out enough, perhaps, to be content to consider more carefully as I move along, and to welcome all manner of thinking other than my own."[126] Bugbee's statement implies a quest for transformation to a degree, though perhaps not as the crucial issue that it is in Merton's writings.

Certainly such openness was part of Merton's own success in actively pursuing diverse approaches to understanding reality. In *The Inner Experience*, for a perfect example, Merton exhibits his appreciation and respect for the teachings of the *Bhagavad Gita*, the wisdom of the Sioux Indians, the teachings of Zen Buddhist masters and Hindu yogis, as well as the wide variety of voices from his own Christian and monastic traditions. "Whatever may be the philosophies and theologies behind these forms of contemplative existence, the striving is always the same: the quest for unity, a return to the inmost self united with the Absolute, a quest for Him Who is above all, and in all, and Who Alone is Alone."[127] Merton found a degree of compatibility with existentialist philosophy, for example, in terms of being able to identify with those who were authentically striving for truth beyond human constructions: "genuine existentialism is, like Zen Buddhism and like apophatic Christian mysticism, hidden in life itself. It cannot be distilled out in verbal formulas."[128]

Merton embraces a mystical perspective in *The Inner Experience*, whereas Bugbee dismisses a mystical definition for his own contemplative outlook. Bugbee acknowledges the power of the ineffable in proposing that "creation is inexpugnably mysterious," but he does not see such a proclamation as necessarily an endorsement of mysticism. Bugbee tends to regard mysticism as being "at times perilously close to abdication of responsibility and a kind of paralytic seizure of the will."[129] "Not out of this world, but in this world, we are," Bugbee declares, sounding very much like Merton.[130] Merton understands this, of course, and shares Bugbee's disdain for any kind of mysticism tending toward escapism or withdrawal from reality, too, adamantly opposing "false mysticism and pseudo-religiosity" as manifestations of "fake interiorization."[131]

Conclusion

Merton and Bugbee share an underlying fundamental concern in the vitalness of listening and response. Bugbee listened to mountains and rivers and heard a call to which he must respond, a call to responsibility. Merton expressed the essence of Bugbee's philosophy best perhaps when he declared that one's whole life can be "a listening."[132] In the end, the crucial difference between Merton and Bugbee is that Merton attributed what he heard to the silent language of God. "My salvation is to hear and respond" to Him, he writes, "[f]or this, my life must be silent. Hence, my silence is my salvation."[133]

In reading both Merton and Bugbee as they write about contemplating reality, I cannot help but reach a distinction that Merton listened a bit more deeply by attending to the inner reality of his life than Bugbee appeared to do. I make this judgment, though, without conclusive evidence. I would have liked to have listened to both these men for myself, face-to-face, in a sacred place akin to what Sigurd Olsen calls a *listening-point*: "Only when one comes to listen, only when one is aware and still, can things be seen and heard. Everyone has a listening-point somewhere. It does not have to be in the north or close to the wilderness, but some place of quiet where the universe can be contemplated with awe."[134]

Notes

1. Henry David Thoreau, *Walden*, (London: J.M. Dent and Rutland VT: Charles E. Tuttle, 1995), p. 78.

2. Henry Bugbee, *The Inward Morning*. (Athens, GA: University of Georgia Press, 1958, 1999); Belden Lane, *Landscapes of the Sacred: Geography and Narrative in American Spirituality*. (1988; Baltimore: Johns Hopkins University Press, 2001).

3. Gabriel Marcel, "Introduction to the 1958 Edition", *The Inward Morning*, p. 26.

4. Nathan Scott, *Visions of Presence in American Poetry* (Baltimore: Johns Hopkins University, 1993), p. 2.

5. Albert Borgmann, "Finding Philosophy," *Falling in Love with Wisdom* (NY: Oxford University Press, 1993), pp. 157-160; David Strong, "The Fragility of Freedom," *Falling in Love With Wisdom*, pp. 180-183.

6. Douglas Burton-Christie, "The Literature of Nature and the Quest for the Sacred," *The Sacred Place: Witnessing the Holy in the Physical World*, W. Scott Olsen and Scott Cairns, Eds. (Salt Lake City: University of Utah Press), pp. 165-177.

7. Edward F. Mooney, Ed., *Wilderness and the Heart* (Athens, GA: University of Georgia Press, 1999).

8. Mooney, *The Inward Morning*, p. xi.

9. Mooney, *The Inward Morning*, pp. xvi, xvii.

10. Bugbee, *The Inward Morning*, p. 33.

11. Bugbee, *The Inward Morning*, p. 33.

12. Edward F. Mooney, 'When Philosophy Becomes Lyric,' *Wilderness and the Heart*, p. 205.

13. Henry David Thoreau, *Walden*, p. 76.

14. Bugbee, *The Inward Morning*, p. 35.

15. Bugbee, *The Inward Morning*, p. 117.

16. Bugbee, *The Inward Morning*, pp. 33-34.

17. Bugbee, *The Inward Morning*, p. 36.

18. See Pierre Hadot, *What is Ancient Philosophy?* Michael Chase, Trans., (Cambridge: Belknap/Harvard, 2002); and *Philosophy as a Way of Life*, Arnold I. Davidson, Ed. (Cambridge: Blackwell, 1995).

19. Thomas Merton, *Zen and the Birds of Appetite* (New York: New Directions, 1968), p. 38, author's emphasis.

20. Thomas Merton, *Thoughts in Solitude* (New York: Noonday, 1958), p. 78.

21. In a similar vein, ecophilosopher David Abram (1996) is interested in this streaming "silent conversation" with reality, especially with the natural world: "Whenever I quiet the persistent chatter of words within my head, I find this silent or wordless dance always already going on—this improvised duet between my animal body and the fluid, breathing landscape that it inhabits"; *The Spell of the Sensuous* (New York: Pantheon,1997), pp 52-53.

22. Bugbee, *The Inward Morning*, p. 38.

23. Bugbee, *The Inward Morning*, p. 10.

24. Bugbee, *The Inward Morning*, p. 139 (author's emphasis).

25. Bugbee, *The Inward Morning*, p. 140.

26. Bugbee, *The Inward Morning*, p. 140.

27. Abram, *The Spell of the Sensuous*, p. 262 (author's emphasis).

28. Thomas Merton, "Hagia Sophia," *Emblems of a Season of Fury* (New York: New Directions, 1963), p. 61. Incidentally, another striking parallel to Bugbee is Merton's title for part one of the poem, in which the reference to hidden wholeness is made; Merton labels the beginning of this poem as: "Dawn. The Hour of Lauds."

29. Max Picard, *The World of Silence* (New York: Gateway, 1948).

30. Bugbee, *The Inward Morning* (1958) p. 79.

31. Bugbee, *The Inward Morning*, p. 79.

32. Merton, *Thoughts In Solitude*, p. 83.

33. For a helpful comparative study of Merton and Thoreau, see Ted Henken's "Henry David Thoreau and Thomas Merton: The Transformation of Individual Experience in Universal Myth" in *The Merton Seasonal*, 22.2 (Summer 1997) pp. 13-22. See also "Thomas Merton as Forester—The Results" by Paschal Phillips, OCSO, in *The Merton Seasonal*, 26.2 (Summer 2001), pp. 25-26.

34. Thomas Merton, *The Sign of Jonas* (New York: Harcourt, Brace, 1953) p. 298.

35. *The Sign of Jonas*, p. 337.

36. *The Sign of Jonas*, p. 340.

37. *New Seeds of Contemplation*, 1961, p. 6.

38. *The Sign of Jonas*, p. 343.

39. Merton, *Sign of Jonas*, p. 362.

40. Merton, *The Monastic Journey* (Kansas City: Sheed, Andrews, and McMeel, 1977), p. 38.

41. Bugbee, *The Inward Morning*, p. 86.

42. Merton, *Sign of Jonas*, p. 311.

43. Bugbee, *The Inward Morning*, p. 39.

44. Bugbee, *The Inward Morning*, p. 40.

45. Bugbee, *The Inward Morning*, p. 40.

46. Bugbee, *The Inward Morning*, p. 196; he borrows the line "the readiness for all" from Shakespeare's *Hamlet*, Act V, Scene II.

47. Bugbee, *The Inward Morning*, p. 133.

48. Bugbee, *The Inward Morning*, p. 176.

49. Bugbee, *The Inward Morning*, p. 175.

50. Bugbee, *The Inward Morning*, p. 155. Bugbee supplies a footnote to this point about "inaction" (or what some authors prefer to call non-action) that is significant for interest in the parallels between him and Merton, explaining that the idea "holds me to the study of such works as the *Gita*, the *Book of Tao*, the literature of Zen, Meister Eckhart's recorded thoughts; and I have found some very interesting cognate material in Jung."

51. Thomas Merton, *The Way of Chuang Tzu* (New York: New Directions, 1965), pp. 9-10.

52. Merton, *The Way of Chuang Tzu*, p. 11.

53. Merton, *The Way of Chuang Tzu*, p. 11.

54. Thomas Merton, "Herakleitos: A Study," *Thomas Merton: Spiritual Master* (ed. Lawrence S. Cunningham, New York: Paulist Press, 1992), pp. 281-282.

55. Merton, 'Herakleitos: A Study', p. 286.

56. Merton, *The Way of Chuang Tzu*, p. 26.

57. Bugbee, *The Inward Morning*, p. 113.

58. Bugbee, *The Inward Morning*, p. 113.
59. Bugbee, *The Inward Morning*, p. 113.
60. Thomas Merton, "Rain and the Rhinoceros," *Raids on the Unspeakable.* (New York: New Directions, 1966), pp. 9-23.
61. Bugbee, *The Inward Morning*, p. 155.
62. Merton, *Raids on the Unspeakable*, p. 9.
63. Lane, *Landscapes of the Sacred*, p. 19.
64. Bugbee, *The Inward Morning*, p. 165.
65. Bugbee, *The Inward Morning*, p. 84.
66. Bugbee, *The Inward Morning*, p. 102.
67. Bugbee, *The Inward Morning*, p. 102.
68. Bugbee, *The Inward Morning*, p. 140.
69. Bugbee's Taoist quest to swim in the river of thinking is similar to physicist David Bohm's distinction between thought and thinking. For Bohm, thinking "implies the present tense" that continues to flow despite our stopping to concentrate on our thoughts, which function as dams in the flow of thinking. Such "thought" leads to the kinds of "fictional thinking" and automatic behavior that Merton railed against as illusions. In this context, Bohm, Marcel, Bugbee and Merton are all linked by their adopting a dialogical approach to understanding reality. See Bohm's *On Dialogue*. Lee Nichol, Ed. (New York: Routledge, 1996); and *Thought as a System*, (New York: Routledge,1994).
70. Bugbee, *The Inward Morning*, p. 83.
71. Bugbee, *The Inward Morning*, p. 82.
72. Thomas Merton, *The Waters of Siloe* (New York: Harcourt, Brace, 1949), p. vii.
73. Bugbee, *The Inward Morning*, pp. 84, 85.
74. Thomas Merton, "Poetry and Contemplation: A Reappraisal," *The Literary Essays of Thomas Merton*, ed. Br. Patrick Hart (New York: New Directions, 1981), p. 348.
75. Merton, *Dancing in the Water of Life*, (Journals, 5; 1963-1965; ed. Robert Daggy; San Francisco: Harper San Francisco, 1997) p. 242.
76. Merton, *Dancing in the Water of Life*, p. 242.
77. Merton, *Thoughts in Solitude*, p. 69.
78. Merton, *Thoughts in Solitude*, p. 69.
79. Lane, *Landscapes of the Sacred*, pp. 19, 29.
80. Bugbee, *The Inward Morning*, p. 41.
81. Bugbee, *The Inward Morning*, p. 41.
82. Bugbee, The Inward Morning, p. 41.
83. Bugbee, *The Inward Morning*, p. 76.
84. Bugbee, *The Inward Morning*, pp. 50-51.
85. Bugbee, *The Inward Morning*, pp. 168, 169.
86. Thomas Merton, *Contemplation in a World of Action* (Notre Dame: University of Notre Dame Press, 1998), p. 142.

87. Merton, *Contemplation in a World of Action*, pp. 151-152.

88. Merton, *Dancing in the Water of Life*, p. 240.

89. Bugbee, *The Inward Morning*, p. 64.

90. Bugbee, *The Inward Morning*, p. 116.

91. Bugbee, *The Inward Morning*, p. 117.

92. Merton, *Dancing in the Water of Life*, p. 241.

93. Lane, *Landscapes of the Sacred*, p. 35.

94. Bugbee, *The Inward Morning*, p. 10.

95. Bugbee, *The Inward Morning*, p. 11.

96. Bugbee, *The Inward Morning*, p. 11.

97. Bugbee, *The Inward Morning*, p. 113.

98. Bugbee, *The Inward Morning*, p. 113.

99. Bugbee, *The Inward Morning*, pp. 161-162.

100. Bugbee, *The Inward Morning*, p. 209.

101. Bugbee, *The Inward Morning*, p. 218.

102. Bugbee, *The Inward Morning*, p. 218.

103. Bugbee, *The Inward Morning*, p. 218.

104. Bugbee, *The Inward Morning*, p. 230.

105. Thomas Merton, *The Inner Experience: Notes on Contemplation* (ed. William Shannon; San Francisco: HarperSanFrancisco, 2003), p. 55.

106. Merton, *The Inner Experience*, pp. 55-56.

107. Merton, *The Inner Experience*, p. 53.

108. Merton, *Raids on the Unspeakable*, p. v. Both Bugbee and Merton appear to be referring to Gabriel Marcel's (1952) concluding argument in *Man Against Mass Society*,(Chicago: Gateway, 1985), p. 257.

109. Merton, *Raids on the Unspeakable*, pp. 2-3.

110. Bugbee, *The Inward Morning*, p. 232.

111. Bugbee, *The Inward Morning*, p. 226.

112. Bugbee, *The Inward Morning*, p. 226.

113. Bugbee, *The Inward Morning*, p. 106.

114. Bugbee, *The Inward Morning*, p. 209.

115. Bugbee, *The Inward Morning*, p. 129.

116. Thomas Merton, *New Seeds of Contemplation.*, p. 107.

117. Bugbee, *The Inward Morning*, p. 216.

118. Bugbee, *The Inward Morning*, p. 222.

119. Bugbee, *The Inward Morning*, p. 222.

120. Albert Borgmann, "Bugbee on Philosophy and Modernity," *Wilderness and the Heart*, p. 126.

121. Merton, *The Inner Experience*, p. 57.

122. Merton, *Thoughts in Solitude*, p. 73.

123. Merton, *The Inner Experience*, p. 33.

124. Bugbee, *The Inward Morning*, p. 172.

125. Merton, *The Inner Experience*, p. 24.

126. Bugbee, *The Inward Morning*, p. 232.

127. Merton, *The Inner Experience*, p. 30.

128. Thomas Merton, "The Other Side of Despair," *Mystics and Zen Masters* (New York: Noonday, 1967), pp. 253-280 (258).

129. Bugbee, *The Inward Morning*, p. 223.

130. Bugbee, *The Inward Morning*, p. 224.

131. Merton, *The Inner Experience*, p. 25.

132. Merton, *Thoughts in Solitude*, p. 74.

133. Merton, *Thoughts in Solitude*, p. 74.

134. Sigurd Olsen, *Listening Point.* (Minneapolis: University of Minnesota Press, 1958), p. 8.

Thomas Merton and George Grant: Hawk's Dream, Owl's Insight

Ron Dart

> When the history of twentieth-century monasticism comes to be written, it is hard not to think that two monks will dominate the story: Thomas Merton and Jean Leclercq.
> Bernard McGinn[1]

> Altogether, his (Grant's) contributions to the CBC probably exceeded those of any other Canadian thinker of his generation, except perhaps Northrop Frye.
> David Cayley[2]

Thomas Merton (1915-1968) and George Grant (1918-1988) were contemporaries. Merton was American and Grant was Canadian, and both grappled with many of the same issues, yet they did not know one another. Merton was a well known public person in his day, and since his death, his books (and many commentaries on them) have grown and flourished. Grant was an equally important public intellectual in his day, and since his death, his books (and a multitude of commentaries on them) have produced a rich and bountiful harvest. The fact that Merton and Grant had many of the same concerns, and the fact that Merton and Grant did not know one another (and the scholarly world of both do not interact) may mean that a more substantive article and book on these men does need to be written. This short essay, in some small way, will attempt to build a needful and necessary bridge between Merton and Grant, and, in doing so, bring together not only Merton and Grant's perspectives, but also the American and Canadian.

It may be most valuable to touch on the four following areas of convergence and overlap between Merton and Grant: 1) the contemplative way of knowing; 2) contemplation and interfaith dialogue; 3) contemplation and the church; and 4) contemplation and prophetic politics. Merton and Grant thought and lived out these issues in a compelling and challenging way. There were differences in the way they handled and dealt with such concerns (and these should not be denied or ignored), but the fact that they, in their wide-ranging and interdisciplinary ways, dared to deal with these areas, speaks much about a way of understanding and interpreting Christian faith that has much to commend it.

Merton was drawn to Robinson Jeffers and Jeffers 'Hawk's Dream'. This poem did much to orient Merton. Grant was drawn to the owl, and the film on his life, *The Owl and the Dynamo*, tells the tale of why Grant turned to the metaphor of the owl for guidance. Merton and Grant were both drawn to artistic and literary traditions as a way of seeing and knowing, and these two metaphors, the dream of the hawk and the insight of the owl can speak much to us as mutually interdependent cultures of seeing.

Contemplation and Theology: Merton and the Contemplative Way

Merton and Grant were quite aware how theology, philosophy and Biblical exegesis could be taken captive by a form of scientific empiricism and, in the process, human subjectivity on our all too human journey could be marginalized. Merton and Grant were not opposed to theology or philosophy; however they did think such disciplines had to go deep, be transformative, and reach personal levels. In their different ways, both sought to return to the Classical and Patristic tradition of mystical/spiritual/contemplative theology as a way of recovering and reclaiming the depths of the Christian faith. Merton turned initially, of course, to the Cistercian tradition at Gethsemani that was, in theory, supposed to be about a contemplative way of knowing and being, but he sometimes found the place was so busy and active that much of the old tradition seemed to have been jettisoned.

Grant taught philosophy and theology all of his academic life at Dalhousie and McMaster Universities, but the contemplative way of knowing in the academy had been replaced and supplanted by a scientific way of knowing in which the thing studied was objectified; this, it was argued, would offer us objective knowledge. Merton and Grant spoke and wrote about this one dimensional and single vision way of knowing, and their turn to the contemplative was, in many ways, counter cultural—a rebellion against the dominant ways of knowing and living the faith journey.

This shift, in the modern world, from the 'vita contemplativa' to the 'vita activa' as a way of knowing and being was duly noted by Hannah Arendt in her classic work in political theory, *The Human Condition* (1958). Arendt's chapter, in *The Human Condition*,

'The Reversal of Contemplation and Action', reflected upon the loss that had occurred with such a reversal. It is significant to note that *The Human Condition* was published at a period of time when Merton and Grant were thinking many of the same thoughts, and Merton commented on this important book in his journal, and most importantly he noted the loss in modern times of the Greek *polis*. The Classical Tradition, for the most part, elevated and prized the contemplative way over and against the active, but, in the modern world, the 'vita activa' has subordinated (and, often banished) the 'vita contemplativa'. Both Merton and Grant attempted, in their different ways, to reverse this. Both men called for a return to the contemplative as the ground, roots, core and center from which the active way could and would authentically emerge and take shape and form in the public realm, place and space. This turn to the contemplative opposed both the hegemony of a thoughtless activism and the dominance of a narrow empirical way of knowing and being. Both Merton and Grant sought to widen the means by which we know, and deepen the source from which we live.

Thomas Merton turned to the monastic way as a means of finding, clarifying and recovering his true self. The monastic way, in principle, was about an openness to be found and transformed by the draw and overtures of God's welcoming grace and goodness. It was in the resulting stillness, waiting, *quies* that the meaning of true theology could and would be known. The contemplative way is about living out the longing for God and making sense of what such a longing means on our human journey.

In 1949, Merton's *Seeds of Contemplation* was published. This text explores, examines and ponders how the soil of the soul can be properly prepared to receive the seeds of the Divine. Merton makes it quite clear, in his inviting and frequently poetic way, that human agency is essential to the contemplative quest. He probes the depths of the contemplative way and its connection to the inner life.

Throughout most of the 1950s, Merton continued to unpack and unravel the meaning of the contemplative way in a variety of books mining the Christian tradition. *Bread in the Wilderness* (1953) addresses Merton's theology of the Cross, and the significance of the crucified Christ for the contemplative journey. The sustained and evocative meditation on the 'Devot Christ' takes us into the depths of Christ's suffering and its significance for us: the bread of the Cross can provide sustained nourishment through the wilderness of time. Merton made it clear that he refused to separate his commitment to contemplative theology from an ever deepening understanding of the Cross. The Bread of Christ is very much, for Merton, the living bread and that which communally feeds and nourishes the soul in the wilderness and desert of time. *The Living Bread* (1956) is a companion piece to *Bread in the Wilderness*. Both books hold high the significance of the Cross, the living bread of the Mass, liturgy as public event of transformation and the essential role of the Psalter in understanding transformation.

In 1962, *New Seeds of Contemplation* appeared. This book builds on the 1949 text *Seeds of Contemplation*, and continues to probe the differences between the false and true self. Merton was dying to ego and opening to the transformed life. The complex and nuanced nature of knowing the difference between the new and old self was front and center for Merton. *New Seeds of Contemplation* clarifies for the attentive reader the nature of the transformative journey. Quite clearly, there is a center and core of Merton's understanding of the contemplative way: it is about becoming a new person. Merton sought to know the difference between the conventional, fiction and false self and the authentic, real and eternal self. The Cross was most instructive in decoding this dilemma; hence Merton's contemplative theology remained focused on the Cross of Christ.

Merton longed to go to the very source and depths of transformation, for he knew, if this journey was not taken, the false and illusory self could and would create a hall of mirrors. Merton was committed to such a death-resurrection quest, and the contemplative way opened for him the doors into how such transition could occur, and the role of God and human agency in this process. Both the West and East, at their contemplative best, saw the ego as something that was a mirage and fiction, a distraction and false face, as something to be free from. Both traditions agreed that to be truly free a letting go had to occur; a dying and leaving behind had to be done. Merton, therefore, as a contemplative theologian, stood against a way of doing theology that was dogmatic and propositional, but lacked serious teaching on the relationship between spirituality and theology. Merton was a contemplative theologian, and this meant he was always in the process of bridging the gap between the Human and the Divine, between human aspiration and longing and Divine grace and welcoming presence.

II. Contemplation and Theology:
Grant and the Contemplative Way

Grant taught philosophy at Dalhousie University in Halifax from 1947-1959, McMaster University from 1961-1980, and he returned to Halifax in 1980 and lived there until his death in 1988. George Grant, like Thomas Merton, sought to retrieve and rediscover the contemplative way as a path of knowing and being. Grant was not a monk, but like Merton, sought to make sense of the contemplative way for the broader public. When George and Shiela Grant became Anglicans in 1956, the contemplative way of High Church Anglicanism at King's College (Halifax) was very much the air they breathed even though Grant had written about the contemplative way before becoming an Anglican. Grant's article, 'Contemplation in an Expanding Economy' in *The Anglican Outlook* (1955) did challenge both the Anglican Church of Canada and her theologians to ponder the fate and future of the church if a certain path was followed and not questioned.

Grant created a storm in the Canadian academic world in 1951 with his article, 'Philosophy', in which he argued that modern and academic philosophy had lost its contemplative dimension, and, as such, had become a lapdog and lackey of a one dimensional way of knowing and being. Modern philosophy had become so subservient to a narrow scientific methodology that human longing had been banished; tinkering with the meaning of language was all that was left for the academy. The commitment by many modern professional philosophers to logical positivism and linguistic analysis was, for Grant, the death knell of philosophy. Grant, in 'Philosophy', called the guild and clan back to the contemplative heritage of philosophy, back to the place of human longing for meaning and purpose, back to the place of inner attention and transformation, back to Plato (and, for Grant, Plato's finest modern interpreter, Simone Weil). Grant was also drawn to existentialism as a more human and humane way than logical positivism to deal with the human condition. Grant's lectures for the CBC, in 1955, on Jean-Paul Sartre and, in 1959, on Fyodor Dostoevsky made it quite clear where and why Grant stood on the contemplative and existential path rather than the more narrow and limited empirical and analytic tradition. It is important to note that Grant was, throughout much of his life, drawn to Heidegger and Heidegger's more receptive and contemplative way of knowing even though, by day's end, Grant did not agree with most of the content and conclusions of Heidegger. Grant was, in his last few years, working on a book on Heidegger and Christianity.

Grant, unlike Merton, taught at public universities, but both walked the extra mile, prophet like, to call both theology and philosophy back to their contemplative roots, to deeper and older sources of knowing God and being transformed by the mystery of God's purifying love. Both Merton and Grant, in their contemplative theology and philosophy, held high the "via negativa" or the apophatic way: both were critical of a form of western rationalism that either sought to master or banish the inscrutable mystery of God. Both realized the deeper contemplative journey was about many deaths, much letting go, many resurrections into the mystery of God's gracious and complete Love. This meant that both men had a certain affinity for the Orthodox distinction between God's 'essence-energies', and the way of a tradition that recognized a holy ground of mystery where none dare speak. Grant wrote much, in his academic career, about the dangers of the way the academy had lost its way, the way wisdom had been trumped by knowledge, *paideia* by *techne*, teaching by research.

Grant, like Merton, connected the contemplative way to the cross of suffering. Martin Luther had made much, in his day, of the theology of glory and the theology of the cross. The theology of glory had a tendency to ignore the suffering of Christ (and our redemption), elevate the resurrection and be insensitive to inexplicable suffering. The triumphalism that often walks hand in hand with a theology of glory was offensive to Grant for a variety of theological, philosophical and political reasons. Grant tended to emphasize Luther's theology of the cross as a corrective to an excessive interest in the theology of glory. Christ, on the cross, plumbed the depths of God's suffering love and the extent to which God would go to illuminate and draw the human race back to unity with Himself. This God was willing to die, to empty all the grandeur and fullness of the Divine in order to serve and suffer, to fail and fall, so new life could be offered. This was not the way of power, of strength, of military might, of mastery and control. The cross both clarified the deeper nature and meaning of goodness, and opened a surer way to understand the meaning of transformation. Shiela Grant's article, 'George Grant and the Theology of the Cross', in *George Grant and the Subversion of Modernity* (1996), and the recent, *George Grant and the Theology of the Cross: The Chris-*

tian Foundations of His Thought (2001), by Harris Athanasiadas, speak clearly to Grant's concerns about the differences between the theology of glory and the theology of the cross, and their implications.

Grant, as indicated, created a storm in the academic world in 1951 with his article, 'Philosophy', and, by 1960, he resigned from York University because the Philosophy Department had so bowed the knee to the empirical way that both Plato and Christianity were banished from the hallowed halls. Grant became a hero to many in the Canadian counter culture of the 1960s because of his willingness to critique the drift and direction of major public universities, and his willingness to resign from York when conscience clashed with expediency.

The recent publication of *Survival or Prophecy? The Letters of Thomas Merton and Jean Leclercq* (2002) delineates Merton and Leclercq's desire to call the monastic traditions back to their contemplative roots. Merton saw such a way as the means of survival for the monastic orders. Both Merton and Grant, in their struggles, spoke to a wide and large audience, and they spoke in such a way that they touched and tapped into the depths of the human condition and human longing. Both Merton and Grant were keenly aware of the fact that there had been a reversal of the contemplative-active dimensions in the West. Both men sought to retrieve, recover and elevate the Classical contemplative way of knowing in opposition to the dominance of the activist and empirical way. Both saw in the contemplative dimensions of the Occident and Orient a way of doing philosophy and theology that the modern West was in danger of losing and forgetting. Both men held to a theology of the cross which grounded the contemplative way.

III. The Contemplative Way: East and West: Merton and Grant

The contemplative turn by both Merton and Grant led them to dialogue between the East and the West. Both men sought the contemplative in the West and East for insight and inspiration. The West had become frenetic and co-opted by *techne* and a technological society, and been taken in by the demands of empirical science as the way of knowing. The soul and the spirit, the inner life of the mind and imagination had become parched, barren and lean in the process. Both Merton and Grant felt this keenly, and they sought for another way to traverse and find the depths of the real and authentic self in a society that had given itself to many illusions and masks of the self.

Merton was interested in the East as early as 1938 when he attended Columbia. It was there he met the Hindu monk, Bramachari, who urged Merton to explore the western contemplative tradition. Merton's deeper journey into the Eastern contemplative way was prompted by two things: the need to discern a way to truly be contemplative, and, in a more important sense, the task of discerning and distinguishing the false from the true self; the ego from the authentic self. Merton found, in the East, insight and wisdom in these areas.

The flowering of Merton's interest and dialogue with the East was at its most intense and mature in the 1960s. The publication of *Gandhi on Non-Violence* (1964), *The Way of Chuang Tzu* (1965), *Mystics and Zen Masters* (1967), *Zen and the Birds of Appetite* (1968) and *The Asian Journal of Thomas Merton* (1973) all make clear that the West must engage the East at a contemplative level, and that the East has much to teach the West about exposing the pretensions of the ego and seeking deep transformation. Merton had met Dr. D.T. Suzuki in 1964, and his correspondence on the relationship between Zen and the Christian contemplative tradition very much spoke to the issues of death, a letting go and a leaving behind of the ego, the old Adam. Merton's death in 1968 at Bangkok, Thailand seems symbolic, and the fact he met the Dalai Lama and Thich Nhat Hanh (who he called 'my brother') before his death also speaks of his affinity with Eastern thought and its leaders. There is a natural unfolding of contemplative thought from *New Seeds of Contemplation* (1961) to interest in the East, and it was the contemplative way of knowing that brought these two traditions together.

Merton's interest in the contemplative aspects of the East placed him very much in the forefront of those (in the past and present) who turned to the East for insight, illumination and enlightenment. Emerson, Thoreau and Whitman before Merton, and many important American Beats (such as Snyder, Ginsberg, Whalen and Kerouac) had turned to the East as a means of countering a West that had lost its contemplative ways. Merton, unlike the American Transcendentalists and the Beats, grounded his contemplative journey in the Roman Catholic way; this makes Merton unique within the American context of the 1960s. Did Merton's turn to the East, though, mean that he saw a unity and convergence at the heart and core of the contemplative traditions of the East and West? Merton, unlike the American Transcendentalists and American Beats, remained both a Roman Catholic and Cistercian monk until his end. It can be argued that Merton turned to the East for aid and insight on what to be free from (the ego), but when asked what he was to be free for (the new self united in Christ and the Church), he was most Christian. *Ace of Freedoms: Thomas Merton's Christ* (1993) by George Kilcourse makes this position quite clear. Merton had, like the Patristic Fathers in the Latin West and Greek East, a generous natural theology, but, as a Christian contemplative theologian, as Merton was, the Grace of Christ did fulfill the longings and desires of other natural religions, just as Christian theology crowned philosophy.

Grant's interest in other religions, like Merton's, was not just for the purpose of information, facts and exotica. He spoke much against the 'museum culture' of the academy, and the tendency of such places to cut out the heart and life of the great and grand contemplative traditions of the religions of the world. Just as Merton was both a teacher to novices and scholastics in the 1950s and 1960s, George Grant taught a generation of students at McMaster how to do theology in a contemplative way. McMaster had one of the largest graduate programs in North America in the 1960s-1970s in the area of Western-Eastern religions, and it was Grant, as chair of the department that had built up the program. Grant did not write as much as Merton on contemplative and interfaith dialogue, but he did address it. *The George Grant Reader* (1998) contains a foreword to Bithika Mukerji's *Neo-Vedanta and Modernity* (1983). Grant praised Mukerji's book, and in his foreword, he highlighted how the modern world had made it difficult to understand the Neo-Vedantic way of joy/bliss. Grant suggested that the modern world had no sense of ontology, no sense of the proper end (or *telos)* from which joy/bliss might be understood. The driven and dynamic world of North America, that is so indebted to those like Locke and Hume, Rousseau and Darwin, has no sense of a deeper way of knowing, hence the contemplative insights of the Neo-Vedanta are outside the pale of many in the political and theological West. Grant argued, in the foreword, that a hearing and heeding of the Indian Neo-Vedanta could teach the West much.

Grant, like Merton, attempted to draw his audience back to the contemplative way and the role the East could play in teaching the West about such a way. Grant sought to hold the University to an older tradition, a tradition closer to the monastic and contemplative way, but, in the age of the dynamo, science and the technological society (and the role of the University in serving such ends); Grant was often ignored and marginalized.

Indian religion taught Grant much, and his attempt to understand the depths of the Christian contemplative tradition was informed by the Gospels and Plato (as interpreted by Simone Weil and Iris Murdoch) and the best of the Indian heritage. Just as Merton's generous natural theology offered him a way to heed the best of the East, so Grant's gracious natural theology opened the doors into the East for him, also. Grant had a real affinity for the contemplative tradition of Hinduism just as Merton was quite drawn to the contemplative traditions of Buddhism (Zen, Tibetan, Vietnamese) and other mystical traditions such as Islamic Sufism and the Jewish Hasidic and Kabalistic traditions. Both men saw in the East (and contemplative traditions) antidotes for the toxins in the West, but both men realized there were immense (although forgotten) resources in the West that they could yet draw from.

IV. Prophets to the Church: Have You Worn the Robes?

The publication of *Thomas Merton's American Prophecy* (1998) and *Survival and Prophecy: The Letters of Thomas Merton and Jean Leclercq* (2002) in the last few years has highlighted the obvious fact that Merton stood very much in the Jewish-Christian prophetic tradition. George Grant stood within the same line and lineage. Merton spoke from within the American context and beyond while Grant did so from within the Canadian context. There are those who have suggested and argued that Merton, in the autumn of 1968, was traveling away from the constraints of the Roman Catholic church.

Merton's graphic and never to be forgotten religious experience at Polonnaruwa so well described in *The Asian Journal*, his visits with the Dalai Lama and his friendship with Thich Nhat Hanh seem to tell the tale of a man on the way to another place. Some have suggested Merton was on his way to Buddhism. But, there is another way to read Merton. If, as I have suggested above, Merton had a generous and truly catholic natural theology, he would have had a sincere interest in the wisdom and insights of other traditions.

Merton was very much a prophet, and this means he was steeped in his own tradition, and that he sought to speak such a tradition in the language of his time. Merton's way, as a prophet, was to find the language of the time, employ such interests and language, and then lead his audience into the fullness of the Christian way.

Merton spoke to the church on a variety of levels, and at each level, he was both welcomed and opposed. Merton was a key figure in the renewal of the monastic way. Merton's commitment to the Cistercian tradition, his interest in the Benedictine, Carthusian and Carmelite ways speak much about his desire to find the centre, core and inner integrity of the contemplative way of the monastic tradition. The correspondence between Merton/Leclercq in *Survival or Prophecy?* explain Merton's crucial role in the renewal of the monastic way within the Roman Catholic tradition. But, Merton's prophetic life and voice went deeper and further than the monastery. Merton spoke, by going deeper into the real message and meaning of the monastic way, to the depths of the human condition and the very purpose of the church. Merton saw the purpose of the church as being profoundly ecumenical, concerned with interfaith contemplative dialogue and engaged (in a non-ideological way) with public and political issues. Merton summed his truly grounded ecumenical vision up in *Conjectures of a Guilty Bystander*:

> If I can unite in myself the thought and devotion of Eastern and Western Christendom, the Greek and Latin Fathers, the Russians and Spanish mystics, I can prepare in myself the reunion of divided Christendom....We must contain all the divided world in ourselves and transcend them in Christ.[3]

A full vision such as this did make certain demands on the church, but it was such a truly catholic approach that was prophetic.

In this, Merton was prophet, although he was often unaccepted in his own tradition (particularly in the pre-Vatican II era). Merton called monks, the church and the world to a deeper contemplative vision of unity, a vision in which the masks, ego and phantoms of the inner life could be exposed and dealt a death blow, and the real and authentic self would be revealed and appear. The new self, hidden in Christ, would speak with a certain consistent ethical vision to the church. Merton had many concerns about the rather right wing leanings of the Roman Catholic church of his time. He duly noted their legitimate concerns for the family, traditional gender roles, their worries and frets about abortion, euthanasia and contraception. But, he spoke out strongly about the Roman Catholic position and silence about the Vietnam war, the American empire, the nuclear policy of the USA, the environmental questions raised by Rachael Carson and the rape of the earth by corporations. The 'Christian realism' of Reinhold Niebuhr disturbed Merton and the 'just war' theory, he feared, could be used to rationalize injustice. Many of Merton's concerns seemed to link him with the 'New Left' of the 1960s, and his willingness to identify himself with Dorothy Day, the Catholic Worker and Dan/Phil Berrigan emphasized that. This did not bode well for him amongst the liberal establishment. When Merton published 'Letter to a White liberal' in 1961, the doyens of the liberal Sanhedrin were displeased.

George Grant was a prophet to the church and the world who shared many of Merton's concerns. Grant was loyal, as was Merton, to the church, and, like Merton, Grant was a vigorous and rigorous critic of the church. Those who only knew how to criticize the many failings and inconsistencies of the church were met with this question by Grant: Have you worn the robes? Those who have taken the time and effort to wear the robes of the ancient tradition (in all its fullness and folly) would and could see things from a much more nuanced perspective. Grant, as an Anglican, did not nod or bow, in an uncritical way, to the High, Broad or Low church traditions within the Anglican Tradition. Grant, who had been involved with C.S. Lewis's 'Socratic Club', while he was at Oxford, was more committed to *'mere Christianity'* than to parties within the Anglican Tradition. It was this *'mere Christianity'*, grounded and rooted in the mystical theology of the Anglican way that interested and held Grant. Grant had his worries and concerns about the broader drift of liberalism in North America (at its most advanced in the USA), and the invasion of liberalism into the Anglican Church of Canada. Both Merton and Grant addressed, intellectually and spiritually, the clash between the ancients and the moderns.

Merton's interest in a fuller, broader ecumenical vision of the church had much affinity with Grant's interest in *'mere Christianity'*. The liberal ecumenism of the day did not grasp their attention as much as an ecumenism that was grounded in the fullness of the Christian Tradition. Both men turned to the Classical past and mined the mother lode of such a heritage for its present influence. Both men, by turning to the Patristic past, had a certain affinity with the Orthodox way. Both Merton and Grant had, in short, an ecumenical and catholic notion of the church that tended to elude the East-West and the Roman Catholic-Protestant schism, and both sought to find the unity at the heart of Christianity.

Grant came to see and argue that at the core of liberalism was a thirst for liberty and individualism, but the dilemma of liberalism was that it had no real grounding or solid way to justify how the individual should use their liberty. Liberalism tended to be insightful and informed on freedom from negative social ills but rather weak on the positive use of freedom. It is this convergence of a rather ill defined and opened ended notion of human nature blended with such principles as liberty, individualism, conscience and equality that made liberalism susceptible to abuse. The actual content of such principles could be as varied as the individual chose to make them. The more the West adopted and adapted such a dogma, the more the church could and would lose its historic voice. Grant saw this on a philosophical level, and he argued, again and again, against the practical implications of not recognizing this fateful and obvious truism. For Grant, the deeper issues were philosophical, and he argued that if issues were not faced by the church at a root level, there would be much confusion and fragmentation at a practical level. This led Grant, by the 1970s, to question the church, as the Anglican Church opened herself more to the questions of abortion and euthanasia. There were for Grant, two levels of discussion: the uncritical social embrace by the church and the secular world of liberal principles and prejudices and, equally important, how these principles played themselves out on such hot button issues as abortion, euthanasia and the family. Grant's position on these issues seemed to collide with his outspoken position against the war in Vietnam, his opposition to militarism, his firm and steady pacifism, his relentless critique of the American empire, his probes into the nature of power elites and the military-industrial complex and the way he illuminated the nature of corporate wealth.

Needless to say, Grant appealed to the political left and right for different reasons, and he was marginalized by the right and left for the same reasons.

Many of Grant's larger social and political positions had much affinity with Merton's. Both men had a broad and fully ecumenical view of the church, and both men had substantive questions about liberalism. Grant tended to be more philosophical than

Merton, and he constantly nudged thinking to the level of political principles. Both men, by turning to the depths of the Christian Tradition, called the church to remember her high calling. Both men spoke from a third way (that was neither right, left nor the sensible centre), and as the church came to reflect the larger culture wars were seen as anomalies. It was this third way that, in many ways, made them prophets to the church and to the world.

V. Merton and Grant: Prophets to the World

Thomas Merton and George Grant were men on the margins. Merton saw his role as a monk in both a literal and metaphorical sense. The monk was very much a man who seemed dead to society, a man on the edge, a misunderstood and alienated person, a person in exile from power and privilege. Merton, as a monk, seeing himself this way, saw other artists and those who protested against the inhumanity of the modern world as his friends and comrades. The monk, in a more metaphorical sense, is the person who says No to the bad faith and false consciousness of the world, lives on the margins for doing so, but speaks a solid and firm Yes to a new vision of life, purpose and meaning. George Grant portrayed a monastic spirituality in the vein of Merton's deeper and more significant sense of it—as one who stands often, alone, against the drift and direction of the world and the church and is faithful, in love, to both.

Both Merton and Grant took positions, on a variety of social, economic and political questions that could not be easily squared with the ideology of the political right, left or centre. Both men stood within the Christian contemplative tradition which was at odds with a secular world that either negated the religious vision, banished it to the private realm or held high contemplative Eastern religious traditions in opposition to the Christian Tradition. Merton and Grant tended to bridge this division and divide, and did it in a way that held out new paths of both approaching Christianity and interfaith dialogue.

Both Merton and Grant had an interest in Mahatma Gandhi, and Gandhi, in his life, threaded together spirituality and justice in a non-violent way and manner. The politics of the right, left and sensible centre tended to dominate the day, and ideologues often marginalized those who did not bow to such positions. Just as Gandhi faced such tensions in his day, Merton and Grant spoke to the world, in a prophetic way, about the horrors of militarism, the

American military industrial complex and the corporate rape of the earth and the environment while taking a faithful stand on the importance of the family and the life of the unborn. The New Left were with Merton and Grant on the former issues, but opposed them on the latter issues just as the New Right were drawn to Grant and Merton on the latter issues but saw them as soft and naïve on the former issues. It was this consistent life ethic that we find in both Merton and Grant that placed them in a unique and distinctive place on the prophetic political spectrum.

Merton tended to side more with the anarchist form of being political, and, in this, he was quite different from Grant. Grant, as a Canadian High Tory, both believed in the need for and commitment to national political parties as a means of bringing into being the common good or the commonweal. Grant was a member of the Progressive Conservative party in Canada for many years, and he was convinced it was the role of the state (with society) to work together in a cooperative way to create a just nation. Merton did not have Grant's commitment to formal party politics, and Merton appealed to the anarchist approach in a way that Grant would have questioned and seriously doubted. It was not that Grant opposed protest and advocacy politics; he did not. He merely thought such a vision of politics was much too reductionistic. But, Merton and Grant did agree that, at that level of theory and hot button issues, there was a need for a political approach that transcended the ideologues of the left, right and center. They did differ on how such ideas could and would be implemented. Merton as an anarchist was strong on protest and moral outrage, but rather weak on serious engagement with political parties. It must be noted that Merton, as a monk, lacked the ability to be engaged in formal party politics. Grant was more involved in the world and, as such, he could and was engaged in national elections and formal party politics. Grant, though, was no uncritical fan of the Progressive Conservative party. In 1988, when the Federal election in Canada was being contested on the 'free trade debate', the Progressive Conservative party was for free trade and the Liberal party was opposed to it. Grant chose to support the Liberal party in their more nationalist stance.

George Grant, like Thomas Merton, spoke to the larger political questions of the 1950s-1960s-1970s and 1980s. The voices of both men continue to live through those who have been drawn to their prophetic vision, a vision that transcends the culture wars and ethos of political correctness that so dominates much public interaction and discourse these days. Both men mined deeply the wisdom of the past, and brought the insights of such a heritage into the present. Merton did not know much about Canada; hence he had little to say about the Canadian context or situation. Grant knew as much about the USA as Canada, and much of his thought sought to disentangle the Canadian way from both American liberal principles and from the New Rome to the south. Grant's classic missive, *Lament for a Nation: The Defeat of Canadian Nationalism* (1965) remains a standard text in Canada that defines the Canadian way in contrast to the American way. Both Merton and Grant were convinced there were profound moral questions that needed to be faced, but they also realized unless a deeper understanding of human identity and human nature was recovered through a contemplative vision, moral posturing and moral outrage would be a futile gesture.

VI. Thomas Merton and George Grant: Hawk's Dream, Owl's Insight

What was Merton's 'Hawk's Dream' and Grant's 'Owl's Insight'? Both men realized that a return to the contemplative depths was the moral and spiritual imperative of the time. A reversal had occurred in the West, and in this reversal the *'vita activa'* had replaced the *'vita contemplativa'* as the core and centre of life. Merton, as the soaring hawk, and Grant, as the observant owl, called North Americans away from the frenetic and driven protestant work ethic back to the contemplative way. It was in and through the contemplative way that the ego, the fiction and phantom within would be exposed and found wanting. It was in the contemplative way that the deeper eternal self would and could be born and resurrected. This is why, for both Merton and Grant, the cross of suffering was foundational to their thought. There is no new life except through the death and resurrection that the cross of Christ so illuminates for us.

Merton and Grant did turn to the East for contemplative wisdom and insight, but ultimately the depths of the Cross (and its transformative meaning) took both Merton and Grant down a different path than the contemplative traditions of the East. The East spoke much wisdom about the illusions we live by and the need to see through them. But, there was more to living from the new self than this. The new life in Christ and the Church defined and shaped what the new person could and would be. Merton and Grant were loyal to the church but critical of her accommodation to much of North American culture. Both men had a broad and full catholic vision of the church that was truly ecumenical and concerned with deeper unity. Both men had, from their understanding and experience of the contemplative, a commitment to the church and a passion for public justice and peace. Both men, in short, were apostles and heralds of the inner depths of the contemplative life and the public and political aspects of the prophetic life. Their perspectives were fully integrated and organic, whole and holy. It was this catholic love of the whole that makes both Merton and Grant so appealing to those who long for something deeper, fuller and more integrated than what is often served up on the religious table.

Notes

1. Thomas Merton and Jean Leclercq, *Survival or Prophecy: The Letters of Thomas Merton and Jean Leclercq* (New York: Farrar, Straus and Giroux, 2002), p. XIX.

2. David Cayley, *George Grant in Conversation* (Toronto: Anansi, 1995), p. VII.

3. Thomas Merton, *Conjectures of a Guilty Bystander* (New York: Doubleday, 1966), p. 21.

"A Humanly Impoverished Thirst for Light": Thomas Merton's Receptivity To the Feminine, to Judaism, and to Religious Pluralism[1]

Edward K. Kaplan

What divides us? What unites us? We disagree in law and creed, in commitments which lie at the very heart of our religious existence. We say no to one another in some doctrines essential and sacred to us. What unites us? Our being accountable to God, our being objects of God's concern, precious in His eyes.

Abraham Joshua Heschel, 1965[2]

The voyage of Thomas Merton, as of that of the Roman Catholic Church, from triumphalism, supersessionism or "replacement theology" to an acceptance of Judaism as spiritually autonomous, beloved by God, was long and very difficult. For the Church, it took about two thousand years; for Merton it began around twenty years after he became a Catholic. The background for this paper is provided by *Merton and Judaism*, a volume in the series on Merton and world religious traditions published by Fons Vitae.[3] The book's two subtitles guide these reflections: first, "Holiness in Words," a phrase from Abraham Joshua Heschel referring to God's presence in the Hebrew Bible; second, "Recognition, Repentance, and Renewal," recognition of past faults, repentance for them, and renewal of Jewish and Christian life both separately and in partnership. We all need renewal.

Recognition and Repentance

Thomas Merton became a partner with Judaism, "the first covenant," as the "old covenant" is now more generously named by Christians, amidst the Second Vatican Council's internal conflicts about the declaration on the Jews. During the turbulent month of September 1964, Merton received a jolt from Rabbi Abraham Joshua Heschel, professor of Jewish ethics and mysticism at the Jewish

Theological Seminary in New York, and author of books on prayer, religious philosophy, and the Hebrew prophets, which Merton taught to the novices at Gethsemani.[4] Heschel sent Merton his recent memorandum (dated 3 September 1964) objecting to the compromised text stalled by the Council Fathers amidst great controversy. The original draft, prepared by the saintly Augustin Cardinal Bea and his Secretariat for Christian Unity, was attacked by members of the Curia for being too favorable to Judaism.[5]

Heschel shared with Merton his outrage that the modern, post-Holocaust Church might still consider Jews to be unfulfilled Christians. I quote a crucial passage from Heschel's rejection of mission to the Jews:

> Since this present draft document calls for "reciprocal understanding and appreciation, to be attained by theological study and fraternal discussion" between Jews and Catholics, it must be stated that *spiritual fratricide* is hardly a means for the attainment of "fraternal discussion" or "reciprocal understanding." A message that regards the Jew as a candidate for conversion and proclaims that the destiny of Judaism is to disappear will be abhorred by the Jews all over the world and is bound to foster reciprocal distrust as well as bitterness and resentment. . . . As I have said repeatedly to leading personalities of the Vatican, I am ready to go to Auschwitz any time, if faced with the alternative of conversion or death.[6]

Merton answered Heschel immediately, on 9 September, for once, almost speechless: "It is simply incredible. I don't know what to say about it. This much I will say: my latent ambitions to be a true Jew under my Catholic skin will surely be realized if I continue to go through experiences like this, being spiritually slapped in the face by these blind and complacent people of whom I am nevertheless a 'collaborator.'"

The following day (10 September) Merton took sides with Heschel in his private journal, as he began to elaborate a theological position with regard to Judaism as a living tradition:

> Abraham Heschel sent a memo on the new Jewish chapter. It is incredibly bad. All the sense has been taken out of it, all the originality, all the light, and it has become a stuffy and point-

less piece of formalism, with the *incredibly* stupid addition that the Church is looking forward with hope to the union of the Jews with herself. As a humble theological and eschatological desire, yes, maybe; but that was not what was meant. It is this lack of spiritual and eschatological sense, this unawareness of the real need for *profound* change that makes such statements pitiable. Total lack of prophetic insight and even of elementary compunction.

It is precisely in prophetic and therefore deeply humiliated and humanly impoverished thirst for light that Christians and Jews can begin to find a kind of unity in seeking God's will together. For Rome simply to declare itself, as she now is, the mouthpiece of God and perfect interpreter of His [God's] will for Jews (with the implication that He in no way speaks to them directly) is simply monstrous.[7]

"Where is the prophetic and therefore deeply humiliated and humanly impoverished thirst for light, that Christians and Jews may now begin to find some kind of unity in seeking God's will together? But if Rome simply declares herself complacently to be the mouthpiece of God and perfect interpreter of God's will for the Jews, with the implication that He in no way ever speaks to them directly, this is simply monstrous!"

Merton dramatically *recognized* a sinful condition within the institutional Church, the absence of even "elementary compunction," and he sought its *repentance* (the "deeply humiliated thirst" of inner transformation) in order to remedy the Church's spiritual blindness. His righteous anger was more than just generous; he himself experienced the pain of Jews persecuted for centuries by the Christian majority. Merton was fully aware of the Roman Catholic Church's millennial "teaching of contempt," propagated at the popular level by pastoral teachings and the old liturgy.[8]

Here I emphasize the positive, however, by exploring Merton's "latent ambition to be a true Jew under his Catholic skin," as he stated to Rabbi Heschel. Merton was already on the road, having been "spiritually slapped in the face." He took courage in his "thirst for light," or more precisely, a "prophetic and therefore deeply humiliated and humanly impoverished thirst for light." Such humility would favor a partnership so "that Christians and Jews can begin to find some kind of unity in seeking God's will together."

Pluralism and Dialogue

Thomas Merton thus asserted the basic premise of authentic inter-faith dialogue: that the will of God is not completely known, nor exclusive to one tradition. Some vision of religious pluralism must attenuate the claim that one's own revelation is absolutely true. The pluralist trusts that if God is God, God is the God of all peoples. Our particular revelations are alive, ongoing, unceasingly calling for response and interpretation. Merton remained committed to his Catholic self while expanding his contemplative awareness, as he sought relentlessly to clarify God's will.

Abraham Joshua Heschel arrived at his pluralistic perspective while retaining his absolute commitment to the Sinai covenant and to the Jewish people. In November 1965 he summarized his view of interfaith cooperation in his inaugural lecture, "No Religion Is An Island," as Harry Emerson Fosdick Visiting Professor at Union Theological Seminary, the liberal Protestant institution.[9] Heschel's impressive opening words define himself, and the Jewish people, in continuity with Biblical tradition:

> I speak as a member of a congregation whose founder was Abraham, and the name of my rabbi is Moses.
>
> I speak as a person who was able to leave Warsaw, the city in which I was born, just six weeks before the disaster began. My destination was New York, it would have been Auschwitz or Treblinka. I am a brand plucked from the fire, in which my people was burned to death. I am a brand plucked from the fire of an altar of Satan on which millions of human lives were exterminated to evil's greater glory, and on which so much else was consumed: the divine image of so many human beings, many people's faith in the God of justice and compassion, and much of the secret and power of attachment to the Bible bred and cherished in the hearts of men for nearly two thousand years.

The *Shoah* gave special urgency to Heschel's celebration of God's presence in the Hebrew Bible. Christians and Jews share his loyalty to that text, with our different understandings of its authority. Our common ancestors, Abraham and Moses, heeded God's call and fathered the ancient Israelites, community of the "first covenant."

Two decades after the allied victory in Europe, Heschel, as "a brand plucked from the fire," echoed the prophet Zechariah (3:2) to assert the sanctity of all humankind. He considered the spiritual consequences of Hitler's intended genocide to be universal, including but surpassing the question of Jewish survival. The death and torture—physical and psychological—of millions of Jews and non-Jews points to a peril from which we continue, increasingly, to suffer: namely, our diminished image of ourselves as living symbols of God.[10] The degradation of what it means to be human is the most insidious danger of our age.

The interfaith environment supported Heschel's proclamation of his Jewish responsibility. Later in his inaugural lecture Heschel summarized his view of interfaith dialogue in a way that reverberates with Merton's defense of Judaism during the Second Vatican Council; this is Heschel:

> I suggest that the most significant basis for meeting of men of different religious traditions is the level of fear and trembling, of humility and contrition, where our individual moments of faith are mere waves in the endless ocean of mankind's reaching out for God, where all formulations and articulations appear as understatements, where our souls are swept away by the awareness of the urgency of answering God's commandment, while stripped of pretension and conceit we sense the tragic insufficiency of human faith.
>
> What divides us? What unites us? We disagree in law and creed, in commitments which lie at the very heart of our religious existence.... What unites us? Our being accountable to God, our being objects of God's concern, precious in His eyes.[11]

Heschel and Merton share the same acute sense of spiritual embarrassment—"humility and contrition"—before God, as they acknowledge "the tragic insufficiency of human faith." Merton calls it a "prophetic and therefore deeply humiliated and humanly impoverished thirst for light that [will allow] Christians and Jews [to] begin to find some kind of unity in seeking God's will together." Such are the elementary pre-conditions, both inward and theological, for a roadmap to peace.

Heschel's task, and that of the post-Holocaust generation, was and remains to revive "the divine image of so many human beings, many people's faith in the God of justice and compassion, and much of the secret and power of attachment to the Bible." The

Jewish people are witnesses, representing by their very existence as Jews loyalty to the living God: *"The Bible is holiness in words. . . .* It is as if God took these Hebrew words and breathed into them of His power, and the words became a live wire charged with His spirit. To this very day they are hyphens between heaven and earth."[12]

The Feminine Unconscious

Thomas Merton's private journals, now published, trace an intriguing connection between his progressive receptivity to Judaism and his late opening to femininity. A cluster of highly charged symbols emerges in Merton's dream life and artistic works around the years of Vatican *aggiornamento* (updating or renewal). In a previous paper I examined the influence of Merton's series of dreams of "Proverb," a young Jewish woman, as they affected his appreciation of Judaism and the world at large.[13] That process of reintegrating *Eros* into his self-conception culminated in the epiphany of Fourth and Walnut, at least at the literary and ideological level of his public persona.

My hypothesis is that Merton's fantasized love for "Proverb," and his celebration of the divine feminine in his prose poem "Hagia Sophia," and, of course, his veneration of the Virgin Mary, are essentially connected with his "latent ambition to be a true Jew under [his] Catholic skin." Merton's new sensitivity to Judaism was part of his evolving pluralism, his ability, and indeed his passion, to participate in the spiritual life of other traditions, Western and Asian.

This line of thought, a focus on the feminine and on Eros, of which my reflections are a part, is familiar to the Merton scholarly community. Among the documents are: Merton's talks to the Contemplative Sisters, *The Springs of Contemplation*[14]; *The Merton Annual* (vol. 13), George Kilcourse's introduction, "Spirituality as the Freedom to Channel Eros"; interview with Jane Marie Richardson, SL; in *The Merton Annual* (vol. 14), Victor A. Kramer's introduction, "Merton's Openness to Change and his Foreshadowing of a Feminist Spirituality"; the interview with Myriam Dardenne, "A Journey into Wholeness"; and Jonathan Montaldo's "Gallery of Women's Faces and Dreams of Women from the Drawings and Journals of Thomas Merton"; studies of Merton's love poems to "M"[15]; the late Myriam Dardenne's presentation of Merton and the feminine at the ITMS meeting held at Bellarmine University in Louisville KY in 2001; *Learning to Love, The Journal of Thomas Merton, vol. 6, 1966-1967*[16]; and much more.

Two recent articles by Judaic scholars suggest that Merton's liberation of *Eros* finds deep historical roots in Jewish mysticism. Arthur Green and Peter Shäfer advance the same bold hypothesis that, in Green's terms, "the unequivocal feminization of the *shekhinah* in the Kabbalah of the thirteenth century is a Jewish response to and adaptation of the revival of devotion to Mary in the twelfth-century Western church."[17] We thus confirm that Thomas Merton's dreams of Proverb, the young Jewish woman, have a significant historical correlative, objective in its existence though intimately personal, subjective in its function.

Merton's feminine imagery parallels the development within ancient and rabbinic Judaism, culminating in the thirteenth-century Kabbalah, of a feminization of God as represented by the *shekhinah*. Put briefly, the Kabbalistic notion of *shekhinah* is the ultimate mediator: she is the indwelling Presence of God in the world, the feminine element within the Godhead, and the *kenesset yisra'el*, the hypostatized Community of Israel, i.e. the Jewish people (not "the Synagogue," a term foreign to Judaism). For example, one of the earliest manifestations of a female consort of God is the figure of Wisdom, *hokhmah*, of Proverbs 8, "identified with the Torah throughout rabbinic literature."[18] There are other womanly entities in Jewish tradition, Mother Rachel, Mother Zion, the Temple, the Holy Ark, the Tent of Meeting, etc., and especially the Sabbath Queen or Bride.

Thomas Merton associates within his inner life a similar cluster of female figures, the most prominent of which are the Blessed Virgin Mary, her mother Saint Anne (in Hebrew, Hannah), Hagia Sophia, Proverb, and M, the real woman with whom Merton the monk fell passionately in love. Green's study provides a precise clue as to why Proverb is embodied, for Merton, as a young Jewish woman, and why that dream accompanied his opening to Judaism and to the world. The Jewish or Biblical foundation of Merton's fantasies may very well be the Song of Songs, "the tradition's prime source for all discussion of sacred *Eros*."[19]

Merton's powerful prose poem, "Hagia Sophia," has been carefully interpreted as a plateau in his relationship to the feminine, a summary of mostly unconscious aspirations for a tender Mother and a fearful yearning to be loved by a real woman, such as he was several years later by M, the student nurse.[20] Merton struggled to reconcile his warring impulses as a man and as a celibate monk: to be loved by his mother, to love his mother, to accept his erotic desire for a woman, body and soul, and in the end to integrate all this with his devotion to God, to Christ, and to the Blessed Virgin. (Not to mention his vow of obedience!) Theologically speaking, Merton's "Hagia Sophia" synthesizes many influences, his dreams (as recounted in the journal), Meister Eckhart, Julian of Norwich, especially mystics of the Eastern Church, and the Song of Songs.

To focus our present reflections on Merton's receptivity to the Other through the feminine, I quote only the two first stanzas, corresponding to the awakening, Dawn, The Hour of Lauds:

> There is in all visible things an invisible fecundity, a dimmed light, a meek namelessness, a hidden wholeness. This mysterious Unity and Integrity is Wisdom, the Mother of all, *Natura naturans*. There is in all things an inexhaustible sweetness and purity, a silence that is a fount of action and joy. It rises up in wordless gentleness and flows out to me from the unseen roots of all created being, welcoming me tenderly, saluting me with indescribable humility. This is at once my own being, my own nature, and the Gift of my Creator's Thought and Art within me, speaking as Hagia Sophia, speaking as my sister, Wisdom. I am awakened, I am born again at the voice of this my Sister, sent to me from the depths of the divine fecundity.[21]

Wisdom is a nurse who awakens the poet in his hospital bed, the Blessed Virgin, earthly mother, and lover—all these females are condensed and elaborated in Merton's meditation. He is being loved; that self-acceptance as a man and as a monk beloved by God made it possible for him to welcome other religions to the feast. There is also a concerted ethical thrust. According to Susan McCaslin, Merton's placing of "Hagia Sophia" in *Emblems of a Season of Fury*, also "calls for the transformation of the world through non-violence and non-retaliation."[22]

Specialists can uncover the deeper stratum of Thomas Merton's progressive receptivity to the feminine by examining the exegetical tradition of the Song of Songs. Green traces popular Christian awareness of the Canticle "in the liturgical settings for the four festivals of Mary found in the old Christian calendar (Nativity,

Purification, Annunciation, and Assumption of the Virgin)[;] verses from the Canticle are often used to depict the love between God, to whom she is both bride and mother, and the Virgin. She is the garden of delight whom God enters and in whom He takes pleasure; she is also the 'sealed fountain' out of whom will flow the living spring of Christ."[23]

For Merton, probably the most important Christian interpreter was Bernard of Clairvaux (1090-1153) whose homilies on the Song of Songs are recognized as "one of the most popular texts of Western Christian mysticism of all time."[24] It is significant that Merton's close friend, Jean Leclercq, OSB, co-edited the Latin collection of Saint Bernard's sermons and wrote a book entitled *Monks and Love in Twelfth-Century France* (not "Monks in love"!).[25] A worthy interfaith research project would clarify Merton's place within Cistercian spirituality and its erotic dimensions, taking into account Jewish interpretations of the Song of Songs, most of which Thomas Merton probably did not directly know.[26] Here is Arthur Green's conclusion:

This rich and varied symbolization of Eros in the Christian texts precedes and provides a context for understanding that which happens a century later in the Jewish mystical sources, especially the Zohar, where images of mother, sister, bride, and a host of others are deeply interlocked. For the Christians this love remains mostly a chaste, maternal Eros, here transformed on the spiritual/hermeneutical plane to that of the virginal, untouched bride. For the Jews, not having a tradition that glorifies virginity or celibacy, the varieties of female imagery in the imagination of the mystic will culminate in the fantasy of a direct sexual coupling. For the Christian sources the love expressed in these readings of the Canticle is that between Christ, who is God, and His human mother Mary, who is not God. For the Kabbalist, whose God is manifest in the ten *sefirot*, *shekhinah* is within the Godhead and the Eros of the Canticle is about the love of God for God. This love is strengthened and supported by human effort, indeed allows itself to be dependent on the energies aroused by Israel in this world, but essentially remains transcendent. Despite these real differences, however, the commonality of symbols, typologies, and structures of thought is truly remarkable.[27]

Merton's life and writings also reflect the quest literature of the twelfth century, a longing for God, for human and spiritual love, and for a pious life. Jews and Muslims in Golden Age Spain shared in this Christian revival of spiritual Eros. Among the Jewish examples cited by Arthur Green are Bahya Ibn Paquda, *The Duties of the Heart*, "Maimonides' description of the love of God [*Mishneh Torah*, hilkhot teshuvah, 10:3; also *Guide of the Perplexed*, 3:51] in which the Song of Songs plays a key role"; the Sufi quest for union with God that influenced his son, Abraham Maimonides; poetry written in Arabic or Hebrew by Jews that was both religious and erotic, and more.

In addition, the studies by Green and Shäfer in themselves contribute significantly to interfaith scholarship, not only because of their content; they develop hypotheses usually ignored by Judaic scholars, a direct and profound influence of Christian practice on Jewish theology and inner experience of God. Accordingly, scholars of Christianity (and Islam) might examine with more objectivity the influence of Jewish traditions.

Pluralistic Theology

This is a time for generosity and hope, but also for sober realism. Neither Merton nor Heschel quickly jumped on the bandwagon of pluralism, pro-actively affirming the preciousness of all religions. But they did so when called upon, and with utmost respect and conviction: Heschel in his inaugural address at Union Theological Seminary, Merton in *Conjectures of a Guilty Bystander* (1966), and especially in Merton's final writings on Asian spirituality. Both men recognized the sanctity of other religions, preparing future cooperation and mutual support against the demons of nihilism, dehumanization, and doubt, our inescapable heritage as fallible human beings.

Mutual respect and "reciprocal understanding and appreciation" first require loyalty to one's own tradition. Neither Merton nor Heschel deviated from or even compromised their sectarian commitments. It is true that many people feared that Merton would leave the Church, but there is no hard evidence that he would have done so. In fact, the conference in Asia during which he met his death was devoted to Christian monastic renewal though dialogue with other traditions, including Marxism. We must not forgot that Merton's stated desire to be a Jew, or a Buddhist or a Hindu, etc., "under his Catholic skin," retains that skin which, after all, held him physically and spiritually together, and defined who he was in the world.

Both Merton and Heschel revered Judaism—ancient and contemporary—as a repository of the Holy Spirit, invigorated by a supernatural Presence both beyond and within our texts, systems, beliefs, and practices. Merton would agree with Heschel that "[t]he essence of Jewish religious thinking does not lie in entertaining *a concept* of God [my emphasis, EK] but in the ability to articulate a memory of moments of illumination by His presence."[28] This is the pluralistic or contemplative approach to religious commitment.

Heschel's loyalty unto death to the Jewish covenant also grounds a pluralistic model. His affirmation of the Mount Sinai event was absolute, although he carefully and deliberately, in *God in Search of Man* (1955), insisted that the original Revelation was witnessed by all mankind. Heschel first asserts, with normative Judaism, that all Jews at all times can bear witness to the <u>original</u> event: "There is no one who has no faith. Every one of us stood at the foot of Sinai and beheld the voice that proclaimed, *I am the Lord thy God*. Every one of us participated in saying, *We shall do and we shall hear*. However, it is the evil in man and the evil in society silencing the depth of the soul that block and hamper our faith."[29] At the very least, his understanding of divine revelation is pluralistic with regard to competing denominations within contemporary Judaism.

Most significantly, Heschel's perspective is both "orthodox" and universal. When he says that "every one of us stood at the foot of Sinai and beheld the voice that proclaimed, *I am the Lord thy God*" he also and especially means Jew and Gentile. Heschel goes on to cite a rabbinical interpretation of the Biblical text, a Midrash that validates this universality: "*Tanhuma, Yitro,* I. The words, according to the Rabbis, were not heard by Israel alone, but by the inhabitants of all the earth. The divine voice divided itself into 'the seventy tongues' of man, so that all might understand it. *Exodus Rabba*, 5,9."[30]

Abraham Joshua Heschel is Thomas Merton's partner because they both straddle the fence between Orthodoxy and Liberalism as they call to the Holy Spirit within all people. Heschel assumes that sensitivity to holiness—a gift emanating from the Divine—is intrinsic to everyone: "Recondite is the dimension where God and man meet, and yet not entirely impenetrable. [God] placed within man something of His spirit (see Isaiah 63:10), and 'it is the spirit in a man, the breath of the Almighty, that makes him understand' (Job 32:8)."[31]

Merton and Heschel invite us all to partake in the Holy Spirit. If the beginning of the Jewish people is God's covenant with Abraham, the foundation of Jewish-Christian dialogue is the Sinai Revelation as we agree to interpret it. These two stories are models of our unfinished business. We cannot forget that Abraham was the father of both Isaac and Ishmael; Jews and Muslims must face and resolve the real conflicts of Sarah and Hagar. Heschel's conviction that God's self-revelation at Sinai was given to all humankind, in its "seventy tongues," reminds us that the Hebrew Bible is a human "report," a midrash, of the Divine message.[32]

Thomas Merton recognized that no human authority, no Church, not even his own, can speak exclusively for God. How many of humankind's "seventy tongues" does the Roman Catholic Church possess? Or any person or institution? Merton's journal entry of 10 September 1964 makes it clear: "It is precisely in prophetic and therefore deeply humiliated and humanly impoverished thirst for light that Christians and Jews can begin to find a kind of unity in seeking God's will together. For Rome simply to declare itself, as she now is, the mouthpiece of God and perfect interpreter of [God's] will for Jews (with the implication that He in no way speaks to them directly) is simply monstrous."[33]

Merton's valiant, lifelong struggle with the feminine within him, his increased support of initiatives by women in religious life, accompanied his affirmation of other traditions, including Judaism. Thomas Merton and Abraham Heschel incite us to renew the Holy Spirit, the Presence of God, in our hearts and in our communities. All of us, Jews, Christians, Muslims, and others, must recover the Spirit of Vatican II, the Holy Spirit (in Hebrew, *ruah hakodesh*) beyond all beliefs, as we nurture, through our irreducible particularity, our reverence for what is universally sacred.

Notes

1. This paper was presented at the ITMS Eighth General Meeting in Vancouver, B.C. June 2003.

2. Abraham Heschel, "No Religion Is An Island," delivered on 10 November 1965 at the Union Theological Seminary; originally pub. *Union Seminary Quarterly* 21:2 (January 1966): 117-34. Reprinted in Susannah

Heschel, ed., Abraham Heschel, *Moral Grandeur and Spiritual Audacity* (New York: Farrar, Straus & Giroux, 1996); hereafter abbreviated as *Moral Grandeur*.

3. Beatrice Bruteau ed., *Merton and Judaism. Holiness in Words. Recognition, Repentance, and Renewal* (Louisville KY: Fons Vitae, 2003); hereafter abbreviated as *Merton and Judaism*.

4. For comparative studies of Merton and Heschel see Edward K. Kaplan, "Contemplative Inwardness and Prophetic Action: Thomas Merton's Dialogue with Abraham J. Heschel," Shaul Magid, "Abraham Joshua Heschel and Thomas Merton: Heretics of Modernity," "Merton-Heschel Correspondence," all in *Merton and Judaism*, pp. 217-268. For foundational works on Heschel see John C. Merkle, *The Genesis of Faith. The Depth Theology of Abraham Joshua Heschel* (New York: Macmillan, 1985) and Edward K. Kaplan, *Holiness in Words. Abraham Joshua Heschel's Poetics of Piety* (Albany NY: SUNY Press, 1996). The Merton-Heschel correspondence with supporting documents quoted below is from *Merton and Judaism*, pp. 217-31.

5. See Brenda Fitch Fairaday, "Thomas Merton's Prophetic Voice: Merton, Heschel, and Vatican II," and Appendix A, "The Successive Versions of *Nostra Aetate*, Translation, Outline, Chronology, Commentary," by James M. Somerville, *Merton and Judaism*, pp. 269-82, 341-72.

6. This and the next quotation from *Merton and Judaism*, pp. 223-25.

7. Thomas Merton, *Dancing in the Waters of Life. The Journals of Thomas Merton* (Journals 5, 1963-1965, ed. Robert E. Daggy; HarperSanFrancisco, 1987), pp. 142-43. Compare with the edited version prepared for publication, quoted by Ron Miller, from *A Vow of Conversation* (p.76), in "Merton: Pioneer of Pluralism," *Merton and Judaism*, p. 293.

8. See the article by Fairaday cited above in note 5 and especially Ron Miller, "Merton: Pioneer of Pluralism," *Merton and Judaism*, pp. 283-96.

9. The next quotation is from Heschel, "No Religion Is An Island," *Moral Grandeur*, p. 235. See Harold Kasimow and Byron Sherwin, eds., *No Religion Is An Island. Abraham Joshua Heschel and Interreligious Dialogue* (New York: Orbis Books, 1991.)

10. Abraham Heschel, *Man's Quest for God* (New York: Charles Scribners Sons, 1955), chap. 5, "Symbolism," pp. 115-44; "Sacred Image of Man," in *The Insecurity of Freedom* (New York: Farrar, Straus & Giroux, 1966), pp. 150-67. For a summary of what I call Heschel's sacred humanism, see A.J. Heschel, *Who Is Man?* (Stanford University Press, 1965). These resources provide a starting point for theological reflection on incarnation in Judaism and Christianity.

11. Abraham Heschel, "No Religion Is An Island," *Moral Grandeur*, pp. 239-40; see also Heschel, "The Ecumenical Movement" (during Cardinal Bea's visit to the United States in 1963), in *Insecurity of Freedom*, pp. 179-83.

12. Heschel, *God in Search of Man. A Philosophy of Judaism* (New York: Farrar, Straus & Giroux, 1955), p. 244.

13. Edward K. Kaplan, "'Under my Catholic Skin,' Thomas Merton's Opening to Judaism and to the World," in *Merton and Judaism*, pp. 109-25.

14. Thomas Merton *The Springs of Contemplation. A Retreat at the Abbey of Gethsemani* (New York: Farrar, Straus & Giroux, 1992; repr. Notre Dame IND: Ave Maria Press, 1997).

15. Kilcourse, *The Merton Annual* 13 (2000), pp. 7-13; Richardson, ibid., pp. 127-43; Kramer, *The Merton Annual* 14 (2001), pp. 7-11; Dardenne, ibid., pp. 33-55; ibid., pp. 155-72. See also Douglas Burton-Christie, "Rediscovering Love's World: Thomas Merton's Love Poems and the Language of Ecstasy," *Cross Currents* (Spring 1989), pp. 64-82; Andrea C. Cook, "The Experience of Romantic Transcendence in Thomas Merton's *Eighteen Poems*," *The Merton Annual* 14 (2001), pp. 121-54; Cynthia Bourgeault, "Merton in Love," *The Merton Seasonal* 27, 2 (Summer 2002), pp. 20-25.

16. *Learning to Love, The Journal of Thomas Merton, vol. 6, 1966-1967*, ed. Christine M. Bochen (HarperSanFrancisco, 1997).

17. Arthur Green, "Shekhinah, the Virgin Mary, and the Song of Songs," *American Jewish Studies (AJS) Review* 26:1 (2002), pp. 1-52; hereafter abbreviated as Green; Peter Shäfer, "Daughter, Sister, Bride, and Mother: Images of the Femininity of God in the Early Kabbalah," *Journal of the American Academy of Religion* 68:2 (June 2000), pp. 221-42. orig. pub. in German, 1998; see Green, p. 21, n88.

18. Green, p. 20, and n83. "The interplay of traditions is manifest in Philo, who depicts the 'Wisdom' of Prov. 8:22 as copulating with the Father and giving birth to the visible universe."

19. Green, p. 1.

20. See Michael Mott, *The Seven Mountains of Thomas Merton* (Boston: Houghton Mifflin Co., 1984), pp. 307-08, 312-13, 361-64 on the prose poem; Therese Lentfohr, *Words and Silence: On the Poetry of Thomas Merton* (New York: New Directions, 1979); and Susan McCaslin, "Merton and 'Hagia Sophia' (Holy Wisdom," *Merton and Hesychasm: The Prayer of the Heart*, ed. Jonathan Montaldo and Bernadette Dieker (Louisville KY: Fons Vitae, 2003), pp. 235-54. See Robert Jingen Gunn, *Journeys into Emptiness. Dogen, Merton, Jung and the Quest for Transformation* (New York: Paulist Press, 2000) for a good survey of Merton's relationships with women, starting with his mother.

21. Merton, *Emblems of a Season of Fury* (New York: New Directions, 1963), 61-69; originally published in a limited edition in January 1962 on Victor Hammer's handpress, Stamperia del Santuccio, then in the magazine <u>Ramparts</u>, March 1963. See *The Collected Poems of Thomas Merton* (New York: New Directions, 1977), 363-71.

22. Susan McCaslin, *Merton and Hesychasm*, p. 252.

23. This and the following quotation from Green, pp. 5-6: "The varied interpretations of the Song of Songs present in the early Church attest to a special fascination with this book and its message. For Origen, God's great gift to us in Creation is *eros*, the power of love that also fuels the journey back to God. For the mature Christian, one who has overcome earthly passions for the sake of still more passionate inner journey, the Song of Songs contains the most important message of the Bible. Of course this is precisely a Christian outgrowth and a Platonic reading of Rabbi Akiva's original claim that the Song of Songs is the 'Holy of Holies.' The Eros that is essential to Neo-Platonic religion finds its Biblical home in this Christianized reading of the Song of Songs."

24. Green, p. 13. See also "When we look at the unabashed eroticism of Bernard's Homilies on the Song of Songs, or that of his Cistercian followers, we wonder where their parallel is in the Hebrew literature, or wonder at the reason for its absence," Green, p. 23. Green refers to E. Anne Matter, *The Voice of My Beloved: The Songs of Songs in Western Medieval Christianity* (Philadelphia: University of Pennsylvania Press, 1990) among several other scholarly studies.

25. See *Survival or Prophecy? The Letters of Thomas Merton and Jean Leclerq*, ed. Patrick Hart (New York: Farrar, Straus & Giroux, 2002).

26. Green, p. 13, n56-57, see esp. Jean Leclercq, *Monks and Love in Twelfth-Century France* (Oxford, Clarendon Press, 1979), and Latin text edited by Jean Leclercq et al., *Sancti Bernardi Opera* (Rome: Editiones Cistercienses, 1955-77). Bernard McGinn, *The Presence of God: A History of Western Christian Mysticis*, vol. 2 (New York: Crossroad, 1996), 158-224. Over 900 manuscripts of Bernard's immensely popular work survived.

27. Green, pp. 21-22.

28. Heschel, *God In Search of Man*, pp. 140-41 for this and the next quotation. See Edward Kaplan, *Holiness in Words*, chap. 9, "Metaphor and Miracle: Modern Judaism and the Holy Spirit," 133-45.

29. Heschel, *God In Search of Man*, pp. 140-41.

30. Heschel, *God in Search of Man*, p. 144, 8.

31. *Ibid.*, p. 137.

32. Cf. Heschel, *God in Search of Man*, p. 185: "We must not read chapters in the Bible dealing with the event at Sinai as if they were texts in systematic theology. Its intention is to celebrate the mystery, to introduce us to it rather than to penetrate or explain it. As a report about revelation the Bible itself is a *midrash*." See Laurence Perlman, "'As a Report about Revelation, the Bible Itself is a Midrash,'" *Conservative Judaism* 55,1 (Fall 2002), pp. 30-37.

33. See above note 7.

Firewatch in the Belly of the Whale: Imagery of Fire, Water, and Place in The Sign of Jonas[1]

David Leigh SJ

Cooled in the flame of God's dark fire
Washed in His gladness like a vesture of new flame
We burn like eagles...
        "The Quickening of John the Baptist" (1949)

May my bones burn and ravens eat my flesh
If I forget thee, contemplation!
        "The Captives—A Psalm" (1949)

When Thomas Merton ends *The Seven Storey Mountain* with a phrase about his vocation to follow "the Christ of the burnt men," he unwittingly foreshadows the primary imagery of his next autobiographical writing in *The Sign of Jonas*. During his first autobiography, he permeates his story with images of water, both the water of cleansing and the water of the abyss, and yet the framework of the narrative is that of climbing the fiery purgative mountain. During his second autobiographical journal, in contrast, the framework suggests the waters which engulf Jonah's whale, but the imagery that permeates the entries is much more redolent of fire than of water. In the prologue written for *The Sign of Jonas*, he describes a young monk during this historic time of monastic transformation as "walking into a furnace of ambivalence."[2] Yet Merton ends the prologue with a mixture of water and fire imagery that, I will show, embodies a number of tensions which Merton was going through between 1947 and 1952 as he sought his right "place" in the world of the monastery: " I feel that my own life is especially sealed with this great sign [of Jonah], which baptism and monastic profession and priestly ordination have burned into the roots of my being . . ."[3]

In this paper, I explore four dimensions of the fire imagery in this journal and their relationship to Merton's four major struggles during this period. First, the imagery of fire as expressing the human need for *purification* during Merton's struggle with the tensions between being a monk and being a writer. Second, the imagery of fire as expressing the painful human *desire for contemplation* in a world of activity, a tension Merton felt throughout this period at Gethsemani. Third, the imagery of fire as embodying the exhausting *consolation of divine presence* in human experience, which Merton experiences during this period along with a great degree of sickness and pressure. Finally, the imagery of fire as used in the Bible to signify *apocalyptic transformation*, and which Merton uses to suggest the final transformation from possessive to pure love of God and all things in God. I then conclude with a few comments on the relationship between his combined use of water and fire imagery in both his autobiographies and his poetry of this period.

In the rough-hewn wooden structure of Gethsemani in the late 1940s, of course, built for seventy but housing two hundred and seventy monks, fire was more than just a poetic image or metaphor. It was a constant physical threat. Although omitted from *Jonas*, Merton records in his posthumously published journal a fire in the gatehouse of the monastery on January 25, 1948, an event that he feared might burn up his own manuscripts.[4] He records the story of a former abbot at Gethsemani who was so upset at a hermit monk who had criticized the monastery that the abbot burned down his hermitage.[5] In May of 1949, he records fires on the hillside and the next month reveals that they had fought similar fires in 1946, a fact that he mentions again near the end of the journal.[6] He seems almost obsessed with the danger of fire to the place of his life as a writer and monk. In mentioning the 1946 fire again on June 27, 1949, he expands on the beauty of the *place* in which his monastic vocation is lived: "Gethsemani looked beautiful from the hill. It made much more sense in its surroundings. We do not realize our own setting and we ought to: it is important to know that you are put on the face of the earth. . . . If we only knew how to *use* this space and this area of sky and these free woods."[7] In December of that same year, he describes himself as "elevated to a position" on the newly formed fire department at the monastery, remarking that "fire fighting [is] serious business."[8] On March 10, 1951, he mentions that he had almost set the woods on fire while burning brush on St. Gertrude's slope near the lake, and concludes: "Many lights are burning that ought to be put out. Kindle no new fires. Live in the warmth of the sun."[9] Except for several mentions of burning manuscripts by Dom Frederic and himself, Merton's final portrait of the danger of fire at the monastery takes place during the famous epilogue titled "Fire Watch, July 4, 1952."

I. The Fires of Purification: Monk and Writer

As Victor A. Kramer has demonstrated in an article on the literary patterns in *The Sign of Jonas*, Merton's primary conflict while writing this journal was between his sense of a vocation to be a contemplative monk and the call of his superiors (and his own talents) to be a writer. Kramer asserts that Merton learned through this conflict that "the secret both for being a successful writer, as well as a good monk, was acceptance of one's place within a particular monastery."[10] But this secret was not learned without several years of great pain and purification, expressed repeatedly through images of fire. As he says on May 23, 1947 in a long discourse on his frustrations over the conflict between writing and contemplation, "At this [Cistercian life] is to be my purgatory."[11] A few weeks later, he extends this burning conflict to include the insufficiency of the entire world in comparison to his contemplative life: "Even the consolations of prayer, lights in the intellect and sensible fervor in the will: everything that touches me burns me at least lightly. I cannot hold on to anything."[12] On September 7, the feast of the Nativity of Mary, after celebrating his happiness in his devotion to the mother of Jesus (a surprising theme throughout his longer journal), Merton complains that everything except solitude with God causes him purifying "pain"—affection, words, singing, writing, reading. The next sentence connects this pain with the "new torches" like "burning hearts upon poles" during Benediction in the monastic chapel.[13] Two weeks later, in a passage that he did not put into *The Sign of Jonas* (about his struggle for solitude), Merton repeats the theme of purification through Cistercian life: "With my whole heart I want all the things in community life that burn and purify me of all my selfishness, of that in me that excludes others and shuts them out. I give myself to those flames with all desire, that the walls of my false solitude may be destroyed . . ."[14]

Throughout his journals, Merton continues to complain about American monasteries becoming not "Eden[s] of contemplation" but "hells of heat and activity."[15] But his use of fire imagery about his own struggles with writing and contemplation disappears after two events during 1948 – the death of Dom Frederic, his first abbot and the one who insisted that he become both a writer and a contemplative, and Merton's first visit to the outside world on a trip to Louisville during which he says "I met the world and I found it no longer so wicked after all. . . . I found that everything stirred me with a deep and mute sense of compassion."[16]   By July 20, 1949, after his ordination, he admits that he has lost his recurrent desire for "running off to the Carthusians" for more solitude: "I no longer have the right to prefer one place to another."[17]   The next day, he is writing: "I am finding myself forced to admit that my lamentations about my writing job have been foolish. . . . The writing is one thing that gives me access to some real silence and solitude. Also I find that it helps me to pray, because when I pause at my work I find that the mirror inside me is surprisingly clear, and deep and serene and God shines there and is immediately found." He recalls singing that day a Latin hymn *Ardens est cor meum*, or "My heart is on fire . . ."[18]   The fire imagery recurs but now as a sign of desire for God and not only of personal purification.

Merton's acceptance of his place at Gethsemani deepens during the rest of 1949 so that by January 18, 1950, he is able to give up dreams of a literal hermitage and admit that "[his] work is [his] hermitage because it is *writing* that helps [him] most of all to be a solitary and a contemplative here at Gethsemani."[19]   The very next entry after this dramatic admission by Merton is a poem on the "Eve of Saint Agnes" which begins with fire imagery: "O small Saint Agnes dressed in gold / With fire in rainbows round about your face / Sing with the seven martyrs in my Canon."[20]   In this poem, the fire of purification has become the rainbow fire of sanctity and joy. Only in a few later references during his illnesses in 1950 does Merton revert to wishing he were free of the fire of conflicts: "now [in the infirmary on Palm Sunday] I burn with a desire to forget all the complex stupidities that my own mind can place between me and God."[21]

II. The Fires of Desire for Contemplative Union with God

As the purgative fire imagery dissipates after the middle of *The Sign of Jonas*, the unitive fire imagery emerges. Here, the conflict within Merton comes in part from what he considers the human desire for contemplative union with God and its conflict with the activism of his personal and monastic life. On May 10, 1947, he turns from his desire for publication to a desire for union with God, "to love God *caste, sancte, ardenter* [chastely, wholly, ardently]."[22] He recalls a verse from John 14:2, "I go to prepare a place for you," and his desire for this place "burns within [his heart] with joy"; he affirms with St. Bernard that "we are made for the mystical marriage, it fulfills our nature."[23] On Sept. 24, 1947, Merton is again taken up with the human desire for contemplation and so enjoys writing about it that he says in his unpublished journal, "My heart burns in my side when I write about contemplation . . . and I want to cast fire on the earth."[24] His desire for contemplative union in the midst of small monastic irritations consumes him a year later: "I want to be poor; I want to be solitary . . . I am all dried up with desire and I can only think of one thing— staying in the fire that burns me."[25] Three weeks later, this consoling desire enlarges itself in his writing to include love for other persons: "The fire of love for the souls of men loved by God consumes you like the fire of God's love, and it is the same love. It burns you up with a hunger for the supernatural happiness . . . of everybody. This fire consumes you with a desire that is not directed immediately to action, but to God."[26] When Merton first gets to use the quiet rare book vault for his writing in January 1949, he enjoys a continuing sense of this consolation, expressing it in a mixture of fire and water imagery: "love, love, love burned in my heart. Still does. Waves of it come and go. I swim on the waves."[27]

When Merton prepares for ordination as a priest several months later, he experiences burning desire for God: "I burn with the desire for His peace, His stability, His silence, the power and wisdom of His direct action, liberation from my own heaviness."[28] This consolation carries over to his first celebrations of the Eucharist as a priest: "the glowing radiance . . . fills the depths of my soul. [Yet it] is a dark radiance—burning in the silence of a faith without images—all the more radiant because I rejoice that it is dark."[29] On August 8, this fiery consolation returns when he reads the Bible outdoors in the natural world: "By the reading of Scripture I am so renewed that all nature seems renewed around me and with me. . . the whole world is charged with the glory of God and I feel fire and music in the earth under my feet."[30] This sense of consoling fire continues with Merton through the end of summer, and he mixes it with water imagery in a powerful entry on Sept. 14, 1949 where he realizes again that he cannot "possess created things":

I try to touch you [created things] with the deep fire that is in the center of my heart, but I cannot touch you without defiling both you and myself. . . . But this sadness generates within me an unspeakable reverence for the holiness of created things, for they are pure and perfect and they belong to God and they are mirrors of His beauty. He is mirrored in all things like sunlight in clean water: but if I try to drink the light that is in the water I only shatter the reflection.[31]

This consoling fire and water imagery associated with transforming reverence re-emerges in Merton's final meditation of *The Sign of Jonas*, the "Firewatch" epilogue.

III. Fire of Consolation from the Divine Presence

Perhaps the most memorable use of fire imagery in his journals comes when Merton uses it to express the power of God's presence that touches and consumes human experience. This common Biblical use of fire begins in two passages from April 26, 1947 that he did not transfer to *The Sign of Jonas* but which embody his feelings after taking solemn vows a month earlier: "I want to live in the middle of Your Trinity and praise You with the flames of Your own praise. . . . You will consume me in Your own immense love."[32] But this usage of fire imagery disappears for almost a year and a half while he is undergoing the fires of purgation and desire. On October 15, 1948, Merton prays to St. Theresa of Avila to "ask our God to consume us with this passionate love [for the salvation of all persons], and fill the world with rivers of the fire of salvation—*fluvius igneus rapidusque egrediebatur a facie Dei!* [a swift stream of fire issued forth before the face of God! (Daniel 7:10)]."[33]

In 1949, as he tries to write a theological treatise on contemplation in the works of St. John of the Cross, Merton chooses a title— *The Cloud and the Fire*—that expresses his own tension about trying to encounter God and letting God encounter him in contemplation. Later that same year, after his ordination, he emphasizes his experience of further purification, but this time not so much from Cistercian life as from divine Love trying to unite with him. As Merton says in his introduction to Part Five of *The Sign of Jonas*, "a priest . . . is bound to be purified by fire . . . the fire of divine charity, in which his soul must become one with the soul of Jesus

Christ. . . . The fire by which he [the contemplative priest] is purified is the fire of God, in solitude."[34] Merton emphasizes this fire
of divine power over him as priest and prophet in a famous passage in which he speaks of his devotion to the prophets and evan-
gelists: "I know well the burnt faces of the Prophets and the Evan-
gelists, transformed by the white-hot dangerous presence of inspiration, for they looked at God as into a furnace and the Sera-
phim flew down and purified their lips with fire."[35]

This encounter with divine love after his ordination causes
Merton a season within what he calls a "hidden volcano" of anxiety, bad health, and new peace and happiness. On February 12,
1950, after passing through this difficult period, he is able to reflect on his experience as "being sealed" by God: "Our souls are
sealed with fire. Our souls are sealed with Life. Our souls are
sealed with the character of God as the air is full of sunshine."[36] A
month later, he reflects on his growth in relation to that of the people
of Israel, who "were afraid to come too close to God. They wanted
Moses to protect them and stand between them and God, lest God
come down too close to them, and lest His fire consume them."[37]

During 1951, Merton begins his assignment as Master of Scholastics, in which he finally assimilates the solitary and community
dimensions of his vocation. The community is no longer so much
a source of purification as a source of contemplative life for Merton.
He recognizes the touch of Christ in both himself and his brothers:
"our souls momentarily spring to life at the touch of His hidden
finger. This flash of fire is our solitude; but it binds us to our breth-
ren. It is the fire that has quickened the Mystical Body since Pentecost so that every Christian is at the same time a hermit and the
whole Church, and we are all members one of another."[38] He concludes that the active work of writing and teaching (which he
thought would interfere with solitude) "is in fact the only true
path to solitude." He resolves this conflict by answering his own
questions: "What is my new desert? The name of it is *compassion.*"[39] As he concludes the journals, Merton expands these theological reflections to explain three levels of his consciousness: the
level of practical thinking and acting, the second level of ordinary
prayer that he writes about in his spiritual books, and the third
level of pure, wordless contemplation. He describes this third level:
"Here is where love burns with an innocent flame, the clean desire for death . . . everything in order. Emergence and deliver-
ance."[40] As he continues, Merton shifts from fire imagery to water

imagery in which the sign of Jonas becomes central to his explanation of one's final entry into the death and resurrection experience. There he meets God "whose pure flame respects all things."[41]

IV. The Fire of Apocalyptic Transformation: Ultimate Union of Love with God

At this point, the journal concludes, and Merton adds an epilogue entitled, significantly, "The Fire Watch." This section becomes a meditative review of his life as a contemplative in the form of a walk through the entire monastery during his duty as night watchman looking for signs of fire. The danger of fire in the monastery had long coincided within Merton's imagination with the apocalyptic fires of a nuclear bomb that might trigger the end of the world. As he wrote on October 10, 1948, as his purification fire began to change to fires of desire for contemplation: "Sooner or later the world must burn, and all things in it . . . . Sooner or later it will all be consumed by fire and nobody will be left—for by that time the last man in the universe will have discovered the bomb capable of destroying the universe . . ."[42] The power of apocalyptic fire becomes important for more personal reasons during Merton's final meditation in his Epilogue, "The Firewatch, July 4, 1952." In this long review of his monastic journey, as Ross Labrie has recently shown, Merton finds himself confronting God's unanswerable question in the darkness and depths of himself and the monastery, a question that cannot be formulated or answered in words. As I would suggest, the question is primarily whether Merton will let God be God. During his meditative walk through the Abbey of Gethsemani, Merton tries to express what he has learned about answering this question during his years of fiery purification, desire, and union. First, he affirms that the answer to the question is beyond words or writing, and in fact beyond all created things.[43] Second, he tells us that the answer is a sort of renunciation of all questions and conceptual thinking, but must still be dealt with in the depths of his being through contemplation and silence: "Silence shall be my answer."[44] Third, he has come to see that this question/answer process itself is a form of "death" and apocalyptic fire that helps Merton transform all things in his monastic life into their final stage in preparation for ultimate union with God. As he concludes his walk, he finds the apocalyptic Eternity of God to be in the monastery at the present moment: "Eternity is in the present. Eternity is in the palm of the hand. *Eternity is a seed of fire*, whose sudden roots break barriers that keep my heart from being an abyss."[45] In this image of a "seed of fire," Merton suggests that God's presence in his life and this world is transforming his possessive love of creatures (including his own monastic life) into a love of God in itself and in all creatures. Just as Job's "answer" was God himself (234-36), so Merton's "answer" to the inexpressible question is God himself, transforming him into the purity of loving communion. In Merton's own words expressing what can only be suggested as being beyond words: "You, Who sleep in my breast, are not met with words, but in the emergence of life within life and of wisdom within wisdom. You are found in communion: Thou in me and I in Thee and Thou in them and they in me."[46] Thus, through the "seed of fire," he has finally reached an apocalyptic sense of time, eternity, and place, which he unites in a final Biblical image of fire and now associates with Gethsemani itself

This is the land where you have given me roots in eternity, O God of heaven and earth. This is the burning promised land, the house of God, the gate of heaven, the place of peace, the place of silence, the place of wrestling with the angel.[47]

Conclusion: Transformation Through the Baptism of Fire, Water, and Spirit

This study of the frequent use of fire imagery in approximately one hundred passages in *The Sign of Jonas* and *Entering the Silence* could well be supplemented by a study of similar fire imagery in the poetry of Merton published in the same period. In *Figures for an Apocalypse* (1947) and *The Tears of the Blind Lions* (1949), Merton uses most of the same fire images in poetry to dramatize the purgative, illuminative/connotative, and unitive stages of the spiritual journey leading toward the apocalyptic transformation.[48] In addition, many of these images derive from or are related to similar images of fire in the Bible.[49] Among these latter, fire imagery can signify a variety of conflicting powers of God—to inspire, to foreshadow judgment, to purify, to symbolize the ultimate, and so forth. This ambiguous use of inspirational, prophetic, purificatory, or apocalyptic fires within the Bible only makes Merton's use of fire imagery more complex in this journal. Finally is the Biblical image of the Holy Spirit coming in tongues of fire as well as through the waters of baptism.

What is more significant, however, for a study of Merton's use of image patterns in this journal is his fusion of water, fire, and place imagery at the beginning and ending of *The Sign of Jonas*. As we have noted, he begins the journal by saying that the sign of Jonas in the belly of the whale is "burned into the roots of [his] being" by means of the water of baptism and by his vow of stability at Gethsemani.[50] This mixing of paradoxical images (water as life-giving and death-dealing; fire as purifying, destroying, and transforming) indicates that Merton is trying to move beyond words toward what can be expressed only dimly through images. It is no surprise, then, that he concludes his journal with another mixed image of the fire of the sun and the water of dew at dawn at the end of "The Fire Watch." These images merge and give way to a traditional symbol of the divine Spirit: "There are drops of dew that show like sapphires in the grass as soon as the great sun appears, and leaves stir behind the hushed flight of an escaping dove."[51]

Notes

1. This paper was delivered in conjunction with Ross Labrie's presentation entitled "The Unanswered Question in Merton's 'Firewatch'" at the 2003 Conference of the International Thomas Merton Society in Vancouver, Canada. Labrie's paper was later published in *Christianity and Literature*, 52 (2003), pp. 557-568.

2. Thomas Merton, *The Sign of Jonas* (New York: Doubleday, 1953), p. 5.

3. *Sign of Jonas*, p. 11.

4. Thomas Merton, *Entering the Silence: Becoming a Monk and Writer* (Journals 2; 1947-52; ed. Jonathan Montaldo; San Francisco: HarperSanFrancisco, 1996), p. 159.

5. *Entering the Silence*, p. 129.

6. *Entering the Silence*, pp. 308, 329, 487.

7. *Sign of Jonas*, pp. 201-202.

8. *Sign of Jonas*, p. 250.

9. *Sign of Jonas*, pp. 324.

10. Victor A. Kramer, "Literary Patterns in *The Sign of Jonas*: Tension between Monk and Man of Letters," in *Toward an Integrated Humanity: Thomas Merton's Journey*, ed. Basil Pennington (Kalamazoo, MI: Cistercian Publications, 1988), p. 8.

11. Merton, *Entering the Silence*, p. 77.

12. *Sign of Jonas*, p. 51; in the original journal he uses the term "cauterizes me," *Entering the Silence*, p. 83.

13. *Entering the Silence*, p. 105; *Sign of Jonas*, p. 62.

14. *Entering the Silence*, p. 120.

15. *Entering the Silence*, p. 190.

16. *Sign of Jonas*, pp. 91-92.

17. *Entering the Silence*, p. 338.

18. *Sign of Jonas*, pp. 207-208.

19. *Sign of Jonas*, p. 269.

20. *Sign of Jonas*, p. 270.

21. *Entering the Silence*, p. 427.

22. *Entering the Silence*, p. 73.

23. *Entering the Silence*, p. 73; this passage is modified and moved to May 14, 1947 in *Sign of Jonas*, p. 47   48.

24. *Entering the Silence, p. 122.*

25. *Sign of Jonas*, p. 121.

26. *Sign of Jonas*, p. 129.

27. *Sign of Jonas*, p. 147.

28. *Sign of Jonas*, p. 191.

29. *Sign of Jonas*, p. 196.

30. *Sign of Jonas*, p. 215-216.

31. *Sign of Jonas*, p. 238.

32. *Entering the Silence*, p. 67.

33. *Entering the Silence*, p. 238; *Sign of Jonas*, p. 130.

34. *Sign of Jonas*, pp. 229-30.

35. *Sign of Jonas*, p. 224.

36. *Entering the Silence*, p. 409; modified without fire imagery in *Sign of Jonas*, pp. 276-77.

37. *Sign of Jonas*, pp. 288-89.

38. *Sign of Jonas*, p. 333.

39. *Sign of Jonas*, p. 334.

40. *Sign of Jonas*, p. 340.

41. *Sign of Jonas*, p. 346.

42. *Sign of Jonas*, p. 122.

43. *Sign of Jonas*, pp. 352-53.

44. *Sign of Jonas*, pp. 354, 358, 361.

45. *Sign of Jonas*, p. 361.

46. *Sign of Jonas*, p. 361-62.

47. *Sign of Jonas*, p. 345

48. The fire and water imagery in Merton's poems from the years he was writing the journal that became *The Sign of Jonas* carries the same range of significance as it does in his journal. In the title poem of *Figures*

for an Apocalypse (1947), the water imagery is subordinated to the purifying and transforming apocalyptic fire imagery, as we note in the opening lines: "Come down, come down Beloved / And make the brazen waters burn beneath Thy feet." The presence of the divine Beloved comes through his eyes, which are "furnaces" that melt the "fireproof rocks" into "diamonds and . . . emeralds," and which make the sea "waters shine like tin / In the alarming light." As the speaker calls the readers to tend their lamps, the cities of Tyre and Sidon "Fall down and drown in foaming seas," a fate similar to that of New York City, "full of sulphur." Meanwhile, "The men on the red horses wait with guns / Along the blue world's burning brim," and the prophet foretells that day: "But when the grey day dawned / What flame flared in the jaws of the avenging mills! / We heard the clash of hell within the gates of the embattled Factory / And thousands died in the teeth of those sarcastic fires." After the apocalyptic destruction of New York, the speaker notes the "quiet fires! . . .after the black night / When flames out of the clouds burned down your cariated teeth." The long meditative poem ends with apocalyptic imagery of the beast who will "brand" survivors so that they are "evermore . . . burned with her disgusting names," and fire shoots from the feet of "impatient horses" and off "those blazing swords." Only in the heavenly city does the destructive fire become in Christ "the new creation's sun." (See Thomas Merton, *The Collected Poems of Thomas Merton* [New York: New Directions, 1977], pp. 135-148.)

In a shorter poem in the same collection, "Two States of Prayer," Merton combines the purgative and transformative power of fire in the contemplative life into a rather awkward stanza:

> Our prayer is like the thousands in the far, forgotten stadiums,
> Building its exultation like a tower of fire,
> Until the marvelous woods spring to their feet
> And raid the skies with their red-headed shout:
> This is the way our hearts take flame
> And burn us down, on pyres of prayer, with too much glory."
> (*Collected Poems*, p. 150).

After extensive use of water imagery in "On the Anniversary of My Baptism" and the two following poems, Merton returns to use fire imagery, this time the prophetic fire he associates with John the Baptist, whom he asks to "kindle in this wilderness / The tracks of those wonderful fires: / Clean us and lead us in the new night . . . / And take us to the secret tents, / The sacred, unimaginable tabernacles / Burning upon the hills of our desire!"(*Collected Poems*, p. 172).

In *The Tears of the Blind Lions*, seventeen poems published in 1949, Merton mixes water and fire imagery throughout the volume. He speaks of Duns Scotus's work on the Trinity as a book that "burns me like a branding iron" (*Collected Poems*, p. 199). He describes his response to John the Baptist as "Cooled in the flame of God's dark fire / Washed in His gladness like a vesture of new flame, / We burn like eagles" (*Collected Poems*, p. 202). In responding to the legend of St. Clement, Merton sees "Words of God blaze like a disaster / In the windows of their prophetic cathedral" but feels their effects on himself: "Your waters shatter the land at my feet with seas forever young" (*Collected Poems*, pp.203-204). On the August feast of St. Clare, he calls to the thunderclouds to "Let five white branches scourge the land with fire" so that "thoughts come bathing back to mind with a new life" (*Collected Poems*, p. 206). During a November on the stormy feast of St. Malachy, he watches as "copper flames fall, tongues of fire fall / The leaves in hundreds fall upon his passing / While night sends down her dreadnought darkness / Upon this spurious Pentecost" (*Collected Poems*, p. 211). In "The Captives—A Psalm," Merton cries out for his most urgent request from his journals and poetry: "May my bones burn and ravens eat my flesh / If I forget thee, contemplation!" (*Collected Poems*, p. 212). He ends this collection with an apocalyptic poem entitled "Senescente Mundo," in which he describes the final days in traditional fire imagery, but then turns to his recent ordination for some of his rare priestly images, before returning to the water imagery with which he names his journal of this period: "Yet in the middle of this murderous season / Great Christ, my fingers touch Thy wheat / And hold Thee hidden in the compass of Thy paper sun ... / I hear a Sovereign talking in my arteries / Reversing, with His Promises, all things / That now go on with fire and thunder ... / Here in my hands I hold that secret Easter ... / Crying like Jonas in the belly of our whale" (*Collected Poems*, p. 222).

49. For brief overviews of the imagery of fire in the Bible, see John McKenzie's *Dictionary of the Bible*, Xavier Leon-Dufour's *Dictionary of Biblical Theology*, or *Eerdmans Dictionary of the Bible*.. These sources list various types of fire in the Hebrew Scriptures: holocaust, purification, divine power (or wrath and jealousy), tribulation and testing, theophanies, judgment, and eschatological transformation. In the New Testament, they find these same Hebrew images but also some new associations of fire with the glory of God, baptism, Pentecost, Christ's desires, etc.

50. *Sign of Jonas*, pp. 20-21.

51. *Sign of Jonas*, p. 352.

Desert Fathers and Asian Masters: Thomas Merton's Outlaw Lineage

Patrick Bludworth

I. The Search for a Teacher

At the end of his life, Thomas Merton was convinced that the key to unlocking the treasures of Christian as well as Asian spiritual traditions was the institution of the guru. Merton recognized great value in the lineage of teacher-student/master-disciple that existed among the early Christian Desert Fathers and continues to exist within various Asian spiritual traditions. He felt that the living presence, from generation to generation, of a specific quality and type of teacher-student relationship was an essential feature in fostering individual spiritual development.

Merton, therefore, saw the need, within the Christian tradition, for a wisdom lineage of spiritual practice, experience, and theoretical and methodological knowledge passed directly from accomplished practitioners to personal disciples. He also recognized that without the existence of such lineage-traditions each generation of sincere seekers was left largely to its own devices in its attempts to discover and experience the goal of enlightenment.

In undergoing training as a monk and priest, Merton went through the formation process at the Trappist Abbey of Gethsemani in which he was taught by the master of novices as well as having various confessors. However, this did not give him the kind of contemplative teaching and experience he sought. From his own long years of struggle toward spiritual growth, Merton came to feel acutely that neither his monastic order nor the Church provided adequate personal guidance and systematic practical training for a would-be saint. The concept of the need for an enlightened teacher as a crucial factor in true contemplative progress is therefore important to an understanding of Merton's mature thought.

As his life unfolded, Merton came to understand the purpose of monastic life and the nature of saintliness very much in terms of the realization, liberation and actualization of the true Self in a state of enlightenment. He viewed the master-disciple relationship as an interpersonal approach to bridging the gap between the sincere but inexperienced seeker and those who have already found or possess more fully this state of enlightened holiness. On the eve of his departure for Asia, Merton told an audience in California,

> The real essence of monasticism is the handing down from master to disciple of an uncommunicable experience. That is to say, an experience that cannot be communicated . . . in words. It can only be communicated on the deepest possible level. And this, it seems to me, with all due respect to everything else that's going on, this to me is the most important thing. This is the only thing in which I am really interested. There is nothing else that seems to me to have the same kind of primary importance.[1]

Merton perceived a crucial advantage in the institution of a lineage of enlightened mentors available to sincere religious and spiritual seekers, not simply for inspirational value but more importantly to serve as adepts knowledgeable about practical methods for accessing the experiential potential of higher stages of spiritual development. He felt that Christianity had at one time upheld the value of such intimate practical mentorship and instruction in spiritual techniques as central to its larger tradition, but had somehow lost this focus, and he believed there was a great advantage to be gained from investigating the various Asian traditions in which the "handing down from master to disciple of an uncommunicable experience" was still a living reality. As he said in Thailand, at the very end of his journey,

> What . . . I think we have to learn from India, is the importance of the guru, the master, the spiritual master. . . . This is something we have lost in our Catholic tradition, and we have to return to it.[2]

The existence of mystical wisdom-practice lineages was an important presence in the life of the early Christian church. With the emergence of Christian monasticism and the Desert Father tradition of Egypt, Syria and Cappadocia in the third and fourth centuries, we find novice hermits seeking out and studying with older experienced hermits. As these novice disciple-hermits matured

spiritually they would in turn become mentors to the next generation of seekers. The younger desert hermit-monks grew toward
saintliness by living closely with, and following the guidance and
instruction of, older hermits who had already realized a more fully
enlightened state of divine union.[3] Merton points out that the
direct person-to-person charismatic transmission of traditional
contemplative methods and teachings aimed at mystical enlightenment goes back through the early generations of Christian
teacher-saints to the original apostles, and thus directly to Jesus,
the divine-human master-teacher and lineage founder.[4] Thus the
heritage of mystical wisdom and practices could be viewed as a
kind of apostolic succession running parallel with, but not dependent upon, the ecclesiastical administrative and sacramental institution of apostolic succession in which generations of diocesan
bishops ordain and supervise priests.

This understanding of a parallel apostolic succession of mystical wisdom-lineages is still present in the Greek and Russian Orthodox and other Eastern Churches. For a number of reasons,
perhaps closely tied to the larger history of social and political
exigencies and crises in Western Europe resulting in the general
loss of intellectual and cultural continuity, this part of the Christian heritage fell into the background in the Western, Latin Church,
even within the monastic communities. By the pre-Vatican II era
of the mid-twentieth century, the concept of a living heritage of
mystical wisdom-practice and teachers of the sort that once thrived
among the early Desert Fathers was all but extinct. As Merton
testified in his Alaskan conferences,

> We used to have in monastic life a sort of guru-disciple rela-
> tionship, something like the idea of a spiritual father in the
> Desert tradition and in the Russian tradition, someone who
> knows intuitively how to bring out what is deepest in a per-
> son and, believe me, . . . that is what we really need—some-
> thing where we don't get a lot of information but a release of
> all that is deepest in us that we would like to have access to.
> We know it is there and yet we can't get to it.[5]

The young Thomas Merton had not yet come to appreciate this
gap between the historical ideal and contemporary reality when
he entered the monastery. Through systematic practice of increasingly profound inward contemplative prayer, which he expected

to learn in the monastery, Merton hoped to achieve mystical union with God, that is, to become whole, to become holy. During the last years of his life, he would emphasize again and again his conviction regarding the supreme importance of this achievement of fully awakened holiness or saintliness in the life of monastics. Speaking in 1968 to a group of nuns gathered for a conference at Gethsemani, Merton made this clear:

> Our religious institutes exist to help form human beings, people who are complete persons. This is our work and our duty, to the human race as well as to God. Our monasteries should be producing people who are fully developed human beings and even saints.[6]

What he discovered not long after settling into life within the cloister, however, was that within his own community there was little if any mature guidance in the kind of effective methods of contemplative prayer in which he was interested, and that this situation prevailed within the monastic orders and the whole of the Western Church at large.

> We may think of ourselves as people who know how to meditate, but the Western Church doesn't really know what meditation is . . . . we have never really gone into it.[7]

The lack of true contemplative education within the monastic life was a continuing source of frustration and disappointment for Merton throughout his many years at Gethsemani. Although he grew quite critical of, and even cynical about, various shortcomings within institutional monasticism and the Western Church in general, this lack of a living heritage of practical assistance and enlightened guidance toward spiritual attainment was the principal issue for him. If life in the Church, particularly in the so-called "contemplative" monastic orders, wasn't a highly expedient, reliable means for developing expert teachers in the higher stages of mystical union, then it was not succeeding in its mission as a school for saints. Merton emphasized this point while addressing a conference of his fellow Catholic contemplatives in Alaska in 1968:

> There is no reason for contemplative monasteries to exist if you are not able, in a contemplative monastery, to develop a different kind of consciousness from that experienced outside.

Not that the outside is bad, but I mean you specialize in a certain kind of awareness. . . . If there is no special advantage in our kind of life, if you don't get any special fruit from it, there is no point to it really. The fact that we just say prayers is not a sufficient justification. I think we have to be deeper people in a certain way. Not just deeper in the sense that we are much wiser than everybody else, but there has to be a deeper experience of life. Our education should lead to that deeper experience.[8]

II. To become a Saint

Before he had joined the Church, Merton expressed a decided interest in Asian as well as Christian mystical traditions. His interest in religion began in earnest during his early twenties while he was a student at Columbia University. While at Columbia, he discovered *The Spirit of Medieval Philosophy* by contemporary French Catholic philosopher Étienne Gilson. Prior to reading Gilson, Merton had found it difficult to embrace the concept of God. Through reading Gilson, Merton came to understand and accept a concept of God as pure Being, and he later claimed that Gilson's work was the first to teach him "a healthy respect for Catholicism."[9]

At around the same time that Merton first read Gilson, Aldous Huxley was enjoying a vogue in intellectual circles, and Merton and a group of his friends at Columbia avidly followed Huxley's developing thought. When Huxley, hitherto a fairly worldly figure associated with the bohemian *literati*, published a work advocating the goal of becoming a saint through the achievement of mystical union, Merton and friends took notice. Huxley's *Ends and Means*,[10] written during the build-up of tensions that erupted into World War II, proposes that it is inner peace achieved through mystical awareness that holds the world together. Huxley believed that if a sufficient percentage of the population came to experience the inner peace of mystical attainment achieved through contemplative practice, many of the world's problems, including the threat of war, could be solved. In *Ends and Means*, the emphasis is on both Asian and Catholic mystical sources. Merton and his Columbia friends were very excited by these ideas, and following Huxley's lead, began to be interested in both Asian and Catholic mysticism. Merton felt that the role which Huxley's book played in his subsequent "conversion" was "quite great."

Merton's interest in both Asian mysticism and Catholicism was further spurred by his pivotal encounter with Dr. M.B. Bramachari, a globe-travelling Hindu monk and scholar of world religions. On Bramachari's enthusiastic recommendation, Merton read the devotional classics of Christian spiritual theology by mystic saints such as Augustine and Thomas à Kempis.[11] The personal example of Dr. Bramachari as a mystic and a monk also helped to inspire Merton to center his life on dedication to the divine goal:

> I became very fond of Bramachari, and he of me. . . . I was trying to feel my way into a settled religious conviction, and into some kind of a life that was centered, as his was, on God.[12]

Another important source for Merton's evolving concept of a life dedicated to saintliness was the French philosopher Jacques Maritain, who Merton had met at a Catholic Book Club. Through Maritain's influence, worldly and sophisticated non-Catholic intellectuals began to view Catholicism as philosophically sound and intellectually provocative. Maritain believed that the major factor responsible for preventing the complete demise of Western civilization during the Dark Ages and for holding it together throughout the Middle Ages, was the influence of the contemplatives in the monastic communities, and he viewed these communities as lighthouses in the darkness and islands of orderliness in a sea of disorder. Along with Huxley, Maritain regarded mystic saints and contemplative communities as crucial energy sources for an enlightened and peace-creating influence in society. For Maritain, as for Huxley, the important thing in life was to be a saint. Merton was very much influenced by Maritain, and became both his student and his friend.

From Gilson, Merton gained a concept of God as pure Being, and through Huxley and Bramachari he came to view life's purpose as a movement toward sainthood and mystical union achieved largely through personal contemplative practice. From Huxley and Bramachari, he learned to value the insights of both Asian and Catholic mystic saints. Maritain reinforced this concept of mystic sainthood and dedication to the contemplative life, albeit with a decidedly Catholic emphasis, and this emphasis was in keeping with Bramachari's advice that Merton read works of the Western spiritual tradition, that is, the Catholic devotional classics. Gilson, Huxley, Bramachari, and Maritain all shared an emphasis on the great value of monasticism as a context for spiritual development. Through this cluster of influences, Merton decided to pursue the goal of mystical enlightenment and sainthood within the Christian monastic tradition.

While completing his studies at Columbia, Merton wrote a master's thesis on William Blake. In his thesis, Merton considered Indian mystical philosophy as an important historical parallel to Blake's vision, and presented Blake's highly individualistic work as a marriage of themes common to classical Indian philosophy and medieval scholasticism. In his preface to this 1939 thesis on Blake, Merton wrote:

> I think that the affinities between Christian thinkers and Oriental mystics are interesting in themselves. To break them up into influences in one direction or another always encourages arbitrary, false, and pigheaded statements, without adding anything at all to our understanding of the way these thinkers and mystics looked at life.[13]

Nonetheless, ten years would pass before his writings would show any evidence of a continuing interest in Asian mysticism and philosophy. In 1949 Merton mentions that he plans to write to a correspondent in India regarding Patanjali's *Yoga Sutras*.[14] Another seven years pass with little further mention of Asian spirituality; then in 1956, Merton's journal records his recent reading of D.T. Suzuki on Zen, and a rich period of interest in both Asian mysticism and the writings of the Desert Fathers ensues.

During this period between his thesis on Blake and his reading of Suzuki, Merton set out on his own monastic path toward mystic sainthood, joining the Trappist community at Gethsemani in 1941. He moved beyond developing an abstract concept of sainthood and embarked on his own process of becoming a saint. At this point, his readings and writings on matters philosophical and spiritual were focused almost exclusively on Catholicism. Archbishop Jean Jadot, described the sequential unfolding of Merton's widening perspective:

> [h]e was a precursor to Vatican II by the way he was opening himself to the other religions. He started first with the very closed Trappist life; he wanted nothing to do with anything but his own faith, and then slowly he opened himself. He

opened...first to non-Catholics and then to non-Christians, and was very much aware of the input and also the influx of the Eastern religions . . . in the United States and even in Europe. All that helped him to see at the beginning that there was something valuable to be found among those people.[15]

Prior to entering monastic life, Merton had developed a somewhat Franciscan approach to the subject of sainthood. He came to feel that certain persons who lived obscure lives of humble means in innocence and purity might very well be anonymous saints. Not surprisingly, his first attempt at entering a monastic order was directed at joining the Franciscans, who refused him, probably because some years earlier he had fathered a child out of wedlock. In the Trappist monastery at Gethsemani, he continued to expand his knowledge of Catholic history and theology. Merton had entered the monastery under the naïve understanding that he was entering a great school for saints. He assumed that the monks regularly engaged in deeply contemplative experience and that through joining this community he would learn a process of attaining deeper and deeper levels of contemplative union. What he found was quite different.

Among his fellow monks at Gethsemani, Merton discovered several that he considered to be saints. Initially, this was both comforting and inspiring, but Merton found that these saintly monks were usually disinclined or unable to express themselves in such a way as to provide others with instruction in achieving saintliness. He was unable to derive any useful guidance from them that could advance him toward his goal. Conversely, Merton discovered that there were a few scholars among the monks, but in general he did not find them to be particularly saintly. For the most part they tended to be academic legalists and formalists focusing on details of church dogma and doctrine, with little or no knowledge of, or interest in, mysticism or the practical aspects of inner spiritual development.

The prayer life at the monastery also proved to be quite different than Merton had imagined. The "contemplative" aspect of Trappist life seemed limited to gatherings in the chapel to sing psalms in Latin and recite traditional prayers. Other than the daily celebration of Mass and the collective singing, the life of Gethsemani monks revolved largely around outdoor farm labor and increasingly around the mechanized indoor factory labor required for the manufacturing of cheese. Merton came to feel that he was not growing in any noticeable way toward increasingly profound spiritual experience, and that no one at the monastery seemed interested, or qualified, to give him help in that direction. He felt that his interest in higher states of mystical development tended to annoy both his fellow monks and his superiors, and that the routine of life in the holy cheese factory was bringing him no closer to his goal. Merton came to realize that he would have to find the way on his own.

This disappointment and frustration with Trappist life eventually led Merton back to the writings of the great saints and mystic teachers. From them he sought a method of prayer and a systematic approach to higher states of mystical union. This was the quest that had originally drawn him toward monastic life. His trajectory had been from the writings of the mystics into the monastery, and now he returned to that original motivating source for guidance.

Merton began to read deeply in mystical Catholic literature and became very interested in mystical theologians such as St. John of the Cross and Meister Eckhart.[16] His investigation ranged across the entire history of Christianity: contemporary theology and living saints, the writers of the Counter-Reformation, medieval mysticism, and the era of the early Desert Fathers. At one point in this process, Merton was particularly attracted to the writings of St. John of the Cross. Part of this saint's special appeal for Merton was the fact that he was one of the few Christian mystical theologians who explicated a detailed account of the highest stages of mystical union and contemplative prayer yet whose orthodoxy remained unquestioned. Merton wrote extensively about the spirituality of this baroque-era mystic and doctor of the Church. A precious relic of St. John was among the few personal possessions he cherished in his hermitage. The saint remained personally significant to Merton as he worked through his own stages of spiritual growth. Nonetheless, Merton came to be publicly so identified with St. John's theology that he grew tired of being pigeonholed in this way. He realized that he need not limit himself to a single approach to sainthood, and that no thinker, even so great a mystical theologian as John of the Cross, represents the vast richness of Catholicism or Christianity, or for that matter, the spiritual traditions of humankind.

Merton then turned to the roots of the Christian monastic tradition and was particularly impressed by the example of the Desert Fathers. Theirs was largely a hermit tradition, and Merton felt that the glaring absence in contemporary monasticism of this crucial aspect of spirituality represented a tragic loss to the Western Christian heritage. In recent centuries the Church had produced plenty of large communal monastic orders, but very few hermits.

Merton felt that the hermit life was necessary to the overall health of the Church. Although he did not consider eremitic solitude to be an absolute prerequisite for the development of saintliness, he did feel that it could be an extremely important factor for many aspirants, including himself. As Merton began increasingly to appreciate the value of solitude as a context for silent contemplative practice, he began to see his own calling as even more specifically that of a hermit than that of a cenobitic monk. For many years he actively sought and was repeatedly refused permission to live as a hermit within the confines of his abbey, nor was he allowed to transfer to a more eremitic monastic order. It is obvious from Merton's writings that while he enjoyed solitude for its own sake, he primarily desired a hermit's life as an expedient means for achieving a profound state of contemplative union, and he viewed the hermit's solitude as the real heart of monastic life, defining the hermit as "the monk par excellence."[17]

For Merton, hermit life did not mean never having any contact with other people; it hadn't meant that for the Desert Fathers, and Merton did not perceive it as meaning that in his own life. For Merton, the hermit life was meant to provide an important benefit for the larger community. Addressing an audience of progressive theologians, academics and other intellectuals at the Center for the Study of Democratic Institutions in Santa Barbara just days before embarking on his journey to Asia in 1968, Merton offered this clear and important attempt to contextualize and justify the hermit life to a contemporary sensibility.

The task of the solitary person and the hermit is to realize within himself, in a very special way, a universal consciousness and to contribute this, to feed this back insofar as he can, into the communal consciousness which is necessarily more involved in localized consciousness, and in such a way that there will be a kind of dialectical development toward a more universal consciousness.[18]

In Merton's view, the hermit life meant freedom from involvement with non-essential ecclesiastical structures and activities. Most of the early Desert Fathers were not priests, and their lifestyle did not depend on church politics or social structure. Their monasticism was chiefly a matter of personal practice and realization of mystical union under the guidance of a qualified and deeply experienced spiritual elder. Merton felt this valuable approach had been overlooked in the more recent history of the Christian Church. Recognizing that it still survived as a living tradition within various Asian spiritual approaches, he felt drawn to learn what he could from these non-Christian sources, viewing this as a possible means to help revive this neglected dimension within the Western Church.

III. The Outlaw Lineage

At about the same time that he was studying the Desert Fathers, Merton began reading works on Zen by D.T. Suzuki. Reading these two schools of mystical literature concurrently, he suddenly saw once again the kinds of parallels that had helped inspire him to join the Church and the monastery in the first place. He was so excited about both the Desert Fathers and his Zen readings that he decided to prepare a volume of translations from the Desert Fathers and sent a copy of it to Dr. Suzuki along with a request that the world-renowned Buddhist scholar write an introduction for the published edition. Suzuki responded favorably, but his response was not suited to the editorial purposes of publication. However, Merton and Suzuki kept up their dialogue through correspondence over the years, and Suzuki eventually invited Merton to visit him in New York. Surprisingly, Merton's abbot, singularly setting aside all his own precedence, gave him permission to accept this invitation. Traveling far from the monastery for the first time in many years Merton enjoyed a wonderful visit with the nonagenarian Suzuki, who joyfully confirmed Merton's intuitions about Zen.

In his pursuit of interfaith dialogue, Merton did not emphasize any need for conversion or change of religious affiliation, but simply wished to avail himself of experiential treasures preserved within the Asian spiritual heritage and to help make them accessible to the Western Catholic Church. At the time of his 1964 meeting with Suzuki, Merton realized that those of a more conservative outlook might question why a Catholic monk would want to meet with someone as seemingly removed from his own religious context and outlook as a Zen master unless it was for the purpose of trying to convert him. Merton, however, saw no reason to necessarily assume that Suzuki was not already a saint, and he readily acknowledged that the great Zen scholar and lay-master had spiritual riches to offer him. Speculating in his journal on the promise of his upcoming meeting with Suzuki, he noted that any conversion process ought to be mutual, helping one another convert "upward" to experience dimensions less clearly brought out already in each other's existing viewpoints:

> [i]f I can meet him on a common ground of spiritual Truth, where we share a real and deep experience of God, and where we know in humility our own deepest selves—and if we can discuss and compare the formulas we use to describe this experience, then I certainly think Christ would be present and glorified in both of us and this would lead to a *conversion of us both*—an elevation, a development, a serious growth in Christ. This conversion "upwards" would be real and fruitful—and a conversion "downwards" (dragging him to a mediocre and exterior acceptance) would be hateful....[19]

Between their initial correspondence and their meeting, Merton had become very interested in the Chinese Taoist sage Chuang Tzu, whose works represent a source for various Zen and Buddhist teachings. When he met with Suzuki, the Zen master concurred with Merton's opinion that Chuang Tzu was in some ways the best of East Asian philosophers. Merton had begun work on his own version of translations from Chuang Tzu, published the following year.[20] The volume created a breakthrough in terms of Merton's literary following, introducing his name and thought to many outside his previous and largely Catholic reading audience, while at the same time serving to announce to both groups the official public beginning of his interest in Asian thought. Merton's dialogues with Prof. Suzuki were published in full four years after they had occurred, when they finally appeared as a major portion of Merton's popular volume *Zen and the Birds of Appetite*.[21]

From the beginning of his interest in spiritual matters, and throughout his many years of struggle with the limitations of monastic life, Merton regularly reminded himself that his ultimate purpose was to be a saint. In this spirit, Merton felt free to embrace a wide variety of sources including a return to his original interest in Asian mysticism. Merton felt acutely the absence of any technical guidance in contemplation from enlightened living teachers within the Church and he was willing to try whatever seemed efficacious in moving him toward becoming whole, becoming holy, even if that meant looking outside his own tradition for such assistance. He began adopting what he could from his readings of the Desert Fathers, Eastern Christianity, and Asian mysticism to help him toward his goal. In his journals of January 1950 he had noted,

> The emphasis on technique, on bodily control, on interior discipline in both Oriental and Orthodox mysticism makes me realize how supremely indifferent we are to techniques. I have never had any method of contemplation. . . . Yet I find I had discovered all by myself many things they talk about and insist on, especially that Hesychian business about attention concentrated in the "heart" and all energies flowing down united there to produce a smooth and effortless absorption that is held in being by God "within our own heart...."[22]

Merton had little or no interest in those aspects of Asian spiritual heritage concerned with religious institutional structure, in-house stylistic politics, theoretical dogmatics, and ceremonial ritual. He was intensely interested, however, in the hermit tradition, the enlightened master-disciple lineage, and any potentially efficacious practices and methodologies leading to mystic union that might be preserved within the semi-independent Asian spiritual traditions. Merton did not feel that any particular religion held a monopoly on sainthood; he acknowledged Hindu saints and Buddhist saints, for instance, as well as Christian saints.

With increasing regularity, Merton's journals began to reflect readings in Yoga, Buddhism, Eastern Christianity, Judaism and Islam. He mentions that he is engaging in Yoga meditation and exercises and in Zen meditation and *koan* practice, all of which he had learned or guessed at only from his readings. He writes of attempting to pass along his growing understanding of Yoga meditation and other Asian spiritual practices to a young fellow Trappist with whom he shared a similar frustration in regard to personal spiritual growth within the monastery. Merton also adopted the central practice of Eastern Christian hesychastic mysticism known as "the Prayer of the Heart" or "the Jesus Prayer" which he recognized as similar to Asian meditative prayer methods. He found these readings in various spiritual traditions very relevant to his personal circumstances and to the general situation in Catholic monastic life and he began corresponding with some of the authors of these works. Merton did not always understand this literature as much as he had hoped, and at times he makes comments that display a Catholic chauvinism or Western insensitivity in regard to one or another of these traditions; yet from the beginning of his exposure to this literature, Merton seems to have recognized a profound value in Asian spiritual traditions. This oddly ambivalent response continued throughout Merton's life.

He did not see this interest as a matter of outwardly "becoming" a Sufi, a Buddhist, or Hindu; rather he sought to take advantage of whatever these traditions might have to offer him as a Christian and a monk. As he noted in his journal,

> It is surprising how much Yoga has in common with St. Bernard—at least in the psychology of mysticism. Self-knowledge is the first step in the ascent. The problem of liberating our deeper energies from base preoccupations which enfeeble and dissipate them....[23]

Merton believed that this commonality of mystical insight among diverse spiritual traditions offered the potential for supplementing Christian spiritual practice, without in any way replacing the unique values at the core of Christian belief. Merton's acquaintance, Papal Nuncio Archbishop Jean Jadot remarked upon this distinction:

> My impression in speaking with him, and reflecting on what he told me, was that he was more convinced that we had something to find in those non-Christian religions on *ways* and *means* rather than on real religious *truths*. If I may make use of an expression: We had more to find from them about *how* to pray than *what* to pray.[24]

Merton was very attracted by the concept of the enlightened person as presented in Chuang Tzu, Suzuki and various other Zen and Taoist sources. The Zen and Taoist model of the saintly or integral person is often expressed in terms of freedom from all boundaries while living immersed in the ultimate dimension. This combination appealed immensely to Merton. He came to view the holiness of the saint as a condition in which, whatever one's outward affiliations and intellectual particularities, one's innermost experience was of freedom from all limitations and integration with divine Reality. Merton recognized that this was also what many of the Christian mystics were saying, if one could understand them correctly. Yet the official attitude of the Christian Church, both historically and in Merton's day, was that one was a saint to the degree that one lived happily—or suffered heroically—within the boundaries prescribed by the Church. An important prerequisite to official (and, of course, posthumous) recognition of candidacy for Catholic sainthood was evidence of overall intellectual and emotional, as well as moral and doctrinal, conformity to the cultural conventions prevailing at a given time and place within the Church. In such a context, sainthood depended to a large degree upon how orthodox and orthopractical one was, whereas from the Taoist and Zen perspectives, the true purpose and goal of orthodoxy and orthopraxy is to produce people who have transcended the boundaries of these and all other outward forms. This transcendence of all boundaries is understood as a process wherein one ultimately becomes both fully individuated and universalized. Merton wryly acknowledged these contrasting standpoints:

> The [Zen] school, with its meditation on the enigmatic and sometimes frankly absurd *koan* riddles, with its resort to violent and unpredictable responses on the part of the master, with its deliberate impieties (one Zen master actually burned a wooden statue of Buddha in order to keep himself warm on a cold winter night), is hardly calculated to inspire confidence in the Christian who is looking for the kind of pious behavior that is traditionally expected in the modern novice or the budding contemplative in a Christian religious order.[25]

From the viewpoints of Taoism and Zen, in spite of whatever wildly idiosyncratic and even seemingly impious behavior may sometimes be in evidence, one is a saint to the degree to which one is truly immersed in, and integrated with, the divine ultimate dimension, such that the saint proves the Church rather than the Church proving or approving the saint. As Merton learned to his joy, this viewpoint is, to a very large extent, both standard and central to most other major classical Asian mystical religious traditions, such as the Yoga, Vedanta and Tantra schools in Hinduism and Buddhism, as well to the somewhat more "Western" schools of Islamic Sufism, Hasidic Judaism, and Hesychastic Eastern Christianity.

One of the great appeals that these traditions, especially Zen and Taoism, held for Merton was that part of their self-identified purpose and value was to transcend their own systems and structures in an experiential realization of the non-dual nature of authentic being:

> The ultimate resolution of the problem of authority, for Zen, is this: "In Zen, true authority is that Self which is itself authority and does not rely on anything.
> . . . True authority is where there is no distinction between that which relies and that which is relied upon."[26]

In our own, as in many an earlier period, this has clearly not been the official attitude of the Catholic Church toward its own systems and structures. Yet Merton would point to historical Christian precedents in support of the Zen-like freedom necessary and inherent to a self-liberating holiness whether of East or West, past or present:

> The least that can be said about some of the Zen masters . . . is that they would hardly meet the norms set up for the canonization of saints by the Church of Rome. . . . But if we take another look, and if we remember some of the stories told of the Christian saints and mystics (the Desert Fathers and the first Franciscans, for example), we will have to admit that they show a spirit of freedom and abandon which is to us less disconcerting only because we have heard the stories so often and they fit into a familiar context. But rather than speculate on the stories that are told about these people, be they Christian mystics or Chinese Zen masters, it is more profitable to examine . . . the ultimate "illumination."[27]

Merton's strong interest in the Desert Fathers was based in part on the fact that they had turned their backs and walked away not only from secular civilization but also from the outward structure of the increasingly decadent Church of the Constantinian empire. They did not view themselves as rejecting the Church itself; on the contrary, they walked into the desert with the quiet realization that they constituted the true remnant and living core of the Church of the apostles and martyrs. The pre-Constantinian Church had been outlawed and persecuted throughout the realm, and the hermit Desert Fathers deliberately resumed a kind of outlaw status as a means of preserving the original spirit and truth of the early Church. Merton would eventually recognize a need to become, in his own way, a similar kind of outlaw and hermit, stepping beyond the boundaries of conventional ideas prevalent within the Church of his day in order to preserve and nurture what he had come to regard as the deeper and fuller spirit of the Church.

For Merton, an immense appeal of Asian religious traditions lay in the fact that they presented an orthodoxy and orthopraxy centered on the concept of a divine ultimate dimension that was beyond all theological constructs, philosophical concepts, and conditioned emotional states, and had preserved a living master-disciple tradition as a means for effectively accessing that dimension. Merton was aware that a very similar mystical understanding and experience of the divine ultimate dimension cropped up again and again in the history of the Christian Church as well. This was not something that had existed only with the Desert Fathers—numerous later Christian saints and mystics also had, by one means or another, arrived at a point where they stepped beyond categories and conditions into a boundless and sanctifying freedom. Many of these individuals had felt no particular need to alter outward conditions and affiliations and often continued to live within the structures designated by their Church, monastic order, or secular society. They lived in a state of inner freedom that they recognized as the true goal and purpose for which both Church and society existed. As Merton explained in his Bangkok address,

> [o]nce [you] penetrate by detachment and purity of heart to the inner secret of the ground of your ordinary experience, you attain to a liberty that nobody can touch, that nobody can affect, that no political change of circumstances can do anything

to. . . . [s]omewhere behind our monasticism, and behind Buddhist monasticism, is the belief that this kind of freedom and transcendence is somehow attainable.[28]

Some Christian mystics did respond to this condition of inner freedom by ceasing to bother with society or Church structure; others were prevented by society or by the Church from making any such choices. Some were condemned, some were canonized. The response of society and/or the Church varied greatly in the cases of individual mystics: Marguerite Porete was burned at the stake and her name all but erased from history; Eckhart was censored, silenced, and ordered to appear in Avignon before the Inquisition. He died before his case was settled, and to date has not been canonized or even officially cleared of all suspicion of heresy. Jan van Ruysbroeck was able to lead a quiet and respectable monastic existence in the forest until a ripe old age, and after his death was beatified. John of the Cross was arrested, imprisoned, tortured, and starved by the "brothers" and "superior" of his own monastic community. He would have undoubtedly died at their hands had he not escaped; yet, he was ultimately canonized. It would seem that for a mystic saint, affiliation with the Christian tradition is very much a matter of taking one's chances.

As an admirer of Eckhart, Ruysbroeck, and St. John of the Cross, Merton was of course aware of the history of the Church's reaction to their mysticism. It is little wonder, therefore, that he found something to admire in Asian spiritual traditions in which mystical realization is an accepted and expected part of religious life, and the saint's state of inner freedom and enlightenment defines the heights of the tradition rather than the tradition defining the saint.

Following his meeting with Suzuki, Merton began to meet with various other Asian seekers and teachers who came to visit him at Gethsemani, but was denied permission by his abbot and other officials of the order when he sought to travel outside the monastery to pursue such interests. This door was suddenly and unexpectedly opened late in Merton's life when—much to everyone's astonishment—his longtime abbot, James Fox, resigned his abbacy and became a hermit living on the grounds of Gethsemani monastery. Flavian Burns, a former student of Merton's from his days as Master of Novices, was elected as the new abbot. As abbot, Burns encouraged Merton to further pursue his studies of Asian spiritual traditions and to look into the potential usefulness of adopting Asian meditative contemplative methods within the Catholic monastic community. Merton was allowed to accept an invitation to travel to Asia and attend conferences there, and was given permission and encouragement to avail himself of opportunities to meet and study with Asian contemplative masters.

During his trip to Asia, Merton was able to meet with various Buddhist masters, including the Dalai Lama, as well as various teachers of Hindu and Sufi traditions. At the time of his death, Merton was strongly considering the feasibility of settling for a while in India or Nepal in order to study intensively with one or more appropriate masters, especially from the Tibetan Vajrayana Buddhist tradition. In this regard, he seems to have had particularly in mind Chatral Rinpoche (Chadral Rimpoche), a married lama (guru) widely-recognized as an expert practitioner and teacher of the ancient Zen-like *Dzogchen* system of meditation and realization still lively at the core of Tibetan Vajrayana practice. A living legend among his peers for his capabilities in subtly transmitting something of the essence of his own comprehensive spiritual realization and understanding, Chadral Rinpoche is also regarded with a certain amount of awe within the Tibetan cultural community because of his unconventional life-style as a freewheeling and sometimes formidable saint-errant much like the ancient *mahasiddhas* ("great perfected yogis"), the revered "outlaw" poet-saints and "crazy-wisdom" masters of early Indian and Tibetan legends. With the encouragement and advice of the Dalai Lama and other advanced lamas, Merton sought out Chadral Rinpoche. Their meeting forms one of the most intimate and stirring episodes in Merton's journal of his Asian pilgrimage.

Although Merton was convinced of many actual and potential benefits to be derived from Asian spiritual traditions, his conversations and private journals record a few reservations and concerns. He realized that these spiritual lineages frequently have historical ties to religious and monastic institutions and social and cultural structures and, therefore, are often replete with in-house politics and intrigue no different from those frequently prevailing in their Western counterparts. This situation extended to aspects of the scene existing around the Dalai Lama, and Merton warned Harold Talbott, his American Catholic friend who was studying at the Dalai Lama's compound, that he should take care not to get caught up in the machinery that is an unfortunate but nonetheless inevitable part of such structures. He advised his friend to adhere to the deeper purpose of deriving inner benefits from the master-disciple relationship and the practice of inward silent meditative techniques. On the eve of his departure for Asia, Merton acknowledged that Western and Eastern traditions alike have these sorts of limitations and extraneous dimensions:

> [y]ou can't base [a monastic] education purely and simply on the rule because a lot of the things in the rule have become irrelevant, a lot of them accidental . . . That is the result of eight hundred years of nonsense. . . . In India, too, there is a lot of this stuff, a mish-mash, but they have preserved much more of the depth. If you go to Asia, a lot of people say you have to break through a lot of superficial stuff in order to get to the real thing, and it isn't easy.[29]

From time to time over the years Merton had experienced periods of concern that his pursuit of Asian practices and methods might be indicative of a loss of faith, that he might be losing his vocation and indeed risking his salvation, moving toward no longer being a Christian. But he ultimately concluded that such concerns were unfounded. Not long before his trip to Asia, during some of the worst periods of his struggles with his longtime abbot, Merton went through a crisis in which he questioned whether there was any advantage to being affiliated with the institutional aspects of the monastery or the Church and any of its theological underpinnings—apart, that is, from the direct, naked, personal experience of a divine dimension, which he never questioned. This crisis was precipitated to a certain degree by his study of Asian spirituality, but even more so by his growing awareness of what he perceived as the moral bankruptcy within the Church. He felt, for instance, that the Papacy's willingness to sell out the Jews to Hitler during World War Two was directly related to the support later given by the Church hierarchy to American military aggression in Vietnam and to various corrupt political power structures around the world. For Merton, this was all of a piece with his personal efforts to rectify the lack of effective and authentically edifying contemplation within the monastery, and his struggles with his abbot and the hierarchy over official censorship of his writings on social, moral, political, racial, and peace issues as well as theological and interfaith subjects:

It all falls into place. Pope Pius XII and the Jews, the Church in South America, the treatment of Negroes in the U.S., the Catholics on the French right in the Algerian affair, the German Catholics under Hitler. All this fits into one big picture and our contemplative recollection is not very impressive when it is seen only as another little piece fitted into the puzzle.[30]

Merton's understanding of Christianity, Catholicism, the priesthood, and the function, purpose and identity of a monk, had all been transformed "upwards" several times since he had first entered the monastery. It had become increasingly internalized, increasingly universalized, less and less institutional, formal, and legalistic. In Merton's mature view, saintliness was not tied to doctrine, dogma, or other sectarian concerns, nor was it necessarily dependent upon the solitude and silence of the hermit's life. Rather, he came to believe that what it all comes down to in the end is that either you have direct experiential access to the divine Reality in some growing, evolving way in your life or you do not, and that the only irreducibly important aspect of a given religious structure or tradition is whether it provides that access and nurtures self-liberation in divine union, that final integration of the human personality which is the holiness of the enlightened saint.

As Merton came increasingly to view true holiness as having little to do with Church structure or monastic routine, so likewise he began more strongly to see the true monk as the marginal person. To be a contemplative was always to be an outlaw because to contemplate successfully is to step *outside* of all laws and structures:

You realize that prayer takes us beyond the law. When you are praying you are, in a certain sense, an outlaw. There is no law between the heart and God.[31]

Society views its main function as activity, and demands that its members self-identify with that activity—family life, profit-making, war, preoccupation with materiality and related concepts and categories. Contemplation requires that one move beyond social and self-imposed identification with such categories and activities and take a stand on the margins, become a witness. Choosing to live the contemplative life is in itself a criticism of structures.

One stands witness to the transcendent value. Merton saw this contemplative stance, taken early in the history of the West by the Desert Fathers, not only as a criticism of secular values, but of ecclesiastical ones, as well.

> The desert life was a life of non-conformity, it was a protest.... When the Church became a respectable establishment, people started going into the desery.... [T]hey simply wanted to get out because they thought that things weren't authentic anymore. They were certainly trying to get away from bishops, although the propaganda never admitted it. . . . Of course, historians play that *down*. The whole picture has really been turned inside out.[32]

For Merton, the contemplative and the saint are the true revolutionaries and, in the spirit of the Desert Fathers, today's contemplatives might also be seen in this special sense as constituting the "authentic church."

> The Church is made up of people who have all different degrees of this kind of awareness of God. . . . [R]eligious should be, whether or not they are saints, people who are striving to keep alive this deepest kind of consciousness in the Church. This is especially so of contemplatives. . . . [They are] recognized instantly by others as somebody who knows, somebody who is tuned in. Here is the Church . . . they have the real "mind of the Church" because they pray and prayer gives them this sense of the realities.[33]

As with the Desert Fathers, Merton felt that an outward official break with all established structures was not necessarily a requirement for continued or renewed personal authenticity and integrity, because the contemplative ultimately transcends categories and structures. The role of the desert hermit, the true monk, the true contemplative, and the true saint is that of the outlaw, the self-liberated sage, the whole person. Once one has grown beyond the conventional institutional and mental categories in an inward way and is living in the divine dimension, then one is living the true meaning of being a Christian, a Hindu, a Taoist, a Buddhist:

The monastic movement is marginal in its denial of the thesis that society has the right answers. . . . The monk has nothing to do with an establishment. But of course as soon as the monk gets into the desert, he discovers a desert establishment, and there is the same problem. You know, in the lifetime of the originators, this problem had already arisen. . . . And it seems to me that, perhaps, what I am doing in this breakthrough to Asia might be a sort of protest in reaction to the present situation within Christian monasticism in this country.[34]

For Merton, the contemplative is the true spiritual revolutionary, the principled outsider, the witness to the Gospel who stands at the margins of conventional secular and ecclesiastical society, often teaching and inspiring others more through the example of his or her life than by verbal preaching.

It is the question of why one becomes a monk, what you become a monk for, and I say this without any qualification: it is an unconditional breaking through the limitations that are imposed by normal society. You become a completely marginal person in order to break through the inevitable artificiality of social life.[35]

By the time he left for Asia, Merton had long since come to feel that being a Catholic hermit-monk and saint-in-training, a decades-long seeker of the divine gift of universal or cosmic unity underlying all duality, made him an honorary Buddhist, Hindu, Jew, Taoist, and Sufi.

You have to experience duality for a long time until you see it's not there. In this respect I am a Hindu. . . . Any moment you can break through to the underlying unity which is God's gift in Christ. . . . Openness is all.[36]

One might think that a person as positively interested in the value of other religious traditions, and as critical of his own tradition as Merton had come to be, might view Asian spirituality as an escape from the strictures of Catholic monasticism. But Merton felt that his own increasingly universal perspective allowed him to be more fully and truly what he already was. Not only did he see no problem with reaching out to embrace, internalize, and integrate teachings, practical disciplines, and methodologies drawn from these other traditions, but he viewed this approach as a move toward fulfillment of his role as a Christian and a Catholic monk and priest.

> I believe that by openness to Buddhism, to Hinduism, and to these great Asian traditions, we stand a wonderful chance of learning more about the potentiality of our own traditions, because they have gone, from the natural point of view, so much deeper into this than we have. The combination of the natural techniques and the graces and the other things that have been manifested in Asia and the Christian liberty of the gospel should bring us all at last to that full and transcendent liberty which is beyond mere cultural differences and mere externals— and mere this or that.[37]

Merton believed strongly that Catholicism would fulfill its role as a genuinely efficacious vehicle for realizing spiritual enlightenment only if it reached beyond its own current limitations to become cross-fertilized by these riches held in trust by other traditions. He felt that his own pursuit of this project was undertaken as a faithful self-identifying Catholic, a Catholic who, in order to live honestly within the Church, the community, and contemporary culture, had been forced to live in some sense as both a stranger and an outlaw. His interest in learning from other traditions was not limited to his own personal spiritual development; beyond this, he sought to bring about a wider integration of these complementary approaches and practices as part of a renewal of Catholic monasticism and Christian spiritual living:

> I need not add that I think we have now reached a stage of (long-overdue) religious maturity at which it may be possible for someone to remain perfectly faithful to a Christian and Western monastic commitment, and yet to learn in depth from, say, a Buddhist or Hindu discipline and experience. I believe that some of us need to do this in order to improve the quality of our own monastic life and even to help in the task of monastic renewal which has been undertaken within the Western Church.[38]

While observing sculptures of the Buddha at an ancient pilgrimage site at Polonnaruwa on the island of Ceylon (Sri Lanka), Merton experienced what he seems to have regarded as the most profound mystical episode of his life, signifying in many ways the culmination of his long search. Standing at the feet of monumental images carved from the rock-face at Polonnaruwa, Merton perceived beyond all categories to the wholeness of reality itself.

> Looking at these figures I was suddenly, almost forcibly, jerked clean out of the habitual, half-tied vision of things, and an inner clearness, clarity, as if exploding from the rocks themselves, became evident and obvious. . . . The thing about all this is that there is no puzzle, no problem, and really no "mystery." All problems are resolved and everything is clear, simply because what matters is clear. The rock, all matter, all life, is charged with dharmakaya...everything is emptiness and everything is compassion. I don't know when in my life I have ever had such a sense of beauty and spiritual validity running together in one aesthetic illumination. Surely, with . . . Polonnaruwa my Asian pilgrimage has come clear and purified itself. I mean, I know and have seen what I was obscurely looking for. I don't know what else remains but I have now seen and have pierced through the surface and have got beyond the shadow and the disguise.[39]

Merton's path to sainthood through becoming and being more fully his true self had taken him beyond boundaries, categories, and problems into unity with divine wholeness, the original unity, and he had come full circle at last. Speaking in those last days in Asia to an audience of Christian, Hindu, Buddhist, and other delegates gathered to exchange thoughts on the future of monasticism, he offered his fully-ripened perspective:

> [t]he deepest level of communication is not communication, but communion. It is wordless. It is beyond words, and it is beyond speech, and it is beyond concept. Not that we discover a new unity. We discover an older unity. My dear brothers, we are already one. But we imagine that we are not. And what we have to recover is our original unity. What we have to be is what we are.[40]

This liberating unity, which he encountered so personally and directly at Polonnaruwa, was in Merton's view, the true goal of both Christian and Buddhist monasticism:

> [The Buddhist monk] is simply opening himself in this interdependence, this mutual interdependence, in which they all recognize that they all are immersed in illusion together, but that the illusion is also an empirical reality that has to be fully accepted, and that in this illusion, which is nevertheless empirically real, nirvana is present and it is all there, if you but see it. I think . . . that this kind of view of reality is essentially very close to the Christian monastic view of reality. It is the view that if you once penetrate by detachment and purity of heart to the inner secret of the ground of your ordinary experience, you attain to a liberty that nobody can touch, that nobody can affect, that no political change of circumstances can do anything to. . . .[41]

In Merton's view, the contemplative monk stands at the margins of society as an outlaw and iconoclast, penetrating the ordinary, going beneath the illusion and discovering the real. His liberation is not a selfish act, for the monk-outlaw distances himself from ordinary engagement in the world, the better to free himself and thereby help his fellow humans to freedom:

> The monk belongs to the world, but the world belongs to him insofar as he has dedicated himself totally to liberation from it in order to liberate it. You can't just immerse yourself in the world and get carried away with it. That is no salvation.[42]

After his epiphany at the Sri Lankan shrine, Merton at first considered that perhaps now he could simply return home, having fulfilled his spiritual quest. He concluded, however, that for the sake of the Christian monastic tradition it was more important than ever that he continue with his plans to study with Asian spiritual masters so as to be able to help make their teachings and techniques available to others in the West. His continuing commitment to this mission was one of the things he spoke of on the day he died, emphasizing the need for a tradition of spiritual masters who can guide others toward freedom and divine union.

[S]omewhere behind our monasticism, and behind Buddhist monasticism, is the belief that this kind of freedom and transcendence is somehow attainable. The essential thing for this, in the Buddhist tradition, is the formation of spiritual masters who can bring it out in the hearts of people who are as yet unformed. Wherever you have somebody capable of giving some kind of direction and instruction to a small group attempting to do this thing, attempting to love and serve God and reach union with him, you are bound to have some kind of monasticism. This kind of monasticism cannot be extinguished. It is imperishable.... I, as a monk—and, I think, you as monks—can agree that we believe this to be the deepest and most essential thing in our lives, and because we believe this, we have given ourselves to the kind of life we have adopted. I believe that our renewal consists precisely in deepening this understanding and this grasp of that which is most real.[43]

Notes

1. Thomas Merton, *Thomas Merton; Preview of the Asian Journey*, ed. Walter Capps (New York: Crossroads, 1991), pp. 34-35.

2. Paul Wilkes, ed., *Merton By Those Who Knew Him Best* (San Francisco: Harper & Row, 1984), p. 156.

3. Thomas Merton, *The Springs of Contemplation: A Retreat at the Abbey of Gethsemani*, ed. Jane Marie Richardson (New York: Farrar Straus Giroux, 1992), pp. 193-94.

4. Thomas Merton, *Thomas Merton in Alaska: Prelude to The Asian Journal; The Alaskan Conferences, Journals and Letters* (New York: New Directions, 1988), pp.120-24.

5. Merton, *Thomas Merton in Alaska*, p. 122.

6. Merton, *The Springs of Contemplation*, p.12.

7. Merton, *Thomas Merton in Alaska*, p. 81.

8. Merton, *Thomas Merton in Alaska*, pp. 126-127.

9. Thomas Merton, *Run to the Mountain* (Journals 1; 1939-41; ed. Patrick Hart; San Francisco: HarperSanFrancisco, 1996), p. 455.

10. See Aldous Huxley, *Ends and Means: An Enquiry into the Nature of Ideals and into the Methods Employed for Their Realization* (London: Chatto & Windus, 1937).

11. Thomas Merton, *The Seven Storey Mountain* (New York: Harcourt, Brace, 1948), p.198.

12. Thomas Merton, *The Seven Storey Mountain*, p. 195.

13. Thomas Merton, *The Literary Essays of Thomas Merton* (ed. Br. Patrick Hart; New York: New Directions, 1985), p. 391.

14. Thomas Merton, *Entering the Silence: Becoming a Monk and Writer* (Journals 2;1941-1952; ed. Jonathan Montaldo; New York: HarperSanFrancisco, 1995), p. 373.

15. Archbishop Jean Jadot quoted in Wilkes, p.156

16. See Anne E. Carr, *A Search for Wisdom and Spirit: Thomas Merton's Theology of the Self* (Notre Dame, IN: University of Notre Dame Press, 1988), p. 96.

17. Thomas Merton, *Contemplation in a World of Action* (Garden City, NY: Doubleday, 1971), p. 296.

18. Merton, in Capps, p. 69.

19. Thomas Merton, *A Search for Solitude* (Journals 3; 1952-60; ed. Lawrence S. Cunningham; San Francisco: HarperSanFrancisco, 1997), p. 273.

20. See Thomas Merton, *The Way of Chuang Tzu* (New York: New Directions, 1965).

21. See Thomas Merton, *Zen and the Birds of Appetite* (New York: New Directions, 1968), pp. 99-138.

22. Thomas Merton, *Entering the Silence* (Journals 2; 1942-52; ed. Jonathan Montaldo; San Francisco: HarpersSanFrancisco, 1997), p. 402.

23. Thomas Merton, *Entering the Silence*, p. 402.

24. Jadot, in Wilkes, p.156.

25. Thomas Merton, *Mystics & Zen Masters* (New York: Farrar, Straus and Giroux, 1967), p. 37-38.

26. Merton, *Mystics and Zen* Masters, p.283. Merton is quoting in this passage from Prof. Shin'ichi Hisamatsu.

27. Merton, *Mystics and Zen Masters*, p. 38.

28. Thomas Merton, *The Asian Journal of Thomas Merton*, ed. Naomi Burton, Patrick Hart, James Laughlin, and Amiya Chakravarty (New York: New Directions, 1973), p. 342.

29. Merton, *Thomas Merton in Alaska*, pp.124-125.

30. Thomas Merton, *Dancing in the Waters of Life* (Journals 5; 1963-65; ed. Robert Daggy; San Francisco: HarperSanFrancisco, 1997), p. 84.

31. Merton, *Thomas Merton in Alaska*, p. 118.

32. Merton, *Springs of Contemplation*, pp. 137-138.

33. Merton, *Thomas Merton in Alaska*, pp. 140-141.

34. Merton, in Capps, pp. 48-49.

35. Merton, in Capps, pp. 42.

36. Thomas Merton, quoted in William H. Shannon, *Thomas Merton's Dark Path: The Inner Experience of a Contemplative* (New York: Farrar Straus Giroux, 1981), p. 224.

37. Merton, *The Asian Journal*, p. 243.

38. Merton, *The Asian Journal*, p. 313.

39. Merton, *The Asian Journal*, p. 233, pp. 235-236.
40. Merton, *The Asian Journal*, p. 308.
41. Merton, *The Asian Journal*, p. 342.
42. Merton, *The Asian Journal*, p. 341.
43. Merton, *The Asian Journal*, pp. 342-343.

Madhyamika and *Dharmakaya*: Some Notes on Thomas Merton's Epiphany at Polonnaruwa*

Joseph Quinn Raab

Introduction

The narrative of Thomas Merton's *The Asian Journal*, if one can seize upon its golden thread, begins with excited anticipation of a great discovery and culminates with the Polonnaruwa experience that confirms and consoles the pilgrim and the reader with the fulfillment of Merton's intense longing just days before his death in Bangkok on December 10, 1968. For many of his Christian readers the Buddhist language Merton employs in his December 4th entry, recounting his experience of December 1st, is both intriguing and challenging for the same reason. It is the writing of a Catholic monk whose account of his intense spiritual vision is shot through with Sanskrit terms and without one explicit comparison or even allusion to a Christian frame of reference. In order to appreciate the extent of his "passing over"[1] into Buddhism I want to consider the Sanskrit terms Merton employed in his journal entry. In accord with Merton's own affinity for integrating seemingly disparate traditions, I would like to consider how this very significant experience can be understood within the context of the larger narrative of his Catholic life.

From the very outset of the *Asian Journal*, Merton prepares himself and his reader for the experience that surprises him in front of the stone Buddhas in Polonnaruwa, Sri Lanka just days before his death. The experience surprised him because he was not especially expecting a great realization on that particular day in that particular place, but still he was anticipating such a break-through in an indeterminate way when he left on his Asian pil-grimage months earlier hoping to "settle the great affair" and to discover "the great compassion, the *mahakaruna*."[2] Indeed, a couple of weeks before he approached those Buddhas in Gal Vihara

* This paper was originally delivered as part of a round-table plenary session entitled *Merton and the East* at the ITMS conference in Vancouver, Canada, June 5-7 2003. The topic of discussion was Thomas Merton's experience at Polonnaruwa. Bonnie Thurston presided over the panel that in-cluded Joseph Q. Raab (Monterey, California), Lucien Miller (Amherst, Massachusetts), and Roger Corless (Benicia, California).

with his shoes off, Merton was discussing *dzogchen* and *dharmakaya* with Chatral Rimpoche and confessing that he had not yet attained to perfect emptiness, but that he was hoping to go out and get lost in a great realization.[3]

On December 1st, as he toured among the artifacts in the park in Polonnaruwa, Merton had a great and powerful realization. A few days later he recreated the scene and the experience in a detailed journal entry. In his account he characterized the monumental bodies of the Buddha figures as "questioning nothing, knowing everything, rejecting nothing" and being filled with "the peace . . . of Madhyamika . . . that has seen through every question." Yet he warned us that, "[f]or the doctrinaire, the mind that needs well-established positions, such peace, such silence, can be frightening." Then he recalled the inner event of being "jerked clean out of the habitual, half-tied vision of things"[4] when everything became clear and evident and obvious. In an instant he had moved to a total affirmation. And his affirmation was this: "all matter, all life is charged with dharmakaya, . . . everything is emptiness and everything is compassion."[5]

It is possible when reading Merton's journal to appreciate the impact and the importance he assigned to this experience without having any clue what he meant by the Buddhist terms he employed. But, since the language Merton used was thoroughly Buddhist, it is the language I want to consider, especially the terms *Madhyamika* and *Dharmakaya*.

Madhyamika

At one level, *Madhyamika* or "the middle way" is simply another name for Buddhism. It suggests the Buddha's realization of *moksha*, or liberation, by navigating through the dialectical extremes of a self-indulgent adolescence and a self-destructive asceticism that characterized his early adulthood. It also names the method for advancing one's liberation as spelled out in the eight-fold path. But the term is richly over-determined; it also refers to a level of systematic reflection developed within the *Mahayana*[6] traditions.

Merton's understanding of *Madhyamika* is largely informed by his reading of T.R.V. Murti's *The Central Philosophy of Buddhism: A Study of Madhyamika System*.[7] This is one of the many texts Merton carted around with him on his journeys from Calcutta, to Darjeeling, to Sri Lanka, and then further east to Bangkok; his journal is generously peppered with quotations from Murti.[8] In this immensely rich work, Murti presents *Madhyamika*, the doctrine of the middle path systematized by Nagarjuna in the 2nd or 3rd century C.E., as a denial of both a monistic reading of the Vedanta and a nihilistic reading of Buddhism. For the Mahayana, Nagarjuna's clarification of *Madhyamika* is a recovery of Buddha's original teaching that had been misunderstood by the Theravadins. For Murti, and consequently for Merton, *Madhyamika* offers a critique of any and all philosophical positions and aims at a spiritual purification of the mind "freeing it from the cobwebs and clogs of dogmatism."[9] No doubt Merton's own approach to Zen resonated with Murti's practical and functional appraisal of Madhyamika. In a letter to Rosemary Radford Ruether dated February 14, 1967 Merton commented, "About Zen: not abstract at all the way I see it. I use it for idol cracking . . . get the dust out quicker than anything I know . . . not piling up the mental junk."[10]

According to a story from the Mahayana tradition, just before the Buddha passed away he said to his *bhikkhus*, "anyone who says I have passed into nirvana cannot be my disciple; anyone who says I have not passed into nirvana cannot be my disciple." This little dictum serves as a nice illustration of *Madhyamika*. *Madhyamika* means "the middle way"; here it is the path between these two statements. What position lies between? Silence or laughter is a better response than offering an explanatory exposition, since humor is a proper fruit of humility; still, Murti's entire book attempts to elucidate just what this middle path is all about, and what is meant by the Buddha's silence.

Methodologically, *Madhyamika* is an approach to any philosophical or ideological position that would disclose the emptiness, impermanence or contingency of the particular view through the dialectical process. The process undermines and exposes the hidden, tacit, or overlooked limitations of any philosophical position. It is avowedly deconstructionist since it offers a negation of any formula; but it is not nihilistic nor agnostic because a commitment to truth still obtains and an ultimate affirmation of life establishes the context within which the deconstruction is carried out. *Madhyamika* espouses the "both/and" and "neither/nor" view always between contraries purporting absolutist positions. *Madhyamika*, then, transcends the "dualistic grasping" inherent in *avidya* (ignorance).[11] Some of Merton's own notations on Murti's text help us to consider what he was gleaning from it, or at least what he found complementary to his own way of thinking. Merton commented:

> Madhyamika does not oppose one thesis with another. It seeks the flaw both in thesis and in antithesis. It investigates the beginningless illusion that holds "views" to be true in so far as they appeal to us and when they appeal to us we argue that they are not "views" but absolute truth. All views are rejected for this reason. " . . . Criticism is Sunyata—the utter negation of thought as revelatory of the real." . . .The empirical, liberated from conventional thought forms is identical with the absolute.[12]

And a couple of pages later Merton wrote, "The purpose of *Madhyamika* is not to convince, but to explode the argument itself. Is this sadism? No, it is compassion! It exorcises the devil of dogmatism."[13]

The insight that engenders *Madhyamika* grasps that our ordinary language (or unenlightened mind) is falsely dichotomous because it implicitly accepts the subject/object division as foundational, primary and basic. When one grasps the unity that precedes, transcends, and conditions the subject-object division that emerges in consciousness, one discovers a new freedom. When the opposition comes together (or dissolves) in a penetrating insight, it often finds expression in the mystical paradox, the *coincidentia oppositorum*; the *todo y nada* of St. John of the Cross; Suzuki's "zero equals infinity, infinity equals zero" or even Eckhart's prayer to God to be free from God. *Madhyamika* denies the final validity of all other positions in order to affirm the illimitability of *rigpa*,[14] the emptiness of mind that gives rise to each limited view. There is an affirmation of transcendence that is essentially performed by *Madhyamika* but not explicitly declared and, thus, translated into a philosophical position. The denying of any particular claim to fully determine the nature of reality amounts to an implicit affirmation of reality as transcendent of any one view. And the affirming of transcendence is simultaneously an affirmation of nature and immanence, because *Madhyamika* refuses to set one up against another. It is both a refusal to reduce reality to monism (a single view) and a refusal to fracture reality into a pluralism of many unrelated, mutually exclusive, or irreconcilable views. In his recollection, Merton sees the peace of *Madhyamika* exploding from the rocks. Merton expresses the realization with the final affirmation, "all life is charged with dharmakaya, . . . everything is emptiness and everything is compassion."

Dharmakaya

Dharmakaya translates as "the body of truth" or more directly, "truth body" and it can be used in numerous ways. Again, we can cull through the many books Merton was toting around with him to find out whence his conception of *dharmakaya* was forming. An important influence seems to have been Evans-Wentz's translations entitled *Tibetan Yoga and Secret Doctrines*;[15] there the term is used in its traditional relation to the two other bodies of the Buddha. In Mahayana Buddhism, Buddha is said to be realized in three distinct ways, or "bodies." This doctrine is called *trikaya*, and the three bodies are (1) *nirmanakaya*, or a living Boddhisatva, or earthly incarnation of the Buddha, (2) *sambhogakaya*, a bodhisattva inhabiting a celestial sphere, in splendid paradise, who imparts wisdom to pilgrims seeking liberation, and finally (3) *dharmakaya*, or "truth body" which means that the essential nature of Buddha is identical with the non-dual, absolute or ultimate emptiness (*sunyata*). This is the Buddha's first body or, for lack of a better term, his true or essential nature, as well as the essential nature of all beings.[16]

Given this meaning of the term *dharmakaya* it is odd for Merton to say, "everything is charged with" it, since this syntax can reify the *dharmakaya* as a "something" that imbues "something else." It is tempting to attribute this odd phraseology to the fact that Merton relied on Evans-Wentz, whose own translations of Tibetan texts were heavily influenced, and in some cases seriously flawed, by his theosophical world-view.[17] In addition, many of the texts Evans-Wentz undertook in translation were texts explicitly reserved for initiated practitioners, and presumably those initiations and practices established contextual parameters for a kind of orthodoxy. However, I would suggest that the odd construction is due in part to the fact that Merton was not writing this with a scholar's concern for technical accuracy, but he was interested in evoking and recalling a response, and his prose is still successful in this regard. Additionally, Merton himself did not go back and edit this (at which point he may well have assumed a more critical posture and noticed the awkwardness of the rendering). At any rate, *dharmakaya*, for *Madhyamika*, is not a spiritual substance permeating a non-spiritual nature, but is identical with both emptiness and form. The book that Evans-Wentz calls "Book II," Donald S. Lopez, Jr. informs us, is a translation of a text originally written by Padma dkar po (1527-1592) entitled *Notes on Mahamudra* (Phyag chen gyi zin bris). Here the original author explicates four ways of realizing *Mahamudra*, or the Great Seal, or enlightenment. Padma dkar po speaks of two ordinary ways and two extraordinary ways. The latter of the extraordinary ways is called the "uncultivated yoga" whereby without meditation and prior dispositional practices the one to be enlightened suddenly "identifies the natural spontaneity of all phenomena as the truth body (*dharmakaya*) . . ."[18] This provides a fairly sound avenue for understanding Merton's experience at Polonnaruwa from within the Buddhist frame of reference he employed. Merton's own description that "everything is charged with dharmakaya" resembles this identification.

Dzogchen and Sacramental Vision

At Polonnaruwa, Merton had a flash of insight into the essential emptiness of nature, and found the insight led to the *mahakaruna*, the great compassion that arises beyond and within the emptiness, and in fact is not separate from the emptiness. Merton's final affirmation that "everything is emptiness and everything is compassion" is clearly consonant with the language of *dzogchen*.[19] Donald S. Lopez, Jr. describes the *Mahamudra* realization of the Great Seal, analogously akin to the Great Perfection of *Nyingma*, or *dzogchen* as "a state of enlightened awareness in which phenomenal appearance and noumenal emptiness are unified" in a single vision.[20] Again, it is quite easy to see this as correlative with Merton's language concerning his experience at Polonnaruwa. Given the linguistic parameters set by the Sanskrit terms, we still wonder about how Merton, who was always concerned to "unite divided worlds" in himself and "transcend them in Christ," might have understood and integrated his Buddhist experience of the "Great Seal" within his own Catholic faith life.

I propose that the language of *dzogchen* as the "unity of emptiness and compassion" and the unity of "noumenal emptiness and phenomenal appearance" would also remind the Catholic monk of St. Augustine's definition of a sacrament as "the visible form of invisible grace."[21] This correlation would have been natural for Merton to make since he had already, in his dialogue with Suzuki, identified the Buddhist experience of "emptiness" with his Christian experience of "grace," however tentative that identification may have been.[22] In this sense we can understand Merton's experience at Polonnaruwa as a sacramental experience as well as an experience of *dzogchen*.

When we acquire the clear vision of faith, we can see the whole world as a sacrament. St. Ignatius Loyola prayed to "see God in all things." Through the eyes of faith the present moment becomes "the great sacrament."[23] Merton enjoyed this sacramental vision of nature more regularly than most. Indeed, if we were to read Merton's nature poems, which are often also his "Zen-mystical" poems, we find that this vision is expressed in poetry long before he was suddenly overwhelmed with the experience at Polonnaruwa. As an example of this, in Merton's 1957 collection of poetry called *The Strange Islands*, he has a poem titled "In Silence" where he expresses a vision of nature as secretly and silently on fire with the presence of God. This poem can be read not only as a sacramental view of creation but even as a foreshadowing of his experience of the burning stones of Polonnaruwa. Merton wrote:

> Be still
> Listen to the stones of the wall.
> Be silent, they try
> To speak your
>
> Name.
> Listen
> To the living walls.
> Who are you?
> Who
> Are you? Whose
> Silence are you? . . .
>
> . . . The whole
> World is secretly on fire. The stones
> Burn, even the stones
> They burn me. How can a man be still or
> Listen to all things burning? How can he dare

> To sit with them when
> All their silence
> Is on fire?[24]

For Merton, we are, and everything is, the silence on fire with God. Merton taught that "there is 'no such thing' as God because God is neither a 'what' nor a 'thing' but a pure '*Who*'."[25] For Merton, the emptiness and compassion of Polonnaruwa are also in a real sense the emptiness of creation and the compassion of Christ, the emptiness and compassion of the Triune God. Thomas Merton's experience at Polonnaruwa was certainly contextualized in the culture of Buddhism, but it is not discontinuous with his Catholic life story. Indeed, Merton thought that Catholicism and Buddhism were mutually complementary since these traditions were dialogically engaged within him in a kind of mystical dance.

Christianity carries forward and makes present the divine Word of the Transcendent Source, who speaks in and through the apostolic *kerygma* and the *koinonia*. Buddhism fiercely debunks the false conceptions we tend to erect about ourselves, and the world, and even the ultimate source, and reveals the essential emptiness or radical contingency of all individual existents. For Merton, the apophatic or iconoclastic function of Buddhism helped till the soil to receive more deeply the good news of Christ, the Word, who becomes incarnate in time in history and community through a process of self-emptying (*kenosis*), and whose acceptance in the world of "rapacious men" demands the utter humility of self-forgetting. Christ is both the *kenosis* and the Word of God, and through our own self-emptying we are transformed by the Spirit; Christ the Word becomes incarnate in us.

The *karuna* (compassion) that Merton declares in union with *sunyata* (emptiness), was for him not something other than the compassion of the Christ, the one who reveals to him exactly what "compassion" can mean. Apart from the life of Christ, the one who willingly suffers with us and for us, and whose suffering heals us, "compassion" can end up being, as Flannery O'Connor once lamented, "a vague and popular word that sounds good in anyone's mouth . . . which no one can put his finger on in any exact critical sense, so it is always safe for anybody to use."[26] This may be the case for all words. The point is, divorced from its context, the word becomes meaningless. The kenotic hymn of Philippians and the passion of the Christ would, for Thomas

Merton, reveal a profound and personal meaning for the *sunyata* and *karuna* of *dzogchen*. Within Merton there is a complementary interpenetration of contexts, Buddhist and Christian, and his interest in the former always included the faith commitments he had made within the latter. Merton's contemplative Catholicism provided him with a place from which to move into the Buddhist world, a first language with which to correlate meanings within a new linguistic frame of reference. But it was always to Christ that Merton would turn to help him define the essential terms and conditions of his own life. The "both/and" and "neither/nor" positions of *Madhyamika* would only support his faith in the paradoxical Christ who is both truly human and truly divine, neither imprisoned by suffering and death nor exempt from it; who is the begotten, incarnate Word of the Absolute, Eternal and Unbegotten.

Notes

1. John S. Dunne uses this term to speak about a form of the spiritual journey that involves temporarily immersing oneself in, or passing over to, a tradition other than one's own in order to deepen one's understanding and appreciation both of the other tradition and of one's own. See *The Way of All the Earth: Experiments in Truth and Religion* (New York: Macmillan, 1972), pp. ix-xii.

2. Thomas Merton, *The Asian Journal of Thomas Merton*, edited by Naomi Burton, et al. (New York: New Directions, 1973), p. 4.

3. Merton, *The Asian Journal of Thomas Merton*, p. 143.

4. Merton, *The Asian Journal of Thomas Merton*, p. 233.

5. Merton, *The Asian Journal of Thomas Merton*, p. 235.

6. According to Roger Corless, Mahayana emerges as a distinct tradition on the Indian subcontinent in the first century C.E. at least in part as a reform movement liberating the Dharma from dogmatic rigidity. Mahayana contains two theoretical traditions: *Madhyamika* and *Yogachara*. I will attempt to elucidate only the former. See Corless's *The Vision of Buddhism* (St. Paul: Paragon House, 1989), p. 290.

7. T. R. V. Murti, *The Central Philosophy of Buddhism: A Study of Madhyamika System* (London: Allen and Unwin, 2nd edition, 1960).

8. *The Asian Journal* also includes a section for complementary reading (pp. 263-292) that incorporates many helpful and poignant snippets from Murti's text.

9. T.R.V. Murti, p. 146.

10. See *At Home in the World: The Letters of Thomas Merton and Rosemary Radford Ruether*, edited by Mary Tardiff, OP (Maryknoll: Orbis, 1995), p. 24.

11. See *Dzogchen: The Heart Essence of the Great Perfection*, Teachings Given in the West by His Holiness the Dalai Lama, Translated by Geshe Thupten Jinpa and Richard Barron, edited by Patrick Gaffney (Ithaca, New York: Snow Lion, 2000), pp. 185-187.

12. Here Merton was reflecting on the material found in pages 140-143 in Murti's text. See *The Asian Journal*, p. 115.

13. This is Merton's synthesis of the material from 145-146 in Murti's text. See *The Asian Journal*, p. 118.

14. *Rigpa* is the dynamic, creative, emptiness of mind that gives rise to both self and world of objects. It is an instance of *sunyata* (emptiness) and not separate from it. See His Holiness the Dalai Lama's *Dzogchen: The Heart Essence of the Great Perfection*, pp. 47-61.

15. W. Y. Evans-Wentz, *Tibetan Yoga and Secret Doctrines: Seven Books of Wisdom of the Great Path* (London: Oxford University Press, 2000), first edition 1935.

16. In the Glossary of *The Asian Journal*, the definition of *dharmakaya* is taken from Murti's text and reads, "the cosmical body of the Buddha, the essence of all beings", (p. 372).

17. Donald S. Lopez, Jr., in his New Foreword to the most recent edition of W. Y. Evans-Wentz's translations of these seven Tibetan books makes the flaws and limitations of Evans-Wentz's work very clear to newer readers while still lauding Evans-Wentz for a work remarkable for its time.

18. See Evans-Wentz, *Tibetan Yoga and Secret Doctrines*, pp. 148-149.

19. It is important here to recall Merton's conversations with Chatral Rimpoche with whom he spoke for a couple of hours about *dharmakaya*, *dzogchen*, and relations among Buddhist and Christian doctrines (*The Asian Journal*, pp. 142-144). Indeed, it was this conversation that led Merton to describe *dzogchen* as the "unity of sunyata and karuna" which means the "unity of emptiness and compassion" the precise terms Merton uses later to recall his experience of December 1st 1968.

20. See Donald Lopez's Foreword to Evans-Wentz, *Tibetan Yoga and Secret Doctrines*, p. I.

21. This broad but classic definition of sacrament commonly attributed to St. Augustine of Hippo was also taught by St. Thomas Aquinas and affirmed by the Council of Trent (Session XIII, Decree on the Holy Eucharist, Chapter 3). It also reminds the Merton reader of the opening line of his poetic essay *Hagia Sophia*, "There is in all visible things an invisible fecundity, a dimmed light, a meek namelessness, a hidden wholeness." See *The Collected Poems of Thomas Merton* (New York: New Directions, 1977), p. 363.

22. In his Final Remarks on the dialogue with Suzuki published in *Zen and the Birds of Appetite* Merton says that the "divine mercy" is grace, not "as a reified substance given to us by God from without, but grace precisely as emptiness, as freedom, as liberality, as gift" (*Zen and the Birds of Appetite*), pp. 136-137.

23. Jean Pierre De Caussade S.J. (d. 1751) wrote *The Sacrament of the Present Moment* wherein he celebrated this Ignatian ideal of seeing God in all things.

24. For the entire poem see *The Collected Poems of Thomas Merton* (New York: New Directions, 1977), pp. 280-81.

25. Thomas Merton, *New Seeds of Contemplation* (New York: New Directions, 1962), p. 13.

26. Flannery O'Connor, *Mystery and Manners*, edited by Sally and Robert Fitzgerald (New York: Noonday Press, 1969), p. 43.

Merton, Cargo Cults and
The Geography of Lograire

Kenelm Burridge

The following essay is a brief excursus into Merton and cargo cults, especially in relation to *The Geography of Lograire* (hereafter *Lograire)*—although cargo cults are only a part of *Lograire's* sustained concern with the underside of the Euro-Christian expansion and civilizing mission.

Cargo cults or movements combine social, political, religious, economic, and magical elements, and have as their overt objective a plentiful and free supply of Western manufactured goods of all kinds, known as cargo or in the Pidgin *kago*. They have been occurring in the South Pacific since the late nineteenth-century and reached their greatest reported frequency in the years after the Second World War. Since the former Papua, New Guinea and adjacent islands amalgamated and became an independent nation, they have been gradually tapering off into a variety of "spirit" rather than cargo cults. Because the kinds of behaviors and symbolisms in cargo movements reach into native mythologies as well as misunderstandings of European or Western modes of thought and techniques, they were, at first, taken to be and repeatedly described as the bizarre activities of a few mentally deranged participants blossoming into particular kinds of mass hysteria: a reaction which reveals European misconceptions of the whys and wherefores of the movements.

Still, Europeans had some basis for describing the activities as bizarre. Some examples may be cited: the attempted use by nonliterates of scribbled pieces of paper as cheques in local stores and banks; the destruction of crops; acts of promiscuous sexuality which act out mythical first beginnings of society and hence a new or fresh start; the making of supposed radios and the aerials to go with them out of forest woods and vines, which would inform the participants of the imminent arrival of cargo; the return of the ancestors in steamships laden with cargo; marching to and fro in military precision with wooden rifles—imitating the European-run police; decorating their houses with flowers as white folk did and do—and many other expedients, including, as we shall see further, a proposed or hopefully expected resurrection.

Yet what is regarded as bizarre by one culture is not necessarily so for the bearers of another tradition. One is reminded of a television skit which opens with a group of men and women sitting on what must have been, from the lilt of speech, a hillside in Wales awaiting the dawn and, one supposes, some sort of climactic event:

> "Did you bring the sandwiches then, Ba?" asks a well wrapped fellow of his neighbour.
> "Sandwiches?" the neighbour echoes indignantly. "In a few minutes now, we'll be sitting at the Heavenly banquet! Sandwiches indeed!"
> "Oh, yes of course" comes the reply. "But you brought the coffee didn't you? I could do with a coffee right now!"
> "Coffee!? Coffee?!" is the exasperated rejoinder. "We're about to drink ambrosia of the gods!"

And so on . . . a hunger cult perhaps? Hunger for what? Not sandwiches and coffee, surely! A Second Coming—but what then? In any case a peculiar mixture of the transcendent, faith and the mundane appetites of everyday.

So it is with cargo cults. Not simply cargo—though that would be reward enough—but the deeper meanings of having free access to cargo. Just before and after World War II, cargo activities began to be interpreted by Westerners in a variety of sociological frameworks and contexts, all having to do with cultural change, colonialism and consequent politico-economic deprivations, adjustments to modernity, and many variants within these general themes. The labels in the extant literature are legion: accommodative, acculturative, adaptive, adjustive (reconciling tradition with intrusive modernity); crisis, disaster (assuming some prior cultural or natural traumatic cause); nativistic, militant, denunciatory (which evoke rebellious responses to foreign rule); dynamic, dynamistic, vitalization, revitalization (emphasizing cultural renewals); or, to further emphasize undoubted Christian missionary influences, charismatic, prophet, Holy Spirit, salvation.

For reasons which may become more evident later on in this paper, especially the inherent similarity of cargo movements to Christian medieval millenarisms, later enthusiasms, adventist movements and more recent Western cultic activities (Jonesville and the Branch Davidians come to mind) all of which contain themes of what fairly clearly seem to be an ultimate redemption, it is useful to think of cargo cults as local variants within a more universal genre, as movements of a millenarian type rather than as psychological aberrations—though of course they may be that as well. Thus, the behavioral peculiarities are as antinomian as one could wish, and receiving the cargo, a plethora of Western manufactured goods, would stand for some sort of acceptable and desired salvation.

Let me say at once that there is precious little in Merton's "Cargo Theology" or "Cargo Cults of the South Pacific,"[1] with which I would disagree. Where Merton goes to myth dream (a collapsing of mythology and dream life, where dreams both derive from and feed back into mythology) and identity, I go to myth dream, new man, and redemption. Both Merton and I regard what used to be a common response, such as there's nothing spiritual about them or they just want the cargo as insufficient. More pointedly, perhaps, in instances where, for example, crops have been destroyed as a condition of, and act of faith in, the arrival of cargo, and the Colonial administration has felt it incumbent to provide all sorts of cargo foodstuffs to prevent a local famine, the rites might seem to an onlooker or even a participant to have worked. But since the people involved in the activities often continue with their cargo beliefs, the point is surely being missed. The cargo is both the actuality as well as the symbol of what is being sought.

Although my *new man* and Merton's *identity* mean something similar, Merton, having written a book on the new man (*The New Man*, 1961), a highly spiritualized and even mystical new man, would be understandably reluctant to use the term in relation to cargo cults. A further difference is that while—together with many other commentators—Merton is hesitant explicitly to class cargo cults together with historical European cults or movements or more recent Western examples (such as the Jonesville or Branch Davidian cults), his verses on the Ranters in *Lograire* as well as other *obiter dicta* elsewhere, persuade me that he might have liked to do so.

With this brief introduction to cargo movements we may perhaps change the idiom of discourse. Instead of rehearsing the usual contexts of colonialism, political and economic difficulties, social deprivations, and the problems of coming to terms with modernity and industrialization, let us try something different. Let us suppose that three interrelated and intertwined archetypal themes seem to inform not only the work, Lograire, but also cargo cults, and Merton's own life experience: the two brothers, Cain and Abel who occur in cargo mythology as older and younger brother; father and son, proto-typically Abraham and Isaac, the son being a willing sacrifice, but also in a variety of other guises; the two brothers as Noah and son Ham, Ham's son (Canaan) and descendants, and Ham's brothers; and the two friends, as in David and Jonathan, often a variant of the two brothers.

Here, it is well to remind the reader of certain pertinent aspects of Merton's life. Merton had a close relationship with his father and mother until his mother died when Merton was six; then his father abandoned Merton with relatives while he went off on his painting trips. When Merton became an adult he had an illegitimate child whom he did not acknowledge and abandoned. In his youth, Merton bullied his younger brother and prevented him from joining in games Merton and friends were playing. The brother's early death in the Second World War, flying with the Royal Canadian Air Force, affected Merton deeply. In young adulthood, Merton had a *coterie* of friends who discussed world affairs and their own feelings and views but did little that was positive—though he did spend some time working at de Hueck's Friendship House for disadvantaged children in Harlem. Perhaps Merton's best friend *cum surrogate* father was his thesis supervisor at Columbia University, Mark Van Doren.

Cain and Abel are explicit in the South canto with the white captain of a ship (Cain?) chasing a runaway slave (Abel?). Why the Lord favoured Abel's lamb over Cain's gift of farm produce has never been clear to me, nor I suspect, to a keen vegetarian, religious or otherwise. But there it is. Merton's frequent mention of the Lamb, son of God, Jesus, would seem to lead into a resolution of the two tensions (father-son/brothers) in the Eucharist, where the Lamb (flesh and blood) inheres in or becomes bread and wine—agricultural products. In cargo mythology, as between the two brothers, one of whom does something—and this varies from a silly mistake (as may be thought of Ham's happening to sight his father's nakedness) to incest or the whim of a Creator figure (as with Cain and Abel)—which entails black skin and no cargo for, more usually, the elder brother, while, again more usually, the younger brother, a smart fellow, has white skin and lots of cargo.

How may this opposition be reconciled? In traditional terms it is scarcely possible. Furthermore, putting their own spin on Bible stories told by missionaries, particularly Noah and the flood, Ham is not only son—identified by Melanesians as the brother who made a mistake—but as brother, cursed by father, whose descendants, black-skinned like Melanesians, are doomed to inferior status. On the other hand, the descendants of Ham's brothers, with white skin, are favoured and so have access to cargo.

Unlike the situation in Polynesia and most of Micronesia, where the father-son relationship is important, the father-son in Melanesia, where the vast majority of cargo cults occur and have occurred, is not as in Freud or Oedipus. Possible problems in the father-son are offset by the disciplinary supervisions and influence of the mother-brother. In Melanesia, one never hears of "Our fathers . . ." but always the ancestors, who are thought of as male, certainly, but never confused with father. In a sense, one feels, without the father-son paradigm, the tension between brothers seems irreconcilable except, perhaps, in this context, through access to cargo—which itself requires a major reconciliation between those with cargo, white people, and those without cargo, black people—or, perhaps and on the other hand, through The Father, *Bigpela antap* (the Big one, God, on high) as the colloquial Pidgin has it. And if a divine Father/God is perhaps a little out of reach, maybe a more tangible and earthy father figure from a native New Guinean political authority is appropriately accessible.

Next, one might look at the Clapcott case in *Lograire*.[2] First, one has to say that Merton's treatment of this—as are his remarks about MacGregor[3] (onetime administrator of what was then Papua or British New Guinea, not Papua New Guinea) and the anthropologist, Bronislaw Malinowski[4]—is overly onesided, concentrating on the brutal whites and the poor and oppressed villagers. In fact, MacGregor was a remarkably good and humane administrator. And Malinowski, a Polish national who accepted the option of going to the Trobriands rather than being incarcerated in an Australian camp for enemy aliens, probably did more for the understanding of other, particularly nonliterate, cultures than anyone else of his time.

Now consider the Clapcott case. He was a single white male, a planter who probably never saw another of his own kind for months at a time. And yes, he took native women into his bed—something that in those days was considered normal and natural, pulling the white stranger into the local web of kin relationships. Suspicion and even alarm might have resulted had he not been so. Further, the woman was usually well rewarded in cash or kind—cargo. In short, such women, usually local villagers' wives, were conduits of cargo, as it were loaned out to lonely whites in exchange for money or cargo or both. It is quite false to think, as Merton seems to do, that this usage was a kind of white-black oppression, although in today's world, of course, it might be seen as a form of male-female oppression however profitable to the woman it might be. In those days, however, a woman found security in being a wife and having the children who would look after her when the husband died or was killed. For a man a wife was valuable not only for dependable sexual relations and children but because she nurtured the crops in the garden and carried loads of ripened tubers (weighing maybe 200 lbs.) as well as babies from garden to village. In short, a wife was a valuable economic asset to husband and kin. Add access to cargo and it was truly a value-added arrangement.

When the wife of an up-and-coming cargo cult leader, whose access to cargo had been augmented by letting his wife out to Clapcott, died, he was of course much put out. Also, having a slight if confused acquaintance with Christianity, he seems to have thought that if Clapcott were killed—read sacrificed—his wife would be resurrected as white with total access to lots of cargo (which might remind one of a recent Californian death cult in which participants in a mass suicide expected to be resurrected into another kind of life as new and superior beings in a spacecraft supposedly cruising above).

Accordingly, Clapcott was done to death—not, be it noted, by the cargo leader, who might be supposed to be the injured party in an adultery, doing so in response to adultery, as Merton would seem to have it, but by henchmen: something alien to and simply not done in traditional Melanesian culture, where no one would support such a personally injured party unless action was first taken by that party.

It is easy to suppose Clapcott was killed for his adultery, for supposedly taking workers or villager's wives by force. What force, one wonders—a man alone among a potentially hostile people? Here, surely, we have an attempt to even the score. Abel killing Cain or Joseph being left in a well by his brothers for being favored by the father but later becoming reconciled, brothers together and united. However, in this case, there was no escape from the well, no resurrection, no cargo; only an administrative posse of police, somebody squealing or informing, and the arrest of those involved in the homicide. There is no reconciliation. Ham's descendants have been left to their fate. The more faithful of the cargo cultists had to wonder what had gone wrong.

Some further points arise from the Clapcott case. In spite of what has already been said about the father-son dimension in Melanesia, sons may fairly frequently encounter both in dream or waking life, the ghost of the dead father, appearing as a pale white cloud. With or without being asked, the ghost-father might give advice to the son. But this advice could well be malicious or maybe at best choked with ambivalences. Just what to do about such advice the son had to figure out for himself. Nevertheless, it was advice, a gift which, like the responses of the oracle at Delphi, had to be treated with circumspection. Able sons benefited; the incompetent made wrong interpretations.

This aspect of the father-son takes us back to the ancestors, thought of as male, pale or white like mist or clouds, who may also bear gifts. Further, males in Melanesia are or were thought to possess a sort of *nous* (my adaptation from the Greek for the Tangu word *gnek)*, seat of thought or intelligence located in the forehead, which is or was considered immortal. That is why males become ancestors and ancestors are regarded as male. Women, on the other hand, are or were thought not to possess such a *nous* or *gnek*. When a woman died, she was envisioned as becoming a mouse or a rat pottering about in the food storage or kitchen. Thus, while living wives actually can or could be conduits of cargo, the ancestors, dead males, like fathers' ghosts, are, on the other hand, frequently figured as the future suppliers of cargo: they make the cargo somewhere far away and load it into ships. But, on the voyage over, someone changes the labels on the packages so that they are addressed only to white folk. To counter this difficulty, cargo cultists assert, the ancestors themselves are going to take charge of the ships and their cargoes, so ensuring that the cargo goes to their descendants. Further, the ancestors might be persuaded to come sooner rather than later if only they, the living, could figure out correctly what would please them. In the Clapcott case, however, it is a resurrected wife, now with a white skin, who is going to become the source of cargo.

Going a little beyond what has already been said, this may be a small facet of what is in fact a quite massive Christian missionary influence. For it is the womenfolk who first become Christians, who take to Euro-education much more readily than the men, who today crowd the meetings of all kinds of local, regional and even international social organizations....Why? Well, perhaps the fact that Christianity gives women an immortal soul and seems to allow them something like a *nous* or *gnek* may have something to do both with their readiness to accept whites' education and with the dead wife's hoped-for resurrection as white with cargo.

Now to something which, on the face it, seems far removed from cargo cults, but which, in its relevance to the father-son relationship, provides an insight into cargo cults: the relation of Ibn Battuta, the North African Muslim traveller in *Lograire*:

A SLAVE
CUTS OFF HIS OWN HEAD
AFTER A LONG SPEECH
DECLARING HOW MUCH
HE LOVES THE SULTAN.[5]

Now Sultan and slave are as father to son, and the slave or son is figured not so much committing suicide as becoming like Isaac, the willing sacrifice to or for love of the Father or Sultan.

Among the Muslim Malays of Malaysia, on party occasions in the villages—weddings, anniversaries and such—evenings could be spent listening to the recital of stories accompanied by the performance of a shadow play, an acting out of suitable stories by puppets placed against a lighted screen. One of the stories of interest to us here concerns a hero, Hang Tuah, who was, together with a friend, a renownedly faithful servant of their Sultan (father), always available for deeds of derring do. One day, the story goes, the Sultan summons Hang Tuah to an audience. Says the Sultan to Hang Tuah:

"Are you the faithful servant I think you are? The time has come to test your loyalty. I want you to bring me the head of your friend—that will show your loyalty to me above all other loyalties."

Sad at heart, Hang Tuah bows to the Sultan: "Your will be done, Sire..."

So Hang Tuah goes to his friend and tells him what he has to do. The friend, the willing sacrifice, replies: "Very well. You must do as the Sultan asks. Behead me."

Albeit reluctantly, with one swipe of his parang, Hang Tuah beheads his friend and, returning to the Sultan, presents him with the head of his friend.

In the past, when this story was told the audience would accept the climax in a silence proper to the tragedy. But in the weeks leading up to *merdeka* or political independence, the story was greeted with growls of disapproval and, as is the wont of storytellers and puppeteers in relation to their audiences, the ending of the story began to change to accord with the mood of the audience.

"No!" exclaims Hang Tuah when the Sultan tells him what he wants done. "I will not kill my friend!"

The cheers of the audience usually drowned out anything further the storyteller had to say. Son has become independent of father as paternal colonialism wanes.

Much the same sort of evolution has occurred in relation to cargo cults. The number of these cults, as such, outside Melanesia—among Polynesians or Micronesians, for example—are so few as to be negligible. Within Melanesia, a very few have occurred among the Highland peoples: polities among these peoples are reasonably stable, the mother-brother is less emphasized, the father-son has a more dynastic relevance than among the coastal peoples where the vast majority of cults have occurred. Unlike the situation in the Highlands, the peoples of the coastal areas received the direct thrust of colonialism. The area was suitable for plantations of coconuts (for the manufacture of cooking oils and soap), and so the need for labor, indentured or, later, contractual, introduced disease-ravaged populations. Unstable indigenous political systems have been the norm.

Today, however, with political independence, and as with Hang Tuah and independence from paternal colonialism, cargo cults have been falling away. Brothers and friends are finding matters other than cargo to quarrel about and, perhaps, finding some sort of reconciliation of their sibling rivalries in the Fatherhood and stabilities of political independence. But if the politico-economic situation of the past has eased, being succeeded by measures of prosperity, stability, and access to cargo, in Melanesia as elsewhere in a world becoming more and more uniform, industrialized, and bringing its own uncertainties, here and there salvation and spirit movements reveal a spiritual void that some feel a need to fill.

To conclude: one cannot but stand in awe and admiration of Merton's breadth of scholarship and depth of insight. But it surely cannot be said that *Lograire* is among the highlights of his work. Personally I enjoyed the Thonga lament and the piece on Ibn Batuta but found most of the remainder to be rather heavy going: the persistent and then fashionable anti-colonial, anti-missionary stance married to racist white-black tensions tends to grate when driven too hard. In *Lograire*, Merton seems to me to emerge as very much a man of his moment and the transient circumstances of the time.

In his *Author's Note* Merton says that *Lograire* is a "purely tentative draft of a longer work in progress."[6] I do not know what Merton had in mind for that longer work, but I like to think he would have left *Lograire* alone and gone on to other things.

Notes

1. See "Cargo Cults of the South Pacific" in Thomas Merton, *Love and Living* (New York: Farrar, Straus, Giroux, 1979) pp 80-94: "Cargo Theology" is an alternate title for this transcribed lecture that is used in the notes of *The Geography of Lograire* (New York: New Directions, 1969) p. 147
2. "Dialogue with Mister Clapcott" ("East" IX), *Lograire*, pp. 113-116.
3. In "Cargo Songs" ("East" III), *Lograire*, p. 91.
4. In "East with Malinowski" ("East" II), *Lograire*, pp. 89-90; see also pp. 91, 93, 95.
5. Prologue to "East" Canto, *Lograire*, p. 81.
6. *Lograire*, p. 1.

What the Machine Produces and What the Machine Destroys: Thomas Merton on Technology*

Paul R. Dekar

Introduction

To discover *all* the social implications of the Gospel not by studying them but by living them, and to unite myself explicitly with those who foresee and work for a social order—a transformation of the world—according to these principles: primacy of the *person*** — (hence justice, liberty, against slavery, peace, control of technology etc.). Primacy of *wisdom and love* (hence against materialism, hedonism, pragmatism, etc.).[1]

In the 1960s Thomas Merton expressed concern for many social issues, including the need for criteria by which to evaluate and control technology. Merton read books by thoughtful writers anxious about social changes engendered by new technological developments. Merton's growing unease intensified after 1964 when he read a pamphlet entitled *The Triple Revolution* in which thirty-two prominent thinkers drew attention to three revolutions. The first had to do with cybernetics. The second with new forms of weaponry that cannot win wars but can obliterate civilization. The third concerned the universal demand for full human rights.[2]

For Merton, *The Triple Revolution* offered an excellent starting point from which to diagnose and ameliorate a pattern of illness in the United States and elsewhere, namely, distortion of our true humanity. Failure to develop a spirituality by which people might resist negative consequences of technology has since given rise to diverse symptoms of human distress. It is therefore worth returning to the 1964 statement.

Merton's reaction to the pamphlet reflects his wider concern with refusing to surrender to the exalted place of technology in western society. His response to technology thus emerges

---

* This article originated as a paper read at the Eighth General Meeting of the ITMS in Vancouver, 2003. Talks with students, monks and scholars, notably Br. Patrick Hart, have been helpful in its preparation. The Shannon Fellowship facilitated research for it.
** I trust that Merton would use bias-free language were he alive now.

as a useful filter by which to read and understand his thought. Merton's views on technology, delineated especially in his later writings, are the subject of growing scholarly interest.[3] Merton remains a helpful companion as humankind wrestles with the ongoing significance of the triple revolution.

Merton on *The Triple Revolution*

In March 1964 Wilbur H. (Ping) Ferry, Vice President of the Center for the Study of Democratic Institutions in Santa Barbara, California, sent Merton a copy of *The Triple Revolution* of which Ferry was the principal author. Replying to Ferry on March 23, 1964, Merton wrote that the message of *The Triple Revolution* was "urgent and clear and if it does not get the right reactions (it won't) people ought to have their heads examined (they won't). (Even if they did, it would not change anything.)" He added, "We are in for a rough and dizzy ride, and though we have no good motive for hoping for a special and divine protection, that is about all we can look for." Merton expressed concern that so-called Christians were totally invested in a "spiritually and mentally insolvent society."[4]

At the time, *The Triple Revolution* reflected widespread anxiety about technology, computers, human rights, war and the environment. The pamphlet grew into a textbook that went through more than one edition.[5] Signatories included activists such as Todd Gitlin and Tom Hayden of the Students for a Democratic Society, and Bayard Rustin, organizer of the August 28, 1963 March on Washington; economists such as Michael Harrington, author of *The Other America*, Robert Heilbroner, author of *The Great Ascent*, and Robert Theobald, author of *Free Men and Free Markets*; and 1962 Nobel peace laureate Linus Pauling. The authors regarded the three revolutions to be so disruptive in magnitude that society's response to them was proving totally inadequate. The authors addressed their concerns to President Lyndon B. Johnson. On April 6, 1964, Lee C. White, Assistant Special Counsel to the President replied that the President was taking steps to deal with the areas of poverty, unemployment and technological change.

The phrase "cybernation revolution" expressed the combination of the computer and automated self-regulating machines. The pamphlet concentrated on this first revolutionary phenomenon because authors anticipated possible abuses of computer systems in the other two arenas. The authors stated that a new era of production had begun. Its principles of organization were as different from those of the industrial era as those of the industrial era were different from the agricultural. A key challenge was the fact that machines can achieve potentially unlimited production without humans. The signatories anticipated that industry would progressively require less human labor, contribute to the loss of jobs and lead to the reorganization of the economic and social system. The authors also recognized a historic paradox, that a growing proportion of the population subsisted on minimal incomes, often below the poverty line, at a time when sufficient productive capacity was available to supply the needs of everyone.

Conventional economic analysis denied or ignored the existence of this inner contradiction. With others, African Americans had marched in Washington for freedom and jobs, yet many were falling behind. Unemployment was far worse than the figures indicated. The gap between rich and poor was growing. This division of people threatened to create a human slag heap but the authors could not tolerate the development of a separate nation of the poor, unskilled and jobless living within another nation of the well-off, the trained and the employed.

The authors called for a new consensus and for major changes in values and institutions. They also called for policies that anticipated the probable long-term effects of the triple revolution such as the large-scale displacement of workers, inadequate public resources for human services and environmental degradation.

Merton shared the conviction of the authors of *The Triple Revolution* that humanity was at a historic moment. A fundamental reexamination of existing values and radical action was needed. To discuss the spiritual roots of protest in the face of technology, Merton met on retreat with some friends at the cottage that would become Merton's hermitage from November 17-19, 1964. The group included Ferry; a Mennonite theologian John Howard Yoder; A. J. Muste, former Executive Director of a pacifist organization, the Fellowship of Reconciliation (FOR), and John Oliver Nelson, one-time FOR national chairperson. Catholics included Dan Berrigan, Phil Berrigan, John Peter Grady, Jim Forest and Tom Cornell. Merton wanted Martin Luther King, Jr., to attend. On the eve of leaving for Oslo, Norway where he was to receive the 1964 Nobel Peace Prize, King could not participate. However, King was aware of the three revolutions and mentioned them in "Remaining Awake through a Great Revolution."[6]

In his formal comments at the opening of the retreat, Merton began by asking, *Quo Warranto?* By what right do we protest? We protest because we have to: "for within me there is something like a burning fire shut up in my bones; I am weary with holding it in, and I cannot." (Jer 20:9). Merton further asked whether technological society by its very nature is oriented to self-destruction or whether it can, on the contrary, be regarded as a source of hope for a new sacral order, a millennial city in which God will be manifested and praised? At the time, Merton did not believe that technology was either morally, or religiously promising. "Does this call for reaction and protest; if so, what kind? What can we really do about it?"[7]

As a partial response to these questions Merton called for *metanoia*. By this Greek word he did not mean conversion, as translators often mistake. Rather, Merton had in mind total personal transformation. Merton believed that a radical turn was needed to the Gospel of peace, sacrifice and suffering in redemptive nonviolent protest. Other participants responded to *The Triple Revolution*. For example, John Howard Yoder commented that Christians must live the Gospel, pure and simple. Yoder proclaimed the Cross, the unique element that Christianity brings to the mystery of the pursuit of peace and justice in a world ruled by perverse power.

The retreat proved to be "near legendary," "a watershed," a "memorable experience" although it did not shape the specific ways Catholic resistance to the culture of technology would subsequently take. Yet, at some point in their lives, most of its participants would serve time in prison for anti-war protests. Merton would be the exception. Indeed, for Merton, the retreat was a last fling. His superiors were not favorable to his continuing to address social issues. In the sense that he did not join movements or take to the streets, Merton was not an activist. This was not simply a matter of obedience. Merton believed in the need, ethically and evangelically, to define his limits. In a letter dated October 10, 1967, he wrote Dan Berrigan,

> In my opinion the job of the Christian is to try to give an example of sanity, independence, human integrity, good sense, as well as Christian love and wisdom, against all establishments and all mass movements and all current fashions which are merely mindless and hysterical.... The most popular and exciting thing at the moment is not necessarily the best choice.[8]

Merton responded to *The Triple Revolution* in ways other than direct action. He developed an analysis of the three revolutions as separate but linked. The cybernation revolution invalidated the general mechanisms of the political economy that had evolved through the industrial revolution. As machines took over production, they absorbed an increasing proportion of resources while the people who were displaced become dependent on minimal and unrelated government measures such as social security, welfare payments or unemployment insurance. The resulting misery could give way to political chaos and undermine civil liberties.

Merton wrote against new weapons that cannot win wars but can obliterate civilization. He warned that modern war is planned and fought not only by people, but also by "mechanical computers."[9] He anticipated a trend away from the deployment of armed troops in combat and towards the use of powerful weapons of mass destruction that could terrorize and destroy an enemy.

People were feeling the full impact of the weapons revolution in such areas as diminished funding of public services for schools, parks, roads, homes, decent cities and clean air and water. To develop new weapons, to deploy them around the world, and to use them in regional wars entailed real costs. In the phrasing of the day, you could not pay for guns and for butter.

With deep pessimism, Thomas Merton responded to such threats as thought control, formalized mechanization of the economy, preemptive attacks and "unquestioning belief in machines and processes which characterizes the mass mind."[10] Merton expressed concern about the spiritual disruption that would occur if humans come to base our moral or political decisions on computers. Merton saw a very serious danger in which most of our crucial decisions may turn out to be no decisions at all, but only the end product of conjectures and games fed to us by computers. He decried "a depressingly inane magazine article" on "the mechanical output" of thinking machines: "[J]ust wait until they start philosophizing with computers!"[11]

Merton was prescient about the growing reach of technology. In a circular letter written for Lent 1967, he expressed awareness of the effects of the cybernation revolution. Merton decried the way resources are diverted away from helping the needy. He dismissed President Johnson's "war on poverty" as "a sheer insult to the people living in our Eastern Kentucky Mountains." Merton therefore took aim at the "universal myth that technology infallibly makes everything in every way better for everybody. It does not."[12] But Merton acknowledged that technology can be good and that humanity has an absolute obligation to use means at our disposal to help people otherwise living in utter misery and dying like flies. For example, modern drugs like penicillin and other medical advances save lives. Modern agriculture can enhance our ability to feed starving people. In short, Merton recognized that technology has the capacity to make the world better for millions of persons. Yet Merton saw technology being used instead to enrich big corporations, spray Vietnamese with napalm and threaten people with genocide.

Merton anticipated a movement towards a "more and more collectivist, cybernated mass culture."[13] Merton's nightmarish vision included such areas as the arts and religion. In "A Letter to Pablo Antonio Cuadra concerning Giants," Merton addressed the Nicaraguan poet and editor of the newspaper *La Prensa* with his concern about "a Christianity of money, of action, of passive crowds, an electronic Christianity of loudspeakers and parades. Magog [a symbol of the United States] is himself without belief, cynically tolerant of the athletic yet sentimental Christ devised by some of his clients, because this Christ is profitable to Magog."[14]

Twenty years later, the Cistercian M. Basil Pennington mentioned the impact the Lent 1967 letter had on readers. Some felt Merton had been too negative in regard to technology. But Pennington believed that Merton wrote what people needed to hear. Pennington concluded that we still need to hear what Merton wrote at the time.[15] Merton spoke truth to the powers and principalities and envisioned the Spirit of God bringing about a new world in which all might live more humanly.

Defining and Evaluating Technology

In a talk "The Christian in a Technological Age," given to novices at the Abbey of Gethsemani, Merton joked, "What do I know about technology? I get into the steel building and I'm lost."[16] Merton continued by defining technology as the application of scientific research to the invention of new tools to assist people in practical ways.

Merton disavowed any special competency or originality on the subject. He followed the derivation of the word from the Greek *techne* (an art or craft) and *logia* (the systematic treatment of). From this definition, people have traditionally regarded technological advances as an appropriate outcome of our using innate, God-given gifts for the common good.

Merton approached technology as inherently neutral. People can use technology for good or evil outcomes. Discernment makes the difference. The malevolent intent and destructive potential of some technologies require self-limitation. Indeed, for Merton some technologies that were developed could have been stopped and should have been refused.

Merton began very early to write about the moral dilemmas and practical consequences of specific developments in the realm of technology. Already in "Tower of Babel," included in *Early Poems: 1940-42* (1971), he had explored the misuse of language to conceal, distort and shape reality and to manipulate people. The poem anticipated a speech by the Professor in part 1, scene 2 of a longer verse drama of the same title published in *The Strange Islands* (1957):

> Now the function of the word is:
> To designate first the machine,
> Then what the machine produces
> Then what the machine destroys.[17]

To evaluate technology, Merton outlined broad-brush guidelines in the passage already quoted at the start of this article. Subsequently, especially in his journals, letters and poetry, Merton articulated several specific ethical criteria: 1) valuing human personality; 2) promoting the common good; 3) protecting the health (including the psychic health) and well-being of citizens; and 4) exercising skepticism towards so-called experts. He was especially worried about the power and wealth concentrated among those who controlled technological innovation.

Merton saw technology as a fact of modern life and a necessity for modern living. But, as a monk, The *Rule* of Saint Benedict had deeply influenced him. Monks were to respect tools and to honor artisans and craftspeople (see chapters 31, 32, and 57): "St. Benedict never said the monk must *never* go out, *never* receive a letter, *never* have a visitor, *never* talk to anyone, *never* hear any news. He meant that the monk should distinguish what is useless or harmful from what is useful and salutary, and *in all things* glorify God." "St. Benedict's principle is that the Rule should be moderate."[18]

Three Baskets of Concern

What specifically bothered Merton about technology? We may gather Merton's concerns in three baskets. First, he believed that human survival was at risk in part because humanity had overreached itself in such areas as military hardware and environmental pollutants. Second, he cautioned that an uncritical embrace of science and technology distorts our true humanity. He believed that, by regarding scientists and technologists as arbiters of the future, humankind ceases fully to love God, self or neighbor. Finally, Merton thought technology had become for many a *divertissement*, the function of which is to stoke our false self through acquiring money, satisfying our appetite for status or justifying society's, "My country right or wrong" thinking. Merton believed that technology anesthetizes individuals and plunges them in the warm, apathetic stupor of a collectivity. These forces threatened *shalom*, a God-given condition of balance, harmony and integrity.

1. Destructive Developments

Unintended and potentially destructive consequences of modern science and technology constitute the first basket of Merton's concerns regarding technology. Merton understood that he lived in revolutionary times. By the nineteen sixties he recognized a society in profound spiritual crisis manifested throughout the world in desperation, cynicism, violence, conflict, self-contradiction, ambivalence and fear. He decried an obsessive attachment to images, idols, slogans and programs that only dull the general anguish for a moment until it bursts out in more acute and terrifying form.

Merton saw specific manifestations of the times—cybernetics, racism, violation of human rights, war, militarism and the eclipse of nature—as incompatible with the norms of God. He wrote, "Certainly there is great risk for a nation which is still playing cowboys and Indians in its own imagination—but with H-Bombs and Polaris submarines at its disposal!"[19]

Merton believed that the technological revolution had degraded and debauched the human spirit. Humanity has been reduced to the condition of a machine responding automatically to diverse stimuli generated by mass communications and political demagoguery. Peering into the future, he was pessimistic about science and technology uncoupled from faith and the processes of radical renewal and reorientation such as Vatican II exemplified. Society will not produce divine faith. In part, this was the work of the contemplative monasteries. There was no reason for Merton to be a monk if he was not able at the Abbey of Gethsemani to develop a kind of consciousness different from that experienced outside. For people to recover their capacity to believe and live more humanly, all Christians must seek such radical healing.[20]

Merton also attributed many achievements to science and technology. However, the priorities of the day did not impress him. When, on his forty-sixth birthday, an ape was sent into space, Merton was not deceived. He discerned what was at stake; not human good but the militarization of space.

> From Mars or the moon we will perhaps someday blow up the world: . . .
> Tra la. Push the buttons, press the levers! As soon as they get a factory on Mars for banana-colored apes there will be no guilt at all.
>
> I am forty-six years old. Let's be quite serious. Civilization has deigned to grace my forty-sixth birthday with this marvelous feat, and I should get ribald about it? Let me learn from this contented ape. He pressed buttons. He pulled levers. They shot him too far. Never mind. They fished him out of the Atlantic and he shook hands with the Navy.[21]

2. Distortion of Our True Humanity

The distinction between the true and false self dominated much of Merton's writings. By false self, Merton described the self that is superficial: alienated, egocentric, exterior, illusory or outward. For Merton, the false self did not exist at any deep level of reality. As for the true self, Merton understood the experience of being united to the image and likeness of God:

> St. Bernard of Clairvaux expanded and implemented the thought of St. Benedict when he called the monastery a school of charity. The main object of monastic discipline, according to St. Bernard, was to restore]to humanity, our] nature created in the image and likeness of God, that is to say created for love and for self-surrender.[22]

But technology can easily manipulate the false self. Technology contributes to alienation from our pilgrimage to our truest selfhood. Conjointly, Merton's sense of social location led him to be very critical of the United States during turbulent times, and he struggled personally with transparency and integrity. As early as 1949 he wrote, "For me to be a saint means to be myself. Therefore the problem of sanctity and salvation is in fact the problem of finding out who I am and of discovering my true self."[23]

Merton's antidote to technology emerges. If technology distorts true human freedom, the spiritual path followed by Merton enables him to find God at the center of his truest selfhood. Over and over again, Merton writes that what really matters in life is the pilgrimage to our true humanity: "Our real journey in life is interior: it is a matter of growth, deepening, and of an ever greater surrender to the creative action of love and grace in our hearts."[24] Merton defends contemplation as a path to realizing one's true self:

> In an age where there is much talk about "being yourself," I reserve to myself the right to forget about being myself, since in any case there is very little chance of my being anybody else. Rather it seems to me that when one is too intent on "being himself" he runs the risk of impersonating a shadow.
> Yet I cannot pride myself on special freedom, simply because I am living in the woods.... We all live somehow or other, and that's that. It is a compelling necessity for me to be free to embrace the necessity of my own nature.[25]

3. *Divertissements*, Diversions and Distractions

Merton believed that one lives more fully, or more humanly when one discovers oneself to be a child of God and that society and technology seek to distract or divert our attention from the reality that we are God's beloved. This is not to say that Merton refused the technological innovation that enhanced life at Gethsemani. It was in the nature of a monastery to use all gifts wisely. On September 21, 1949 he reported a new machine that aided the monks in their agricultural work: "Things have changed greatly in the six years since I was a novice. But since there is much more work, we can do with a few machines."[26] In a February 16, 1965 journal entry, Merton welcomed new power lines and with them tools that eased the workload of his brothers and allowed him to have electricity in his hermitage. "I was glad of American technology pitching in to bring me light," but he had no brief for an excess of useless technology.[27]

In a December 12, 1962 letter to Ray Livingston of Macalester College in St. Paul, Minnesota, Merton wrote that he had to some extent abandoned any intransigent position of complete hostility to machines as such.[28] In an April 22, 1967 journal entry Merton noted how helpful it was to use a tape recorder: "It is a very fine machine and I am abashed by it. I take back some of the things I have said about technology."[29]

But Merton feared the impact of technology in the area of human relationships and freedoms. French thinker Jacques Ellul's discussion of mass society especially influenced him. Others have detailed Merton's reflections on Ellul. I want to highlight Merton's concern that having things imparted a false sense of security. Merton criticized frivolous materialism as follows:

> The tragedy of a life centered on "things," on the grasping and manipulation of objects, is that such a life closes the ego upon itself as though it were an end in itself, and throws it into a hopeless struggle with other perverse and hostile selves competing together for the possessions which will give them power and satisfaction. Instead of being "open to the world" such minds are in fact closed to it and their titanic efforts to build the world according to their own desires are doomed in the end by the ambiguity and destructiveness that are in them. They seem to be light, but they battle together in impenetrable moral darkness.[30]

In spite of the Christian elements that survive in the West, Merton believed that he lived in an essentially atheistic society. In a civilization that at best tolerates God and religion, our values – materialism, status, power – distract us from Christian values and prevent us from receiving God's grace. As a cure, Merton taught that only as we come to live in God can we resist the *divertissements* of society at large, even those of the monastery. Technology had the capacity to numb a person to the danger of idolatry. Merton wrote,

> Technology was made for man, not man for technology. In losing touch with being and thus with God, we have fallen into a senseless idolatry of production and consumption for their own sakes. We have renounced the act of being and plunged our-

selves into *process* for its own sake. We no longer know how to live, and because we cannot accept life in its reality life ceases to be a joy and becomes an affliction.[31]

Peering into an abyss, Merton could be quite despairing. He believed that the fixation with technology in the West blinds people to the reality of the spiritual world. Technological civilization such as people now live is without angels or God. Where angels and God used to be, humanity has replaced them with machines. Today, it is hard if not impossible to find God, angels, self or neighbor.

Merton's Prophetic Diagnosis

Welling up with compassion for a world caught up in pursuit of the false self, a world of hallucinogenic drugs, consumerism, propaganda, technology and war, Merton sought to bring people to their senses. To shape an alternative vision, Merton probed the monastic traditions as well as other religions, world-views, communal experiments and twentieth-century literature. Especially significant was his role in introducing myriad readers to the spiritual teachings of South and East Asia, of Islam and of the ancient wisdom of Africa, Australasia and native America. Imaginatively, Merton also mediated his knowledge of traditional knowledge systems and modern technology through art, photography, literary criticism and poetry.

Believing that technology had evolved to such an extent that some form of religious idealism was necessary to sustain humanity, Merton did not look primarily to organized religion for hope. He turned to contemporary artists. In "Day of a Stranger," Merton ironically gives a picture of a "suspension of modern life in contemplation that *gets you somewhere!" TMR* p. 430 (his emphasis).

Merton asked if technology would usher in a new kind of jungle, an electronic labyrinth. Or if it would somehow overcome the myths of science and technology and come to an eschatological culture of peace.[32] Merton anticipated the latter. This culture of peace could be the fruit of the convergence of diverse sources, most notably brought together by Merton in his poetry.

Emblems of a Season of Fury (1963) contains some of Merton's most moving poems including "And the Children of Birmingham," a "freedom song," and "Hagia Sophia," which introduces readers to the feminine Merton. He explores alienation of the individual and the breakdown of communication between the individual and

God, leading ultimately to the breakdown in community and communion. Whatever positive things Merton says elsewhere about technology, Merton is critical here. The lead poem "Why Some Look Up to Planets and Heroes," is eerily topical;

> Brooding and seated at the summit
> Of a well-engineered explosion
> He prepared his thoughts for fireflies and warnings. . .
>
> Until at last the shy American smiles
> Colliding once again with air fire and lenses
> To stand on noisy earth
> And engineer consent
>
> Consent to what? Nobody knows
> What engine next will dig a moon
> What costly uncles stand on Mars
>
> What next device will fill the air with burning dollars
> Or else lay out the low down number of some Day
> What day? May we consent?
> Consent to what? Nobody knows.
> Yet the computers are convinced
> Fed full of numbers by True Believers.[33]

Another poem in the collection, "Chant To Be Used in Processions around a Site with Furnaces," is a commentary on the technological sophistication of the Nazis. "I was born into a Catholic family but as these people were not going to need a priest I did not become a priest I installed a perfectly good machine it gave satisfaction to many." He concludes his meditation with a caveat, "Do not think yourself better because you burn up friends and enemies with long-range missiles without ever seeing what you have done." In this poem, Merton condemns not only the Nazis. As in his early novel published posthumously, Merton indicts the whole of Western civilization.[34]

Emblems of a Season of Fury includes "A Letter to Pablo Antonio Cuadra Concerning Giants," an essay which uses symbolism to critique the prevailing relationship between the United States and the world and especially Latin America:

... The vertigo of the twentieth century needs no permission of yours or mine to continue.... It has sprung unbidden out of the emptiness of technological [humanity]. It is the genie he has summoned out of the depths of his own confusion, this complacent sorcerer's apprentice who spends billions on weapons of destruction and space rockets when he cannot provide decent meals, shelter and clothing for two thirds of the human race. Is it improper to doubt the intelligence and sincerity of modern [people]? ... The truth is that there is a little of Gog and Magog even in the best of us.[35]

For Merton, Magog and Gog were symbols of the United States and the Soviet Union. Merton pronounced the greatest sin of the "European-Russian-American complex which we call 'the West' as not only [its] greed, cruelty, not only moral dishonesty and infidelity to truth, but above all *its unmitigated arrogance towards the rest of the human race.*"[36] With great urgency, Merton was saying, be unlike these giants.

With stunning language and visual imagery *Cables to the Ace* (1968) and *The Geography of Lograire* (1969) celebrated a new myth-dream that represents Merton's understanding of a new world coming into being. In an essay on "Poetry and Contemplation," Merton reflected on his identity as poet, contemplative and co-creator with God:

In an age of science and technology, in which [we] find [ourselves] bewildered and disoriented by the fabulous versatility of the machines [we have] created, we live precipitated outside ourselves at every moment, interiorly empty, spiritually lost. . . .At such a time as this, it seems absurd to talk of contemplation. . . .The contemplative is not just a [person] who sits under a tree with. . . . legs crossed, or one who edifies [herself or] himself with the answer to ultimate and spiritual problems. He [or she] is one who seeks to know the meaning of life not only with [one's] head but with [one's] whole being, by living it in depth and in purity, and thus uniting himself to the very Source of Life.... the whole world and all the incidents of life tend to be sacraments—signs of God, signs of [God's] love working in the world.[37]

Merton appreciated technologies that blessed his life and added joy to the lives of others. He valued appropriate uses of technology, a position he shared with Gandhi. He liked simple technology, which accounts for his fascination with Shaker furnishings. Even as he spent much of the last years of his life in a hermitage, Merton resourcefully used means at his disposal to share widely his vision of a better world.

> The artist and the poet seem to be the ones most aware of the disastrous situation, but they are for that very reason the closest to despair. If man is to recover his sanity and spiritual balance, there must be a renewal of communion between the traditional, contemplative disciplines and those of science, between the poet and the physicist, the priest and the depth-psychologist, the monk and the politician. . . .[i]f the contemplative, the monk, the priest, and the poet merely forsake their vestiges of wisdom and join in the triumphant, empty-headed crowing of advertising men and engineers of opinion, then there is nothing left in store for us but total madness.[38]

Merton was not a pessimist. He probed many sources and concluded that the final outcome of our current fetishisms—pseudo-mysticism, technology, violence—rests neither with the scientist and technician, nor with artist and poet. He proclaimed that our hope rests with God and God's angels:

> Surely, if we are to rebuild the temporal order by the dedication of our own freedom and our science to truth and to love, we need our good angels to help us and to guide us. Who knows? Maybe our technology itself calls for angelic guardians who are ready to come if we let them. We need not fear that they will revive obsessions that died with the Middle Ages. It is not for us to imagine them, to explain them, to write them bodily into the details of our blueprints. It is for us to trust them, knowing that more than ever they are invisible to us, unknown to us, yet very powerful, very propitious and always near.[39]

Merton was prescient. He warned humanity about a disastrous trajectory along which he understood the reigning science-technology paradigm is leading us. He sensed a "responsibility to be in all reality a peacemaker in the world, an apostle, to bring people to truth, to make my whole life a true and effective witness to God's Truth."[40]

Conclusion and Summary

With reference to Western society, Merton made a physician-like diagnosi: "Our times manifest in us a basic distortion, a deep-rooted moral disharmony against which laws, sermons, philosophies, authority, inspiration, creativity, and apparently even love itself would seem to have no power." Merton identified "the sickness of disordered love, of the self-love that realizes itself simultaneously to be self-hate and instantly becomes a source of universal, indiscriminate destructiveness."[41]

Merton traced the sources of this illness to ideas prevalent in the nineteenth century when people came to believe in indefinite progress, in the supreme goodness of the human person and in the capacity of science and technology to achieve infinite good. He then challenged these principles. As evidence, Merton cited the abject misery of the poor, the persistence of racism and the scourge of war. Merton never ceased to struggle with the allure of technology or to warn others about its effects. Out of solidarity with marginalized peoples, Merton offered a vision of a better world.

Merton still addresses the disquiet of at least four groups of his readers: religious seekers for whom Merton opens a window into Christian contemplative traditions and other spiritual traditions; those for whom materialism and noise have become a *tsunami*; those for whom a society that prepares for war, violates rights, or abuses the environment is worrisome; and those who are part of the current uprising against the globalization of the world's economy and planetization of United States culture. Merton acknowledges that technological change is a reality. As humanity develops newer technologies, Merton invites us to consider carefully the choices before us, to use technology mindfully to meet basic human needs, to refuse to acquiesce to evil, to find community and to honor God.

Notes

1. Thomas Merton, *Turning Toward the World* (Journals 4: 1960-63; (ed. Victor A. Kramer, San Francisco: HarperSanFrancisco, 1966), p. 9, entry for June 6, 1960, Merton's emphasis.

2. "The Triple Revolution," *Liberation* (April 1964), pp. 9-15. The text is available at http://www.pa.msu.edu/people/mulhall/mist/Triple.html.

3. Ross Labrie, *Thomas Merton and the Inclusive Imagination* (Columbia: University of Missouri, 2001); William H. Shannon, "Technology," *Thomas Merton Encyclopedia* (Maryknoll: Orbis, 2002), pp. 466-470; Phillip M. Thompson, "The Restoration of Balance: Thomas Merton's Technological Critique," *Merton Annual* 13 (2000): 63-79 and "'Full of Firecrackers': Jacques Ellul and the Technological Critique of Thomas Merton," *Merton Seasonal* 25.1 (Spring 2000): 9-16; John Wu, Jr., "Technological Perspectives: Thomas Merton and the One-Eyed Giant," *Merton Annual* 13 (2000): 80-104.

4. *The Hidden Ground of Love: Letters on Religious Experience and Social Concerns* ed. William H. Shannon (New York: Farrar, Straus, Giroux, 1985), p. 216. Hereafter, *HGL*.

5. Robert Perrucci and Marc Pilisuk, *The Triple Revolution Emerging. Social Problems in Depth* (Boston: Little, Brown, 1971).

6. *A Testament of Hope. The Essential Writings of Martin Luther King, Jr.* ed. James M. Washington (San Francisco: Harper & Row, 1986), March 31, 1968 sermon at the National Cathedral, Washington, D.C. *A Knock at Midnight: Inspiration from the Great Sermons of Reverend Martin Luther King, Jr.* ed. Clayborne Carson and Peter Holloron (New York: Time Warner Audio, 1998). (audiocassette)

7. Thomas Merton "Retreat, November, 1964: Spiritual Roots of Protest," *Thomas Merton on Peace* (ed. Gordon C. Zahn; New York: McCall, 1971), pp. 259-260. Merton wrote of the retreat to FOR coordinator for religious groups John C. Heidbrink, *HGL*, p. 417. Tom Cornell, *Fellowship* 40, 1 (January 1974): 23; Jim Forest, "A Great Lake of Beer," *Apostle of Peace. Essays in Honor of Daniel Berrigan*, (ed. John Dear; Maryknoll: Orbis, 1996); Michael Mott, *The Seven Mountains of Thomas Merton* (Boston: Houghton Mifflin, 1984), pp. 406-407; Murray Polner and Jim O'Grady, *Disarmed and Dangerous. The Radical Lives and Times of Daniel and Philip Berrigan* (New York: Basic, 1997), pp. 106-108.

8. *HGL*, p. 98.

9. Thomas Merton, "Nuclear War and Christian Responsibility," *Passion for Peace. The Social Essays* ed. William H. Shannon (New York: Crossroad, 1995), p. 43.

10. "Introduction," *Breakthrough to Peace* (New York: New Directions, 1962), p. 11.

11. *Conjectures of a Guilty Bystander* (Garden City: Doubleday, 1966), p. 8. Hereafter *CGB*. See Donald P. St John, "Technological Culture and Contemplative Ecology in Thomas Merton's *Conjectures of a Guilty Bystander*," *Worldviews* 6, 2 (2002), pp. 159-182.

12. *The Road to Joy: The Letters of Thomas Merton to New and Old Friends* (New York: Farrar, Straus, Giroux, 1989), p. 98, 99. Hereafter, *RJ*.

13. *CGB*, p. 258.

14. *The Collected Poems of Thomas Merton* (New York: New Directions, 1977), p. 382. Hereafter, *CP*.

15. M. Basil Pennington, *Thomas Merton*. *Brother Monk* (San Francisco: Harper & Row, 1987), pp. 189-190.

16. June 5, 1966, tape, Thomas Merton Center, Louisville. As sources of his talk, Merton cited the thought of Lewis Mumford and an article by Hyman George Rickover, "A Humanistic Technology," *Nature* 208 (November 20, 1965), reprinted in Noel de Nevers, ed., *Technology and Society* (Reading: Addison-Wesley, 1972). See also Merton's "Technology," *Collected Essays* 6, pp. 53-59.

17. *CP*, p. 21 and p. 255-56. The title of this article is taken from this poem.

18. *CGB*, p. 6, Merton's emphasis; pp. 82-83.

19. *The Literary Essays of Thomas Merton*, ed. Patrick Hart (New York: New Directions, 1981), p. 169. Hereafter, *LE*.

20. *Life and Holiness* (New York: Herder and Herder, 1963), pp. 106-107; *Thomas Merton in Alaska* intro. Robert E. Daggy (New York: New Directions, 1989), pp. 126-27.

21. *CGB*, p. 49.

22. Thomas Merton, *Monastic Peace* (Trappist: Abbey of Gethsemani, 1958), p. 19.

23. *Seeds of Contemplation* (New York: New Directions, 1949), p. 26.

24. *RJ*, September 1968 Circular Letter, p. 118.

25. "Day of a Stranger," *A Thomas Merton Reader*, Revised Edition (New York: Image, 1974), pp. 431-432.

26. *The Sign of Jonas* (New York: Harcourt, Brace, 1953), p. 241.

27. Thomas Merton, *Dancing in the Water of Life. Seeking Peace in the Hermitage* (Journals 5; 1963-65, ed. Robert E. Daggy; San Francisco: HarperSanFrancisco, 1997), p. 206.

28. *Witness to Freedom. The Letters of Thomas Merton in Times of Crisis*, ed. William H. Shannon (New York: Farrar, Straus, Giroux, 1994), p. 246. Hereafter *WF*.

29. Thomas Merton, *Learning to Love. Exploring Solitude and Freedom* (Journals 6: 1966-67; ed. Christine M. Bochen; San Francisco: HarperSanFrancisco, 1997), p. 222.

30. *Zen and the Birds of Appetite* (New York: New Directions), p. 82.

31. *CGB*, p. 202, Merton's emphasis.

32. *Ishi Means Man* (Greensboro: Unicorn, 1968), pp. 70-71.

33. *CP*, pp. 305-7.

34. *Ibid.*, pp. 346-9. Cf. Thomas Merton, *My Argument with the Gestapo* (Garden City: Doubleday, 1969).

35. *Ibid*, pp. 372-3.

36. *Ibid.*, p. 380. Elsewhere Merton commented, "It is taken for granted that the U.S. is universally benevolent, wise, unselfish and magnanimous in her dealings with Latin American countries" and concluded that this was not the case. *The Secular Journal of Thomas Merton* (New York: Farrar, Straus and Cudahy, 1959, pp. 47-48.

37. *LE*, pp. 339-40, 345.

38. "Symbolism, Communication or Communion," *New Directions in Prose and Poetry* (Norfolk: New Directions, 1968), p. 15.

39. "The Angel and the Machine," *Merton Seasonal* 22., (Spring,1997): 6.

40. Thomas Merton, *A Search for Solitude* (Journals 3: 1952-1960, ed. Lawrence S. Cunningham; San Francisco: HarperSanFrancisco, 1996) p. 356, entry for December 27, 1957.

41. *CGB*, p. 55.

"A Very Disciplined Person"...
from Nelson County:
An Interview with Canon A.M. Allchin
about Merton"

Conducted by *Victor A. Kramer*
Edited and Transcribed by *Glenn Crider*

Conducted in Atlanta, Georgia, following the Conference on "Thomas Merton and Ecumenism" at Emory University, November, 1998.

Kramer: We are going to talk some about Thomas Merton. We want to go back to 1963 and talk about when you first were there at [The Abbey of] Gethsemani. I thought it might be good if you gave a bit of information about your background and how you became interested in Merton.

Allchin: Well, I don't remember which of Merton's books I read first. I think it was *Seeds of Contemplation*. It certainly wasn't *The Seven Storey Mountain* (or *Elected Silence*, as it was called in the English edition, which was even more abbreviated). And I'm glad because as a young Anglican and rather tender, I would have been rather put off by *The Seven Storey Mountain*. But I think *Seeds of Contemplation* was the first one that I read and I loved it very much. I remember vividly reading *The Sign of Jonas* when I was making a retreat in a small retreat house in the countryside. Then I had this feeling—which I suppose lots of people have reading Merton's books—as if he was in the room talking to me. There seemed to be this immediate contact. This account of how it was like living inside a Cistercian monastery was so fascinating and so absolutely unexpected at that time. That was part of the fascination of the book for me. But I never dreamt I'd meet him.

Kramer: Were you teaching in New York City?

Allchin: No, the first time I went to Louisville was before I'd been to New York. It was my first visit to the United States. In 1962 Dale Moody, who was a Professor at the Baptist Theological Seminary in Louisville, had a sabbatical year in Oxford. And most days of the week he used to come to Pusey House where I was on the staff—because he was using our library—and he would come to have lunch with us, an informal lunch. We got to know each other rather well. I was an Anglican delegate to the Faith-And-Order conference at Montreal. I think it was in July 1963 and it was my first ever visit to North America. When I told Dale I was coming to Montreal he said, "You must come to the United States and stay with us." So I went to the Montreal conference and then I came to Louisville.

Kramer: How did you get out to Gethsemani? Did one of the monks meet you?

Allchin: I spent three or four days at the seminary as a guest of Dr. Moody and his wife and family. Dale Moody drove me around; we went to all kinds of places in Kentucky. I learned much about the history of Kentucky and its role in the Civil War and how they were on both sides. I learned quite a lot about the Revival of 1802 and 1803 and the Camp Meetings. I began to get a feeling of the kind of place it was. But the thing that impressed me most was the Shaker Village—Pleasant Hill—[near Lexington]. It was Dale who had written to Merton, made an arrangement, and he took me out there [to Gethsemani]. He left me there and I spent three or four days at the monastery. And that was my first visit to a Cistercian monastery.

Kramer: So when you went to the Guesthouse did you have some time there before you met Merton?

Allchin: Well, I think Merton must have been there to meet us because I remember, for a brief time, there were the three of us together. There was Dale Moody, myself, and Merton and we sat and talked. Then Dale drove off. And Merton took me up into what I suppose was his office. I think it must have been his office because I remember the conversation began and very soon got on to the question of Shakers. Because Merton said "What have you been doing in Kentucky and what have you seen?" I said I've seen all kinds of things but what impressed me most was the Shaker Village because I thought the architecture was so absolutely wonderful. There was a kind of purity and simplicity about it. And he at once went over to his filing cabinet, pulled out the drawer, pulled out a file full of photographs and said, "Look at these photographs!"—which were very beautiful. He said he wanted to write a book about the Shakers. So we started talking about Shakers and that broke the ice between us, because I was feeling a bit nervous being face to face with this world-famous author whom I'd never met before. And then I didn't feel nervous anymore because we were both so enthusiastic about Shakers.

Kramer: When you were there at Gethsemani, did you participate in the liturgy? Were you invited to be there in the choir stalls?

Allchin: No, at that time I was up in the balcony. And I don't think at that time there was any thought that I would receive Communion. I don't think it would have entered into my head nor anybody else's. The liturgy was very impressive but what struck me was the heat of the church, which was fearful. I was there in early August. It struck me that the physical asceticism of the community must have been very real because at that time there was no air conditioning in the monastery. There was air conditioning in the Guest House, thank goodness. Living through that heat and wearing those clothes must have been a kind of penance in itself which was enough for anybody.

Kramer: Did you have occasion to talk with other monks while you were there?

Allchin: Yes I did. The awful thing is that I don't have a very vivid memory of it. But I'm sure that I met Fr. John Eudes Bamberger and Fr. Chrysogonus Waddell. And I'm sure I met one or two other people too. But most of my conversation was with Merton. It was very fascinating. We wandered over all kinds of topics. He very much wanted to have news of friends and things going on in England. I suppose, in a way, that was one of the primary things I could bring. Because not very many people from England came to Gethsemani or to Louisville.

Kramer: Did you two have any mutual acquaintances?

Allchin: No, I don't think so. But obviously the people he knew in Oxford and corresponded with, he wanted information about. I don't remember if he knew Etta Gullick already at that stage. I think that came later. But as you know from the correspondence, there's a very full set of letters to her. And I knew her very well. But it was a little bit of time before we realized we were both in correspondence with Merton.

Kramer: After you left there in '63 did you start corresponding with Merton with any regularity?

Allchin: Yes I did. And I think also that it was the first time I went to St. Meinrad's to meet Fr. Polycarp Sherwood—the monk there who was a great expert on Maximus the Confessor. There were very few people who were experts on Maximus then. And I had a great friend in Sweden, Lars Thunberg, who was writing his doctoral thesis on Maximus. Wherever I went people who were interested in Maximus tried to help the cause. In those days, the number of people in the English-speaking world who were working on Maximus was about two!

Kramer: What did Merton know about Maximus?

Allchin: At that stage, Merton certainly knew quite a lot about Maximus. I, of course, had no idea what was in his Lectures on Ascetical and Mystical Theology, which I think he gave in '61. The chapter on Maximus seems to be one of the most remarkable chapters in that book because he expounds Maximus' quite difficult theology with wonderful clarity. And he uses the example of the Shakers to explain Maximus' theory of natural contemplation and the Logos, the work of God in the whole created world.[1]

Kramer: I think it was in 1960 when he did that course. So he'd been thinking about these things for three or four years by the time you came to visit.

Allchin: Yes. And, of course, one of the things we must have talked about on that first visit was the Russians in Paris. For instance, the question of Paul Evdokimov came up, and I explained that Paul was a layman, not a priest, although I didn't know Paul personally. Then I told Merton about the Lossky family. Vladimir Lossky, who wrote *The Mystical Theology of the Eastern Church*, which certainly Merton had read by 1950; there was a very early reference to that in his correspondence with Jean Leclercq. Vladimir had died in '58. And his widow, Madeline, was a very, very remarkable person—a Jewish Christian with all the kind of emphasis and intensity of some Jewish-Christian people. So I was able to give him some kind of personal contact and anecdotes about that whole Russian emigration world where he'd read so much. And he was already in touch with Olivier Clément, a young Frenchman. So there was a kind of network of contacts there, which I suppose were useful and interesting to him.

Kramer: Often, when people talk about Merton they stress that he had this kind of intensity where you felt that he was totally focused upon the conversation he was having with that particular person. What kind of remembrances do you have of his mannerisms when you first met him?

Allchin: Well, the first thing which struck me was how wonderfully ordinary he was. It's quite true that he gave you his absolute, undivided attention. And we had wonderful conversations. We both had, you might say, lateral-thinking minds, or butterfly minds drifting from one thing to another. And that's one reason I found it terribly difficult to make notes of our conversations. We talked about so many things and moved from one subject to another so quickly. There was never any kind of systematic conversation. We went over all kinds of subjects. It was fascinating talking to him. He had this wonderful sense of humor and a wonderful sense of the ridiculous. I saw that he was excited by all kinds of things. It was always a delight being with him.

Kramer: What kind of scholarly interests were you pursuing at this particular time? And do you think things that you were able to talk about with Merton had any influence upon what you were then able to write yourself in those years?

Allchin: Yes. If I go right back to my first degree at Oxford, which was in History, I did a special subject on St. Bernard and the beginning of the Cistercian Reform. I wanted at that time to be a medieval historian. I thought that's what I was going to be. In the end, I wrote my thesis not in medieval history but in nineteenth-century history. But I did write it in monastic history, which was the revival of religious and monastic communities in the Church of England in the nineteenth-century in the aftermath of the Oxford movement. So I was already interested in monastic history, and I was interested in the history of spirituality. And that was one reason why Dale Moody said to me, "You must go and see Merton. There are so many interests that you two would have in common." So I think we talked a lot in that field. And, as I said, we talked about the Russians in Paris but we also talked about the whole theological situation in France. Because it was just towards the end of Vatican II, and I was very much involved in going back and forth from France because contact between Anglicans and

Catholics no longer had to be clandestine and secret and hidden as it had been before the Council. Suddenly, it was approved of and encouraged by the authorities in Rome.

Having a fair fluency in French, I was constantly invited to go to France by different kinds of groups—some clergy, some lay—to talk about Anglicans and Christian unity. It was a kind of spring-time for all that. And of course, [Merton] being half-French and having such a fluency in French and obviously having contacts with people like Jean Leclercq, he was very much in touch with the French theological scene which was, at that time, an extraordinarily vital and lively one. And this kind of rediscovery of the Fathers, the return to the sources, was such an important part of French theology at that time. So, I'm sure we talked about that. I don't know that in the first meeting we talked so much about English poetry as we certainly did in the '67 and '68 time. But I'm pretty sure we must have done—again, without looking at the correspondence I don't remember when the first letters were written. I don't think I introduced him to David Jones that time, but when that came up it was an extraordinary common interest. That was certainly during my later visits.

I remember in the earliest visit there was an elderly monk from France—I forget from what monastery—who was busy trying to teach plain-chant to the community at Gethsemani. And we had quite a long conversation. We talked French together. I was on my first visit to America and I was full of enthusiasm. He had been a number of times and he was very French and rather skeptical about it [America]. He said, "In two- or three-hundred year's time America will be a remarkable country, very interesting indeed." But he didn't have much hope about what it was then! I remember a lot of conversations with American people who asked me if I was a Redemptorist because I wore my cassock most of the time and it was the kind of wrap-over cassock which Redemptorists would wear, and which Anglicans would also wear. And I said, "No I'm not a Redemptorist, I'm an Anglican. And they said, "Well, what kind of order is that?" Of course, it was interesting and surprising to be in a place that had not even heard of Anglicans, and probably never seen one before and wouldn't have known that they were basically the same as Episcopalians. But that was all to the good, because coming out of England where one is the center of things, it's good to be on the margin.

Kramer: Had you visited Cistercian monasteries in France before you went to Gethsemani?

Allchin: I don't think I had. I would love to have gone to Cistercian monasteries but I don't think at that time I had any contacts. Certainly in England at that time I never visited a Roman Catholic monastery because I was sure they would have tried to convert me. And I wanted to avoid that kind of situation. I think I had already stayed at the monastery at Bec in Normandy. So I had some experience with a Catholic monastery in France—although a Benedictine one. Later I got to know the monastery at Mont des Cats in France which was the Cistercian monastery I've known best over the last thirty years and have visited regularly. I think it was '69—the year after Merton died. So, no, this was a new experience for me—being in a Cistercian monastery—and a very fascinating one, having already read a good deal about them and about Merton.

Kramer: You went back to visit Gethsemani in 1967?

Allchin: Yes, and again in 1968.

Kramer: If you think back on that four-year period, did you notice any difference in terms of the way Gethsemani seemed in those four years?

Allchin: Oh yes. I have to say that 1963 was the only time I went to the hermitage. We went up and spent one afternoon in the hermitage. In '67 and '68, Merton came down to the Guest House and we always met in the Guest House. He didn't take me to the hermitage then. But in '67, I already felt that things were much more relaxed in the life of the community. And the Guest House was more comfortable, and I think that the restoration and renovation of the church had taken place. And as far as I can remember, there was air conditioning by then. I had the feeling that the place was being adapted and modernized. It was the second time I was there that we were sitting together one afternoon and suddenly someone came in—perhaps the phone rang—and Merton went out and spoke, and he came back and said, "That was Fr. Abbot on the phone. He wants you to talk to the community before Compline. Will you do so?" I agreed. Then I said, "What should I tell them about?" He said, "Tell them about the monastic life and that it is worthwhile." I said, "They know about that better than I do." He said, "Yes, but it is good for them to hear it from someone outside." So, that's what I did. And at the end of my talk, Dom James said, "We're going to have a little celebration now called 'Compline.' I suppose you've never heard of that, but you can come if you'd like to."

Kramer: What did you think of Dom James?

Allchin: Well, that was the only time I met him. Naturally, I was in awe of him—he was the Abbot. But I knew very little about him. My conversations with Merton would range very widely over things. But he never said anything that was the slightest bit critical of him. He was very loyal.

Kramer: Did you ever have the feeling when you were talking with Merton that he had criticisms to make of Gethsemani?

Allchin: Yes. Of course, by the time I came back [in 1967] *Conjectures of a Guilty Bystander* was out and I had read it. So that gave me an idea of where he was and what he thought about Gethsemani. For instance, we talked about the whole question as to whether there should be some provision for people to live the monastic life temporarily. Some may come to the monastery not necessarily intending to make a life commitment, but wanting to spend two or three years there and then go back into the world. We thought about the possibility of a community like Gethsemani—having a lay community alongside it where guests could be received, where postulants could be received. It would be a kind of decompression chamber between the outside world and the community itself. We talked of the need for a greater variety of monastic institutions.

We also talked about the question of smaller communities. Certainly, in my second two visits I talked to Merton about the community of the Sisters of the Love of God in Oxford at Fairacres. Because by '67 I had become the spiritual companion to them which I hadn't been, of course, in '63. We talked quite a lot about what he thought about the development of the contemplative life in the Church of England. I remember him saying you're so lucky as an Anglican. You're not tied to Canon Law; you don't have any laws on the subject! And we didn't really. We didn't know how lucky we were.

Kramer: In late '67 he gave a retreat for some women—abbesses and prioresses—and later those tapes were transcribed into [manuscripts].

Allchin: I think he talked about that. I think it was then that we went to Loretto one time. In '68 I came with a friend—a student from General Theological Seminary. And we had a car, and Jerry drove, because I've always been a bit nervous about driving on the right-hand side of the road. In the '68 visit we went out during the day. And again, we'd never done that before. And I always said to people—and I still say to people—if you read about Merton you know about all the occasions when he went out. Most of the time he wasn't going out. Even in '67 and '68 with all the various disturbances there were, he was still living basically a very regular life. That was what always impressed me; he was a very disciplined person.

Kramer: So how was it in 1967 that you had planned to visit him. Were you in the United States for some particular reason?

Allchin: Yes, in both years I was invited for a semester to be a visiting lecturer at General Theological Seminary. I was lecturing in what we should nowadays call "Spirituality." In those days it was called "Ascetical Theology." Most students thought it was "Aesthetical Theology!" But I came in '67 and I knew I was coming back in '68, and I'm sure we talked about the possibility of coming again.

Kramer: When you came back in '68 various combinations of events conjoined to make that very special. You were with him on a trip to Lexington, is that right?

Allchin: Well, we went out for the day; it was towards the end of March. [Martin Luther King, Jr., died April 4th.] And we went first to the Shaker Village—Pleasant Hill. From there we went into Lexington where we went into a restaurant. After that we went and called Caroline Hammer and sat there and talked a bit. Then we began to drive back to Gethsemani and heard on the radio that Martin Luther King [Jr.] was in Memphis and things seemed to be rather dangerous and unhappy. We also heard a rather amusing report on the television news about Christian Barnard—the surgeon in a hospital in Cape Town who had just performed the first successful heart transplant. And there was some really rather amusing and absurd discussion in the film with Christian Barnard about the man who received the heart because he had the heart of a black man. Merton, in his diaries, seemed surprised that Jerry and I did not catch on to this. The reason why I didn't catch on was because my sister was head of the Radiology Department in that hospital and the last time she was in England I had asked her about Christian Barnard. She said he was a famous and brilliant surgeon but was extremely difficult to work with. He was a very difficult colleague. My fantasy was that I would be sitting in this roadside café and I'd see my sister speak [on television]. But that didn't happen. That's very much a footnote!

Then we drove on from there and while driving off we heard over the car radio that Martin Luther King had been shot. And Merton's immediate reaction was that we must go into Bardstown and go and call Colonel Hawk and see how he is. I think two of his children were away at college and would therefore be away from home and the whole possibility of rioting and violence was a concern. So we went to the restaurant—Hawk's Diner—and had a wonderful evening and a fascinating meal.

Kramer: So you were at the restaurant for quite a while?

Allchin: Oh yes. Some customers came and talked with us including Hawk himself. I suppose it was the first time I had had a serious conversation with a black American, and I must say he was a very impressive person and I had this impression—I already had quite a bit of contact with Eastern Europe—that people who belong to nations which have suffered, suffered history rather than made history, are often people of great depth because not only personally but somehow nationally, socially and culturally they have a kind of experience of adversity which very often we English-speaking people don't have, because we belong to nations which have been, on the whole, quite successful outwardly.

Kramer: Do you think Merton was aware of that too?

Allchin: Merton was intensely aware of that. I'm sure Merton had a great deal of respect for him, for the family, for the place. I don't know how many local contacts [he had] with black people who were Catholic. Probably not very many because I think there weren't very many black people in that part of Kentucky.

Kramer: Do you think this fed into Merton's writing?

Allchin: Sure it did. He has in those writings, in the 60s where he is writing about the relationship of black and white people, a very deep empathy and a typical Merton-kind-of-understanding of the feelings and thoughts of black people.

Kramer: Do you know that song cycle where he takes a Psalm and re-writes some Psalms thinking just below the surface of Civil Rights issues?

Allchin: Yes, I've never heard them but I've read about them. John Howard Griffin had already written *Black Like Me* at that time. So, there again was another person whom Merton obviously knew very well, who affected him in that matter.

Kramer: Do you think any of this feeds into the poetry in *The Geography of Lograire*?

Allchin: Oh yes, indeed, it does. But what I notice more in *The Geography of Lograire* is the opening section where he says there are two seas in here—a German sea and a Celtic sea. And it seems to me that the opening of the poem is clearly influenced by David Jones and by *The Anathemata*. He had discovered David Jones about a year before and he had written to him saying it was a really great discovery. I, myself, was also in the process of discovering David Jones.

Kramer: I do not think much has been written about Merton's awareness of David Jones. That would be an important thing to follow-up.

Allchin: I think it would, yes. It's something that happened the last year of his life—or the last 18 months of his life. But clearly it made a very great impression. And David Jones is a very great writer.

Kramer: Did Merton ever talk to you about the kinds of books he was reading because he was a poet and because of his relationship with James Laughlin—the New Directions editor—and the fact that Laughlin would have been sending him books by some of the people he was publishing like William Carlos Williams and Ezra Pound and Denise Levertov, people like that. Did he ever mention any of those people?

Allchin: Yes. My own very limited knowledge of American poetry, I suppose, in a way, restricted our conversation. As I said, I certainly talked about Edwin Muir and he was interested in R. S. Thomas and quite appreciated him. I talked probably on the first occasion about Edwin Muir whom I already liked very much. And certainly on the last occasion we talked about Denise Levertov whose poems I knew a little bit—not very much. But I had begun to appreciate [Levertov] and he gave me a very nice, large photograph of himself and Denise and Eugene Meatyard on some kind of picnic expedition.

Kramer: I guess Meatyard was taking photographs. Or, I think there was one picnic where Wendell Berry and Merton and Levertov were there and Meatyard was taking photographs. That would have been in 67, I think.

Allchin: Unfortunately, I can't find that photograph. I was looking for it recently, but my memory is certain that the photograph had Merton and Meatyard and Denise. He also told me on that occasion about Joan Baez's visit. And I had great enthusiasm for Joan Baez in those days. And Merton told me about his singing "Silver Dagger" when he was getting up in the morning. At the time he was living in a hermitage and could sing without disturbing anybody. He might disturb the frogs and sometimes they disturbed him!

Kramer: What did he say about Joan Baez? What did he think she was doing that was original?

Allchin: Well, I had the impression that he very much enjoyed her visit and admired her work.

Kramer: Could I change the subject? If you had to think for a moment about Merton's facial expressions, what kind of things come to mind?

Allchin: Well, first of all, of course, is that he didn't look at all like the traditional image of a Christian ascetic saint or even like the traditional Catholic image of St. Bernard. He looked round and somewhat like a Buddha. Secondly, the thing that you see as soon as you look at the spread of photos of him in John Howard Griffin's book is that his face is extraordinarily mobile. He looked different at different times. I was never surprised that the photographs showed such a variety of faces because that is in a sense how he was. But I suppose the thing which struck me most the third time, which was March '68—I think it had been quite a hard winter in the hermitage—was that he looked very weather-beaten. He looked like a man, a farmer who had been in the fields a good deal and it had been a hard winter. So he looked red-faced, in fact, weather-beaten. When we were in the restaurant in Lexington I was very correctly dressed in a black suit with a clerical collar. And my voice proclaimed me as not coming from Lexington. And a rather elegant lady came up and asked me if I came from England. I said, "Yes, I do." She said, "Have you met our bishop here?" And I said no I hadn't. She said, well you should meet him and all these things. She then turned to this curious, weather-beaten-looking character in a red-checked shirt who was sitting at

the table with me and said: "Do you come from England too?"
And he replied, "No, I come from Nelson County, lady." She was
puzzled that I had a British accent, and he didn't!

Kramer: If you think back on that '68 moment and the last times
you were with Merton, can you remember when that last moment
was?

Allchin: No, I can't exactly. I remember Merton's reaction to the
news as we heard it on the car radio that Martin Luther King [Jr.]
was shot. It was one of not being surprised. I had the impression
that he—and also a lot of other people—had a kind of intuitive
sense that something was going wrong. And somehow when the
tragedy happened it seemed to have a kind of inevitability about
it. I remember that rather distinctly. I also remember that the next
day—the day afterwards—he came down to the Guest House—
whether he said Mass at the Guest House or whether we went
over to a chapel in the Novitiate, I am not sure. But certainly he
said Mass. He said the Mass of Our Lady of Sorrows. It was the
week before Holy Week, and he said Mass for Martin Luther King
and a particular prayer for his wife and the family. As you know,
the Yungbluts were in the process of trying to organize a visit for
Martin Luther King to the monastery.

So, in that sense he [Merton] obviously was very closely involved in the whole thing. I think he may actually have [corre-
sponded with] Martin Luther King by that time. So I think it was
probably after he said Mass that we left and he went back to the
hermitage. And that was the last time we talked.

Kramer: If you think about his writing and his influence upon
monastic communities, do you think that other monks have absorbed Merton's writing or do you think he has had some kind of
concrete influence upon the way monasticism has developed? Do
you think that some of his fellow monks have been somewhat reluctant to acknowledge his presence?

Allchin: Well, insofar as I know the monastic world in England—
and I know more about the Catholic monastic world now but not
so well as the Anglican one—I've thought that in England he has
had a very great influence. Not everybody admires him. People
disagree with him about this and that—it is not difficult to do that.
But I think he's had a great influence within monasteries and within
religious communities in England.

In France, I do not think he has been so much of an influence mainly because many of his writings have not been translated into French. Also, there is within the French Cistercian and Benedictine world such a strong tradition of monastic thinking and monastic commentary because there is a whole kind of monastic world there which still has a very traditional strength to it. Although his name is certainly known [within this French tradition] I don't think he has had a very great influence.

Kramer: So, do you think in France Merton would be considered more of a kind of American curiosity and someone that you would not take with much seriousness?

Allchin: I may be wrong. This may even have changed within the last few years, but before five or ten years ago not very much of his writing was available in French. I think quite a lot was translated in the '50s. Then after that I don't think very much was translated. So I don't think he's been such an influence there as far as I know.

Kramer: But in England you feel people have read him and think he is important?

Allchin: Oh certainly.

Kramer: Can you give examples of particular monastic influences?

Allchin: I can't think off-hand although I'm sure if I went back and looked through periodicals I could find examples of articles by members of religious communities and monastic communities about his work. But I know his books are very widely read and I think the whole development of his monastic understanding from the rather self-centered view of enclosure [being cloistered] (which you get in the earlier writing) to the much more open understanding of monastic life (which is seen in his later writing) has had a very great influence. Surely that is part of the whole rethinking and reliving of monasticism which maybe has not changed the lives of those inside so much, but has certainly changed their lives in relation to the outside world and church. Monks and nuns are in a much more direct and open relationship with people who come and stay than they were. And they are much more open and concerned with the affairs of the world than they were thirty or forty years ago. I am sure his influence there has been considerable. I think contemplatives almost naturally think of Christianity's relationship with other religions. They are almost instinctively interested in Zen and yoga and they are not frightened of it like many of the more intellectual and activist Christians are. There again, Merton's influence has been very great.

Kramer: When you go back to those visits in '67 and '68, did he talk about non-Christian religions much?

Allchin: Oh yes. I think in ['65] *The Way of Chuang Tzu* had just come out and he gave me a copy of it and he talked a lot about it. I was a little bit shocked. I thought, "I would much rather see you writing a new book about St. Antony or St. Gregory of Nyssa or St. Bernard. Why are you writing about this curious Chinese author?" But that just shows you how narrow-mindedly Christian I was at that time myself! But he certainly was already fascinated and it was quite clear that he was fascinated by Chuang Tzu. And, of course, having heard him talk about it, then having read his book, my own eyes began to open and my views were widened. But, yes, he was clearly very interested in that whole world. I think he probably saw that I was not all that interested or very well informed. So he did not press the matter. I am sure we talked more about it in '67 and '68.

[By '68] he had this contact with R. S. Thomas and he got interested in the Welsh background in his own family tree. And although at that stage I was still pretty much a novice in Welsh things, I was beginning myself to become much more interested in Welsh. I sent him copies of the English translation of the hymns of Anna Griffith. He was very interested in Anna Griffith, and he was very interested in things to do with Wales. The postcard that he sent from New Delhi said that he hoped to get permission to come back through England. He said he would come to England and then we would go to Wales. And now I've been living in Wales for ten years.

Kramer: Do you have particular works of his that you feel are especially valuable in relation to questions about ecumenism. Are there particular books that you feel are of value?

Allchin: In terms of Christian ecumenism, I think that the discussion with Bonhoeffer and Barth in *Conjectures of a Guilty Bystander* is quite exceptionally valuable. I must say that *Conjectures of a Guilty Bystander* is almost my favorite Merton book. I was fascinated by it when I first read it and I've been fascinated by it ever since. I have been very interested since his Journals were published to discover how much he was reading of the [Orthodox] Russians in Paris. Although we certainly talked about it, I do not think I realized it until I read those journals quite how much he had read of them. But it is quite clear that although he did not write about them and it does not [necessarily] appear in his own productions, the influence of the Russians in Paris was quite considerable. Naturally, some of the things he wrote in his letters to me were about the seventeenth-century Anglicans and how he felt they were important if people could assimilate them. But he was not very hopeful that [people could assimilate them] because they were too remote from most American Catholics. But he certainly hoped that perhaps they would be assimilated. And he was particularly interested in Henry Vaughan and Thomas Traherne and the other Metaphysicals. I sent or tried to provide books that would help him in that particular interest.

Kramer: But he never could really pursue much of that.

Allchin: No. He said in a letter that he thought of making an edition of one of Henry Vaughan's translations [It was of Eucharius' *De Contemptus Mundi*, according to Working Notebook #5.], but he had many projects at one time or another. I don't think that was a project which would have been a top priority to him.

Kramer: Now, if we could change the subject just a bit and think in terms of your own work which has been really amazing in so many ways. Do you see any relationships between what you learned from Merton and what then subsequently you were able to do with all of your research and writing with regard to ecumenism and so forth?

Allchin: I think undoubtedly that if I've been able to hold together many interests, he has helped greatly. Some of my friends have told me that I look too widely and on too many subjects and never actually get anything finished. They have not said it quite like that but they point into that direction. If I have managed to hold together a rather diverse group of interests within the realm of Christian spirituality and Christian theology, I think the example of Merton was and has been terribly, terribly important for me. I don't for a moment think that I have anything like his intellect or capacity or ability. In my own kind of way, I have myself tried to branch out—not much beyond the Christian world—at least not in my writings but within the Christian world: Anglican, Catholic, Orthodox, Methodist, Lutheran. I've read a certain amount—especially [about] Sufism and to some extent Jewish Mysticism—but I have not written anything on those subjects, nor have I done anything like what Merton did. But again, in the whole thing about the relationship of faith to poetry and faith to literature, I've done a certain amount. But, not having Spanish and Portuguese, I have never investigated the Latin American world in the way that he did. I have (perhaps) a little more explored than he did through translation the Eastern European, Polish, Russian and Romanian worlds and, with my Celtic interests, at least tried to follow contemporary writing in Irish and Welsh which I suppose he didn't do. But in both cases, yes, clearly his example has been an immense inspiration and encouragement.

Kramer: You were recently in contact with people in Moscow and an International Thomas Merton Chapter has been set up and people are beginning to read Merton in Russia right now. He had had correspondence with Boris Pasternak and so on. What do you think Merton can offer Russia right now?

Allchin: Oh, I think Merton could be of immense value to Russia. I think but I'm not certain that his correspondence with Pasternak is now translated—I'm not sure that it's been published. But I'm sure it will draw much interest when it is published. As you know, the Russian Orthodox Church suffers from the kind of polarization of progressives and traditionalists which all churches seem to suffer from at the moment. But the Russians suffer in a very bad way. The extreme conservatives have the upper-hand and shout louder and, of course, get all of the attention from the press. But there are—in the Orthodox world in Russia—plenty of people who are thinking in a very ecumenical way. Many of them are directly inspired by Fr. Alexander Men.

Kramer: Who is Fr. Alexander Men?

Allchin: Fr. Alexander Men was a priest of the Orthodox Church who was murdered under very strange circumstances, probably by some extreme right-wing group about five or six years ago in Moscow. He was an exceptionally gifted man. He came from a Jewish family background which made him even more unacceptable to some of the anti-Semitic groups in Russian Orthodoxy. He had a very great gift as a popular expositor of Christianity. And when, in 1988 and 1989, it was possible for the first time to speak about Christian and religious questions openly on television and on radio, Fr. Alexander Men was one of the very few people who had the kind of preparation or the kind of intellectual and communicative capacities to do that. So for a brief period of two or three years, I think he became a very famous person in Russia as a spokesman for Russian Orthodoxy. And he represented a very open, ecumenically-minded kind of Orthodoxy which I would think of myself as the most authentic kind of Orthodoxy. But certainly he was criticized and he has been very much criticized since his death by the more traditionalist kinds of Orthodox groups. But there are many people in Russia who greatly admire him. There is an Alexander Men University which is a small, private university in Moscow which is teaching theology and studying theology. And it is in those kinds of circles that Merton's writings are being translated. I think of Merton as a monastic author, who is at the same time not at all a rigidly traditionalist but a profoundly traditional writer who will have an immense contribution to make to Russia.

Three or four years ago we had—I give this just as an example—in our Center at Oxford a very brilliant, young, Russian academic teaching philosophy who had re-discovered Christian faith about three or four years before he came to England. [He was] exploring Christian doctrine with passionate interest and excitement, discovering, as if for the first time, those things that have been there for fifteen hundred years. He was absolutely thrilled in England to be able to stay in the Russian Orthodox Monastery in Essex which is a small community of about fifteen monks. He was fascinated and happy to be there. He said, "I'd longed to have the opportunity to live in a monastic community for a time to share in prayer and understand more about Orthodox monasticism." He said, "In Russia the monasteries are so rigid—theologically and intellectually—and so afraid of someone like myself, who comes in and asks them to read Heidegger or listen to The Beatles. They think I must be a heretic by the fact that I know the names of such people!" That told me something about the problems in Russia at the moment, where the Church is struggling with a situation where for seventy years there was no publishing and therefore no possibility for the development of a well-informed and well-educated Christian leadership. It is in that kind of situation that I think Merton's writing will come into play.

Kramer: I'd like to talk more particularly about Merton's influence in the monastic world.

Allchin: Well, I do not know that I have a great deal to say except for one particular book I did not mention, which I think has been very important to many people inside monasteries rather than outside. That is, of course, *The Climate of Monastic Prayer*. That, I think, is a book which has been very—maybe not widely but—deeply read because it speaks so directly to the experience of prayer of other people whether they are living within monasteries or outside monasteries. This, I think, is one of Merton's greatest gifts. He has a great gift of communicating traditional material. It is often quite difficult to get at and to summarize a twelfth-century or a fourth-century author and to make them accessible to you, but he also has a way of expressing the particular experiences and dynamics and agonies of our twentieth-century world. And he gives words to experiences which people have which they find it difficult to name. I suppose that is one of the reasons why he is so widely read and so valued.

Kramer: I think so. This book *The Climate of Monastic Prayer*—which is now published as *Contemplative Prayer*—it is a very dark book and it is a book which some people find very discouraging because it forces the reader to think in terms of how you have to deal with your own disappointments.

Allchin: Yes. I think that is why it is such a useful and helpful book! It seems to me that the kind of spiritual writing and religious poetry which is able to face and name some of those dark, difficult experiences, and disappointments in ourselves, and the apparent absence of God, and living within a world from which God seems withdrawn—the people who can write about that and name those experiences are enormously helpful to others. Because if we do not confront those dark sides of the Christian experience openly, we are paralyzed by feelings of guilt about them. When we begin to discover that there are people who seem to be getting through a similar kind of "Dark Night," it is an enormous liberation and we begin to understand the situation a little more.

This is particularly characteristic in Great Britain [of] the poetry of R. S. Thomas. I know he is not very well known [in the United States] for one reason or another, but Merton very much appreciated [R. S. Thomas]. Well, this is thirty years ago. Over the last thirty years, Ronald Thomas' poetry has more and more turned into a poetry about the struggle with God. It is certainly a struggle and many of the poems represent a very dark kind of picture of the life of faith and the life of prayer—a picture which suggests at times that the whole thing is more or less impossible. But people find him, in a way, extraordinarily helpful and encouraging because he is so willing to express [carefully] dark elements of their own experience which are more easily lived with and coped with when they are named.

I remember an occasion some years ago when I had to do a kind of study weekend for some military chaplains. I decided to start with two or three of these rather dark poems of R. S. Thomas and my intuition for once was absolutely right because it released amongst the priests there—most of whom, as I say, were Army chaplains—a kind of honesty of discussion and recognition of our own doubts and difficulties in prayer and sense of darkness which made the whole weekend more open and, I think, much more personally honest and profound. And I think it is the same with that book [*Contemplative Prayer*] which translates much of the same sense of darkness which I think anybody who is living a life of prayer and faith in our age must come to because we are living a life of prayer and faith in a society that does not at all help us live [that sort] of life.

Kramer: I think that Merton's final writings (some of the poetry toward the end; some of the Journal material toward the end) is planned to force people to realize that you have to deal with the complexity of [a] life which is full of disappointments.

Now, I would like to ask a question. This is a theory that has not been systematically tested but I think that in the Journals towards the end, that is, beyond the Fourth Volume or so Merton has somehow made up his mind that his job is not to simply provide edification but to record the difficulties he is having with his own life. Therefore the Journals become less and less a matter of providing helpful advice and more of a kind of record of Merton's own difficulties. Some would say this is not going to be very helpful. Have you thought about what is going on in those Journals—Volumes Five, Six, Seven and towards the end?

Allchin: I think I agree with you with what is going on. And I think the result is that they are genuinely edifying and genuinely encouraging in a way that they could never have been if he had been offering advice and edification which had covered up the personal difficulties and anxieties and problems he had been going through. He is teaching us to live with immense uncertainties—to live in a very apophatic kind of way. This is perhaps, to some extent, a sign of personal maturity. Maybe earlier in one's life one has to have more clear boundaries of practice and doctrine and as time goes on one can learn to be a bit freer about those things and learn to hold less to particular formulations and more to some inward experience and knowledge which is very difficult to name. That seems to me to be what is going on inside [Merton]. The later volumes are very helpful because of their very great honesty. There are perplexing things about Merton—I mean he is so interested in what is going on in himself and he is obviously somewhat aware that other people are going to be. And he has this extraordinary rapport with things in the immediate past and in the remote past.

In that sense the comparison with John Henry Newman is, I think, very interesting. Newman seemed to have an extraordinary rapport with things in his childhood and his adolescence and different periods of his life which he can write about. And he also seemed to know people were going to be interested in him. Merton seems to have the same kind of intuition. That is perplexing to most of us because we are not those kinds of people and we feel that people who do that must be doing it in a rather self-conscious way. But Merton, for the most part, seems pretty un-self-conscious about it. When he gets self-conscious about it he becomes very ironical and self-critical and he makes many jokes.

Kramer: I think that is sufficient. Thank you.

Note
_____

1. See *Merton and Hesychasm: The Prayer of the Heart/The Eastern Church* edited by Bernadette Dieker and Jonathan Montaldo (Louisville, KY: Fons Vitae, 2003), pp. 409-45.

An Obscure Theology Misread
2003 Bibliographic Review

David Joseph Belcastro

All theology is a kind of birthday
Each one who is born
Comes into the world as a question
For which old answers
Are not sufficient.

Birth is question and revelation.
The ground of birth is paradise
Yet we are born a thousand miles
Away from our home.
Paradise weeps in us
And we wander further away.
This is the theology
Of our birthdays.

Obscure theology
On the steps of Cincinnati Station:
I am questioned by the cold December
Of 1941.

So begins the second poem of *Eighteen Poems* with the rather ambiguous title (not, presumably, given by Merton himself) of *Untitled Poem*.[1] This title, vague as it might at first appear, nonetheless aptly introduces a poem that glimpses the hidden work of God in the public life of Thomas Merton. Within these lines, Merton's biography unfolds as an obscure theology that draws the reader into the illuminating darkness of unknowing wherein the transcendent wholeness of our common life, the ground of our birth that is both question and revelation, the paradise from which we have wandered and for which we long, is experienced.

It is difficult to read this poem without thinking of George Steiner's book entitled *Real Presences*.[2] Here he argues that transcendent reality grounds all genuine art and human communica-

tion. Consequently, a poem, for example, may become an opportunity for a reader to return to the source of creation, not only of
the poem but of his or her own life. Steiner describes this experience as a "wobble" in our consciousness of time, a sense of home-
coming rooted in the fact that the arts are mimetic of the original
act of creation so that the mystery of any authentic art form is the
mystery of creation itself. Furthermore, he believes that there is
an inherent human longing for this ineffable dimension of human
experience that he identifies as the "real presence of God." I imagine, however, that he would have little difficulty talking about the
experience along the lines of Rilke's "first world," Eliot's "still point
of the turning world," or Merton's "paradise of question and revelation." However it may be named, all four writers would agree
that works of art, whatever form they might take, are expressions
of that longing. Perhaps, then, it could also be said that all art is a
kind of birthday and each one who is born comes into the world
as a form seeking expression for which old expressions are not
sufficient. This variant reading of a few lines from "Untitled Poem"
brings us to what is relevant for this bibliographic review.

Rather than a critical examination of a work that intentionally
distances itself in order to view the work objectively, Steiner proposes a creative response that approaches a work with the intention of creating from it a new work that is simultaneously analytical and imaginative. His proposal is based on a belief that each
"performance of a dramatic text or musical score is a critique in
the most vital sense of the term; it is an act of penetrative response
which makes sense sensible."[3] Unlike an exclusively analytical
response, a creative response "makes sense sensible" by carrying
out the "potentialities of meaning" of the original work into a new
work so that we once again may experience with all our senses
and thereby more fully understand what was then and there but
is here and now revealed anew. The evaluation of a book, for example, would take the form of new literary works, or, possibly,
alternative forms provided by the visual or performing arts. In
this way, the older work comes to live in and against the newer
work. Steiner illustrates what he has in mind:

Virgil reads, guides our reading of Homer as no external critic
can. The *Divine Comedy* is a reading of the *Aeneid*, technically
and spiritually 'at home', 'authorized' in the several and inter-
active senses of the word, as no extrinsic commentary by one

who is himself not a poet can be. The presence, visibly solicited or exorcized, of Homer, Virgil and Dante in Milton's *Paradise Lost*, in the epic satire of Pope and in the pilgrimage upstream of Ezra Pound's *Cantos*, is a 'real presence', a critique in action. Successively, each poet sets into the urgent light of his own linguistic and compositional resources, the formal and substantive achievement of his predecessor(s). His own practice submits these antecedents to the most stringent analysis and estimate. What the *Aeneid* rejects, alters, omits altogether from the *Iliad* and the *Odyssey* is as critically salient and instructive as that which it includes via variant, *imitatio* and modulation.[4]

Writers, therefore, begin as readers who eventually get around to arranging their dislocated reflections on texts to which they feel compelled to respond. Even though Steiner refers to this process as "misreading," he does so with something positive in mind. Misreadings, according to Steiner, provide glimpses into the transcendent dimension of the human experience that is, while always obscure, nonetheless present. Acknowledging that even a good reading will fall short of the text by a "perimeter of inadequacy," he sees that perimeter as the luminous "corona around the darkened sun."[5] In other words, misreadings illuminate, not distort, the meaning of the original work. For a misreading to be illuminating, however, it must be accountable to the original work. As Steiner explains:

> The authentic experience of understanding, when we are spoken to by another human being or by a poem, is one of responding responsibility. We are answerable to the text, to the work of art, to the musical offering, in a very specific sense, at once moral, spiritual and psychological.[6]

It should be noted, however, that even when we dare to respond to a text with body and soul, "there always will be a sense in which we do not know what it is we are experiencing and talking about" even while we are experiencing and talking "about that which is."[7] Consequently, the conversation remains and must remain open-ended and allowed to unfold in unexpected ways as each new generation, while working with old insights and questions, continues the inquiry.

Real Presences provides us with a perspective from which to consider the books to be reviewed in this essay. Merton scholarship, these works in particular, are excellent examples of misreadings as misreading is defined by Steiner. Each author and editor has read texts earlier constructed by Merton that drew him or her into a conversation not only with Merton but with those with whom Merton had conversed, corresponded and/or read. They have responded responsibly to his work with creative weavings of their own. While different in perspective and design, they are all playful misreadings that provide a luminous corona around the obscure theology of Merton's life. Here we witness a postmodern monasticism without walls that continues Merton's interest in the contemplative life and its relation to the arts, the environment, and social justice, as well as his engagement of the world in a serious discussion of what it means to be authentically human, and all of this from diverse religious perspectives.

Cincinnati Station

Woven into the first part of the title of Paul Elie's book entitled *The Life You Save May Be Your Own, An American Pilgrimage: Flannery O'Connor, Thomas Merton, Walker Percy, Dorothy Day*[8] is the title of a short story by Flannery O'Connor that refers to a sign forewarning Tom T. Shiftlet as he drove off in an old car that he had saved from the junkyard: DRIVE CAREFULLY—THE LIFE YOU SAVE MAY BE YOUR OWN. Shiftlet is a drifter who prefers the open road and desolate places. His "composed dissatisfaction" with the world and unusual "moral intelligence" provide him with the wherewithal to offer wry insights into the human predicament and to search for redemption in unforeseen byways. Even though Flannery O'Connor, Walker Percy, Dorothy Day, and Thomas Merton bear some resemblance to Shiftlet, the connection between the titles of these works by Elie and O'Connor is to be found elsewhere.

The story's title serves as a roadside sign indicating the direction in which Elie intends to take the reader. It is more than just a ride along an old road recalling past events and accomplishments in the lives of four American writers. Elie has woven the stories of O'Connor, Percy, Merton, and Day into the narrative of a pilgrimage. By framing the stories as a pilgrimage, Elie has defined the act of reading in a way that is reminiscent of Steiner:

A pilgrimage is a journey undertaken in light of a story. A great event has happened; the pilgrim hears the reports and goes in search of the evidence, aspiring to be an eyewitness. The pilgrim seeks not only to confirm the experience of others firsthand but to be changed by the experience. Pilgrims often make the journey in company, but each must be changed individually; they must see for themselves, each with his or her own eyes. And as they return to ordinary life the pilgrims must tell others what they saw, recasting the story in their own terms. In the story of these four writers, the pattern of pilgrimage is also a pattern of reading and writing.[9]

On the one hand, it is the pilgrimage of the author who grew up as a Roman Catholic trying to work out from his religious tradition and experiences how faith, belief and knowledge were integrated into and gave shape to his life. To do this, he turned to the literary works of Percy, O'Connor, Merton, and Day. On the other hand, it is a story of others who, like Elie, are curious and perplexed about religious experience, or, unlike Elie, indifferent or altogether hostile to the notion. Hearing of *The Seven Storey Mountain, The Last Gentleman, Wise Blood,* or *From Union Square to Rome,* they became readers in search of evidence, aspiring, according to Elie, to be eyewitnesses not only to confirm what they had heard but perhaps to be changed by the experience of integrating the stories of the four writers into their own lives. The literary works of these four writers provide a point of entrance and departure for this transformative experience. Each of the writers dramatizes his or her experiences in such a way that readers are able to enter into the narrative personally, testing the work against their own life experiences, and vice versa.[10] It is writing that invites the reader into a process of questioning whereby abstract beliefs become lived experiences from which the "ground of our birth" is rediscovered. Elie sees these writers as having created texts that "reach us at the center of ourselves, and we come to them in fear and trembling, in hope and expectation— reading so as to change, and perhaps to save, our lives."[11] Consequently, *The Life You Save May Be Your Own, An American Pilgrimage* is more than an account of four writers. It is about the relationship that exists between writers and their readers. It is about how art, life, and religious faith converge and give shape to a person's life. It is about the way four individuals who glimpsed the transcendent in their reading and evoked it in their writing, have encouraged their readers to go and do likewise.

With regard to Merton, Elie sees him as a distinct religious type; a rebel, excitable and prone to anxiety, who threw himself at God headlong raging "against the contradictions within himself."[12] For Merton, the pilgrimage was not so much about finding himself but losing himself, which as Elie rightfully points out, was a lifelong endeavor:

> Merton's sense of self is so strong that he is moved to rebel against it, to cast it off and start over. He will conclude that a false, modern self stands in the way of his true self, rooted in the old French Catholic tradition to which he is heir. To recover his true self, he must recover the lost world of the Catholic past—and then eventually renounce this, too, believing that he has begotten a false self which stands between him and the experience of God.[13]

Elie believes that Merton approached this task in a manner that was at once religious and literary. He traces the development of this approach to Merton's reading of the St. Ignatius' *Spiritual Exercises*. Under the guidance of this spiritual master, Merton's way of reading was shaped by the practice of "composition of place." This meditative practice requires a person to develop his or her faculty of imagination to recollect sacred stories from the past. This hermeneutic allows the person to enter and thereby experience and be transformed by what was, then and there, but is here and now revealed. It was a meditative practice that he would eventually extend to Joyce, Blake, Hopkins, Rilke, Camus, and others. In doing so, as Elie points out, his meditation on sacred and secular texts became a meditation on his own personal history[14] and the way in which the landscape of his interior life took shape. Consequently, we are here reminded that when reading Merton we enter a literary world composed of creative misreadings, complex and sometimes contradictory, but, as a consequence, more often than not rich and vibrant as a painting by Cézanne. The comparison with Cézanne is not without justification or importance for this essay. In *The Seven Storey Mountain*, Merton, before telling us that he had inherited his father's way of looking at things, describes the way in which his father saw the world:

> My father painted like Cézanne and understood the southern French landscape the way Cézanne did. His vision of the world was sane, full of balance, full of veneration for structure, for the relations of masses and for all the circumstances that impress an individual identity on each created thing. His vision was religious and clean, and therefore his paintings were without decoration or superfluous comment, since a religious man respects the power of God's creation to bear witness for itself.[15]

Needless to say, this is not simply a childhood recollection but an early memory informed by later experiences, in particular, his education at Columbia where he was introduced to theories about Paul Cézanne.[16] While this is not the place to fully explore this idea, it is important to note that the comparison of Merton with Cézanne suggests possibilities for not only understanding what Merton longed to express in his life and work but also the complex literary structures that resulted from his method of reading that was shaped by St. Ignatius' *Spiritual Exercises.*

As you may have imagined by now, Elie's story of Merton is the story of the coming together of monk and writer, monastic community and literary world, liturgical life and the life of literature. Even though Waugh's evaluation was that Merton was more monk than writer,[17] Elie sees the publication of *The Seven Storey Mountain* as clear evidence of his vocation as monk and writer.

> *The Seven Storey Mountain* is the best evidence, perhaps the only evidence necessary, that Merton was meant to be both a monk and a writer. His confidence in his religious calling has given his life "wholeness, harmony, and radiance," the Scholastic formula for an achieved work of art. It has given his life a story, one that imitates, which is to say participates in, the larger Christian story, that of the individual soul's peregrination to God. Through this story, he understood his life for the first time.[18]

Even though it can be said that Merton's vocation provided his life with "wholeness, harmony, and radiance," it was also, as acknowledged by Elie, "a quandary forever unfolding."[19] Writing became the way in which he was able to find his way through these quandaries and discern patterns in the obscure theology of his own life. Gifted with an "extraordinary imagination" he was able to see the gray stones of Gethsemani "as the center of the universe, a stray shard of medieval France, a Kentucky equivalent of an outpost of prayer in the Himalayas."[20] It was also this imagination that enabled him to create a coherent narrative of his experiences, obscure and incongruous as they might sometimes appear.

Elie offers an interesting perspective on Merton as a creative writer who captures the imaginations of his readers; so much so that he sometimes gives the impression that they are welcome anytime to drop by the hermitage, as more than a few have, and, later, walk with him "into the cloister or the woods or the ideal monastery of his imaginings, and to retreat there awhile in the company of a spiritual master." Because of this, however, Elie felt a need to sound a warning, as O'Connor does in "The Life You Save May Be Your Own," of "narrow roads that drop off on either side." It is clearly a necessary warning. It attempts to waylay problems that may arise from a less than nuanced reading of his message "to read and do likewise." He raises this warning sign by telling Merton's story of an ex-Trappist monk who wrote to Merton explaining that the strength of Merton's faith was what made him become a monk and had kept him a monk all those years.[21] Elie finds in Merton's angry response a message for his own readers:

> This model religious never really believed in God—as he has at last discovered. And a good thing that he has, for he has now taken the first step towards believing. He entered the monastery on somebody else's faith and lived there on somebody else's faith and when he finally had to face the fact that what was required was his own faith he collapsed. As many others could, or will, collapse when they find out how they stand.

Merton's anger, however, was clearly rooted deeper than that which can be explained by one letter by one ex-monk. Merton was concerned that his old friend was only one of many such admirers and that his writing might likewise "legitimize other people's bad faith." Elie has identified one of the dangers of reading Merton, whose "gift of radical identification with others, and his way of inspiring others to identify with him, could lead his readers to see him as a surrogate believer—lead us to bury our unbelief in his belief, to remain religious novices sitting humbly in the presence of the master." I believe that this problem is serious enough to warrant the printing of this warning on the side of every Merton book or recitation of it at every gathering of the International Thomas Merton Society or the posting of it at his hermitage. If this is too much to expect, perhaps something needs to be published on how to read Merton, not unlike the interesting little book he wrote entitled *Opening the Bible*[22] that addresses similar concerns with regard to the reading of this sacred text. Merton says the Bible "reads us."

Obscure Theology

Camera Obscura is a dark room or box with a hole in one end that allows sufficient light to cast an inverted image on paper laid out opposite the entrance of the light. Daniel Barbaro, a Venetian who lived at about the same time as Leonardo da Vinci, described the image as revealing "the whole view as it really is, with its distances, its colours and shadows and motion, the clouds, the water twinkling, the birds flying. By holding the paper steady you can trace the whole perspective with a pen, shade it and delicately colour it from nature." I mention this, of course, for a reason. After reading the following two books, three of Merton's interests converged in such a way that I remembered an old experience of entering a Camera Obscura while visiting the George Eastman House in Rochester, New York. Holding both thoughts together, I came to wonder whether entering the interior life is not unlike entering one of these dark rooms. The light that passes through the small opening of contemplation casts a shadow revealing a divine presence that tends always to surprise us, regardless of how many times we have traced its patterns in our lives. This unexpected reflection led to further thoughts on how Zen enlightenment and apophatic shadows might have been at work within Merton's monastic world. Is this too fanciful of a notion to be further considered? I will leave it to the reader to decide as we examine Merton's book on the inner experience of the contemplative life and a publication that introduced a recent exhibit of his photography. Before doing so, however, two further points should be made. First, Merton's life may not be fully understood, as suggested in "Untitled Poem," without reference to the apophatic tradition within and out of which he lived. Both books remind us of this. Second, both books are, for the most part, by Merton. That is to say, he wrote the drafts and notes that preceded the publication of the first book and he took the photographs that are considered in the second. The two publications that are before us, however, are the works of others who selected, arranged, and contextualized the contents.

Because Merton had not given permission to his literary executors to publish an unfinished manuscript on the contemplative experience, it was some time before drafts and notes could be reconstructed into this complete and authorized edition of *The Inner Experience: Notes on Contemplation* by William Shannon.[23] Shannon provides an account of the changes undergone by the text from 1948 to its publication in 2003. He also provides critical apparatus of italics, footnotes and changes in typeface that assist the reader in observing subtle shifts in emphasis and interest that took place during the twenty years in which Merton worked on this manuscript.

Even with all the changes, one thing remained the same. According to Merton, while times have changed and man with them,

> . . . he is always man, and as long as he has a human nature, human freedom, human personality, he is the image of God, and is consequently capable of using his love and freedom in the highest of all his activities—in contemplation. But, as I say, times have changed, and in the education of modern man the fact that he is the image of God does not carry much weight. Indeed, nothing could be treated with less concern *today* than man's innate capacity to be a contemplative.[24]

In addition to this lack of interest in the contemplative dimension of the human experience, Merton believed that there was another contemporary problem that needed to be addressed.

> There are in fact too many books which look at the spiritual life exclusively from the standpoint of a virginal or priestly life, and their needless multiplication is, in fact, the reason why there is so much sterile spiritual writing. At the same time, this sterile influence makes itself felt in the interior life of those married Christians who should have the greatest influence for good in keeping the Christian mind fully and sanely *incarnate*.[25]

The modern world's lack of interest in the contemplative life and the barrenness of spiritual writing being published at this time, were two of the reasons, perhaps primary reasons, for Merton to write *The Inner Experience*. He had come to realize that if people at the end of the twentieth-century were to rediscover the transcendent in their lives, spiritual writing would have to change. This manuscript represents one of his many attempts to offer to his generation what he perceived was very much needed at the time. While heading off in the right direction, however, it does not, in my estimation, reach its destination. Merton's holding back on its publication may suggests that he too thought something more was needed. But what?

To be sure, there is much about this book that is right. First, Merton judiciously shares with his readers what he had found of value in his own readings. He does so without confusing them with theological lines of thought that never seem to quite come together; as was the case for many who attempted to read through his *The Ascent to Truth*. Second, he is equally cautious when sharing insights from his own life experiences. Here he avoids as much as possible the mistake earlier pointed out by Elie. The focus is seldom on himself but rather on the reader who, unlike himself, is not monastic but domestic, with his or her own sacred vows to keep.

Merton's interests over the years had shifted from bringing the world into the monastery to taking the monastery out into the world; a shift in emphasis and interest that is more than apparent in this book that provides laypersons an opportunity to consider the contemplative life. Thirdly, even though he insists on the simplicity of this way of life, he does not do so at the expense of the tradition he represents. While emphasizing that the contemplative experience is something very real, he nonetheless forewarns that it is elusive and therefore difficult to define and fully grasp.

It takes place in the depths of the subject's own spiritual being, and yet it is an "experience" of the transcendent, personal presence of God. This experience has to be carefully qualified, because its paradoxical character makes it an *experiential awareness* of what cannot be experienced on earth. It is a knowledge of Him Who is beyond all knowledge. Hence, it knows Him as unknown. It knows "by unknowing."

This "dark knowledge," this "apophatic" grasp of Him Who Is, cannot be explained in a satisfactory way to anyone who has not come to experience something of the sort in his own inner life.[26]

Because the way of unknowing requires experiential learning, Merton also offers practical guidelines for establishing a contemplative life. He suggests that the person desiring true spiritual poverty and detachment should move to the country or small town in order to reduce the conflict and frustration of coping with the world. It is also here that the needs for pleasure, comfort, recreation, prestige, and success may be more easily reduced. The person should find a job that is "off the beaten track" but pays well enough to provide for basic needs. Within this setting, the person should establish a practice of waking around at four or five a.m. to enjoy the silence and solitude of the small hours of the morning and if possible, attend mass during this time, pointing out that it is at this time the poor go to pray before work. The Sabbath, of course, should be a day for contemplation. In order to protect and foster contemplative spirituality, informal gatherings with others who share the same interest should be arranged. And, if married, recognize the sacramental nature of your relationship.

With so much done right, where does the book fall short? I believe it is with the last point. While laying out the above plan, Merton from time to time reminds the reader who may be seeking this "elementary" level of contemplative life that if he or she is one of the few who succeeds, it will only happen by a minor miracle. And, even then, it must be kept in mind that you are not a real monk and must accept that your prayer life will be correspondingly humble and poor.[27] While there can be no doubt that living the contemplative life outside a monastic community would be impossible for many and difficult for the few who perdure, it seems odd to be saying this when one is trying to encourage people to rediscover the contemplative dimension of their lives. With that said, however, given Merton's understanding of the contemplative life, this was all that he could say and as far as he could go at that time. Peter Feuerherd recognized this shortcoming and in his review of *The Inner Experience*, he takes issue with Merton's suggestion that those seeking contemplation must move to small towns and farms since cities are nearly impossible places to live as a contemplative. Feuerherd counters by pointing out that anyone who has ridden New York's subways can spot commuters who are quietly reading their Bibles and prayer books and obviously contemplating something.[28] Feuerherd is correct with regard to what Merton is saying in *The Inner Experience*. It should be noted however, that during the latter part of Merton's life, Merton also entertained thoughts of monastic communities that would live and work within urban and even large metropolitan settings. Perhaps more telling was his appreciation for "worldly" monks like Albert Camus whom he referred to as that "Algerian Cenobite" or the comedian Lenny Bruce that he called a "monk in reverse" or those strange Beats with whom he shared a common history and sense of community.[29] And, then, of course there are those references in *The Asian Journal* that record his admiration for Buddhists, monks and laypersons, praying in public places. So, it is clear, that while he was looking for a way to integrate the contemplative life into the public lives of ordinary people and that he did in fact have a few odd and end insights into how this might be done, he did not have the opportunity to work out such an idea nor sufficient experience of his own to see his way through the situation and to finish *The Inner Experience*.

The Paradox of Place: Photography of Thomas Merton, edited by Paul M. Pearson,[30] offers the reader four short but noteworthy essays that suggest ways in which Merton's photography may be appreciated and understood. "The Joyful Face Behind the Camera" by Paul Quenon, "The Paradox of Place: Thomas Merton's Photography" by Paul Pearson, "An Enduring Spirit: The Photography of Thomas Merton" by Anthony Bannon, and "With Eyes to See: Thomas Merton: Contemplative Photographer" by Marilyn Sunderman introduce an exhibition of thirty-one photographs at the McGrath Art Gallery, Bellarmine University, Louisville, Kentucky from October 10th to November 11th 2003 in celebration of the 40th Anniversary of the Thomas Merton Collection of thirteen hundred photographs that are preserved in the Thomas Merton Center at Bellarmine University. While different in perspective, each essay focuses on Merton's ability to create profoundly affecting images that reveal his rich interior vision of the world.

Merton's travels during the final year of his life, provided him with significant opportunities to photograph places far beyond the walls of Gethsemani and the knobs of Kentucky; thus the first part of the title, *The Paradox of Place*. Pearson explains:

> The photographs in this exhibit reflect these paradoxical poles in Merton's life and writing. On the one hand, the images of the places associated with his monastic life, the minute things he observed around him everyday at the Abbey of Gethsemani in the rural Kentucky countryside, images which in his photo-

graphs became prayers. Then, in contrast, the images from his travels of 1968, images of California, New Mexico, Alaska and Asia—images of places very different to his monastery, yet still seen with the same eye that captured those images of Gethsemani.[31]

Is this not what we would expect? Is this not what makes his photographs so valuable to us who see through very different eyes; eyes trained by driving on expressways, scanning shelves for groceries, and staring at computer screens; eyes trained to see only what meets the eye from the surface of the object viewed? Merton's eyes were different. He saw the world as Gethsemani had taught him to see it. He saw the world in a deeper and more authentic way than we usually do. He saw the world through contemplative eyes and his photographs now allow us to see in the same way.

Quenon identifies Merton's photography as part of a "tradition of visual contemplation."[32] As such, it is a different kind of language that provides us with an opportunity to do far more than simply think about the contemplative life. If Merton's writings inform us of the contemplative life, it is his photography that invites us into the experience of contemplation; an experience that, as Merton reminds us in *The Inner Experience*, is necessary if we are to understand the way of unknowing. Bannon, referring to several of the photographs in this exhibit, draws our attention to how the "variety of textures across a limited palette of black and white, the deep shadow and decisive light, these elements of his work call" us to "informed reflection"[33] where we discover a "language for contemplation"[34] that opens us to see the apophatic shadows that are cast by Zen enlightenment.

While this is not the place to sort out the relation between two traditions that shaped Merton's contemplative vision, the following may be sufficient to hint at what may be found here. Sunderman believes that Merton's contemplative photography

attests to the truth of the Zen insight that being fully awake or enlightened entails awareness of one's unity with all that exists, and, hence, the cherishing of each created thing. According to Zen, emptiness is fullness and vice versa. By giving himself over, as completely as possible, to the reality of what he saw through his camera lens, Merton sought to empty himself of self in order to become attuned to the fullness of each object that he contemplated. Merton's photographs capture some of his experiences of "transformed consciousness," that is, the state of Zen enlightenment that is utter awakeness to the *isness* of reality.[35]

Bannon seems to be suggesting something more; a kind of symbiotic relation between Zen enlightenment and Apophatic shadows that is similar to the way in which a camera functions. Focused on the dialectic of the shadow in Merton's photography, he sees

> the play of light against dark, the twinning of the thing and its thrown image, the notion of presence and absence, of self and other, the thing and its trace, the object and its abstraction, the drawing out an image. And these conceits find an echo in the thousands of quick-lined Zen-like drawings he also made during his lifetime. Interestingly, the implied transformation of the thrown image is one carried by photography itself, and is one of the medium's defining attributes. For photography, with its near magical qualities, is designed to carry the trace of light reflected from the represented thing and impress it upon the light sensitive emulsion of film negative, which, in turn, renders light as darkness, just like a shadow. The photograph as transformation, then, as a kind of shadow itself, fits Merton's work like a glove.[36]

Whether there is anything to this notion of mine, it is nonetheless clear that Merton's photography has much to offer us. This publication and the exhibition that it introduced remind us that in addition to the many images of Merton that we have of him as a monk at prayer, a writer sitting at a desk, a hermit in the woods, and an ordinary man with friends, the image of him as photographer needs to be included to round off our understanding of him and his work. Fortunately, Quenon has preserved a story that does just that:

> I was told by a nun at the Redwoods monastery in California that a neighbor of theirs saw Fr. Louis photographing on the empty beach nearby. He did so with such energy and enthusiasm that he thought that man must either be a madman or a saint.[37]

Misreadings

Still other new books demonstrate how Merton's life and work continue to draw people together to think deeply and in new ways about contemplation and the implications of a contemplative life for the postmodern world. These publications also indicate the various ways in which other writers have responded to his work. Each in its own way, bears out much that was said by Steiner in *Real Presences* regarding the relation between writers and readers who write. The authors and editors of these books provide us with much more than a critical examination of the Merton corpus. While they respond responsibly to the texts, they do so with a freedom that Merton would have appreciated; an intellectual, spiritual, and aesthetic freedom that has allowed them to continue the inquiry that was initiated by a monk interested in awakening his world to the obscure but nonetheless real presence of God.

The first three books, *Seeking Paradise: The Spirit of the Shakers* edited by Paul M. Pearson,[38] *When the Trees Say Nothing* edited by Kathleen Deignan,[39] and *Seeds* edited by Robert Inchausti,[40] are creative rearrangements of works and excerpts from works previously published by Merton. The first two of these three books include photographs or drawings that remind us of the "tradition of visual contemplation" and the significance of weaving text and image for comprehending the hidden presence to which his work witnesses. The second set of books, *Merton and Hesychasm: The Prayer of the Heart*[41] edited by Bernadette Dieker and Jonathan Montaldo and *Judaism: Holiness in Words: Recognition, Repentance, and Renewal*[42] compiled and edited by Beatrice Bruteau bring together papers previously published by Merton and articles by a new generation of scholars and contemplatives on subjects of mutual concern. The effect of such editing is a sense of the abiding presence of Merton at conferences where old questions unfold to reveal new questions and insights for which old answers are no longer sufficient. The third set of books, *The Vision of Thomas Merton*[43] edited by Patrick F. O'Connell and *Mystery Hidden Yet Revealed*[44] by Marie Theresa Coombs are, as the titles suggest, two very different approaches to clarifying Merton's contemplative vision. Equally interesting is the way in which these two books provide readers with new perspectives from which to view Merton. With *The Vision of Thomas Merton*, we see him through the eyes of Robert Daggy, first archivist and director of the Merton Center in

Louisville, Kentucky. With *Mystery Hidden Yet Revealed*, we see Merton as if sitting at dinner with Georgia O'Keeffe in her home in New Mexico. Having not heard of her dinner guest, she had difficulty remembering his name.[45] Nevertheless, *we* know both of their names. As a consequence of seeing them together, we come to know Merton and O'Keeffe in a new way. Something like a stage play entitled *After Dinner with O'Keeffe* would be both entertaining and revealing as Daggy tries to explain to the famous artist who the unknown monk was that she had invited to her home.

Seeking Paradise: The Spirit of the Shakers represents Merton's interest in Pleasant Hill, an abandoned site of a Shaker community located not far from Gethsemani, and the tradition to which it belonged. Pearson identifies three "foundations" for this interest.[46] First, there was Merton's interest in clarifying the "ideal of monasticism" and the Shakers provided an excellent example of one community's effort to realize such an ideal. Second, his "paradise consciousness" that is evident in his later poetry found expression not only in Shaker beliefs but in their way of life, the communities they formed, and the furniture and other things they made. Third, his "Blakean rebellion" against modern culture and prophetic witness to the reality of God's presence in the world was characteristic of the way the Shakers were present in the world of their day. These three interests form a unified theme for this publication of Merton's essays, conference talk, selected letters, and photographs brought together here for the first time. *Seeking Paradise: Thomas Merton and the Shakers* is not, as Walt Chura has pointed out, a critical study of the Shakers.

Readers of this collection, coming fresh to the Shakers, however, need to be cautioned. Thomas Merton was remarkable in his ability to extract gold from shallow pools. Nevertheless he had limited access to resources for his studies. Even for those resources he depended on the good offices of friends "in the world," as the Shakers say. Most of these friends were well versed in the subject area with which they aided him, and he was able to gain significant illumination from their material. Yet, Merton sometimes had no means to recognize, let alone critique, the bias, limitations or accuracy of his sources.[47]

Chura is, of course, correct. A critical study of Merton's work on the Shakers along the lines indicated in Chura's review is still needed. But, as Chura himself points out, Merton was a "seeker" and not a historian.[48] Merton's primary concern was to explore and discover what this lost tradition might have to offer contemporary contemplatives by creating misreadings of his own that were, as Chura writes, "meant not simply to inform but to help transform the reader."[49] Pearson's reworking of Merton's work on the Shakers contributes significantly to this objective. It is, therefore, more than just an account of that interest. Pearson's skillful editing and finely written introduction have created a work that evokes an awareness of the spirituality of a bygone tradition that is nonetheless relevant for our times. Here we discover how prayer may become an art form and work a form of prayer; how the deepest pleasures of life are simple and plentiful; how peace becomes a reality when people live charitably and kindly with one another, grounded in the love of God; how a community may be productive and prosperous without destroying the environment; and how a Christian community that is willing to risk and struggle to live out the Gospel in this way becomes a prophetic voice crying in the wilderness of our times that are marked by alienation, consumerism, and violence.

Seeking Paradise: The Spirit of the Shakers offers readers a vision of an alternative way of life. To become a Shaker is, of course, no longer a possibility. To once again, however, catch a glimpse of their vision, may be nonetheless beneficial. As Merton recognized, the Shakers apprehended something totally original about the spirit and vocation of America that has, unfortunately, remained hidden to most everyone else.[50] This book reveals what has been hidden. It does so in such a way that readers become aware of a religious vision that now haunts their imaginations to think deeply on old and forgotten questions that, if lived, may open them to a more authentic religious life.

When the Trees Say Nothing is a collection of over three hundred quotations gathered like wild flowers from Merton's writings on nature. This florilegium of selected texts is arranged to represent Merton's panoramic view of the natural world. The arrangement is illustrated with fine drawings by John Giuliani. Texts and images invoke a sacramental awareness of the divine presence that Merton witnessed in the changing seasons, the woods at Gethsemani, and the mountains of Asia. This format is, perhaps, the most appropriate genre for representing Merton's interest in the environment. Thomas Berry, in his foreword to this publication, reminds us that Merton's response to nature was "neither academic nor overly critical but spiritual in the most demanding sense of the word."[51] It is a spirituality that seeks to experience, not analyze, our relationship with nature. Such an experience is, as Berry points out, essential for finding a way out of the ecological quandary that the modern world has created for itself.[52] And, because the sacramental awareness of nature is so lacking today, a book such as this one is needed. Deignan's introduction provides a different but nonetheless related perspective. Here she traces in Merton's biography the "rich and overlooked sub-theme" of his "marriage to the forest." This theme reveals how Merton came to understand his relation to nature and the importance of that relation to his spiritual formation.

When the Trees Say Nothing is not a book by Merton even though the quotations are his. Nor is the book about Merton even though Berry and Deignan provided valuable insights into Merton's life and work. It is a collaborative work that brings together the talent and insights of the above mentioned writers and artist. What kind of book is it? If this is determined by how it reads, I would say it is a kind of prayer book. I say "kind of prayer book" because it is not a book of prayers. Rather it is a book that, according to Deignan, may:

> . . . awaken the naturalist in us, or the poet, or the creation mystic. Perhaps he will aid us in recovering our senses that were fashioned to behold the wonders all around us. Indeed these meditations will aid in healing the hurried, harried soul that has become divorced from the encompassing fullness in which divinity resides—at once concealed and revealed in the incarnate realm. In this as in those many other matters of the sacred, Merton is a spiritual master for us, offering a way to practice the art of natural contemplation by reading with delight and awe the scripture of creation unfolding moment by moment all about us. With him we enter into the liturgies of rain and autumn and dawn, discovering our own "thin places" where earth becomes diaphanous to Eden and finding there the sanity and refreshment that brings us true vitality.[53]

While *When the Trees Say Nothing* is an appropriate misreading of Merton's thoughts on nature, a critical study is nonetheless in order. One place to begin would be the correspondence between Merton and Czeslaw Milosz.[54] Within this exchange of letters, Milosz criticizes Merton for writing about Nature as too idyllic,

rich in symbols, a veil of divine presence without paying sufficient attention to the ruthlessness of Nature that necessitates continuous rounds of suffering.[55] While Merton's immediate response
to Milosz affirms much of what is said in *When the Trees Say Nothing*, it fails to respond to the questions that Milosz raises.[56] I imagine, however, that Merton may very well have kept those questions in mind and from time to time he addresses them with the
hope of eventually working out a position that does take into consideration the violence that is inherent in the created order of things.

Seeds is a book of selected paragraphs from Merton edited by
Robert Inchausti. The paragraphs are organized according to four
dimensions of Merton's spiritual formation: Real and False Selves,
The World We Live In, Antidotes to Illusion, and Love in Action.
Together they present an image of Merton as "the harbinger of a
still yet to be realized contemplative counterculture—offering us
a vision of an interior life free from rigid philosophical categories,
narrow political agendas, and trite religious truisms."[57] As this
quotation from the introduction indicates, Inchausti is presenting
something more here than just a selection of readings from Merton.
While never directly said, it may have something to do with the
"still yet to be realized contemplative counterculture." Perhaps
Inchausti is the one planting seeds this time and the seeds are those
ideas so carefully packaged into paragraphs by Merton. For this
reason, Inchausti decided to work with paragraphs rather than
essays believing that they are always "accessible, poignant, and
revelatory" and thereby allow the reader to not only see Merton's
ideas but the reflective thought processes by which single ideas
grew "thematically, lyrically, and dialectically out of themselves,
making unexpected connections, and then emerging into surprising new epiphanies."[58] Inchausti sets before us a compelling image of Merton who "combined the rigor of the New York intellectuals with the probity of the Desert Fathers—speaking directly to
our solitude through a rigorous examination of his own." As a
consequence, Seeds is a book that "undermines our illusory ambitions, questions our values, and assaults our complacency[;] he
also gives solace to our impoverished souls by reminding us of a
larger, more inclusive, transcendent reality of which we are all a
part."[59]

What Inchausti has identified with Merton, is true for himself.
He too has created something new that hints at "unexpected connections" and "surprising epiphanies." Furthermore, he invites

the reader to do the same; that is to say, to make connections of their own. *Seeds* provides the reader with an opportunity to observe how Merton, "an explorer on the frontiers of human self-understanding," reflected on old truths in light of new experiences. As such, it is an excellent lesson on how to resolve ambiguities, refine ideas, and rediscover old truths in new contexts where they may be once again fully appreciated and understood.[60] There should be no confusion as to how Inchausti wants the reader to approach this collection of paragraphs. He sends the reader in the right direction with a quote printed at the outset from Merton's *New Seeds of Contemplation*.

> The purpose of a book of meditations is to teach you how to think and not to do your thinking for you. Consequently if you pick up such a book and simply read it through, you are wasting your time. As soon as any thought stimulates your mind or your heart you can put the book down because your meditation has begun. To think that you are somehow obliged to follow the author of the book to his own particular conclusion would be a great mistake. It may happen that his conclusion does not apply to you. God may want you to end up somewhere else. He may have planned to give you quite a different grace than the one the author suggests you might be needing.[61]

Merton & Hesychasm: The Prayer of the Heart and *Merton & Judaism: Holiness in Words: Recognition/Repentance/Renewal* are new additions to the Fons Vitae Thomas Merton Series. Fons Vitae is committed to the publication of books that contribute to mutual understanding and respect among religious communities "by sharing matters of spiritual sustenance." Merton's contributions in this area are well known as recognized by the editors who note Ewert Cousins who:

> ... has called Merton an "axial figure" who bridges within his own experience and theological work the contemporary estrangements between religious and secular perspectives. Dr. Cousins has publicly shared his opinion that Thomas Merton means almost more today to many than he actually did in his lifetime. He is becoming an iconic figure who models interreligious dialogue for those who are seeking a common ground

of respect for the varied ways in which human beings realize the sacred in their lives. Merton's life and writing, especially when it focuses on the contemplative practices common to the world's major religions, have indeed become a forum, or a "bridge" in Cousins' term, upon which those engaged in inter-religious dialogue can meet and engage one another.[62]

Merton intentionally set out to become a forum for inter-religious dialogue by approaching his work as monk and writer in a particular way:

If I can unite *in myself*, in my own spiritual life, the thought of the East and the West, of the Greek and Latin Fathers, I will create in myself a reunion of the divided Church, and from that unity in myself can come the exterior and visible unity of the Church. For, if we want to bring together East and West, we cannot do it by imposing one upon the other. We must contain both in ourselves and transcend them both in Christ.[63]

What is here said regarding the Roman Catholic Church and the Orthodox Church, may also be said regarding nearly every other set of historical differences that divide and set humankind against itself. (Perhaps the distinction between humankind and nature should also be included.) Once again Merton explains how he reads and what he is about when writing. Having heard reports of traditions other than his own, he seeks not only confirming evidence but to be changed by what he discovers; changed into a more authentic human person.

Merton & Hesychasm: The Prayer of the Heart is the second in the series. The first, published in 1999, was entitled *Merton & Sufism: The Untold Story.* This book on Orthodox spirituality is divided into three parts. Part one, "Hesychasm: the Gift of Eastern Christianity to Spiritual Practice," is an introduction to "prayer of the heart" as present in the theology, liturgy, and practice of the Eastern Orthodox Churches. Part two, "Thomas Merton and Eastern Christianity," presents essays that clarify what Merton found so attractive in this tradition. The *hesychast* method of prayer contributed significantly to his effort to connect the contemplative and active dimensions of his life. Here was a tradition that provided Merton a way to integrate contemplation and action by revealing the divine presence in the world and thereby suggesting ways for being in the world that are more authentic and effective. Part three, "Hesychasm in the Writing of Thomas Merton," presents Merton's essays, lectures, correspondence in which he discusses the *Hesychast* tradition and the ways in which he incorporates it into his life of prayer and understanding of the mystical tradition. Reading the sayings of the Desert contemplatives and the writings of the Greek theologians opened for Merton a "balanced, humane, and liberating vision of authentic Christian life."

Merton's interest in the Eastern Orthodox Church, however, served more than just his spiritual formation. Albert J. Raboteau, in his review of the volume, states, from the perspective of a member of the Orthodox tradition, what Merton's interest and this collection of essays, means to him:

> At a time when ecumenical relations between Orthodoxy and Roman Catholicism seem to have stalled, it is heartening to reflect on these words and to recall Merton's devotion to icons, to St. Seraphim of Sarov, and his personal observance, as early as 1960, of the anniversary of St. Silouan the Athonite. This volume, as the general editors hope, could serve as an inspiration to renewed dialogue between Eastern and Western Christians.[64]

Merton & Judaism: Holiness in Words: Recognition/Repentance/Renewal is more than a book by or about Merton. It is collection of writings that represents an effort to engage Christians and Jews in an open and honest conversation about the past that has separated them and the future that may offer possibilities for mutual respect, appreciation, and cooperation. As such, it demonstrates, as pointed out by Victor A. Kramer in the foreword, "Merton's prophetic role in being able to pursue a particular line of interest which then shines as a beacon to guide others in the decades following."[65] The organization of writings is intended to show thematic unity and development. The editor, Beatrice Bruteau, explains:

> It is launched with James Carroll's account of his and Merton's journey from innocence of the Christian/Jewish history to this strong call for Christian *teshuva*, a thorough **recognition** of the ill done and deep **repentance** for it. Then we move through several papers that examine this in some detail and approach

the central climax, Merton's interaction with Abraham Joshua Heschel and their common concern for the production of *Nostra Aetate* during Vatican II. It is in connection with this, Merton's most crucial relation to Judaism—and the hope and the challenge growing out of it—that the appendices are so important; they reveal the struggle within the Church, in the context of which Merton's intervention was significant.[66]

Richard E. Sherwin, in his review of the book,[67] notes that Merton's understanding of Judaism is limited by two factors. First, Merton's reading was primarily limited to Martin Buber and Abraham Heschel, who were in many ways most like Merton himself, sharing as they did an interest in mysticism. Second, Merton tended to look for connections with his own tradition. As a consequence, that which is "foreign, indigestible but radiant" in Judaism becomes lost. While both have, as Sherwin says, their "up and downsides," he recognizes that Merton does not present himself as a Jewish scholar but as a Christian monk interested in this tradition, as he was interested in all traditions, i.e., to initiate conversations that eventually allow us to see our own religious traditions "from an angle that freshens everything, and stretching our faith healthfully in the process."

The Vision of Thomas Merton is a new collection of essays similar to the two previous collections of essays entitled *The Message of Thomas Merton*[68] and *The Legacy of Thomas Merton*.[69] This collection was published in honor of the late Robert E. Daggy, curator of the Thomas Merton Collection and director of the Thomas Merton Studies Center at Bellarmine University. The impressive bibliography of articles and essays by Daggy on Merton printed as an appendix would be sufficient evidence for recognizing him as one of the "great authorities on the life and writings of Thomas Merton." Perhaps more importantly, however, is what he came to mean to those who study Merton. Patrick O'Connell explains from his own experience:

In the summer of 1998, when I came across some unpublished poems of Thomas Merton in the Columbia University Library archives, my spontaneous response was to think, 'Won't Bob Daggy be interested in this'! Of course I knew that the former director of the Bellarmine College (now University) Thomas Merton Center had died the previous December, but he had

been so much a part of my own study of Merton, as he had
been for so many others, that it was difficult to realize that he
was no longer there to offer insight and encouragement.[70]

The relation that existed between Daggy and authors of the articles in *The Vision of Thomas* Merton is important to note for this
essay. These were friends and colleagues of Daggy's. Their articles tell us one of two things. Either we learn something of the
relationship they enjoyed with Bob, or something of an aspect of
Thomas Merton that was often inspired by Daggy. In either case,
it is important. While it is a collection of articles about Merton, it
is in many ways about Merton with the assistance of Daggy. In
other words, it is a collection of misreadings that illuminate like a
corona around two darkened stars; an illumination that not only
casts shadows of Daggy and Merton but of what both men
glimpsed and we now behold. The articles, written by the editors
of the recently published volumes of Merton's journals and letters, offer new insights into Merton's complex vision of life and
faith. Their insights once again allow us to see the expansive geography of inquiry that was earlier explored by Merton and
mapped out by Daggy.

Mystery Hidden Yet Revealed is a book on Merton and O'Keeffe
and that concludes this essay and, by virtue of its thesis, brings us
back to Steiner and the notion of the immanent transcendence of
God. Coombs begins by exploring the theme of mystery hidden
yet revealed from the perspective of the interrelationship of transcendence, self-actualization and creative expression and then proceeds to describe the interplay of those three elements in the lives
and works of Thomas Merton and Georgia O'Keeffe. She believes
that while Merton personified the contemplative as artist, O'Keeffe
was the artist as contemplative. With regard to Merton, she concludes:

Up to a certain threshold in his life, Thomas Merton proceeded
generally from wordless, imageless, loving encounter with God
to awareness of the divine presence in nature and in the world
around him. In other words, he went from communing with
God in an apophatic way to a sense of God's presence in the
created realities around him. As Merton matured spiritually,
his manner of approaching the divine presence expanded. He
continued to move from encounter with God in darkness and

emptiness to beholding the mystery of God within the created world. Yet, increasingly his involvement with creation became itself an opening for encounter with the transcendence of God. Moving back and forth in a rhythm between those two basic approaches to the divine, Merton developed a sense of God's immanent transcendence everywhere, in everything and in everyone. His whole life became a contemplation of God.[71]

The book has taken shape over the years from the author's ministry of spiritual direction and was later developed recently into a doctoral dissertation. As a consequence, it is a book that reflects critical attention to her subjects and pastoral concern for her readers. With regard to the critical aspect of the book, it is important to note that this is not a critical study of the works by Merton and O'Keeffe but rather a study of the process by which transcendence, self-actualization, and creative expression are at play in their lives and works. In some ways, it is a rather awkward book to read. Perhaps the author is trying to do too many things at the same time. Whatever may be the case, it represents another interesting misreading of Merton; one that is enriched not only by the writer's interests but by the addition of O'Keeffe who adds a certain erotic dimension to the spiritual life that is often times lacking.

Question and Revelation

Elie's focus on reading Merton as a pilgrimage in quest of confirming evidence and transforming experiences makes questioning an essential aspect of reading. Perhaps an adaptation of the Buddha's teaching to "believe nothing that you have not found to be true in your own experience" to "believe nothing you have read until you have found it to be true in your own experience," would be an appropriate way to summarize, at least in part, what Elie is saying in *The Life You Save May Be Your Own, An American Pilgrimage*. The other part of Elie's message is echoed in Rilke's advice to a young poet:

. . . be patient toward all that is unsolved in your heart and to try to live the *questions themselves* like locked rooms and like books that are written in a very foreign tongue. Do not now seek the answers, which cannot be given you because you would not be able to live them. And the point is, to live everything. *Live* the questions now. Perhaps you will then gradually, without noticing it, live along some distant day into the answer.[72]

Questions and readings that invoke questioning are to be lived. If lived, they become the way by which we live make unexpected connections, experience epiphanies, and discover answers. These answers, however, are not ones that may be printed on paper but must be, by their very nature, embodied within our lives. Reading a text in this way, requires readers to tend to the text, responding responsibly, to recall Steiner, to what is before them. It is both a critical and creative process that allows for misreadings that provide new insights about old questions.

Questioning of this sort is an important aspect of the apophatic tradition that was central to Merton's obscure theology. This is evident in "Untitled Poem." Finding the question that seeks us, is, as Merton narrates, the way back to the paradise where we were born, a paradise of question *and* revelation. In *Opening the Bible*, Merton suggests a way for understanding how question and revelation may be opposite sides of the same experience.

In the progress toward religious understanding, one does not go from answer to answer but from question to question. One's questions are answered, not by clear, definitive answers, but by more pertinent and more crucial questions.[73]

New questions open a new horizon from which larger fields of vision emerge. Perhaps this is what Merton had in mind when he imagined paradise as question and revelation. If so, the books considered in this essay represent a returning to this paradise. Each of the authors and editors took up old questions raised by Merton decades ago. In so doing, they have made them their own, pressing out of the old questions, new insights that will in turn invoke new questions.

Notes

1. Thomas Merton, *Eighteen Poems* (New York: New Directions, 1985).
2. George Steiner, *Real Presences* (Chicago: University of Chicago Press, 1989).
3. Steiner, *Presences*, p. 8.

4. Steiner, *Presences*, pp. 12-13.

5. Steiner, *Presences*, p. 175.

6. Steiner, *Presences*, p. 8.

7. Steiner, *Presences*, p. 215.

8. Paul Elie, *The Life You Save May Be Your Own, An American Pilgrimage: Flannery O'Connor, Thomas Merton, Walker Percy, Dorothy Day* (New York: Farrar, Straus, Giroux, 2003).

9. Elie, *The Life You Save*, p. x.

10. Elie, *The Life You Save*, pp. x-xiii.

11. Elie, *The Life You Save*, p. xiv.

12. Elie, *The Life You Save*, p. 32.

13. Elie, *The Life You Save*, p. 77.

14. Elie, *The Life You Save*, pp. 103-105.

15. Thomas Merton, *The Seven Storey Mountain* (New York: Harcourt, Brace and Company, 1948), p. 3.

16. Paul Portuges, "Allen Ginsberg's Paul Cézanne and the *Pater Omnipotens Aeterna Deus*," *On the Poetry of Allen Ginsberg* ed. Lewis Hyde (Ann Arbor; University of Michigan Press, 1984), pp. 131-140.

17. Elie, *The Life You Save*, p. 181.

18. Elie, *The Life You Save*, pp. 150-151.

19. Elie, *The Life You Save*, p. 428.

20. Elie, *The Life You Save*, p. 466.

21. Elie, *The Life You Save*, pp. 467-8.

22. Thomas Merton, *Opening the Bible* (Collegeville, Minnesota: The Liturgical Press, 1970).

23. Thomas Merton, *The Inner Experience: Notes on Contemplation*, (ed. William Shannon; San Franciso: HarperSanFrancisco, 2003).

24. Merton, *Inner Experience*, p. 128.

25. Merton, *Inner Experience*, p. 141.

26. Merton, *Inner Experience*, p. 115.

27. Merton, *Inner Experience*, p. 136.

28. Peter Feuerherd, *National Catholic Reporter* (October 10, 2003).

29. David Belcastro, "Thomas Merton and the Beat Generation; A Subterranean Monastic Community," *Thomas Merton: The World in My Bloodstream* (ed. Angus Stuart; Abergavenay, Wales: Three Peaks Press, 2004), pp. 79-91.

30. *The Paradox of Place: Thomas Merton's Photography* (ed. Paul M. Pearson; Louisville, Kentucky: Thomas Merton Center at Bellarmine University, 2003).

31. Pearson, "The Paradox of Place: Thomas Merton's Photography," *Paradox of Place*, p. 8.

32. Quenon, "The Joyful Face Behind the Camera," *Paradox of Place*, p. 5.

33. Bannon, "An Enduring Spirit: The Photography of Thomas Merton," *Paradox of Place*, p. 15.

34. Bannon, "An Enduring Spirit: The Photography of Thomas Merton," *Paradox of Place*, p. 14.

35. Sunderman, "With Eyes to See: Merton: Contemplative Photographer," *Paradox of Place*, pp. 19-20.

36. Bannon, "An Enduring Spirit: The Photography of Thomas Merton," *Paradox of Place*, p. 11.

37. Quenon, "The Joyful Face Behind the Camera," *Paradox of Place*, p. 5.

38 *Seeking Paradise: The Spirit of the Shakers* (ed. Paul M. Pearson; New York: Orbis Books, 2003).

39. *When the Trees Say Nothing* (ed. Kathleen Deignan; Notre Dame, IN: Sorin Books, 2003).

40. *Seeds* (Boston & London: Shambhala, 2002).

41. *Merton and Hesychasm: The Prayer of the Heart* (eds. Bernadette Dieker and Jonathan Montaldo; Louisville, Kentucky: Fons Vitae, 2003).

42. *Merton and Judaism; Holiness In Words: Recognition, Repentance, and Renewal* (ed. Beatrice Bruteau; Louisville, Kentucky: Fons Vitae, 2003).

43. *The Vision of Thomas Merton* (ed. Patrick F. O'Connell; Notre Dame, Indiana: Ave Maria Press, 2003).

44. Marie Theresa Coombs, *Mystery Hidden Yet Revealed* (Eugene, Oregon: Wipf and Stock Publishers, 2003).

45. Coombs, *Mystery Hidden Yet Revealed*, p. 95.

46. Merton, *Seeking Paradise*, pp. 16-17.

47. Walt Chura, "The Tree of Life for the Healing of the Nations," *The Merton Seasonal* 29:1 (Spring 2004), p. 27.

48. Chura, "The Tree of Life," p. 26.

49. Chura, "The Tree of Life," p. 28.

50. Merton, *Seeking Paradise*, p. 122.

51. Merton, *When the Trees Say Nothing*, p. 14.

52. Merton, *When the Trees Say Nothing*, p. 18.

53. *When Trees Say Nothing*, pp. 40-41.

54. *Striving Towards Being: The Letters of Thomas Merton and Czeslaw Milosz*, (ed. Robert Faggen: New York: Farrar, Straus and Giroux, 1997).

55. *Striving Towards Being*, pp. 64f.

56. *Striving Towards Being*, pp. 69f.

57. *Seeds*, p. xi.

58. *Seeds*, p. xvi.

59. *Seeds*, p. xvii.

60. *Seeds*, p. xvi.

61. *Seeds*, p. vii.

62. *Merton and Judaism: Holiness in Words*, p. 13.

63. *Merton and Hesychasm*, pp. ix-x.

64. Albert J. Raboteau, "Transcending Divided Worlds," *The Merton Seasonal* 28.3 (Fall 2003), p. 30.

65. *Merton and Judaism: Holiness in Words*, p. 15.

66. *Merton and Judaism: Holiness in Words*, pp. 25-26.

67. Richard E. Sherwin, "Graced by Passion and Compassion," *The Merton Seasonal* 29:1 (Spring 2004), pp. 29-32.

68. Patrick Hart, *The Message of Thomas Merton* [*Cistercian Studies Series Number 42*] (Kalamazoo, MI: Cistercian Publications, 1981).

69. Patrick Hart, *The Legacy of Thomas Merton* [*Cistercian Studies Series Number 92*] (Kalamazoo, MI: Cistercian Publications, 1986).

70. *Vision of Thomas Merton*, p. 9.

71. *Mystery Hidden Yet Revealed*, p. 298.

72. Rainer Maria Rilke, *Letters to a Young Poet* (New York: W.W. Norton, 1954), p. 35.

73. Merton, *Opening the Bible*, pp. 19-20.

The Merton Annual:
Index to Volumes 1 (1988)-16 (2003)*

by *Patricia A. Burton*

Notes:

The **main list** of authors, titles, reviews, etc. is in alphabetic order.

The reader is referred to **specialized sections** within the main list:
Bibliographic Reviews
Editors' Introductions
Interviews
Merton, Thomas: (1) works by, published in *The Merton Annual*.
Merton, Thomas: (2) works by, as subject of Essays.

A special section entitled "**Subjects, Themes, People**" appears after the main list, for those researching a particular area of study. Title entries in the main list are also often useful in finding subjects.

Author entries are sorted as follows:
The author's own essays, reviews etc. are listed in date order first.

Cross-references to books by the author (which appear in Reviews) are listed in italic after essays, by book title in alphabetical order, with the note: *See* Reviews:...

Reviews are split into three categories: Merton's Books, Books about Merton, and Other Books. Each category is sorted alphabetically by the book title. The book title is stated most fully in the Reviews list, and in a shorter form as a cross-reference.

*This comprehensive Index to all the materials included in *The Merton Annual* is a tribute to Merton, to all the scholars, reviewers, and former editors of *The Merton Annual*, as well as to the diligence of Patricia A. Burton whose careful work will prove to be of great value for future investigators.

V.A.K., Editor

"'Abundant, Multiple, Restless': Levertov and Merton in the 1960s," by Emily Archer. 10 (1997) 131-175

Albert, John OCSO.
"Lights across the Ridge: Thomas Merton and Henry David Thoreau."
1 (1988) 271-320
"To Merton through Augustine: Images, Themes and Analogies of Kinship."
5 (1992) 65-94

Allchin, A. M.
Review of *Thomas Merton on Prayer* (ed. Castle), and of *The Shining Wilderness: Daily Readings with Thomas Merton*, (ed. Taylor). 3 (1990) 310-311
"The Worship of the Whole Creation: Merton and the Eastern Fathers."
5 (1992) 189-204
"Our Lives, a Powerful Pentecost: Merton's Meeting with Russian Christianity." 11 (1998) 33-48

Altany, Alan. "Thomas Merton's Poetic Incarnation of Emptiness."
10 (1997) 109-130

"Alternative Frameworks for Spirituality: The Frontier of Merton Studies," by George A. Kilcourse Jr. 12 (1999) 207-232

"'Although It Is Night': A Carmelite Perspective on Spirituality at the Juncture of Modernity and Postmodernity," by Steven Payne OCD. 6 (1993) 134-159

"Animated Outsiders: Echoes of Merton in Hampl, Norris, Dillard, and Ehrlich," by Claire Hoertz Badaracco. 8 (1995) 150-161

Apel, William D.
"Ninevah to Calvary: Thomas Merton and a Spiritual Geography of the Bible." 13 (2000) 235-244
"Mystic as Prophet: The Deep Freedom of Thomas Merton and Howard Thurman." 16 (2003) 172-187

Aprile, Dianne. Review of *A Seven Day Journey with Thomas Merton* (de Waal).
7 (1994) 181-185

Archer, Emily.
Review of *Evening Train* and of *New and Selected Essays* (Levertov).
6 (1993) 219-227
"'Abundant, Multiple, Restless': Levertov and Merton in the 1960s."
10 (1997) 131-175
Review of *Ezekiel: Vision in the Dust* (Berrigan). 12 (1999) 248-249

"The Associates of the Iowa Cistercians, Sowing New Seeds of Contemplation," by Patricia and Dennis Day. 16 (2003) 111-128

"'Aware and Awake and Alive': Interview with Brother Paul Quenon," by George A. Kilcourse Jr., transcr. Susan Merryweather. 15 (2002) 210-231

Axtell, Rick. Review of *Disarming the Heart* (Dear). 8 (1995) 264-271

Baciu, Stefan. "Latin America and Spain in the Poetic World of Thomas Merton."
2 (1989) 13-26

Badaracco, Claire Hoertz.
  "Animated Outsiders: Echoes of Merton in Hampl, Norris, Dillard, and Ehrlich." 8 (1995) 150-161
  "Cultural Resistance and Literary Identity: Merton's Reading Notebooks." 10 (1997) 193-204
  "The Influence of 'Beat' Generation Poetry on the Work of Thomas Merton [*Cables to the Ace* used for comparison]." 15 (2002) 121-135

Baker, Kimberly F. "'The Great Honesty': Remembering Thomas Merton." Interview with Timothy Kelly OCSO, by George A. Kilcourse Jr., ed. Kimberly F. Baker. 9 (1996) 193-220

Baker, Rob. *Merton and Sufism* (ed. Baker and Henry). *See* Reviews: Books About Merton

Bamberger, John Eudes OCSO.
  Review of *Thomas Merton, Brother Monk* (Pennington). 1 (1988) 347-351
  "Merton's Vocation as a Monastic and Writer." Interview by Victor A. Kramer, ed. Dewey Weiss Kramer. 4 (1991) 21-38
  "Monasticism and Thomas Merton, Monk-Priest and Author: His Contributions to a Wider Understanding of Spirituality." 12 (1999) 22-37

Barron, Robert. *The Strangest Way: Walking the Christian Path. See* Reviews: Other Books

Bathanti, Joseph. Review of *Woman and the Sea: Selected Poems* (Mott). 14 (2001) 275-277

Baumann, Steven L. Review of *The Merton Tapes*: Fifth Release of Lectures. 7 (1994) 176-178

Bear, Virginia. "A Woodshed Full of French Angels: Multilingual Merton." 15 (2002) 136-154

Belcastro, David.
  "Czeslaw Milosz's Influence on Thomas Merton's 'Notes for a Philosophy of Solitude'." 7 (1994) 21-32
  "Merton and Camus on Christian Dialogue with a Postmodern World." 10 (1997) 223-233

"Bells in Thomas Merton's Early Poetry, 1940-1946," by Sheila M. Hempstead. 2 (1989) 257-287

Benner, David G. *Sacred Companions. See*: Reviews: Other Books

Berrigan, Daniel J. SJ.
  "What, Then, Must We Do?" [Merton and Dorothy Day]. 11 (1998) 49-66
  Ezekiel: Vision in the Dust. See Reviews: Other Books
  The Writings of Daniel Berrigan (Labrie). *See* Reviews: Other Books

Berry, Wendell
  Selected Poems of Wendell Berry. See Reviews: Other Books
  A Timbered Choir: The Sabbath Poems, 1979-1997. See Reviews: Other Books
  Watch With Me and Six Other Stories.... See Reviews: Other Books

"'The Best Retreat I Ever Made': Merton and the Contemplative Prioresses," by Bonnie B. Thurston. 14 (2001) 81-95

Betz, Margaret Bridget. "Merton's Images of Elias, Wisdom, and the Inclusive God." 13 (2000) 190-207

Biallas, Leonard J.
  Review of *The Intimate Merton* (ed. Hart and Montaldo). 13 (2000) 257-263
  "Merton and Basho: The Narrow Road Home." 15 (2002) 77-102

Bibliographic Reviews
1987. "The Merton Phenomenon in 1987: A Bibliographic Survey," by Robert E.
  Daggy. 1 (1988) 321-337
1988. "Merton and 1988: A Survey of Publications and Commemorations," by
  Robert E. Daggy. 2 (1989) 291-308
1989. "The Continuing Tsunami: 1989 in Merton Scholarship and Publication," by
  Robert E. Daggy. 3 (1990) 277-289
1990. "'What They Say': 1990 in Merton Scholarship and Publication," by Robert
  E. Daggy. 4 (1991) 259-271
1991. "Wandering in the Merton Dimension: A Survey of Scholarship and
  Publication in 1991," by Robert E. Daggy. 5 (1992) 357-360
1992. "Critical Turn Ahead!: 1992 in Merton Scholarship and Publication," by
  Michael Downey. 6 (1993) 194-202
1993. "'Easter Fugue' out of a 'Great Spiritual Silence': 1993 in Merton Scholarship and Publication," by George A. Kilcourse Jr. 7 (1994) 156-173
1994. "Thousands of Words: A Bibliographic Review," by Victor A. Kramer.
  8 (1995) 221-245
1995. "Posthumous Prolificacy: A Bibliographic Review Essay," by Michael
  Downey. 9 (1996) 237-251
1996. "A Haven for 'Homeless Religious Minds': 1996 Bibliographic Review," by
  George A. Kilcourse Jr. 10 (1997) 303-325
1997. "'Non-Public' Writing in Journal and Correspondence: A Core Radiating
  Outward. 1997 Bibliographic Review," by Victor A. Kramer.
  11 (1998) 174-195
1998. "Alternative Frameworks for Spirituality: The Frontier of Merton Studies,"
  by George A. Kilcourse Jr. 12 (1999) 207-232
1999. "Connecting the Spiritual and the Cultural: Patterns within Merton's
  Writings," by Victor A. Kramer. 13 (2000) 144-164
2000. "Inertia, Idiosyncrasy and Incubation: The Range of Current Merton
  Studies," by George A. Kilcourse Jr. 14 (2001) 223-243
2001. "'Contemplation's Shadow and Merton's Act: Becoming a Saint Through
  Words': 2001 Bibliographic Review," by Victor A. Kramer.
  15 (2002) 232-262
2002. "Merton's 'True Spirit' or a Calculated 'Official Pedestal'?" by George A.
  Kilcourse Jr. 16 (2003) 221-244

Biddle, Arthur W.
  Review of *The Way of the Dreamcatcher...Robert Lax* (Georgiou).
  16 (2003) 255-257
    When Prophecy Still Had a Voice (ed. Biddle). *See* Reviews: Merton's Books

"Blazing in the Spark of God: Thomas Merton's References to Meister Eckhart,"
  by Erlinda G. Paguio. 5 (1992) 247-262

"Blessed Are the Meek: The Nonviolence of Thomas Merton," by John Dear SJ.
  5 (1992) 205-213

Bochen, Christine M.
"A Time of Transition. Selection of Letters from the Earliest Correspondence of
Thomas Merton and Ernesto Cardenal," ed. and introd. Bochen, transl.
Roberto S. Goizueta. 8 (1995) 162-167
"A Journey into Wholeness." Interview with Sr Myriam Dardenne at Red-
woods Monastery (with Victor A. Kramer, ed. Bochen). 14 (2001) 33-55
"From Faith to Joy: Studying the Church and Thomas Merton": Interview with
William H. Shannon, by Christine M. Bochen and Victor A. Kramer. 16
(2003) 85-110
   At Home in the World: Letters of Merton and Ruether, Afterword by Christine
   M. Bochen. *See* Reviews: Merton's Books
   The Courage for Truth: Letters of Thomas Merton (ed. Bochen). *See* Reviews:
   Merton's Books
   Learning to Love: Journals of Thomas Merton, ed. Christine M. Bochen. *See*
   Reviews: Merton's Books
   The Thomas Merton Encyclopedia (Shannon, Bochen, O'Connell). *See* Reviews:
   Books About Merton.
   Thomas Merton: Essential Writings (ed. Bochen). *See* Reviews: Merton's Books
Bock, David OCSO. Review of *The Cloister Walk* (Norris). 10 (1997) 345-347
Bonazzi, Robert. *Man in the Mirror: John Howard Griffin and the Story of Black Like
Me. See* Reviews: Other Books
Bondi, Roberta. Review of *Illuminated Life: Monastic Wisdom for Seekers of Light*
(Chittister). 14 (2001) 263-264
Bourget, Dom M. Laurence OCSO. "Thomas Merton: A Monk Who 'Succeeded'."
Interview by Jonathan Montaldo. 12 (1999) 38-61
Brame, Grace Adolphsen. *The Ways of the Spirit* (Underhill, ed. Brame). *See*
Reviews: Other Books
Breit, Marquita E. Review of *Merton Vade Mecum* (Burton). 13 (2000) 269-271
Bridgers, Lynn. Review of *Thomas Merton: Essential Writings* (sel. and ed. Bochen).
14 (2001) 251-252
"'Bringing the Earth to Flower': A Tribute to Robert Lax (1915-2000) Poet,
Pilgrim, Prophet," by Jeannine N. Mizingou. 15 (2002) 23-60
Bruteau, Beatrice.
"Eucharistic Cosmos." 10 (1997) 77-107
"Eating Together: The Shared Supper and the Covenant Community."
16 (2003) 17-26
   What We Can Learn from the East. See Reviews: Other Books
Burnham, Christopher C.
"Out of the Shadows: Merton's Rhetoric of Revelation." 9 (1996) 55-73
"Merton's Ethos in *The Seven Storey Mountain*: Toward a Rhetoric of Conver-
sion." 11 (1998) 110-120
Burns, Flavian OCSO. "Merton's Contribution as Teacher, Writer and Community
Member." Interview by Victor A. Kramer, ed. Dewey Weiss Kramer.
3 (1990) 71-89
Burrell, David B. CSC "On Discovering Divine Foolishness: Merton as Bridge-
Person." 2 (1989) 121-129

Burton-Christie, Douglas. Review of *Witness to Freedom: Letters of Thomas Merton* (ed. Shannon). 8 (1995) 246-254

Burton, Patricia A. *Merton Vade Mecum*. *See* Reviews: Books About Merton

Cahaney, Elizabeth. Review of *A Stay Against Confusion* (Hansen). 15 (2002) 276-278

Callahan, Annice RSCJ.
  Review of *Merton: Mystic at the Center of America* (King). 6 (1993) 205-208
  Spiritual Guides for Today. *See* Reviews: Books About Merton

Capps, Walter. *Preview of the Asian Journey* (Merton, ed. Capps). *See* Reviews: Merton's Books

Cardenal, Ernesto. "Time of Transition: A Selection of Letters from the Earliest Correspondence of Thomas Merton and Ernesto Cardenal," ed. and introd. Christine M. Bochen, transl. Roberto S. Goizueta. 8 (1995) 162-200

"The Cardinal and the Monk: Literary and Theological Convergences in Newman and Merton," by Michael W. Higgins. 5 (1992) 215-225

Carrere, Daniel OCSO.
  Review of *Turning Toward the World: Journals of Thomas Merton* (ed. Kramer). 10 (1997) 334-338
  "Standing before God: Merton's Incarnational Spirituality." 16 (2003) 56-72

Carr, Anne E.
  Review of *Evelyn Underhill: Artist of the Infinite Life* (Greene), and of *The Ways of the Spirit* (Underhill, ed. Brame). 4 (1991) 298-300
  A Search for Wisdom and Spirit. *See* Reviews: Books About Merton

Casey, Michael OCSO.
  "Merton's Teaching on the 'Common Will' and What the Journals Tell Us." 12 (1999) 62-84
  Sacred Reading: The Ancient Art of Lectio Divina. *See* Reviews: Other Books
  Toward God: The Ancient Wisdom of Western Prayer. *See* Reviews: Other Books

Castle, Tony. *Thomas Merton on Prayer*, ed. Castle: *See* Reviews: Merton's Books

"'A Certainty of Tread': Grace Unfolded in Thomas Merton's Contemplative Experience and Poetry," by George A. Kilcourse Jr. 15 (2002) 7-13

Chittister, Joan D. OSB.
  "Of Moses' Mother and Pharoah's Daughter: A Model of Contemporary Contemplation." 3 (1990) 61-70
  "Thomas Merton: Seeder of Radical Action and the Enlightened Heart." 12 (1999) 103-116
  Illuminated Life: Monastic Wisdom for Seekers of Light. *See* Reviews: Other Books

"The Christian Exploration of Non-Christian Religions: Merton's Example and Where It Might Lead Us," by Roger Corless. 13 (2000) 105-122

"The Christian Mystic as *paganus redevivus*: A Hermeneutical Suggestion," by Roger Corless. 3 (1990) 203-216

Clark, Benjamin OCSO.
  "Thomas Merton's Gethsemani: Part I, The Novitiate Years." 4 (1991) 223-256

"The Continuing Tsunami: 1989 in Merton Scholarship and Publication," by Robert E. Daggy. 3 (1990) 277-289

Cook, Andrea C. "The Experience of Romantic Transcendence in Thomas Merton's *Eighteen Poems.*" 14 (2001) 121-154

Cooper, David D.
"From Prophecy to Parody: Thomas Merton's *Cables to the Ace.*" 1 (1988) 215-234
"Thomas Merton and James Laughlin: Two Literary Lives in Letters." 10 (1997) 177-191
Review of *Thomas Merton's American Prophecy* (Inchausti). 12 (1999) 239-241
The Alaskan Journal of Thomas Merton (pref. Cooper). *See* Reviews: Merton's Books
Thomas Merton and James Laughlin: Letters (ed.Cooper). *See* Reviews: Merton's Books
Thomas Merton in Alaska (pref. Cooper). *See* Reviews: Merton's Books
Thomas Merton's Art of Denial. *See* Reviews: Books About Merton

Corless, Roger.
"The Christian Mystic as *paganus redevivus*: A Hermeneutical Suggestion." 3 (1990) 203-216
Review of *Freedom in Exile: The Autobiography of the Dalai Lama.* 4 (1991) 295-297
"In Search of a Context for the Merton-Suzuki Dialogue." 6 (1993) 76-91
Review of *Thomas Merton and Chinese Wisdom* (Lee), and of *What We Can Learn from the East* (Bruteau). 9 (1996) 277-280
Review of *The Gethsemani Encounter* (ed. Mitchell and Wiseman). 12 (1999) 242-244
"The Christian Exploration of Non-Christian Religions: Merton's Example and Where It Might Lead Us." 13 (2000) 105-122
Buddhist Emptiness and Christian Trinity (Corless and Knitter). *See* Reviews: Other Books

Crews, Clyde F. Review of *The Impact of Divine Love*: 8 cassette tapes. (Morneau). 5 (1992) 389-392

Crider, Glenn.
Review of *Poetry as Prayer: Thomas Merton* (Waldron). 14 (2001) 252-257
(with Victor A. Kramer) "An Editorial Note concerning the Tape 'The Irish Tradition of Mysticism' and 'About Contemplative Life Today'." 16 (2003) 13
"From Faith to Joy: Studying the Church and Thomas Merton": Interview with William H. Shannon, by Christine M. Bochen and Victor A. Kramer, ed. and transc. by Glenn Crider. 16 (2003) 85-110
Review of *Sacred Companions* (Benner). 16 (2003) 257-260

"Critical Turn Ahead!: 1992 in Merton Scholarship and Publication," by Michael Downey. 6 (1993) 194-202

Culbertson, Diana OP. [part of] Review Symposium of *Ace of Freedoms: Thomas Merton's Christ* (Kilcourse). 7 (1994) 203-207

"Cultural Resistance and Literary Identity: Merton's Reading Notebooks," by Claire Hoertz Badaracco. 10 (1997) 193-204

"Culture and the Formation of Personal Identity: Dilemma and Dialectic in Thomas Merton's Teaching," by Thomas Del Prete. 8 (1995) 105-121

Cunningham, Lawrence S.

Review of *The Alaskan Journal of Thomas Merton* (ed. Daggy). 1 (1988) 343-347
Review of *A Search for Wisdom and Spirit* (Carr). 2 (1989) 329-332
"Thomas Merton: The Monk as a Critic of Culture." 3 (1990) 187-199
"Harvesting New Fruits: Merton's 'Message to Poets'." 9 (1996) 21-33
   A Search for Solitude: Journals of Thomas Merton (ed. Cunningham) *See*
      Reviews: Merton's Books
   Thomas Merton and the Monastic Vision. See Reviews: Books About Merton
   Thomas Merton: Spiritual Master (ed. Cunningham). *See* Reviews: Merton's
      Books

"Czeslaw Milosz's Influence on Thomas Merton's 'Notes for a Philosophy of Solitude'," by David Belcastro. 7 (1994) 21-32

Daggy, Robert E.

Editors' Introduction (with P. Hart, D. W. Kramer, V. Kramer). 1 (1988) ix-x
"The Merton Phenomenon in 1987: A Bibliographic Survey." 1 (1988) 321-337
"Merton and 1988: A Survey of Publications and Commemorations."
   2 (1989) 291-308
Editors' Introduction (with P. Hart, D. W. Kramer, V. Kramer). 2 (1989) ix-x
Editors' Introduction by Robert Daggy, P. Hart, D. W. Kramer, V. Kramer.
   3 (1990) xi
"The Continuing Tsunami: 1989 in Merton Scholarship and Publication."
   3 (1990) 277-289
"'What They Say': 1990 in Merton Scholarship and Publication."
   4 (1991) 259-271
Editors' Introduction (with P. Hart, D. W. Kramer, V. Kramer). 4 (1991) xi
"Wandering in the Merton Dimension: A Survey of Scholarship and Publication in 1991." 5 (1992) 357-360
   The Alaskan Journal of Thomas Merton (ed. Daggy). *See* Reviews: Merton's
      Books
   Dancing in the Water of Life: Journals of Thomas Merton (ed. Daggy). *See*
      Reviews: Merton's Books
   Encounter: Thomas Merton and D. T. Suzuki (ed. Daggy). *See* Reviews:
      Merton's Books
   "Honorable Reader": Reflections on my Work (ed. Daggy). *See* Reviews:
      Merton's Books
   Monks Pond: Thomas Merton's "Little Magazine" (ed. Daggy). *See* Reviews:
      Merton's Books
   The Road to Joy: Letters of Thomas Merton (ed. Daggy). *See* Reviews: Merton's
      Books
   Thomas Merton in Alaska (ed. Daggy). *See* Reviews: Merton's Books

Dalai Lama.

   The Gethsemani Encounter (ed.Mitchell and Wiseman), foreword by the Dalai
      Lama. Review by Roger Corless. 12 (1999) 242-244

"Penning Patterns of Transformation: Etty Hillesum and Thomas Merton." 4 (1991) 77-95

Review of *An Anthology of Christian Mysticism* (Egan). 5 (1992) 394-395

"Critical Turn Ahead!: 1992 in Merton Scholarship and Publication." 6 (1993) 194-202

"Daughter of Carmel; Son of Cîteaux: A Friendship Endures." Interview with Angela Collins OCD, ed. Andrew Hartmans. 8 (1995) 201-220

"Collision Course 101: The Monastery, the Academy, and the Corporation." 8 (1995) ix-xii

"Posthumous Prolificacy: A Bibliographic Review Essay." 9 (1996) 237-251

The New Dictionary of Catholic Spirituality (ed. Downey). *See* Reviews: Other Books

My Song Is of Mercy: Writings of Matthew Kelty (ed. Downey). *See* Reviews: Other Books

"'Easter Fugue' out of a 'Great Spiritual Silence': 1993 in Merton Scholarship and Publication." Bibliographic Review 1993, by George A. Kilcourse Jr. 7 (1994) 156-173

Eastman, Patrick.

"The Dangers of Solitude." 7 (1994) 14-20

[part of] Review Symposium of *Ace of Freedoms: Thomas Merton's Christ* (Kilcourse). 7 (1994) 198-203

"Eating Together: The Shared Supper and the Covenant Community," by Beatrice Bruteau. 16 (2003) 17-26

"Editing the Journals of Thomas Merton," by Patrick Hart OCSO. 9 (1996) 221-225

Editors' Introductions

Note: Vols. 1 to 4 were edited jointly by Robert E. Daggy, Patrick Hart OCSO, Dewey Weiss Kramer, and Victor A. Kramer: page references as follows: 1 (1988) ix-x; 2 (1989) ix-x; 3 (1990) xi; 4 (1991) xi.

1992. Introduction by Victor A. Kramer. 5 (1992) ix-x

1993. "Spirituality after 'A Prayer Lip Stumbles'," by George A. Kilcourse Jr. 6 (1993) 1-5

1994. "Solitude Leads toward Apostolate in and for the World," by Victor A. Kramer. 7 (1994) ix-xiv

1995. "Collision Course 101: The Monastery, the Academy, and the Corporation," by Michael Downey. 8 (1995) ix-xii

1996. "News of a More Complex Merton Industry," by George A. Kilcourse Jr. 9 (1996) ix-xxii

1997. "Fragmentation and the Quest for the Spiritual in the Late Twentieth Century," by Victor A. Kramer. 10 (1997) ix-xiv

1998. "The Religious Ethic at the Heart of Merton's Spirituality," by George A. Kilcourse Jr. 11 (1998) 7-11

1999. "Thomas Merton's Commitments to Community: The Need for Courtesy, Exchange and Engagement," by Victor A. Kramer. 12 (1999) 7-12

2000. "Spirituality as the Freedom to Channel Eros," by George A. Kilcourse Jr. 13 (2000) 7-15

"Fire Watch Epilogue and *Life and Holiness*: Opposing Rhetorics in the Writings of Thomas Merton," by Mary Murray. 7 (1994) 45-57

Fisher, James T. *The Catholic Counterculture in America, 1933-1962. See* Reviews: Other Books

Fitzpatrick-Hopler, Gail. "The Spiritual Network of Contemplative Outreach Limited." 16 (2003) 188-196

Flynn, James E. Review of *The Sound of Listening* (Dear). 13 (2000) 271-272

Ford, John H. "'Not Himself, but a Direction'," Interview with John (Jack) H. Ford, by George A. Kilcourse Jr., ed. David King. 6 (1993) 175-193

Forest, James H.
    Review of *Thomas Merton on Nuclear Weapons* (Powaski). 2 (1989) 336-339
    Living With Wisdom: A Life of Thomas Merton. See Reviews: Books About Merton

Foster, Diane. Review of *Thomas Merton in Alaska* (ed. Daggy). 3 (1990) 305-309

"Foundations for Renewal: An Analysis of Shared Reflections of Thomas Merton and Ernesto Cardenal," by Douglas R. Letson. 3 (1990) 93-106

Fox, Ruth OSB.
    "Merton's Journey from *Seeds* to *New Seeds.*" 1 (1988) 249-270
    Review of *Prayer and Commitment in Thomas Merton* and of *Prophecy and Commitment in Thomas Merton* [2 cassette tapes] (Tobin). 5 (1992) 377-384

"Fragmentation and the Quest for the Spiritual in the Late Twentieth Century," by Victor A. Kramer. 10 (1997) ix-xiv

Friesen, Duane K. "A People's Movement as a Condition for the Development of a Just Peacemaking Theory." 9 (1996) 182-191

Frohlich, Mary. *The Lay Contemplative* (ed. Manss and Frohlich). *See* Reviews: Other Books

"From Faith to Joy: Studying the Church and Thomas Merton": Interview with William H. Shannon, by Christine M. Bochen and Victor A. Kramer, ed. and transc. by Glenn Crider. 16 (2003) 85-110

"From Prophecy to Parody: Thomas Merton's *Cables to the Ace*," by David D. Cooper. 1 (1988) 215-234

Fuller, Roy D.
    Review of *Exiles from Eden* (Schwehn). 7 (1994) 188-190
    "The Virtuous Teacher: Thomas Merton's Contribution to a Spirituality of Higher Education." 8 (1995) 59-74

Funk, Mary Margaret OSB. Review of *Toward God* (Casey) and of *Sacred Reading*(Casey). 10 (1997) 341-344

Furlong, Monica. *The Shining Wilderness* (ed.Taylor). *See* Reviews: Merton's Books

"A Gallery of Women's Faces and Dreams of Women From the Drawings and Journals of Thomas Merton," Introduction by Jonathan Montaldo. 14 (2001) 155-158

"Geography of Solitude: Thomas Merton's 'Elias—Variations on a Theme'," by Patrick F. O'Connell. 1 (1988) 151-190

Georgiou, S.T. *The Way of the Dreamcatcher...Robert Lax. See* Reviews: Other Books

Henry, Patrick G. *For the Sake of the World* (Henry and Swearer). *See* Reviews: Other Books

Hensell, Eugene OSB. Review of *Thomas Merton and the Monastic Vision* (Cunningham). 13 (2000) 263-265

"'Hiding the Ace of Freedoms': Discovering the Way(s) of Peace in Thomas Merton's *Cables to the Ace*," by Lynn Szabo. 15 (2002)103-120

Higgins, Michael W.
"Merton and the Real Poets: Paradise Re-Bugged." 3 (1990) 175-186
"The Cardinal and the Monk: Literary and Theological Convergences in Newman and Merton." 5 (1992) 215-225

Hinson, E. Glenn.
"Social Involvement and Spirituality." 3 (1990) 217-229
"Rootedness in Tradition and Global Spirituality." 6 (1993) 6-22
"'Thomas Merton, my Brother': The Impact of Thomas Merton on my Life and Thought." 11 (1998) 88-96
Spirituality in Ecumenical Perspective (ed. Hinson). *See* Reviews: Other Books

Hotchen, Stephen J. Review of *The Spark in the Soul* (Tastard). 4 (1991) 291-295

Huda, Qamar-ul. Review of *Merton and Sufism* (ed. Baker and Henry). 13 (2000) 266-268

"The Human Way Out: The Friendship of Charity as a Countercultural Practice," by Paul J. Wadell CP. 8 (1995) 38-58

"Humanizing the University: Adding the Contemplative Dimension," by Julia Ann Upton RSM. 8 (1995) 75-87

Imperato, Robert. *Merton and Walsh on the Person*. *See* Reviews: Books About Merton

"In Memoriam: Mahanambrata Brahmachari (23 December 1904-18 October 1999)," by Francis X. Clooney SJ. 13 (2000) 123-126

"In Search of a Context for the Merton-Suzuki Dialogue," by Roger Corless. 6 (1993) 76-91

"In the Company of Prophets? Merton's Engagement with the World," by Francis Kline OCSO. 12 (1999) 117-128

Inchausti, Robert. *Thomas Merton's American Prophecy*. *See* Reviews: Books About Merton

"Inertia, Idiosyncrasy and Incubation: The Range of Current Merton Studies," by George A. Kilcourse Jr. 14 (2001) 223-243

"The Influence of 'Beat' Generation Poetry on the Work of Thomas Merton," by Claire Hoertz Badaracco. 15 (2002) 121-135

Interviews
Bamberger, John Eudes OCSO. "Merton's Vocation as a Monastic and Writer." Interview by Victor A. Kramer, ed. Dewey Weiss Kramer. 4 (1991) 21-38
Bourget, M. Laurence OCSO. "Thomas Merton: A Monk Who 'Succeeded'." Interview by Correspondence cond. and ed. Jonathan Montaldo. 12 (1999) 38-61

Interviews cont'd

Burns, Flavian OCSO. "Merton's Contribution as Teacher, Writer and Community Member." Interview by Victor A. Kramer, ed. Dewey Weiss Kramer. 3 (1990) 71-89

Collins, Angela OCD. "Daughter of Carmel; Son of Cîteaux: A Friendship Endures." Interview by Michael Downey, ed. Andrew Hartmans. 8 (1995) 201-220

Collins, Frederic OCSO. "Merton's Quiet Influence, A Testimony of Continuing Conversion." Interview by Victor A. Kramer. 5 (1992) 169-186

Dardenne, Myriam OCSO. "A Journey into Wholeness." Interview at Redwoods Monastery, by Christine M. Bochen with Victor A. Kramer; ed. Bochen. 14 (2001) 33-55

Ferry, W. H. "Action at the Center." Interview by Gregory J. Ryan. 4 (1991) 205-219

Ford, John H. "'Not Himself, but a Direction'." Interview by George A. Kilcourse Jr., ed. David King. 6 (1993) 175-193

Kelly, Timothy OCSO. "'The Great Honesty': Remembering Thomas Merton." Interview by George A. Kilcourse Jr., ed. Kimberly F. Baker. 9 (1996) 193-220

Kelty, Matthew OCSO. "Looking back to Merton: Memories and Impressions." Interview by Victor A. Kramer, ed. Dewey Weiss Kramer. 1 (1988) 55-76

Padovano, Anthony T. "Spirituality, Scholarship and Biography." Interview by Jonathan Montaldo. 10 (1997) 285-302

Quenon, Paul OCSO. "'Aware and Awake and Alive': Interview" by George A. Kilcourse Jr., transcr. Susan Merryweather. 15 (2002) 210-231

Richardson, Jane Marie SL. "Life Through the Lens of Inner and Outer Freedom." Interview by George A. Kilcourse Jr., ed. Paul Stokell. 13 (2000) 127-143

Seitz, Ron. "The Climate of Humor and Freedom." Interview by George A. Kilcourse Jr., ed. Matthew McEver. 7 (1994) 129-155

Shannon, William. "From Faith to Joy: Studying the Church and Thomas Merton." Interview by Christine M. Bochen and Victor A. Kramer, ed. and transc. Glenn Crider. 16 (2003) 85-110

Tobin, Mary Luke SL. "Growing into Responsibility." Interview by Dewey Weiss Kramer, ed. Victor A. Kramer. 2 (1989) 43-56

Waddell, Chrysogonus OCSO. "Truly Seeking God...in Christ." Interview by Victor A. Kramer. ed. George A. Kilcourse Jr. 11 (1998) 148-173

Johmann, Michael.
Review of *My Song Is of Mercy: Writings of Matthew Kelty* (ed. Downey). 8 (1995) 271-274

Review of *Dancing in the Water of Life: Journals of Thomas Merton* (ed. Daggy). 11 (1998) 196-199

Johnson, Timothy J. OFM Conv. Review of *The New Dictionary of Catholic Spirituality* (ed. Downey). 7 (1994) 194-197

Johnston, William. *'Arise My Love...': Mysticism for a New Era.* See Reviews: Other Books

"A Journey into Wholeness." Interview with Sr Myriam Dardenne at Redwoods Monastery, by Christine M. Bochen with Victor A. Kramer. 14 (2001) 33-55

"The Joy of Being Catholic: The Relationship of the Conversion of Thomas Merton to the RCIA," by Mitch Finley. 13 (2000) 171-189

Juen, Helge J. Review of *The Dawn of the Mystical Age* (Tuoti). 12 (1999) 246-247

Kang, Kun Ki. "Prayer and the Cultivation of Mind: An Examination of Thomas Merton and Chinul." 2 (1989) 221-238

Kardong, Terrence G. OSB, Review of *Survival or Prophecy? Letters of Merton and Leclercq* (ed. Hart). 16 (2003) 245-246

Katz, Jon. *Running to the Mountain. See* Reviews: Books About Merton

Keating, Thomas OCSO. *Healing our Violence...Centering Prayer* (Rohr and Keating). *See* Reviews: Other Books

Kelly, Timothy OCSO.
"'The Great Honesty': Remembering Thomas Merton." Interview by George A. Kilcourse Jr. 9 (1996) 193-220
Photograph of the Dalai Lama and Abbot Timothy Kelly at Thomas Merton's Grave, April 25, 1994, taken by Amy Taylor. 9 (1996) 192

Kelty, Matthew OCSO.
"Looking back to Merton: Memories and Impressions." Interview by Victor A. Kramer. 1 (1988) 55-76
Review of *Brother and Lover: Aelred of Rivaulx,* by Brian Patrick McGuire. 8 (1995) 274-276
My Song is of Mercy: Writings of Matthew Kelty [ed. Downey]. *See* Reviews: Other Books

"The Kenotic Convict: A *Divertissement* on Contemporary Contemplative Spirituality in its Social Context," by Jens Söring. 16 (2003) 152-171

Kilcourse, George A. Jr.
"The Monk as a 'Marginal' Person." 2 (1989) 175-189
"'A Shy Wild Deer': The 'True Self' in Thomas Merton's Poetry." 4 (1991) 97-109
Review of *Spiritual Guides for Today* (Callahan). 5 (1992) 384-386
"Spirituality after 'A Prayer Lip Stumbles': Introduction to *Merton Annual* 6 (1993) 1-5
"'Not Himself, but a Direction'." Interview with John (Jack) H. Ford, ed. David King. 6 (1993) 175-193
"'Easter Fugue' out of a 'Great Spiritual Silence': 1993 in Merton Scholarship and Publication." 7 (1994) 156-173
"The Climate of Humor and Freedom." Interview with Ron Seitz. 7 (1994) 129-155
Author's Response (to Review Symposium on *Ace of Freedoms*). 7 (1997) 221-226
"News of a More Complex Merton Industry." Introduction to *Merton Annual* 9 (1996) ix-xxii
"'The Great Honesty': Remembering Thomas Merton." Interview with Timothy Kelly OCSO, ed. Kimberly F. Baker. 9 (1996) 193-220
"A Haven for 'Homeless Religious Minds": 1996 Bibliographic Review 10 (1997) 303-325
"The Religious Ethic at the Heart of Merton's Spirituality." Introduction to *Merton Annual* 11 (1998) 7-11

Kramer, Victor A. cont'd

"Merton's Quiet Influence, A Testimony of Continuing Conversion." Interview with Frederic Collins OCSO, ed. Dewey Weiss Kramer. 5 (1992) 169-186

Foreword to second series of *Merton Annual*. 6 (1993) ix-x

"Solitude Leads toward Apostolate in and for the World." Introduction to *Merton Annual* 7 (1994) ix-xiv

"Thousands of Words: A Bibliographic Review." 8 (1995) 221-245

"Fragmentation and the Quest for the Spiritual in the Late Twentieth Century." Introduction to *Merton Annual* 10 (1997) ix-xiv

"'Non-Public' Writing in Journal and Correspondence: A Core Radiating Outward." 1997 Bibliographic Review. 11 (1998) 174-95

"Thomas Merton's Commitments to Community: The Need for Courtesy, Exchange and Engagement." Introduction to *Merton Annual* 12 (1999) 7-12.

"Connecting the Spiritual and the Cultural: Patterns Within Merton's Writings." 1999 Bibliographic Review. 13 (2000) 144-164

"Introduction: Merton's Openness to Change and his Foreshadowing of a Feminist Spirituality." 14 (2001) 7-11

"A Journey into Wholeness." Interview with Sr Myriam Dardenne at Redwoods Monastery, by Christine M. Bochen with Victor A. Kramer. 14 (2001) 33-55

"'Contemplation's Shadow and Merton's Act: Becoming a Saint Through Words': 2001 Bibliographic Review." 15 (2002) 232-262

"Introduction: Merton's Contemplative Presence within Contemporary Society" 16 (2003) 7-12

(With Glenn Crider), "An Editorial Note concerning the Tape 'The Irish Tradition of Mysticism' and 'About Contemplative Life Today'." 16 (2003) 13

"From Faith to Joy: Studying the Church and Thomas Merton": Interview with William H. Shannon, by Christine M. Bochen and Victor A. Kramer. 16 (2003) 85-110

"Postscript: A Statement about the Publishing History of *The Merton Annual*." 16 (2003) 267-269

Turning Toward the World: Journals of Thomas Merton (ed. Kramer). *See* Reviews: Merton's Books

Kristoff, Donna OSU. "'Light That Is Not Light': A Consideration of Thomas Merton and the Icon" [incl. illustrations of icons, 109-114]. 2 (1989) 85-114

Kropf, Richard W. "The Mysticism of Merton and Teilhard Compared." 5 (1992) 227-245

Labrie, Ross.

Review of *Thomas Merton's Art of Denial* (Cooper). 3 (1990) 321-324

"Merton and the American Romantics." 9 (1996) 34-52

"Merton and Time." 11 (1998) 121-137

Review of *Walker Percy: A Life*, by Patrick H. Samway SJ. 11 (1998) 211-213

Review of *At the Crossroads... Walker Percy*, by John F. Desmond. 11 (1998) 213-214

Review of *The Thomas Merton Encyclopedia* (Shannon, Bochen, O'Connell). 16 (2003) 246-250

McGuire, Brian Patrick. *Brother and Lover: Aelred of Rivaulx. See* Reviews: Other Books

McKenna, Thomas F. CM.
"Thomas Merton and the Renewal of Religious Life." 3 (1990) 107-118
Review of *Song for Nobody* (Seitz). 7 (1994) 178-181
"A Voice in the Postmodern Wilderness: Merton on Monastic Renewal."
   8 (1995) 122-137

McMillan, Allan M. "Thomas Merton's Seven Lessons for Interfaith Dialogue."
   15 (2002) 194-209

Meatyard, Ralph Eugene. *Father Louie: Photographs by Meatyard* (ed. Magid). *See*
   Reviews: Books About Merton

Meinert, Barbara Dolan. Review of *The Lay Contemplative* (ed. Manss and
   Froelich). 14 (2001) 266-267

Merryweather, Susan. "'Aware and Awake and Alive': Interview with Brother
   Paul Quenon," by George A. Kilcourse Jr., transcr. Susan Merryweather.
   15 (2002) 210-231

"Merton and Basho: The Narrow Road Home," by Leonard J. Baillas.
   15 (2002) 77-102

"Merton and 1988: A Survey of Publications and Commemorations," by Robert
   E. Daggy. 2 (1989) 291-308

"Merton and Blake: The Heretic Within and the Heretic Without," by Susan
   McCaslin. 14 (2001) 173-183

"Merton and Camus on Christian Dialogue with a Postmodern World," by David
   Belcastro. 10 (1997) 223-233

"Merton and Loretto: Background of Tape Recording [Comments about the
   Religious Life Today]," by Jane Marie Richardson SL. 14 (2001) 12-13

"Merton and the American Romantics," by Ross Labrie. 9 (1996) 34-52

"Merton and the Celtic Monastic Tradition: Search for the Promised Land," by
   Paul M. Pearson. 5 (1992) 263-277

"Merton and the Living Tradition of Faith," by William H. Shannon.
   1 (1988) 79-102

"Merton and the Mysticism of the Mind," by Robert Faricy SJ. 11 (1998) 138-147.

"Merton and the Real Poets: Paradise Re-Bugged," by Michael W. Higgins.
   3 (1990) 175-186

"Merton and the Tiger Lily," by Chrysogonus Waddell OCSO. 2 (1989) 59-79

"Merton and Time," by Ross Labrie. 11 (1998) 121-137

"Merton as Voluntary Prisoner," by James M. Somerville. 16 (2003) 148-151

"Merton Lecture, Columbia University, November 15, 1995," by Margaret
   O'Brien Steinfels. 9 (1996) 8-20

"Merton of Gethsemani and Bernard of Clairvaux," by Chrysogonus
   Waddell OCSO. 5 (1992) 95-130

"Merton Phenomenon in 1987: A Bibliographic Survey," by Robert E. Daggy.
   1 (1988) 321-337

"Merton, Friend of God and Prophet," by Sandra M. Schneiders IHM.
7 (1994) 81-86

"Merton, Moore, and the Carthusian Temptation," by Johan Seynnaeve.
10 (1997) 251-265

"Merton, Nonviolence and the Bishops' Pastoral," by Paul E. Dinter.
1 (1988) 129-148

Merton, Thomas: (1) works by, published in *The Merton Annual*
"About Contemplative Life Today" (transcript of audiotape, part of Credence
Cassette #AA2268). 16 (2003) 14-16

"Answers for Hernan Lavin Cerda," ed. Patrick Hart OCSO. 2 (1989) 5-12

"A Balanced Life of Prayer," ed. Patrick Hart OCSO. 8 (1995) 4-21

"The Black Sheep," foreword by Paul M. Pearson. 11 (1998) 17-32

"Comments about the Religious Life Today" (transcript of tape made by
Merton for Sisters of Loretto). 14 (2001) 14-32

DRAWINGS AND PRAYERS: "Gallery of Women's Faces and Dreams of Women
from the Drawings and Journals of Thomas Merton," sel. and introd. by
Jonathan Montaldo. 14 (2001) 159-172

"He Is Risen." 9 (1996) 1-7

JOURNALS: "Four Merton Journal Transcriptions, Two Missing Sheets of Merton
Journal Discovered," ed. Patrick Hart OCSO. 9 (1996) 225-236

LETTERS:
"Letter to a Poet about Vallejo." 2 (1989) 27-28

"Thomas Merton and Jean Leclercq: A Monastic Correspondence," ed.
Patrick Hart OCSO. 3 (1990) 5-35

"Correspondence 1962-1968" [with Douglas V. Steere], ed. Patrick
Hart OCSO. 6 (1993) 23-53

"Time of Transition: A Selection of Letters from the Earliest Correspondence
of Thomas Merton and Ernesto Cardenal," ed. Christine M. Bochen,
transl. Roberto S. Goizueta. 8 (1995) 162-200

"List of Works [in progress, to Superiors]." Transl. from French by William H.
Shannon. 2 (1989) 80-84

The Man in the Sycamore Tree [Fragment of an Early Novel]. Ed. Patrick
Hart OCSO. 5 (1992) 7-38

"Monastic Courtesy," ed. Patrick Hart OCSO. 12 (1999) 14-21

"The Neurotic Personality in the Monastic Life," ed. Patrick Hart OCSO.
4 (1991) 5-19

"The Ox Mountain Parable of Meng Tzu," with introductory note by Merton.
15 (2002) 20-22.

"The School of the Spirit," foreword by Patrick Hart OCSO. 10 (1997) 5-34

"*The Sign of Jonas*: Variant Drafts in a Manuscript of *The Sign of Jonas*," ed.
Jonathan Montaldo. 13 (2000) 16-26

"Three Prayers on Sacred Art," Appendix B of "Light That Is Not Light" by
Donna Kristoff. 2 (1989) 115-117

"Vocations to the Lay Apostolate" [1941 essay], ed. Patrick F. O'Connell.
7 (1994) 6-13

"The Zen Insight of Shen Hui," ed. Patrick Hart OCSO. 1 (1988) 3-16

Moon, Gary W. Review of *The Contemplative Heart* (Finley). 14 (2001) 267-269

Morneau, Robert F.
"Thomas Merton and the Vocation of the Cultural Critic: Prophetic and Poetic Imagination." 7 (1994) 68-80
The Impact of Divine Love (8 cassette tapes). *See* Reviews: Other Books

Morrin, Peter. Review of *Dialogues with Silence: Prayers and Drawings* (Merton, ed. Montaldo). 15 (2002) 270-271

Mossi, John P. SJ. Review of *Merton: An Enneagram Profile* (Zuercher). 10 (1997) 339-341

"Mother of All the Living: The Role of the Virgin Mary in the Spirituality of Thomas Merton," by Kenneth M. Voiles. 5 (1992) 297-310

Mott, Michael. *Woman and the Sea: Selected Poems. See* Reviews: Other Books

Murray, Harry. "Dorothy Day, Welfare Reform and Personal Responsibility." 12 (1999) 189-206

Murray, Mary. "Fire Watch Epilogue and *Life and Holiness*: Opposing Rhetorics in the Writings of Thomas Merton." 7 (1994) 45-57

"Mystic as Prophet: The Deep Freedom of Thomas Merton and Howard Thurman," by William D. Apel. 16 (2003) 172-187

"The Mysticism of Merton and Teilhard Compared," by Richard W. Kropf. 5 (1992) 227-245

Neuman, Matthias OSB. "Revisiting *Zen and the Birds of Appetite* after Twenty-five Years." 8 (1995) 138-149

"News of a More Complex Merton Industry: Introduction," by George A. Kilcourse Jr. 9 (1996) ix-xxii

"Ninevah to Calvary: Thomas Merton and a Spiritual Geography of the Bible," by William D. Apel. 13 (2000) 235-244

"'Non-Public' Writing in Journal and Correspondence: A Core Radiating Outward. 1997 Bibliographic Review," by Victor A. Kramer. 11 (1998) 174-195

Norris, Kathleen.
The Cloister Walk. See Reviews: Other Books
Dakota: A Spiritual Geography. See Reviews: Other Books

"Notes after First Visit and Correspondence [with Merton] 1962-1968," by Douglas V. Steere. 6 (1993) 23-53

O'Brien, Kevin J. Review of *Healing our Violence...Centering Prayer* (Rohr and Keating). 16 (2003) 263-266

O'Connell, Patrick F.
"Geography of Solitude: Thomas Merton's *Elias*—Variations on a Theme." 1 (1988) 151-190
Review of *Thomas Merton and the Education of the Whole Person* (Del Prete). 4 (1991) 284-288
Review of *Pilgrim in the Ruins: A Life of Walker Percy* (Tolson). 6 (1993) 227-234
"Eight Freedom Songs: Merton's Sequence of Liberation." 7 (1994) 87-128
Editor's Note to "Vocations to the Lay Apostolate" (Merton) 7 (1994)1-5

[part of] Review Symposium of *Run to the Mountain: Journals of Thomas Merton* (ed. Hart). 9 (1996) 288-298

"'What I Wear is Pants': Monasticism as 'Lay' Spirituality in Merton's Later Life and Work." 10 (1997) 35-58

"Thomas Merton's Wake-up Calls: Aubades and Monastic Dawn Poems from *A Man in the Divided Sea*." 12 (1999) 129-163.

Review of *When Prophecy Still Had a Voice: Letters of Merton and Lax* (ed. Biddle). 14 (2001) 244-251

    The Thomas Merton Encyclopedia (Shannon, Bochen, O'Connell). *See* Reviews: Books About Merton.

O'Hanlon, Daniel J. SJ. Review of *Encounter: Thomas Merton and D. T. Suzuki* (ed. Daggy). 2 (1989) 311-314

O'Hara, Dennis Patrick.

"'The Whole World...Has Appeared as a Transparent Manifestation of the Love of God': Portents of Merton as Eco-Theologian." 9 (1996) 90-117

Review of *Earth Community, Earth Ethics* (Rasmussen). 11 (1998) 208-211

"Thomas Merton and Thomas Berry: Reflections from a Parallel Universe." 13 (2000) 222-234

O'Keefe, Mark OSB. "Merton's 'True Self' and the Fundamental Option." 10 (1997) 235-250

"Of Moses' Mother and Pharoah's Daughter: A Model of Contemporary Contemplation," by Joan D. Chittister OSB. 3 (1990) 61-70

"On Discovering Divine Foolishness: Merton as Bridge-Person," by David B. Burrell CSC. 2 (1989) 121-129

"Otherness Has a Face...and It Is Not a Pretty Face," by Roberto S. Goizueta. 6 (1993) 92-114

"Our Lives, a Powerful Pentecost: Merton's Meeting with Russian Christianity," by A. M. Allchin. 11 (1998) 33-48

"Out of the Shadows: Merton's Rhetoric of Revelation," by Christopher C. Burnham. 9 (1996) 55-73

"The Ox Mountain Parable: An Introduction," by Paul M. Pearson. 15 (2002) 14-19

Padovano, Anthony T.

Review of *A Vow of Conversation: Journals 1964-1965* (Merton, ed. Stone). 2 (1989) 320-323

"Spirituality, Scholarship and Biography." Interview by Jonathan Montaldo. 10 (1997) 285-302

    Conscience and Conflict: A Trilogy of One-Actor Plays. See Reviews: Books About Merton

Paguio, Erlinda G.

"Blazing in the Spark of God: Thomas Merton's References to Meister Eckhart." 5 (1992) 247-262

Review of *A Catch of Anti-Letters* (Merton and Lax). 8 (1995) 254-257

Palmer, Parker J. "Contemplation Reconsidered: The Human Way In." 8 (1995) 22-37

Parry, Richard D.
  Review of *Passion for Peace: The Social Essays* (Merton, ed. Shannon).
    9 (1996) 255-264
  Review of *Peace Is the Way* (ed. Wink). 14 (2001) 269-270

Patnaik, Deba P. Review of *Father Louie: Photographs by Meatyard*, (ed. Magid).
    5 (1992) 373-377

"The Pattern in Thomas Merton's *Cables to the Ace*," by Gail Ramshaw.
    1 (1988) 235-246

Patterson, Richard B. *Becoming a Modern Contemplative*. *See* Reviews: Other Books

Payne, Steven OCD. "'Although It Is Night': A Carmelite Perspective on Spiritual-
    ity at the Juncture of Modernity and Postmodernity." 6 (1993) 134-159

"The Peacemaker: Merton's Critique and Model," by David Steindl-Rast OSB.
    1 (1988) 117-128

Peake, Frank A. "Self, Sexuality and Solitude in John Cassian and Thomas
    Merton: Notes from a Retreat." 2 (1989) 241-256

Pearson, Paul M.
  "Merton and the Celtic Monastic Tradition: Search for the Promised Land."
    5 (1992) 263-277
  "Thomas Merton in Search of His Heart: The Autobiographical Impulse of
    Merton's Bonaventure Novels." 9 (1996) 74-89
  Foreword to "The Black Sheep" by Thomas Merton. 11 (1998) 13-16
  "The Ox Mountain Parable: An Introduction." 15 (2002) 14-19
  Review of *Reading Thomas Merton: A Guide to His Life and Work* (John
    Laughlin). 15 (2002) 271-272

"Penning Patterns of Transformation: Etty Hillesum and Thomas Merton," by
    Michael Downey. 4 (1991) 77-95

Pennington, M. Basil OCSO.
  A Retreat with Thomas Merton. *See* Reviews: Books About Merton
  Thomas Merton, Brother Monk. *See* Reviews: Books About Merton
  Thomas Merton, My Brother. *See* Reviews: Books About Merton
  Toward an Integrated Humanity. *See* Reviews: Books About Merton

"A People's Movement as a Condition for the Development of a Just Peacemak-
    ing Theory," by Duane K. Friesen. 9 (1996) 182-191

Percy, Walker.
  At the Crossroads...Walker Percy, by John F. Desmond. *See* Reviews: Other Books
  Pilgrim in the Ruins: A Life of Walker Percy, by Jay Tolson. *See* Reviews: Other Books
  Walker Percy: A Life, by Patrick H. Samway SJ. *See* Reviews: Other Books

Pippin, Tina. "Standing on the Edge of the Abyss: A Postmodern Apocalyptic
    Spirituality." 6 (1993) 160-174

Plank, Karl A.
  Review of *Thomas Merton: First and Last Memories*, by Patrick Hart OCSO.
    1 (1988) 351-353
  "Thomas Merton and Hannah Arendt: Contemplation after Eichmann."
    3 (1990) 121-144
  "Appendix: Sources for Thomas Merton's 'Epitaph for a Public Servant'."
    3 (1990) 145-150

"Pleading for Sanity: Cosmic Heart in a Sea of Fire," by John Wu Jr.
10 (1997) 267-284

Poks, Malgorzata. "Thomas Merton's Poetry of Endless Inscription: A Tale of Liberation and Expanding Horizons." 14 (2001) 184-222

Porter, J. S.
"Last Journals of Thomas Merton and Anaïs Nin." 5 (1992) 279-295
"Thomas Merton's Late Metaphors of the Self." 7 (1994) 58-67
The Thomas Merton Poems: A Caravan of Poems. See Reviews: Books About Merton

"Posthumous Prolificacy: A Bibliographic Review Essay," by Michael Downey.
9 (1996) 237-251

Powaski, Ronald E. *Thomas Merton on Nuclear Weapons*. See Reviews: Books About Merton

"Prayer and the Cultivation of Mind: An Examination of Thomas Merton and Chinul," by Kun Ki Kang. 2 (1989) 221-238

Prevallet, Elaine SL. Review of *Spirituality in Ecumenical Perspective* (ed. Hinson).
7 (1994) 185-188

Pycior, Julie Leininger. "We Are All Called to be Saints: Thomas Merton, Dorothy Day and Friendship House." 13 (2000) 27-62

Quenon, Paul OCSO.
"Shadows at the Redwoods: Merton Remembered." 2 (1989) 31-42
Review of *Learning to Love: Journals of Thomas Merton* (ed. Bochen).
11 (1998) 199-203
"'Aware and Awake and Alive': Interview," by George A. Kilcourse Jr., transc. by Susan Merryweather. 15 (2002) 210-231

Quinn, Archbishop John R. *The Reform of the Papacy*. See Reviews: Other Books

"The Rain Speaks On: Contradiction in Thomas Merton's View of Peace," by Linnell Roccaforte. 4 (1991) 131-152

Ramon [Brother] SSF. *Soul Friends*. See Reviews: Books About Merton

Ramshaw, Gail. "The Pattern in Thomas Merton's *Cables to the Ace*."
1 (1988) 235-246

"Recreated Innocence in *The Sign of Jonas*," by Michael Rukstelis. 4 (1991) 69-74

Rasmussen, Larry L. *Earth Community, Earth Ethics*. See Reviews: Other Books

Reinders, Eric. Review of *Journeys into Emptiness* (Gunn). 14 (2001) 257-259

Reiser, William SJ. "Solidarity and the Reshaping of Spirituality." 11 (1998) 97-109

"The Religious Ethic at the Heart of Merton's Spirituality," by George A. Kilcourse Jr. 11 (1998) 7-11

"Remembering Merton and New York," by Robert Lax, ed. Paul J. Spaeth.
5 (1992) 39-61

"The Restoration of Balance: Thomas Merton's Technological Critique," by Phillip M. Thompson. 13 (2000) 63-79

Reviews: Merton's Books
The Alaskan Journal of Thomas Merton, ed. and introd. Robert E. Daggy, pref. David D. Cooper. Review by Lawrence S. Cunningham. 1 (1988) 343-347

Reviews: Merton's Books cont'd

At Home in the World: The Letters of Thomas Merton and Rosemary Radford Ruether, ed. Mary Tardiff OP, introd. Rosemary Ruether, afterword Christine M. Bochen. Review by Clare Ronzani. 9 (1996) 252-255

A Catch of Anti-Letters, by Thomas Merton and Robert Lax. Review by Erlinda G. Paguio. 8 (1995) 254-257

The Courage for Truth: The Letters of Thomas Merton to Writers, ed. Christine M.Bochen. Review by Elena Malits CSC. 7 (1994)174-176

Dancing in the Water of Life: Finding Peace in the Hermitage. The Journals of Thomas Merton, vol. 5, 1963-1965, ed. Robert E. Daggy. Review by Michael Johmann. 11 (1998) 196-199

Dialogues with Silence: Prayers and Drawings by Thomas Merton, ed. Jonathan Montaldo. Review by Peter Morrin 15 (2002) 270-271

Encounter: Thomas Merton and D. T. Suzuki, ed. Robert E. Daggy. Review by Daniel J. O'Hanlon. 2 (1989) 311-314

Entering the Silence: Becoming a Monk and Writer. The Journals of Thomas Merton, vol. 2, 1941-1945, ed. Jonathan Montaldo. Review by Jim Grote. 10 (1997) 326-330

"Honorable Reader": Reflections on my Work, ed. Robert E. Daggy. Review by Michael Downey. 3 (1990) 293-295

The Intimate Merton: His Life from His Journals, ed. Patrick Hart and Jonathan Montaldo. Review by Leonard J. Biallas. 13 (2000) 257-263

Learning to Love: Exploring Solitude and Freedom. The Journals of Thomas Merton, vol. 6, 1966-67, ed. Christine M. Bochen. Review by Paul Quenon OCSO. 11 (1998) 199-203

The Merton Tapes: Lectures by Thomas Merton. Review by Victor A. Kramer. 2 (1989) 314-319

The Merton Tapes 2 [Second Series], Review by Dewey Weiss Kramer. 3 (1990) 311-320

The Merton Tapes 3 [Third Series], Review by Victor A. Kramer. 5 (1992) 362-368

The Merton Tapes 4 [Fourth Series], Review by Dewey Weiss Kramer. 6 (1993) 235-236

The Merton Tapes 5 [Fifth Series], Review by Steven L. Baumann. 7 (1994) 176-178

The Merton Tapes 6 [Sixth Series], Review by Richard D. Parry. 9 (1996) 264-266

The Merton Tapes 7 [Seventh Series], Review by David King. 12 (1999) 235-239

Monks Pond: Thomas Merton's "Little Magazine" (facsimile, ed. Robert E. Daggy). Review by Jonathan Greene. 3 (1990) 295-298

The Other Side of the Mountain: The End of the Journey. The Journals of Thomas Merton, vol. 7, 1967-68, ed. Patrick Hart OCSO. Review by Thomas Del Prete. 12 (1999) 233-235

Passion for Peace: The Social Essays, ed. William H. Shannon. Review by Richard D. Parry. 9 (1996) 255-264

Preview of the Asian Journey, ed. Walter Capps. Review by Bonnie B. Thurston. 3 (1990) 298-300

The Road to Joy: Letters of Thomas Merton to New and Old Friends, ed. Robert E. Daggy. Review by Jane Marie Richardson SL. 3 (1990) 300-304

Run to the Mountain: The Story of a Vocation. The Journals of Thomas Merton, vol. 1, 1939-1941, ed. Patrick Hart OCSO. Review symposium by Patrick F. O'Connell, William H. Shannon, David King, with editor's response by Patrick Hart OCSO. 9 (1996) 288-315

The School of Charity: The Letters of Thomas Merton on Religious Renewal and Spiritual Direction, ed. Patrick Hart OCSO. Review by Jonathan Montaldo. 4 (1991) 275-284

A Search for Solitude: Pursuing the Monk's True Life. The Journals of Thomas Merton, vol. 3, 1952-1960, ed. Lawrence S. Cunningham. Review by Robert Ellsberg. 10 (1997) 331-333

The Shining Wilderness: Daily Readings with Thomas Merton , ed. Aileen Taylor, introd. Monica Furlong. Review by A. M. Allchin. 3 (1990) 310-311

The Springs of Contemplation: A Retreat at the Abbey of Gethsemani, ed. Jane Marie Richardson SL, introd. Mary Luke Tobin SL. Review by Mary Damian Zynda CSSF. 6 (1993) 215-219

Survival or Prophecy? The Letters of Thomas Merton and Jean Leclercq edited by Patrick Hart OCSO. Review by Terrence G. Kardong OSB. 16 (2003) 245-246

Thomas Merton: Essential Writings, sel. and ed. Christine M. Bochen. Review by Lynn Bridgers. 14 (2001) 251-252

Thomas Merton and James Laughlin: Selected Letters, ed. David D. Cooper. Review by Bradford T. Stull. 11 (1998) 203-206

Thomas Merton in Alaska: Prelude to the Asian Journal; The Alaskan Conferences, Journals and Letters, introd. by Robert E. Daggy, pref. David D. Cooper. Review by Diane Foster. 3 (1990) 305-309

Thomas Merton: Spiritual Master—The Essential Writings, ed. and introd. Lawrence S. Cunningham. Review by Walter E. Conn. 6 (1993) 203-205

Turning Toward the World: The Pivotal Years. The Journals of Thomas Merton, vol. 4, 1960-63, ed. Victor A. Kramer. Review by Daniel Carrere OCSO. 10 (1997) 334-338

A Vow of Conversation: Journals 1964-1965, ed. Naomi Burton Stone. Review by Anthony T. Padovano. 2 (1989) 320-323

When Prophecy Still had a Voice: The Letters of Thomas Merton and Robert Lax, ed. Arthur W. Biddle. Review by Patrick F. O'Connell. 14 (2001) 244-251

Witness to Freedom: The Letters of Thomas Merton in Times of Crisis, ed. William H. Shannon. Review by Douglas Burton-Christie. 8 (1995) 246-254

Reviews: Books About Merton

Ace of Freedoms: Thomas Merton's Christ, by George A. Kilcourse Jr. Review Symposium by Patrick Eastman, Diana Culbertson, Donald J. Goergen, and Jean-Marc Laporte, with Author's Response. 7 (1994) 198-226

Christian Conversion: A Developmental Interpretation of Autonomy and Surrender, by Walter E. Conn. Review by Dewey Weiss Kramer. 1 (1988) 353-357

Conscience and Conflict: A Trilogy of One-Actor Plays: Thomas Merton; Pope John XXIII; Martin Luther, by Anthony T. Padovano. Review by Richard Moir. 3 (1990) 324-327

Father Louie: Photographs of Thomas Merton by Ralph Eugene Meatyard, ed. Barry Magid. Review by Deba P. Patnaik. 5 (1992) 373-377

Reviews: Books About Merton cont'd

15 Days of Prayer with Thomas Merton, by André Gozier OSB. Review by Anne K. Walter. 13 (2000) 272-273

Journeys into Emptiness: Dogen, Merton, Jung and the Quest for Transformation, by Robert Jingen Gunn. Review by Eric Reinders. 14 (2001) 257-259

Keeping a Spiritual Journal with Thomas Merton, ed. Naomi Burton Stone. Review by Mary Luke Tobin SL. 1 (1988) 341-343

Living With Wisdom: A Life of Thomas Merton, by Jim Forest. Review by Gordon Zahn. 5 (1992) 368-370

Merton and Sufism: The Untold Story, ed. Rob Baker and Gray Henry. Review by Qamar-ul Huda. 13 (2000) 266-268

Merton and Walsh on the Person, by Robert Imperato. Review by William H. Shannon. 2 (1989) 323-326

Merton Vade Mecum: A Quick-Reference Bibliographic Handbook, by Patricia A. Burton. Review by Marquita E. Breit. 13 (2000) 269-271.

Merton: An Enneagram Profile, by Suzanne Zuercher. Review by John P Mossi, SJ. 10 (1997) 339-341

Merton: Mystic at the Center of America, by Thomas M. King SJ. Review by Annice Callahan RSCJ. 6 (1993) 205-208

Monks Pond, Old Hermit, Hai!! A Haiku Homage to Thomas Merton, by Ron Seitz. Review by John Leax. 3 (1990) 328-330

Poetry as Prayer: Thomas Merton, by Robert Waldron. Review by Glenn Crider. 14 (2001) 252-257

Prayer and Commitment in Thomas Merton and *Prophecy and Commitment in Thomas Merton*, by Mary Luke Tobin (cassette tapes). Review by Ruth Fox OSB. 5 (1992) 377-384

Reading Thomas Merton: A Guide to His Life and Work by John Laughlin. Review by Paul M. Pearson. 15 (2002) 271-272

A Retreat with Thomas Merton, by M. Basil Pennington OCSO. Review by Donald St. John. 2 (1989) 326-328

Running to the Mountain: A Journey of Faith and Change, by Jon Katz. Review by Donald Grayston. 13 (2000) 273-274

A Search for Wisdom and Spirit: *Thomas Merton's Theology of the Self*, by Anne E. Carr. Review by Lawrence S. Cunningham. 2 (1989) 329-332

A Seven Day Journey with Thomas Merton, by Esther de Waal. Review by Dianne Aprile. 7 (1994) 181-185

Silent Lamp: The Thomas Merton Story, by William H. Shannon. Review by Francis Kline OCSO. 6 (1993) 208-214

Something of a Rebel: Thomas Merton, His Life and Works—An Introduction, by William H. Shannon. Review by David Kocka. 11 (1998) 206-208

Song for Nobody: A Memory Vision of Thomas Merton, by Ron Seitz, foreword by Patrick Hart OCSO. Review by Thomas F. McKenna CM. 7 (1994) 178-181

Soul Friends: A Journey with Thomas Merton, by Brother Ramon SSF. Review by Valerie M. Lagorio. 4 (1991) 289-291

The Spark in the Soul: Spirituality and Social Justice [variant subtitle *Four Mystics on Justice*], by Terry Tastard. Review by Stephen J. Hotchen. 4 (1991) 291-295

Spiritual Guides for Today: Evelyn Underhill, Dorothy Day, Karl Rahner, Simone Weil, Thomas Merton, Henri Nouwen, by Annice Callahan RSCJ. Review by George A. Kilcourse Jr. 5 (1992) 384-386

Reviews: Books About Merton cont'd

Thomas Merton and Chinese Wisdom, by Cyrus Lee, fwd. by Robert E. Daggy. Review by Roger Corless. 9 (1996) 277-280

Thomas Merton and the Education of the Whole Person, by Thomas Del Prete. Review by Patrick F. O'Connell. 4 (1991) 284-288.

Thomas Merton and the Inclusive Imagination, by Ross Labrie. Review by Bradford T. Stull. 15 (2002) 263-267

Thomas Merton and the Monastic Vision , by Lawrence S. Cunningham. Review by Eugene Hensell OSB. 13 (2000) 263-266

Thomas Merton and Thich Nhat Hanh: Engaged Spirituality in an Age of Globalization by Robert H. King. Review by J. Milburn Thompson. 15 (2002) 267-269

Thomas Merton as Writer and Monk: A Cultural Study 1915-1951, by Peter Kountz. Review by Richard (Columban) Weber OCSO. 5 (1992) 370-373

Thomas Merton, Brother Monk: The Quest for True Freedom, by M. Basil Pennington OCSO. Review by John Eudes Bamberger OCSO. 1 (1988) 347-351

A Thomas Merton Curriculum, Terrance A. Taylor, (ed.). Review by Thomas Del Prete. 16 (2003) 250-255

The Thomas Merton Encyclopedia, William H. Shannon, Christine M. Bochen, and Patrick F. O'Connell. Review by Ross Labrie. 16 (2003) 246-250

Thomas Merton: First and Last Memories, by Patrick Hart OCSO. Review by Karl A. Plank. 1 (1988) 351-353

Thomas Merton in Search of His Soul: A Jungian Perspective, by Robert G. Waldron. Review by Joann Wolski Conn. 8 (1995) 258-261

Thomas Merton, My Brother: His Journey to Freedom, Compassion, and Final Integration. Review by Raymond Wilkie. 9 (1996) 269-271

Thomas Merton on Nuclear Weapons, by Ronald E. Powaski. Review by James H. Forest. 2 (1989) 336-339

Thomas Merton on Prayer, ed. and introd. by Tony Castle. Review by A. M. Allchin. 3 (1990) 310-311

Thomas Merton Remembered: Dialogues with Various People Who Knew Him, produced by Michael Toms [tape cassette of radio program]. Review by Dewey Weiss Kramer. 9 (1996) 267-269

Thomas Merton's American Prophecy, by Robert Inchausti. Review by David D. Cooper. 12 (1999) 239-241

Thomas Merton's Art of Denial: The Evolution of a Radical Humanist, by David D. Cooper. Review by Ross Labrie. 3 (1990) 321-324

Thomas Merton's Paradise Journey: Writings on Contemplation, by William H. Shannon. Review by Marilyn Sunderman RSM. 14 (2001) 259-263

Toward an Integrated Humanity: Thomas Merton's Journey, ed. M. Basil Pennington OCSO. Review by Columban (Richard) Weber OCSO. 2 (1989) 333-336

Up and Down Merton's Mountain: A Contemporary Spiritual Journey, by Gerald Groves. Review by Frank X. Tuoti. 2 (1989) 339-343

Reviews: Other Books

An Anthology of Christian Mysticism, by Harvey Egan SJ. Review by Michael Downey. 5 (1992) 394-395

'Arise My Love...': Mysticism for a New Era, by William Johnston SJ. Review by M.Thomas Thangaraj. 14 (2001) 273-274

Reviews: Other Books cont'd

At the Crossroads: Ethical and Religious Themes in the Writings of Walker Percy, by John F. Desmond. Review by Ross Labrie. 11 (1998) 213-214

Becoming a Modern Contemplative by Richard B. Patterson. Review by Paul Wise. 9 (1996) 272-277

Buddhist Emptiness and Christian Trinity, ed. Roger Corless and Paul F. Knitter. 4 (1991) 308-310

Brother and Lover: Aelred of Rivaulx, by Brian Patrick McGuire. Review by Matthew Kelty OCSO. 8 (1995) 274-276

The Catholic Counterculture in America, 1933-1962, by James Terence Fisher. Review by Victor A. Kramer. 4 (1991) 301-308

The Cloister Walk, by Kathleen Norris. Review by David Bock OCSO. 10 (1997) 345-347

The Contemplative Heart, by James Finley. Review by Gary W. Moon. 14 (2001) 267-269

Dakota: A Spiritual Geography, by Kathleen Norris. Review by Bruce H. Lescher CSC. 7 (1994) 190-194

The Dawn of the Mystical Age: An Invitation to Enlightenment, by Frank X. Tuoti. Review by Helge J. Juen. 12 (1999) 246-247

Disarming the Heart: Toward a Vow of Nonviolence, by John Dear SJ. Review by Rick Axtell. 8 (1995) 264-271

Earth Community, Earth Ethics (Ecology and Justice Series), by Larry L. Rasmussen. Review by Dennis Patrick O'Hara. 11 (1998) 208-211

Evelyn Underhill: Artist of the Infinite Life, by Dana Greene. Review by Anne E. Carr. 4 (1991) 298-300

Evening Train, by Denise Levertov. Review by Emily Archer. 6 (1993) 219-227

Exiles from Eden: Religion and the Academic Vocation in America, by Mark R. Schwehn. Review by Roy D. Fuller. 7 (1994) 188-190

Ezekiel: Vision in the Dust, by Daniel Berrigan. Review by Emily Archer. 12 (1999) 248-249

For the Sake of the World: The Spirit of Buddhist and Christian Monasticism, by Patrick G. Henry and Donald K. Swearer. Review by William H. Slavick. 3 (1990) 330-334

The Foundations of Mysticism: Origins to the Fifth Century, by Bernard McGinn. Review by Paul Lachance OFM. 9 (1996) 280-287

Freedom in Exile: The Autobiography of the Dalai Lama. Review by Roger Corless. 4 (1991) 295-297

Fruit of the Spirit: Growth of the Heart, by Bonnie B. Thurston. Review by Lynn Szabo. 14 (2001) 271-272

The Gethsemani Encounter: A Dialogue on the Spiritual Life by Buddhist and Christian Monastics, ed. Donald W. Mitchell and James Wiseman OSB, fwd. by the Dalai Lama, pref. Pierre François de Béthune OSB. Review by Roger Corless. 12 (1999) 242-244

The Growth of Mysticism: Gregory the Great through the Twelfth Century, by Bernard McGinn. Review by Paul Lachance OFM. 9 (1996) 280-287

Healing our Violence through the Journey of Centering Prayer, by Richard Rohr OFM and Thomas Keating OCSO. Review by Kevin J. O'Brien. 16 (2003) 263-266

Reviews: Other Books cont'd

The Spirituality of the Celtic Saints, by Richard J. Woods OP. Review by Dana Greene. 14 (2001) 264-266

A Stay Against Confusion: Essays on Faith and Fiction, by Ron Hansen. Review by Elizabeth Cahaney. 15 (2002) 276-278

The Strangest Way: Walking the Christian Path, by Robert Barron. Review by Alice G. Weber. 16 (2003) 262-263

A Taste of Water: Christianity through Taoist-Buddhist Eyes, by Chwen Jiuan A. Lee and Thomas G. Hand. Review by Bonnie B. Thurston. 4 (1991) 308-310

A Timbered Choir: The Sabbath Poems, 1979-1997, by Wendell Berry. Review by Stephen Whited. 12 (1999) 250-253

To Everything a Season: A Spirituality of Time, by Bonnie B. Thurston. Review by Lynn Szabo. 14 (2001) 271-272

Toward God: The Ancient Wisdom of Western Prayer, by Michael Casey. Review by Mary Margaret Funk. 10 (1997) 341-344

Tranquillitas Ordinis, by George Weigel. Review by Gordon Zahn. 2 (1989) 344-349

Walker Percy: A Life, by Patrick H. Samway SJ. Review by Ross Labrie. 11 (1998) 211-213

Watch With Me and Six Other Stories of the Yet-Remembered Ptolemy Proudfoot and his Wife, Miss Minnie, née Quinch, by Wendell Berry. Review by Irwin H. Streight. 8 (1995) 262-264

The Way of the Dreamcatcher: Spirit Lessons with Robert Lax , by S.T. Georgiou. Review by Arthur W. Biddle. 16 (2003) 255-257

The Ways of the Spirit, by Evelyn Underhill, ed. Grace Adolphsen Brame. Review by Anne E.Carr. 4 (1991) 298-300

What We Can Learn from the East, by Beatrice Bruteau. Review by Roger Corless. 9 (1996) 277-280

Why Not Be a Mystic? by Frank X. Tuoti. Review by Paul Wise. 9 (1996) 272-277

Woman and the Sea: Selected Poems, by Michael Mott. Review by Joseph Bathanti. 14 (2001) 275-277

The Writings of Daniel Berrigan, by Ross Labrie. Review by Victor A. Kramer. 4 (1991) 301-308

"Revisiting *Zen and the Birds of Appetite* after Twenty-five Years," by Matthias Neuman OSB. 8 (1995) 138-149

Richardson, Jane Marie SL.

Review of *The Road to Joy: Letters of Thomas Merton* (ed. Daggy). 3 (1990) 300-304

"Life Through the Lens of Inner and Outer Freedom." Interview by George A. Kilcourse Jr., ed. Paul Stokell. 13 (2000) 127-143

"Merton and Loretto: Background of Tape Recording [Comments about the Religious Life Today]." 14 (2001) 12-13

The Springs of Contemplation (ed. Richardson). *See* Reviews: Merton's Books

"The Road to Simplicity Followed by Merton's Friends: Ad Reinhardt and Robert Lax," by Paul J. Spaeth. 13 (2000) 245-256

Roccaforte, Linnell. "The Rain Speaks On: Contradiction in Thomas Merton's View of Peace." 4 (1991) 131-152

Shannon, William H. *cont'd*
  Silent Lamp: The Thomas Merton Story. See Reviews: Books About Merton
  Something of a Rebel. See Reviews: Books About Merton
  The Thomas Merton Encyclopedia (Shannon, Bochen, O'Connell). *See* Reviews:
   Books About Merton.
  Thomas Merton's Paradise Journey. See Reviews: Books About Merton
  Witness to Freedom: Letters of Thomas Merton (ed. Shannon). *See* Reviews:
   Merton's Books

"'A Shy Wild Deer': The 'True Self' in Thomas Merton's Poetry," by George A.
  Kilcourse Jr. 4 (1991) 97-109

"*The Sign of Jonas*: A Jungian Commentary," by Robert G. Waldron. 4 (1991) 59-68

Slavick, William H.
  Review of *For the Sake of the World* (Henry and Swearer). 3 (1990) 330-334
  Review of *The Nonviolent Movement* (Kownacki). 16 (2003) 260-262

Smock, Frederick. Review of *In Commemoration of Monuments* and of *Instructions
  for Silence* by Regina Derieva. 13 (2000) 274-276

"Social Involvement and Spirituality," by E. Glenn Hinson. 3 (1990) 217-229

"'A Soft Voice Awakens Me': Merton's Spirituality of Human Communication,"
  by Marilyn King SM. 2 (1989) 193-220

"Solidarity and the Reshaping of Spirituality," by William Reiser SJ.
  11 (1998) 97-109

"Solitude Leads toward Apostolate in and for the World," by Victor A. Kramer.
  7 (1994) ix-xiv

Somerville, James M. "Merton as Voluntary Prisoner" 16 (2003) 148-151

Söring, Jens. "The Kenotic Convict: A *Divertissement* on Contemporary Contemplative Spirituality in its Social Context." 16 (2003) 152-171

"The Sound of Sheer Silence: A Study in the Poetics of Thomas Merton," by Lynn
  Szabo. 13 (2000) 208-221

Spaeth, Paul J.
  "The Road to Simplicity Followed by Merton's Friends: Ad Reinhardt and
   Robert Lax." 13 (2000) 245-256
  "Remembering Merton and New York," by Robert Lax, ed. Paul J. Spaeth.
   5 (1992) 39-61

"The Spiritual Network of Contemplative Outreach Limited," by Gail
  Fitzpatrick-Hopler. 16 (2003) 188-196

"Spirituality after 'A Prayer Lip Stumbles'," by George A. Kilcourse Jr.
  6 (1993) 1-5

"Spirituality as the Freedom to Channel Eros," by George A. Kilcourse Jr.
  13 (2000) 7-15

"A Spirituality of Mercy: Aelred of Rievaulx," by Katherine M. TePas.
  6 (1993) 115-133

"Standing before God: Merton's Incarnational Spirituality," by Daniel
  Carrere OCSO. 16 (2003) 56-72

"Standing on the Edge of the Abyss: A Postmodern Apocalyptic Spirituality," by Tina Pippin. 6 (1993) 160-174

Stassen, Glen. "Abbey Center for the Study of Ethics and Culture Conference: To Develop a Just Peacemaking Theory." By Edward LeRoy Long, Jr., Glen Stassen, and Ronald Stone. 9 (1996) 170-181

Steere, Douglas V. "Notes after First Visit and Correspondence 1962-1968" [letters to Thomas Merton]. 6 (1993) 23-53

Steindl-Rast, David OSB. "The Peacemaker: Merton's Critique and Model." 1 (1988) 117-128

Steinfels, Margaret O'Brien. "Merton Lecture, Columbia University, November 15, 1995." 9 (1996) 8-20

Stokell, Paul. "Life Through the Lens of Inner and Outer Freedom." Interview with Jane Marie Richardson SL, by George A. Kilcourse Jr., ed. Paul Stokell. 13 (2000) 127-143

Stone, Naomi Burton (ed.)
   Keeping a Spiritual Journal with Thomas Merton. See Reviews: Merton's Books
   A Vow of Conversation: Journals 1964-1965. See Reviews: Merton's Books

Stone, Ronald. "Abbey Center for the Study of Ethics and Culture Conference: To Develop a Just Peacemaking Theory," by Edward LeRoy Long, Jr., Glen Stassen, and Ronald Stone. 9 (1996) 170-181

Streight, Irwin H. Review of *Watch with Me and Six Other Stories...*, by Wendell Berry. 8 (1995) 262-264

Stull, Bradford T.
   "Metaphors and Allusions: The Theopolitical Essays of Thomas Merton." 10 (1997) 205-221
   Review of *Thomas Merton and James Laughlin: Selected Letters* (ed. Cooper). 11 (1998) 203-206
   "Wild Seeds: Thomas Merton and Dorothy Day." 12 (1999) 164-167
   Review of *Man in the Mirror: John Howard Griffin and the Story of* Black Like Me (Bonazzi). 12 (1999) 244-245
   Review of *Thomas Merton and the Inclusive Imagination* (Labrie). 15 (2002) 263-267

St. John, Donald P.
   Review of *A Retreat with Thomas Merton* (Pennington). 2 (1989) 326-328
   "Deep Geography: Nature and Place in *The Sign of Jonas*." 4 (1991) 39-58

Sunderman, Marilyn RSM.
   "Thomas Merton and Dorothy Day on Prayer, Conscience and Christian Social Responsibility: A Comparative Study." 12 (1999) 168-188
   Review of *Thomas Merton's Paradise Journey* and of *Silence on Fire* (Shannon). 14 (2001) 259-263

Suzuki, Daisetz T. *Encounter: Thomas Merton and D. T. Suzuki* (ed. Daggy). *See* Reviews: Merton's Books

Swearer, Donald K. *For the Sake of the World* (Henry and Swearer). *See* Reviews: Other Books

Szabo, Lynn.
"The Sound of Sheer Silence: A Study in the Poetics of Thomas Merton."
13 (2000) 208-221
Review of *To Everything a Season* and of *Fruit of the Spirit* (Thurston).
14 (2001) 271-272
"'Hiding the Ace of Freedoms': Discovering the Way(s) of Peace in Thomas
Merton's *Cables to the Ace*." 15 (2002) 103-120

Tardiff, Mary OP. *At Home in the World: Letters of Merton and Ruether* (ed. Tardiff).
See Reviews: Merton's Books

Tastard, Terry. *The Spark in the Soul. See* Reviews: Books About Merton

Taylor, Aileen (ed).*The Shining Wilderness. See* Reviews: Merton's Books

Taylor, Amy. Photograph of the Dalai Lama and Abbot Timothy Kelly at Thomas
Merton's Grave, April 25, 1994, taken by Amy Taylor. 9 (1996) 192

Taylor, Terrance A. (ed.), *A Thomas Merton Curriculum. See* Reviews: Books About
Merton

"'Teaching is Candy': Merton as Teacher at Columbia and Bonaventure," by
Thomas Del Prete. 9 (1996) 152-169

"Technological Perspectives: Thomas Merton and the One-Eyed Giant," by John
Wu Jr. 13 (2000) 80-104

"Tension between Solitude and Sharing in the Monastic Life of Thomas Merton,"
by James Conner OCSO. 3 (1990) 47-59

TePas, Katherine M. "A Spirituality of Mercy: Aelred of Rievaulx."
6 (1993) 115-133

Thangaraj, M. Thomas. Review of *'Arise My Love...': Mysticism for a New Era*
(Johnston). 14 (2001) 273-274

"Thomas Merton: A Monk Who 'Succeeded'." Interview by Correspondence with
Dom M. Laurence Bourget OCSO, by Jonathan Montaldo. 12 (1999) 38-61

"Thomas Merton and Confucian Rites: 'The Fig Leaf for the Paradise Condition'," by John Wu Jr. 9 (1996) 118-141

"Thomas Merton and Dorothy Day on Prayer, Conscience and Christian Social
Responsibility: A Comparative Study," by Marilyn Sunderman RSM.
12 (1999) 168-188

"Thomas Merton and Education: The Theme of Self-Discovery," by Thomas Del
Prete. 2 (1989) 145-174

"Thomas Merton and Hannah Arendt: Contemplation after Eichmann," by Karl
A. Plank. 3 (1990) 121-144

"Thomas Merton and James Laughlin: Two Literary Lives in Letters," by David
D. Cooper. 10 (1997) 177-191

"Thomas Merton and St. Bernard of Clairvaux," by Jean Leclercq OSB.
3 (1990) 37-44

"Thomas Merton and the Grey Man," by Michael Rukstelis. 3 (1990) 233-250

"Thomas Merton and the Renewal of Religious Life," by Thomas F.
McKenna CM. 3 (1990) 107-118

Thompson, Phillip M. "The Restoration of Balance: Thomas Merton's Technological Critique." 13 (2000) 63-79

"Thousands of Words: A Bibliographic Review," by Victor A. Kramer. 8 (1995) 221-224

Thurston, Bonnie B.
"Zen Influence on Thomas Merton's View of the Self." 1 (1988) 17-31
Review of *Preview of the Asian Journey* (Merton, ed. Capps). 3 (1990) 298-300
Review of *Buddhist Emptiness and Christian Trinity* (ed. Corless and Knitter), and of *A Taste of Water* (Lee and Hand). 4 (1991) 308-310
"'The Best Retreat I Ever Made': Merton and the Contemplative Prioresses." 14 (2001) 81-95
Fruit of the Spirit: Growth of the Heart. See Reviews: Other Books
To Everything A Season: A Spirituality of Time. See Reviews: Other Books

"A Time of Transition." Selection of Letters from the Earliest Correspondence of Thomas Merton and Ernesto Cardenal, ed. and introd. by Christine M. Bochen, transl. by Roberto S. Goizueta. 8 (1995)162-200

"To Merton through Augustine: Images, Themes and Analogies of Kinship." by John Albert OCSO. 5 (1992) 65-94

"To See the Beauty of their Hearts: The Contemplative Aesthetics of Thomas Merton." Introduction to ITMS papers in *Merton Annual* 13, by Dorothy LeBeau. 13 (2000) 165-170

Tobin, Mary Luke SL.
Review of *Keeping a Spiritual Journal with Thomas Merton* (ed. Stone). 1 (1988) 341-343
"Growing into Responsibility." An Interview with Mary Luke Tobin SL, by Dewey Weiss Kramer. 2 (1989) 43-56
Prayer and Commitment in Thomas Merton and *Prophecy and Commitment in Thomas Merton* (2 cassette tapes). *See* Reviews: Books About Merton
The Springs of Contemplation (ed.Richardson, introd. Tobin) *See* Reviews: Merton's Books

Tolson, Jay. *Pilgrim in the Ruins: A Life of Walker Percy. See* Reviews: Other Books

Toms, Michael (producer). *Thomas Merton Remembered: Dialogues with Various People Who Knew Him* [tape cassette]. *See* Reviews: Books About Merton

"Truly Seeking God...in Christ." Interview with Chrysogonus Waddell OCSO by Victor A. Kramer, ed. George A. Kilcourse Jr. 11 (1998) 148-173

Tuoti, Frank X.
Review of *Up and Down Merton's Mountain* (Groves). 2 (1989) 339-343
"Contemplative Prayer: Antidote for an Ailing Generation." 16 (2003) 27-40
The Dawn of the Mystical Age. See Reviews: Other Books
Why Not Be a Mystic? See Reviews: Other Books

Underhill, Evelyn.
Evelyn Underhill: Artist of the Infinite Life (Greene*). See* Reviews: Other Books
The Ways of the Spirit (Underhill, ed. Brame). *See* Reviews: Other Books

Upton, Julia Ann RSM. "Humanizing the University: Adding the Contemplative Dimension." 8 (1995) 75-87

Reviews

MERTON, Thomas, *The Inner Experience—Notes on Contemplation*. Edited [and introduced] by William H. Shannon (San Francisco: HarperSanFrancisco, 2003), pp. xvi + 176. ISBN 0-06-053928-3 (hardcover). $22.95.

As readers of *The Merton Annual* undoubtedly know, *The Inner Experience—Notes on Contemplation* is the recent publication in book form of Thomas Merton's last work: a major revision and expansion of *What is Contemplation?*, originally released in 1948, that was still in progress at the time of his death in 1968. Many Merton aficionados will in fact already have purchased and read *The Inner Experience* by the time this review is published. So what is there left to say now, in these pages?

Merton himself, as a practitioner of contemplation, would probably have recommended silence. For mystics, fewer words and more quiet are always the preferred option. Since that is not practicable here, however, allow me to offer a few personal reflections on *The Inner Experience* that may help put this work into context.

Context is particularly important with this book because it quite definitely is not a unified and complete literary product. For writers, this gives *The Inner Experience* a peculiar charm: editor William Shannon's excellent endnotes and the use of three different fonts—for the 1948 original, the 1959 additions, and the 1968 revisions—allow us to follow Merton's creative process at work over the course of twenty years. But if that were all there is to this book, it would perhaps be only of limited interest, a scholarly curiosity to be filleted by earnest graduate students and a few fellow authors.

I would like to see *The Inner Experience* rescued from that fate and placed in a broader context, however. What The Merton Trust, HarperSanFrancisco and William Shannon have given us here is in fact a unique kind of almost personal spiritual journal: not a sequential, chronological record of Merton's inner development, but a continual overlaying of one evolutionary stage upon the other. Instead of looking at the staircase of his soul's journey from the side, step-by-step, as it were, we see it top-down, with the steps telescoped into and sometimes on top of one another. Those strata of Merton's growth, revealed through Shannon's three fonts, show us how Merton kept refining his answer to the central question of his life, the question he posed at the very beginning of his literary career: just what is contemplation?

In some ways, there is no one set answer to that question, which undoubtedly is why Merton did not want to see *The Inner Experience* published. But I think the fact that he loaned the manuscript of this work-in-progress to a convent of Carmelite nuns just before his death gives a clue on how to approach these unfinished pages, now that they have been released as a book. Those nuns were fellow pilgrims on the long journey into the inner desert, after all, and it is surely significant that Merton chose them as confidants in this matter. Who would better understand the indeterminate nature of these *Notes on Contemplation*—the manuscript's subtitle—than other practitioners of silent prayer?

Perhaps, then, *The Inner Experience* is best read as a fireside monologue by a brother hermit whose path we have crossed on our own sojourn into the Sahara of the soul. Among the sand dunes and scorpions, we rejoice in each other's company for one night and listen to a Bedouin's musings on where to find Living Water, burning bushes and manna. He gives us no maps or GPS-coordinates, of course, but the wisdom of his own experiences, some general directions, and much needed encouragement. Even he, after all these years, is still seeking God's face in the desert—holy man, crazy man, seeking, always seeking. *What is contemplation? What is it?*

Just how many of us pilgrims there are who ask this question alongside Merton is a subject he takes up toward the end of *The Inner Experience* in a section particularly meaningful to me. Elsewhere in the book, earlier in his own development, he suggests that contemplation should only be attempted by an especially gifted elite living in cloistered communities; but on page 137, he suggests the formation of a "contemplative Third Order, connected with the Cistercians or the Carthusians" that "could provide [its] members with books, conferences, directions and perhaps a quiet place in the country where they could go for a few days of meditation and prayer."

This is, of course, precisely the kind of ministry practiced by Fr. Thomas Keating's Contemplative Outreach, Ltd., since the 1970's, joined in more recent years by Fr. Richard Rohr's Center for Action and Contemplation. Thanks to the work of these men and their associates, the kind of prayer Thomas Merton wrote of so eloquently has now been made accessible even to the unlikeliest subjects. That, in turn, has created a much broader readership for Merton's books than, for example, the little convent of nuns to whom he passed the manuscript of *The Inner Experience* in 1968. Everywhere, the seeds of contemplation are finding fertile soil; everywhere, great trees of silent prayer are growing, giving rest to all kinds of different birds—even jailbirds like me!

What is contemplation? Perhaps it is not just an *inner* experience, but a shared experience by contemplatives across the world, across the ages. Perhaps contemplation will eventually become the blood that feeds the body of Christ everywhere—not inner but outer, not invisible but visible, not incorporeal but incarnate. Perhaps that would have been the next step on Merton's journey— the one that, sadly, he was not able to take.

Jens Söring

MERTON, Thomas, *Seeking Paradise: The Spirit of the Shakers*. Edited and introduced by Paul M. Pearson (Maryknoll, NY: Orbis Books, 2003), pp. 125. ISBN 1-57075-501-9 (hardcover). $24.00.

The opening words, "This book is a celebration of Merton's love of the Shakers," begin the preface by Paul M. Pearson (9). This work collects together in one volume several disparate pieces of Merton's thought: excerpts from his article on the Shaker Village at Pleasant Hill (1964); the introduction Merton wrote for Edward Deming Andrews's book *Religion in Wood: A Book of Shaker Furniture* (1964); "Work and the Shakers: A Transcript of a Conference Given by Thomas Merton at the Abbey of Gethsemani on July 22, 1964"; and "Selected Correspondence" from Merton to the Shaker scholar Edward Deming Andrews, Ralph McCallister – Executive Director of the Pleasant Hill project of restoration, and Mary Childs Black, convener for a discussion on the influence of religion on American folk art. In addition to these chapters, there is one entitled, "Pleasant Hill: A Shaker Village in Kentucky," which draws on material from Edward Deming Andrews's books, *Shaker Furniture* and *The People Called Shakers*.

One of the delights of the book is its many photographs of Shaker houses and furniture, most of which were taken by Merton himself. The clear simple lines of architecture and craftsmanship in the furniture illustrate well Merton's deep appreciation for "the Edenic innocence which is the special glory and mystery of Shaker work" (79). Elsewhere, Merton had written in his Introduction to *Religion in Wood* the following:

> One feels that for the Shaker craftsmen, love of God and love of truth in one's own work came to the same thing, and that work itself was a prayer, a communion with the inmost spiritual reality of things and so with God, not as if the "spirit" of the thing were something distinct from the thing itself, but in a full realization that everything that is, is in a certain sense "spirit," since "spirit," "form," and "actualization" are all one and the same. The Shakers thus had a deeply existential approach to reality (81).

Merton's words to the novices of his community, on a Shaker maxim, ring true today with respect to attitudes toward work, which allow the monk to be in communion with God while one works.

> One of the Shakers' chief maxims was 'Put your hands to work and your hearts to God.' Well, of course, this is normal for us. You work and your heart is lifted up to god while you are working and you are working for God. Now, to work for God means not this business of working and looking at God, but working in such a way that your work is your union with God....[I]f I work properly, with my heart set on the truth of the work, this counts as a prayer because in this I am united with God. Not just that I am doing his will but that I am also seeking him in the truth of what I'm doing (92, 93).

In his December 12, 1960 letter to Andrews, Merton expressed the hope of writing a book on the Shakers; to that end he had borrowed two of Andrews' books. Merton indicated that he would not rush through the project because he needed to honor the "careful and honest principles" of the Shakers through a deep, reverent and loving study of them (108). Moreover, he wrote, "I feel all the more akin to them because our own Order, the Cistercians, originally had the same kind of ideal of honesty, simplicity, good work, for a spiritual motive" (108).

Besides the simplicity of architectural line and their work ethic, Merton also loved [the Shaker] dance. In fact, he wrote "The General Dance," as the final chapter of *New Seeds of Contemplation* (1961) when he became interested in the Shakers. That section is a perennial favorite, which at the current time of Holy Easter 2004, calls for repetition of its theme of new life.

> The Lord plays and diverts Himself in the garden of His creation, and if we could go out of our own obsession with what we think is the meaning of it all, we might be able to hear His call and follow Him in His mysterious, cosmic dance...when, like the Japanese poet Basho we hear an old frog land in a quiet pond with a solitary splash—at such times the awakening, the turning inside out of all values, the 'newness', the emptiness and the purity of vision that makes themselves evident, provide a glimpse of the cosmic dance.
>
> For the world and time are the dance of the Lord in emptiness. The silence of the spheres is the music of a wedding feast...no despair of ours can alter the reality of things, or stain the joy of the cosmic dance which is always there. Indeed, we are in the midst of it, and it is in the midst of us, for it beats in our very blood, whether we want it to or not.
>
> Yet the fact remains that we are invited to forget ourselves on purpose, cast our awful solemnity to the winds and join in the general dance (52-53).

This little work is a precious treasure for meditation and reflection by one of America's best known monks. Its editor, Paul Pearson, captures well the spirit of Shaker and Cistercian spirituality in his own Preface and opening chapter.

Mary Foreman, OSB

O'CONNELL, Patrick F. (ed.), *The Vision of Thomas Merton: Essays in Honor of Robert E. Daggy* (Notre Dame: Ave Maria Press, 2003), pp. 253. ISBN 0-87793-991-8 (paperback). $14.95.

Following two previous collections of essays—*The Message of Thomas Merton*[1] and *The Legacy of Thomas Merton*,[2] both edited by Brother Patrick Hart—*The Vision of Thomas Merton* marks an important continuation of such studies. This particular set of sapid essays demonstrate Merton's almost global applicability as well as his ongoing relevance some thirty-six years after his death. Under the editorship of Patrick F. O'Connell, this book offers a dynamic, multifaceted look at one of the twentieth-century's most influential spiritual writers. Dedicated to the late Robert E. Daggy, the Publications Committee of The International Thomas Merton Society would be hard-pressed to find a better qualified team of contributors to write *The Vision of Thomas Merton*. The twelve featured essays come from friends and colleagues of Robert Daggy—all of whom represent the best of Merton interest and scholarship of the last twenty-five plus years. Readers will undoubtedly gain new insights and realizations about Merton as they hear from Bob Daggy's fellow editors of the two primary Merton publication projects, the five volumes of selected letters, the seven volumes of the complete journals as well as those who served as presidents or General Meeting program chairs of the Merton Society.

Although each contributor discusses Merton from quite different perspectives, a central theme throughout reveals Merton was much more than a monk and spiritual writer and that his influence both extends well beyond the cloistered walls of Gethsemani and crosses into a variety of disciplines, topics and interests. Even though he obviously remained a Trappist upon his commitment to Gethsemani in 1941, Merton's literal identity as monk and writer was but a starting point from which he eventually grew into an engagingly paradoxical seeker of Truth, a Catholic solitary with mass appeal. Robert Daggy's essay on Merton's bohemian/artistic parents—Owen and Ruth Jenkins—suggests that Merton's rocky yet progressive childhood served as a catalyst for his interests in nature, poetry, relationships, God, ideas, and politics, to name a few. Merton's childhood was likely instrumental when he (later on) began to earnestly explore key concepts inherent to monasticism: emptiness and mystery.

From a more literary perspective, Victor A. Kramer suggests that Merton's methodology changed dramatically as he matured: "...the complete journals subtly shift in the 1960s toward a far greater emphasis upon acceptance of mystery along with concurrently less emphasis on personal assurance" (78). Thomas Del Prete underscores Merton's acceptance of mystery in his appealing essay, "On Mind, Matter, and Knowing: Thomas Merton and Quantum Physics," which stresses that quantum physics excited Merton because of its interconnectedness to contemplation and the spiritual life. For Merton saw in Werner Heisenberg's "uncertainty principle"[3] a particular correlation with St. John of the Cross and his "dark soul" hypothesis. Although operating from traditionally conflicting worldviews, Heisenberg and St. John ultimately share the same assumption about human life: mystery, not certainty, is its primordial sustenance.

As Merton progressed in the monastic life, he began to see more and more that most of his surroundings—both literal and metaphorical—were spiritual reservoirs waiting to be tapped for such nourishment and growth. Monica Weis, in her essay, "Dancing with the Raven: Thomas Merton's Evolving View of Nature," says Merton's contact with nature was a strongly significant influence that functioned in many distinct ways:

> ...as weather report, as trigger for memory, as analogy to explain the conundrums of life, as vehicle for his poetic eye, as language to mediate the ineffable experience of prayer, and finally, as healing influence to provide Merton with a sense of coming home (140).

This example is emblematic of Merton's ontological openness which is essential for understanding why he remains such a compelling guide and mentor for such a wide audience. Merton more or less embodied his influences, and he did so in a way that others could easily relate to.

Lawrence S. Cunningham says that in *The Asian Journal*[4] Merton identifies three elemental characteristics of monastic values that, ideally, should apply to anyone interested regardless of their religious tradition or lack thereof.[5] Merton coincidentally presented these fundamental elements to an interreligious group in Calcutta. The point is that this represents one of many examples throughout *The Vision of Thomas Merton* where Merton made himself and, more importantly, his message readily available and appealing to virtually any interested persons. Merton's uncanny ability to articulate his wide interests sets him apart. Erlinda Paguio examines his interest in the work of Indian art historian and philosopher Ananda Coomaraswamy. William H. Shannon emphasizes Merton's relationship with Eastern wisdom as Bonnie Thurston explores Merton's contemplative awareness primarily through his *Thirty Poems* (1944). Jonathan Montaldo and Christine Bochen's essays remind us that Merton's faith journey was both fulgent and wearing. Merton articulates his faith well including struggle and doubt. Montaldo uses this point to show why Merton's vision remains timeless: "Merton witnesses our dilemma for us and suggests its hard cure by exposing his weaknesses as an essential means of identifying with his life's only spiritual master, Jesus Christ" (106). Merton's relationship to Eastern thought, his growing ecological and sacramental consciousness, his sapiential theology and spirituality as well as his contemplative journey via poetry, prose, journals and photography show Merton's expansive, pluralistic vision as edification for virtually anyone willing to explore his life and writings.

Notes:
1. Patrick Hart, *The Message of Thomas Merton* [*Cistercian Studies Series Number 42*] (Kalamazoo, MI: Cistercian Publications, 1981).
2. Patrick Hart, *The Legacy of Thomas Merton* [*Cistercian Studies Series Number 92*] (Kalamazoo, MI: Cistercian Publications, 1986).
3. Through quantum physics, Heisenberg's "uncertainty principle" undermined Newtonian physics because it suggests that, at the subatomic level, matter cannot be seen, controlled or measured. See pp. 119-133 for further discussion.
4. Thomas Merton, *The Asian Journal of Thomas Merton* (New York: New Directions, 1973).
5. The three characteristics are: "(1) a certain distance or detachment from the ordinary secular concerns of life; a solitude of varying intensity and duration; (2) a preoccupation (Merton's word) with the radical inner depth of one's religious and philosophical beliefs, and their spiritual implications; (3) a particular concern with inner transformation and the deepening of consciousness of a transcendent dimension of life beyond the empirical self and of 'ethical and pious observances'" (70).

Glenn Crider

RINGMA, Charles R, *Seek the Silences with Thomas Merton: Reflections on Identity, Community and Transformative Action* (London: SPCK; Vancouver, BC: Regent College Publishing, 2003), pp. xxv + 229. ISBN 0281056048 (British) (hardcover); 1553610911 (Canadian) (paperback). £9.99; $24.95 CAN.

This engaging and attractive book consists of a series of short meditations on key dimensions of the Christian life, grouped in six sections, each with a brief introduction: "Being–The Search for Self-Identity" focuses on conversion and spiritual growth as a journey of self-discovery; "Being and Transcendence–The Search for Ultimate Meaning" examines the encounter with God in the person of Jesus through the power of the Holy Spirit; "Being With–The Search for Friendship and Community" discusses community as sign and sacrament of the reign of God present in the world; "Being Against–The Search for a Prophetic Voice" considers the distinctive Christian commitment to social critique as an integral dimension of the life of faith; "Being For–The Search for Transformative Action" looks at both personal and social renewal as responses to the redemptive mystery of Christ's death and resurrection; "Being and Hope–The Search for an Eschatological Vision" emphasizes not only the final victory of the risen Lord but the call to make the redemptive healing of the nations a reality.

The individual meditations, each a page to a page and a half in length, develop a vision of Christian witness rooted in a deep personal relationship with Christ that leads to a commitment both to building authentic Christian community and to being agents for transforming the world. Charles Ringma criticizes the Church's failure to be "a servant, witness and sacrament of the reign of God" (xviii) and encourages his readers to find in solitude and the disciplines of prayer and meditation on scripture the resources for announcing and living the Gospel. Though not primarily autobiographical, the book does provide fascinating vignettes of the author's own quite remarkable life on four different continents: born in Holland, an immigrant to Australia as a boy, a teacher and social activist both there and in the Philippines, and now Professor of Mission and Evangelism at Regent College in Vancouver, Ringma clearly comes across as someone who has genuinely tried to put his faith into action, and as someone who is therefore able to put that faith into words as well. He draws on his own successes and failures, frustrations and struggles, insights and graced moments, yet the focus is always on God's work not his own. The progression of the meditations from personal conversion to social transformation is evident without being too rigid or constricting–many of the same themes recur in the different sections, suggesting the integration and interrelationships of the various dimensions of Christian living. Written in a conversational style devoid of jargon or abstract theorizing, the book is challenging without being at all self-righteous or confrontational. The author simply considers what the call to authentic discipleship entails in the present day, and invites the reader to take part in this process of discernment.

Aimed primarily, though by no means exclusively, at an audience that shares Ringma's own Protestant Evangelical perspective, the book rejects a conventional religiosity that focuses primarily on interior piety and privatized morality without seeing the implications of the Christian message for issues of peace, human rights, concern for the poor and protection of the environment. It also repudiates a narrow sectarianism: his ecumenical appreciation for the insights and contributions of other streams of Christian tradition, particularly for the Catholic commitment both to contemplative stillness and to active social engagement, is evident throughout the book, and is reinforced by the presence of his "conversation partner," Thomas Merton.

The actual contribution of Merton to the overall impact of the book may initially seem, despite the title, to be somewhat less than central. There is a brief initial overview of Merton's life and teaching (xxi-xxv) that emphasizes his "incarnational spirituality" (xxv) and the relevance for other Christians of his monastic commitment to solitude and community, to prayer and work, to sapiential insight and prophetic critique, as well as a concluding, not completely accurate chronology of Merton's life (215-19). (Merton is said to have begun teaching at St. Bonaventure in 1939 rather than 1940; Mother Berchmans becomes Berkmans, and St. Lutgarde of Aywières, Lutgarte of Aywiues; *Cables to the Ace* becomes–shades of Eldridge Cleaver!–*Cables on Ice*; the listing of posthumous publications stops abruptly in 1992, omitting all the complete journals, even though passages from both *Entering the Silence* and *The Intimate Merton* are quoted in the book itself.) Each of the meditations of the book proper contains a single brief quotation from Merton, typically a single sentence or less, never more than two or three sentences. Occasionally, as in the reflection on "Conformity: Resisting its subtle power" (132-34), Ringma begins with a Merton quotation, in this case his warning not to allow "the noble Christian concept of duty and sacrifice" (132) to be equated with a passive servility to government dictates, and then continues with his own commentary on the same topic. More typically the Merton quotation is inserted in the middle of the meditation, and if it were omitted the reader would never miss it. For example, in the section entitled "An unremarkable source: Seeing the small beginnings" (32-34), Ringma recalls his trip as a teenager in Australia to the rather unimpressive headwaters of the Coomera River, and sees this as a metaphor for easily overlooked beginnings that nonetheless are of great potential significance. In the midst of his reflection he quotes Merton's observation from *Disputed Questions* that "it is not sufficient to know the water is there–we must go and drink from it" (33), and then continues with his own considerations of the human tendency to mistake the outwardly impressive for the truly meaningful. Removing the Merton quotation would have little effect on the overall message of the section.

The fact that there is always one and only one Merton quotation for each of the 139 meditations might give the impression that his presence in the book is somewhat contrived and mechanical–perhaps even to some degree a marketing strategy–and the fact that Ringma has published similar volumes focused on other figures, including Jacques Ellul, Dietrich Bonhoeffer and his fellow Dutch native Henri Nouwen (as well as a forthcoming one on Mother Teresa) might reinforce this impression of a standardized, formulaic approach. Such a conclusion, however, would be hasty and superficial, a misjudgment. While it is true that Ringma could have written most of the book with no explicit reference to or citation of Merton at all–and that such a book would still be well worth reading for Ringma's own insights into the struggles and joys of the Christian life–it is nonetheless equally true that Ringma resonates deeply with Merton's holistic spiritual vision, his integration of contemplation and social critique, his engagement both with the tradition and with contemporary challenges. Ringma knows his Merton well–he includes quotations from 32 different Merton works, and the passages chosen, generally not ones already quite familiar to Merton "fans," are always to the point. One senses that Merton has really been a valued companion from Ringma on his journey, serving both as an antidote to the rather rigid Dutch Reformed Calvinism of his youth and as a complement to the more expansive but sometimes socially disengaged Evangelical Protestantism of his maturity. The presence of Merton in the book is thus not exclusively in the specific quotations, but to some extent at least in the overall perspective, the incarnational and contemplative vision, that Ringma has come to share with Merton. For someone totally unacquainted with Merton, Ringma's book does provide an admiring and appreciative introduction that may encourage such a reader to seek out some of Merton's own writings; for those already familiar with Merton, perhaps the main advantage of his presence in the title and in the book itself would be to draw them to make the acquaintance of Charles Ringma, who is himself someone well worth meeting, an unassuming but wise and engaging spiritual guide.

Patrick F. O'Connell

MORNEAU, Robert F., *Poetry As Prayer: Jessica Powers* (Boston: Pauline Books & Media, 2000), pp. 150. ISBN 0-8198-5921-4 (paperback). $8.95.

Robert Morneau's book, *Poetry As Prayer: Jessica Powers*, is a wonderful starting point for those looking for new or alternative ways to pray. Morneau, auxiliary archbishop of Green Bay, and a poet himself, believes that "Prayer, the dialogue between God and humankind, has many sources. God speaks and elicits a response through the mystery of creation (xvi)." He suggests that "poetry written or read in faith can be a form of deep prayer…(it) helps us name experiences and feelings that are often illusive and ambiguous…(and) helps us know that we're not alone."

In this compact, attractive volume, Morneau reveals the power of poetry to inspire by featuring the poetry of the Carmelite nun, Jessica Powers (1905-1988). Powers, whose religious name was Sr. Miriam of the Holy Spirit, was born in Cat Tail Valley, Wisconsin, and lived forty-seven years at the Carmel of the Mother of God in Milwaukee, where she served as prioress for several years. Sometimes referred to as "Wisconsin's Emily Dickinson," Powers lived her entire life in conversation with God. Writing from reverence, thankfulness, wonder, and love, she took the words God gave her and gave them back to Him as poetry.

Morneau first read Powers' work in 1985 and was "astounded by…the clarity of verse, its simplicity, its insight, its rootedness in nature and grace (37)." Powers' poems are completely accessible. Grounded in the present, she saw God in the everyday, and offered her thankfulness to God in poems alive with images that reflect a quiet attentiveness to her natural surroundings: "To live with the Spirit of God is to be a listener./ It is to keep the vigil of mystery, earthless and still./ One learns to catch the stirring of the Spririt,/ strange as the wind's will./…The soul is all activity, all silence;/ and though it surges Godward to its goal,/ it holds, as moving earth holds sleeping noonday,/ the peace that is the listening of the soul (87-88)."

Morneau has selected Powers' poems as centering themes for ten short "prayer periods": each meditation focusing on a single topic: Freedom, Mercy, Spirituality, Death, God's will, Providence, Eucharist, The person of Jesus, Simplicity, and Community. For each "prayer period," he suggests the reader take a quiet 20 minutes to read the poem slowly, allowing it to sink in and act as a catalyst for the reader's own thoughts, reactions, and prayers.

Morneau follows each poem with commentary and suggested prayers; these short meditations, accompanied by Joseph Karlik's inspiring artwork, complement the Powers' poems beautifully. Without lecturing or telling the reader what to think, Morneau serves as a thoughtful, easily understood guide to the spirit of Powers' transformative poetry. This delightful collaboration of poetry, art, and meditation results in a lovely, accessible book that creates possibilities for new avenues of personal prayer.

Catherine Senne Wallace, OblSB

SÖRING, Jens, *The Way of the Prisoner: Breaking the Chains of Self Through Centering Prayer and Centering Practice* (New York: Lantern Books, 2003), pp. xxx + 317. ISBN 1-59056-055-8 (paperback). $17.95.

This book is full of riches. In fact, it is three books in one: it contains the story of Jens Söring leading to his present situation and discovery of Centering Prayer; it shows in detail how he has applied Centering Prayer to his own life; and it shows how readers can adapt Centering Prayer and Centering Practice to their own lives to break the chains that bind them as prisoners to the self.

Reading Söring's book takes real discipline. He challenges the reader, at times with a specialized vocabulary, with a detailed organization, and with his personal history, and with his understanding of Centering Prayer. It is well worth the effort it will take to follow all of these. It is important to realize that the book really begins with the Foreword, Preface, and Introduction. Neglecting these may frustrate the reader. Above all, the Introduction must be read. It sets the stage, gives a helpful overview, and explains some of the difficulties readers might encounter.

I highly recommend taking seriously Söring's suggestion that the reader first read Söring's personal story contained in clearly identified sections. This will cut distractions when reading Söring's detailed account of his Centering Prayer experience and how it became his desire to encourage others to follow that practice. It will also be helpful to read the "Brief Postscript on Centering Terminology" at the conclusion of the text and also the appendix containing a brief and accurate outline of Centering Prayer as developed by Thomas Keating, OSCO. This will be especially helpful for readers not familiar with Centering Prayer. For readers familiar with the practice, reading Keating's outline may help in understanding just how Söring adapts Centering Prayer in and to his own circumstances.

In writing his book, Jens Söring wants to share what has helped to transform his own life and help others to do the same. In his words, he wants readers to learn this way of breaking the fetters that bind us all as prisoners, no matter what those fetters might be. He wants us to see that if he can do it, so can we. He says, "My aim is to give you all the spiritual tools you need to revolutionize your life, to introduce you in depth to these tools' history and theory and to give you beginning, intermediate and advanced training in their use" (xxix). He realizes that the book may be difficult for some, but he also believes it is worth the effort it will take to learn Centering Prayer. I agree with Söring.

While the journey Söring describes is solitary, it is possible to draw on the collective wisdom of the Western contemplative tradition, which Söring does. First, however, he rightly begins with the instruction Jesus left us in Scripture. Söring relies here on the pattern of *lectio divina* of ancient monastic tradition. This consists of four parts: *lectio*: in which we listen to the Word of God in Scripture; *meditatio*: where we reflect on the message this Scripture reading brings today; *oratio*: by which we respond to God through prayer; and *contemplatio*: where we rest in Christ's peace. This is the outline Söring then uses throughout his book, detailing each of these with examples.

Söring is always encouraging; he knows the pitfalls, the distractions, the loneliness, and the sheer drudgery of what he encourages readers to do. His tone shows the truth in his claims for Centering Prayer in his life. It is obvious that he has learned and grown through his own efforts with Centering Prayer, and his only desire is to help others to do the same. Perhaps in time he will be able to restrain his desire to give the reader all of the fruits of his labor and write a simpler book for beginners that will encourage without perhaps overwhelming them. For this reason I recommend *The Way of the Prisoner* especially to readers already familiar with Centering Prayer. To beginners I recommend reading the book slowly by sections rather than all at once in a hurry. Then relax in God's presence, open to whatever gift might come your way. Centering Prayer does take effort, but it cannot be hurried or forced. What comes is a gift. Söring understands this.

Stefanie Weisgram, OSB

DERKSE, Wil, *The Rule of Benedict for Beginners, Spirituality for Daily Life* (Collegeville: Liturgical Press, 2003), pp. index + 90. ISBN 0-8146-2802 (paperback). $9.95.

DEWAAL, Esther, *Lost in Wonder; Rediscovering the Spiritual Art of Attentiveness* (Collegeville: Liturgical Press, 2003), pp. 168. ISBN 0-8146-2992 (hardback). $14.95.

These two books reflect the widening interest in lay involvement in contemplative ways of life as fostered by Benedictine attitudes. Indirectly, Merton has set the stage, as was demonstrated in many of the articles about lay people and prayer in the preceding Vol. 16 of *The Merton Annual*. Merton has clearly had an influence on DeWaal's work, and she in turn has clearly made an impression on Derkse who includes a note listing three of her books on related topics.

Derkse's book, *The Rule of St. Benedict for Beginners, Spirituality for Daily Life*, consists of interrelated essays which provide both an overview of how the Benedictine lifestyle is, in a sense, always at the point of beginning again, and also a compendium of suggestions about how persons new to the Benedictine tradition can convert its patterns into a life lived within a contemporary secular setting. DeWaal's *Lost in Wonder; Rediscovering the Spiritual Art of Attentiveness*, builds on her earlier studies of the Benedictine life and on her admiration of Thomas Merton as someone systematically attentive to the Spiritual as it appears in many surprising settings. Both Derkse and DeWaal remind us of the continuity of the contemplative dimension within Western spiritual life, both historically and holistically.

The topics in Derkse's book are arranged in four parts with sub-sections: "A First Acquaintance with Benedictine Spirituality;" "Basic Patterns" (Way of Life, Listening); "Leadership"; and "Benedictine Time Management." These topics call attention to the Benedictine Rule (RB) and flow into one another. They demonstrate that time-honored patterns developed in a particular monastic place, such as at Hildegard of Bingen's monastery, are still being lived there today and as well have meaning for non-monastics to "strengthen the quality of societal living" (ix). Specific references to visiting Hildegard's Abbey in Eibingen focus on the living tradition which exists there today, and from which we can learn.

DeWaal's structures her book in nine sections: 1) "The Starting Point" and "The Pattern of the Retreat"; 2) "Seeing with the Inner Eye"; 3) "Silence"; 4) "Attention"; 5) "Change"; 6) "Dark and Light"; 7) "Mystery"; 8) "Gift"; and 9) "Epilogue." A short section of "Prayers and Reflections" (approximately four pages) follows each chapter. Thus, this book includes thirty-four pages of poems, psalms, prayers which can be used to build on the many ways of being attentive which DeWaal examines. She also provides 18 short biographical sketches of the "Fathers and Friends" she mentions in her text, including Merton and Hildegard of Bingen.

Both books will assist readers to appreciate the fact that the Rule of Benedict can be adapted to the contemporary moment. *Stabilitas, conversatio morum, obedientia*—commitment, engagement, listening (at many different levels) are the keys. In a parallel way the second part of Derkse's book provides suggestions about how the Benedictine way of life illustrates how "Listening Attentively to Gain Results" works. The same is true with stability, hospitality, decision making, *not* grumbling, and *lectio*. Such forms, he argues, help the development of the "Spirituality for daily life."

This text could be of use to individuals to absorb, slowly, or for groups (such as oblates of a particular community, or ITMS book discussion groups). Both books are meant to be read at a slow and prayerful pace and digested as food to nourish the life of those willing, like all Benedictines, to begin over and over.

DeWaal suggests that her book might be used as a "retreat"—read in a set pattern of days, or even slower increments. Her reflections, drawing often on Merton, cultivate respect for the present moment and a sense of awe. She urges us to look, wake up, wonder. A major theme is the relationship between the inner and the outer, "[the] connection between my outer environment and my inner life of prayer" (9). Merton's insistence on the use of the imagination to get closer to God (23)—his poem "This flower" (51); his camera and love of photography (63-66); his life always "open to new and different orientations" (83-36)—are blended into this "tapestry" of attentiveness.

Because such considerable insight is packed into this text, it would lend itself well to use as manual or guide for reflection and watchfulness. Readers could easily re-use the book on a regular basis. In Chapter 6, relying upon Psalm 126 to set the tone, De Waal shows how particular moments of darkness and examples which she has gleaned from literature (Fr. Christian of the Trappist monastery, Tibhirine; Philip Toynbee; J. K. Rowling; T. S. Eliot; Alan Paton; Rowan Williams; St. Catherine of Siena) can well serve as models for readers to be aware of God's grace and light, even as all things dim, die, and change!

Dewey Weiss Kramer

MARETT-CROSBY, Anthony (ed.), *The Benedictine Handbook* (Collegeville: The Liturgical Press, 2003), pp. 320. ISBN 1-8146-2790-0 (hardback). $24.95.

RIGER, Kate E. and Michael Kwatera, OSB (eds.), *Prayer in All Things: A Saint Benedict's St. John's Prayer Book* (Collegeville: Liturgical Press, 2004), pp. 136. ISBN 0-8146-6298-14 (paperback). $9.95.

These two new volumes are designed for distinct audiences—one for Oblates and those who represent the extended "Benedictine Family"; the other, a prayerbook which has grown out of a college context, done by editors at St. John's University and at the College of St. Benedict, two schools which have forged a remarkable cooperative venture. Both of these volumes can and will serve persons far beyond their primary audiences. Any person associated with a Benedictine or Cistercian monastery, or persons with a college or university connection. Indeed, anyone seeking the "love of learning" could find both of these books of value.

The section in the *Handbook* by Mary Foreman about "Prayer" (110-113) is a good example of how the *Handbook* works. Only four pages long, the words are carefully chosen:

> Prayer for Benedictines is a relationship with God which opens one to the awareness of God's permeating presence all of one's life . . . .
> Prayer is an invitation to 'listen with the ear of your heart' the first words of the Prologue that open the Rule of St. Benedict—

This essay is carefully written and gives a good overview of what Benedictines (or Cistercians) do best. Similarly the prayers put together by the two editors of *Prayer in All Things* reflect concentrated focus, yet also are valuable as a collection of a wide variety of types of prayer – suitable for a broad audience differing in age, needs, and concerns. These prayers will feed the need for a spirituality suitable to the contemporary moment.

The *Handbook* is arranged with an overview of the goals of the book; a new translation of the Rule by Patrick Barry, OSB. Then helpful, yet succinct articles over topics including: "The Work of God," "The Art of *Lectio Divina*," "Prayer," "Work," "Perseverance," "The Vows," and "Hospitality." Each makes connections between the tradition and the present moment.

This book is designed to be "a lifelong companion." It is a reference work and as well a compendium of basic information. Section V contains "A Short History," then a section about Benedictines worldwide, plus an article on "the Cistercian tradition."

Part Six is a useful glossary of "Benedictine terms" with good definitions from "Abbot/abbess" to "Vows."

Parts Nine and Four are especially useful: "The Benedictine Experience of God" including "A Simple Daily Office" and a "Who's Who Section" (226-268). In Part Four strong, useful articles about "Living the Rule," "In Community," "In Solitude," "As an Oblate, and "In the World" are provided. Each could be returned to again and again.

Prayer in All Things is organized in six sections:

1) "Ask and It Will Be Given"; for peace, families, students, ministries. . . .
2) "Pray in the Spirit at All Times"; for times of quiet. . . .
3) "Do Not Worry about Anything"; for help, for protection. . . .
4) "Rejoice Always"; for praise, for thanksgiving. . . .
5) "Keep silent"; for hearing God's word. . . .
6) "My Words Abide in You"

While one could quibble about some of the prayers, perhaps too many by a few contributors, all are good. This idea of a book of new and traditional prayers gathered as a prayer book for a college community is an excellent idea. A Bibliographical listing is provided for the contents and the combination of new prayers by faculty and students along with prayers by famous saints and writers makes the book live.

Thomas Merton, with his thirst for making connections with the world would definitely be pleased to see these two books. Neither would have been dreamt fifty years ago. They remind us that the traditions of Benedict –sometimes forgotten in the past— are alive and well. They remind us that there are many ways to transmit the living traditions of the Church and St. Benedict.

Anthony Feuerstein

Contributors

Arthur MacDonald Allchin, former Canon of Canterbury Cathedral, was also Director of the St. Theosevia Center at Oxford University, Oxford, England. He is author of several books including *The World is a Wedding: Explorations in Christianity* (1978). He has published widely on ecumenism and has served as President of the Thomas Merton Society of Great Britain and Ireland.

David Belcastro is Professor of Religious Studies and Chair of the Religion and Philosophy Department at a Lutheran University in Bexley, Ohio. He has been presenting and publishing papers on Merton for the past fourteen years . . . most recently at the Merton Conference in England on "Chanting on the Rim of Chaos; Sane Language in an Insane World."

Patrick Bludworth is an artist and retired founding retreat director of Alpine Living Arts Institute, Alpine, California, and the Desert Academy of Meditation, Soboba Hot Springs, California. He holds an MA in Art and Literature from Goddard College, Vermont, and studied Creation Spirituality with Matthew Fox at Loyola University, Chicago. He is currently pursuing an MA in Asian Religions from Skidmore College, New York.

Ken Burridge is an anthropologist who taught for many years at the University of British Columbia. He is the author of *Mambu: A Melanesian Millennium* (1960), the book which prompted Merton to write his well-known essay on the cargo cults of the South Pacific.

Patricia A. Burton has been developing indexes and bibliographies of Thomas Merton's works since 1996. Her publications include *Merton Vade Mecum: A Quick-Reference Bibliographic Handbook* and *'About Merton': Secondary Sources 1945-2000* (in collaboration with Marquita E. Breit and Paul M. Pearson), both distributed by the Thomas Merton Foundation. Her research work, begun in 1998, assisted in the publication of Thomas Merton's *Peace in the Post-Christian Era* by Orbis Books in 2004. She is currently working on an annotated bibliography of Thomas Merton's books. She is retired, living in Toronto, Canada.

Glenn Crider holds an MA in psychology and a Master of Divinity from Emory University's Candler School of Theology. He is the Production Manager and an editorial contributor for *The Merton Annual* and was Chair of the Atlanta Chapter of the International Thomas Merton Society, 2001-2003.

Ron Dart teaches in the Department of Political Science, Philosophy, and Religious Studies at University College of the Fraser Valley, British Columbia. He has published a number of books and volumes of poetry and is currently working on a study of Stephen Leacock and George Grant.

Paul R. Dekar has served as Niswonger Professor of Missions and Evangelism at Memphis Theological Seminary, Memphis, Tennessee since 1995. Over a nineteen-year tenure at McMaster University in Hamilton, Ontario, he introduced Merton in courses on peace and spirituality. He received a grant from the Shannon Fellowship Committee that facilitated research at The Thomas Merton Center, Bellarmine University, Louisville.

Anthony Feuerstein attended St. Edward's University in Austin, Texas and has been interested in writings about spirituality and prayer since he first read Merton's *Seeds of Contemplation* in 1958. He is familiar with Centering Prayer both through instruction at the Abbey of the Holy Spirit, Conyers, Georgia, and through an eight-day intensive workshop at Sacred Heart Monastery in Cullman, Alabama.

Mary Foreman, OSB, School of Theology-Seminary, Saint John's University, Collegeville, MN., not only teaches Monastic Studies but is a scholar of the Rule of Benedict, lecturer and retreat director on topics of monastic history and spirituality. Her latest publication is "Benedict's Use of Scripture in the Rule: Introductory Understandings" in the *American Benedictine Review*.

Edward K. Kaplan is Kaiserman Professor in the Humanities and Chair of the Program in Religious Studies at Brandeis University. In addition to his work in French literature, he has published essays on Martin Buber, Thomas Merton, Howard Thurman, and books on Abraham Joshua Heschel. Papers presented at the conference he organized on Thomas Merton and Judaism have just been published as a book by Fons Vitae.

Deborah Kehoe is from Oxford, Mississippi. She is on the faculty of Northeast Mississippi Community College where she teaches English Composition and British and World Literature.

Victor A. Kramer, a founding editor of *The Merton Annual*, was a Research Scholar at the Institute for Ecumenical and Cultural Research at St. John's University in Collegeville, Minnesota, 2003-2004. Currently he is writing about Walker Percy and sacramentality.

Dewey Weiss Kramer, a founding editor of *The Merton Annual*, has participated in many ITMS meetings. She has presented several workshops on Merton's journals and was Vice President of the ITMS for four years. During 2003-2004 she was a Resident Scholar at The Institute for Ecumenical Culture and Research, St. John's University, Collegeville, MN where she studied and lectured on Hildegard of Bingen, as well as on a translation of Johann Tetzel's 1518 response to Luther's Ninety-five Theses.

David Leigh, SJ, is Professor of English at Seattle University, where he has taught for twnty years. He is the author of *Circuitous Journeys: Modern Spiritual Autobiography* (Fordham UP, 2000), and dozens of articles on literature and theology. He has also taught courses on Thomas Merton.

Gray Matthews is an Assistant Professor of Communication at The University of Memphis and the coordinator of the Memphis Chapter of the ITMS. Gray also teaches courses on Merton for the diocesan Liturgical Ministry Institute. His essay on "The Healing Silence: Thomas Merton's Contemplative Approach to Communication" was recently published in *The Merton Annual*.

Patrick F. O'Connell teaches Religious Studies at Gannon University in Erie, Pennsylvania. He has published extensively about Thomas Merton and is a past president of the International Thomas Merton Society. He is the editor of *The Merton Seasonal* and one of the authors of *The Thomas Merton Encyclopedia*.

Joe Raab is currently serving as the Chair of the Religious Studies Department at Santa Catalina School in Monterey, CA. He holds an MA in Theological Studies from the University of Dayton, and he received his PhD in Systematic Theology from the University of St. Michael's College in Toronto. Joe's research interests include Thomas Merton, Buddhist-Christian dialogue, Mysticism, and the Philosophy of Bernard Lonergan.

Jens Söring, inmate ID 179212, has served eighteen years of his two life sentences for double-murder. His most recent book, *The Way of the Prisoner—Breaking the Chains of Self through Centering Prayer and Centering Practice* was published by Lantern Books, 2003. His current address can be obtained at 1-800-467-4943. The Department of Corrections spells his name 'Soering.' His website is http://www.jenssoering.com/

Angus Stuart holds degrees in Geography and Theology from the Universities of London and Durham respectively. Since 1996 he has been Senior Anglican Chaplain at the University of Bristol. In 2000 he became Chair of the Thomas Merton Society of Great Britain & Ireland and has presented papers on Merton and the Beats at the Society's conferences.

Lynn Szabo is Associate Professor of American Literature and Creative Writing at Trinity Western University, Vancouver, Canada. Her scholarly interest in Thomas Merton has focused on his poetry in relation to his mysticism. She is currently producing a new anthology of Merton's poems for New Directions Books and is completing a book on his poetics. She teaches a number of courses and regularly leads retreats on Thomas Merton as a spiritual mentor. She is a member of the Boards of the Thomas Merton Society of Canada and the International Thomas Merton Society.

Catherine Senne Wallace, Minneapolis MN, is a poet and oblate associated with St. John's Abbey, Collegeville MN. Her poetry has appeared in numerous journals, anthologies, newspapers, and sound recordings.

Stefanie Weisgram, OSB, is a member of Saint Benedict's Monastery, St. Joseph, Minnesota. Former book review editor for *Sisters Today*, she is collection development librarian for The College of Saint Benedict and St. John's University, Collegeville, Minnesota, and cataloging librarian for the Abadia de Jesucristo Crucificado in Esquipulas, Guatemala.

Index